THE
TEMPLE
OF
HIGH
WITCHCRAFT

ABOUT THE AUTHOR

Christopher Penczak is an award-winning author, teacher, and healing practitioner. Beginning his spiritual journey in the tradition of modern witchcraft and Earth-based religions, he has studied extensively with witches, mystics, shamans, and healers in a variety of traditions from across the globe to synthesize his own practice of magick and healing. He is an ordained minister, herbalist, flower essence consultant, and certified Reiki Master (Teacher) in the Usui-Tibetan and Shamballa traditions. Christopher has been involved with the Gifts of Grace Foundation and is a faculty member of the North Eastern Institute of Whole Health, both in New Hampshire. He is the author of many books, including *Ascension Magick*, *Magick of Reiki*, *Spirit Allies*, *The Mystic Foundation*, *Instant Magick*, and *The Inner Temple of Witchcraft*. For more information, visit www.christopherpenczak.com.

THE TEMPLE OF HIGH WITCHCRAFT

CEREMONIES, SPHERES AND THE WITCHES' QABALAH

CHRISTOPHER PENCZAK

Llewellyn Publications

Woodbury, Minnesota

First Edition
Third Printing, 2011

Book design and format by Donna Burch
Cover background © Photodisc
Cover design by Lisa Novak
Editing by Andrea Neff
Interior illustrations by Llewellyn Art Department
Tarot cards from the *Universal Tarot* by Roberto De Angelis © 2000 by Lo Scarabeo and reprinted with permission from Lo Scarabeo

For a complete list of credits, please see page 558.

Library of Congress Cataloging-in-Publication Data
Penczak, Christopher.
    The temple of high witchcraft : ceremonies, spheres, and the witches' qabalah /
       by Christopher Penczak.—1st ed.
    p. cm.
    Includes bibliographical references and index.
    ISBN 13: 978-0-7387-1165-2
    1. Witchcraft. 2. Magic. 3. Cabala. I. Title.

BF1566.P453 2007
133.4'3—dc22   2007020774

Llewellyn Publications
A Division of Llewellyn Worldwide Ltd.
2143 Woodbury Drive
Woodbury, MN 55125-2989
www.llewellyn.com
Llewellyn is a registered trademark of Llewellyn Worldwide Ltd.
Printed in the United States of America

Other Releases by Christopher Penczak

City Magick (Samuel Weiser, 2001)

Spirit Allies (Samuel Weiser, 2002)

The Inner Temple of Witchcraft (Llewellyn Publications, 2002)

The Inner Temple of Witchcraft Meditation CD Companion (Llewellyn Publications, 2002)

Gay Witchcraft (Samuel Weiser, 2003)

The Outer Temple of Witchcraft (Llewellyn Publications, 2004)

The Outer Temple of Witchcraft Meditation CD Companion (Llewellyn Publications, 2004)

The Witch's Shield (Llewellyn Publications, 2004)

Magick of Reiki (Llewellyn Publications, 2004)

Sons of the Goddess (Llewellyn Publications, 2005)

The Temple of Shamanic Witchcraft (Llewellyn Publications, 2005)

The Temple of Shamanic Witchcraft Meditation CD Companion (Llewellyn Publications, 2005)

Instant Magick (Llewellyn Publications, 2005)

The Mystic Foundation (Llewellyn Publications, 2006)

Ascension Magick (Llewellyn Publications, 2007)

The Temple of High Witchcraft Meditation CD Companion (Llewellyn Publications, 2007)

The Living Temple of Witchcraft Volume One (Llewellyn Publications, 2008)

The Living Temple of Witchcraft Volume One CD Companion (Llewellyn Publications, 2008)

The Living Temple of Witchcraft Volume Two (Llewellyn Publications, 2009)

The Living Temple of Witchcraft Volume Two CD Companion (Llewellyn Publications, 2009)

The Witch's Coin (Llewellyn Publications, 2009)

The Witch's Heart (Llewellyn Publications, 2011)

Acknowledgments

To my husband, Steve, who sparked my interest in ceremonial magick, got me over my fear of delving into magickal realms I thought were beyond me, and most especially for climbing the sacred Tree by my side.

To the modern magicians who continue to deepen my knowledge, understanding, and experience of the Tree of Life: Donald Michael Kraig, Alan Moore, Jason Augustus Newcomb, Lon Milo DuQuette, John Michael Greer, and my sweet soul sister Kala Trobe.

To all the amazing people who have contributed to this work and my views on magick, including Alixaendreia, Leandra Walker, Olivette Aviso, Jean Pando, S. Rune Emerson, Penney L. Robinson, Diane Gatchell, Ian Corrigan, and Laurie Cabot.

Special thanks to Adam Sartwell for his inspiration, insight, and rituals.

EVERY MAN AND EVERY WOMAN IS A STAR

—from *The Book of the Law*

Contents

CHAPTER NINE

CHAPTER TEN

CHAPTER ELEVEN

CHAPTER TWELVE

CHAPTER THIRTEEN

CHAPTER FOURTEEN

CHAPTER FIFTEEN

CHAPTER SIXTEEN

CHAPTER SEVENTEEN

EXERCISES

CHARTS AND FIGURES

Charts

Figures

Introduction

WHAT IS THE TEMPLE OF HIGH WITCHCRAFT?

Once I had delved into the more primal shamanic arts of the witch and integrated them into my practice, I still felt a gap in my magickal education. My first teachers each had a vast magickal library, with both the popular, modern books and the classic magickal texts, the old grimoires of Solomon and the medieval books of occult philosophies. I thumbed through these old books and must admit that, even though they were written in old-style English, they might as well have been written in Greek, Latin, or Hebrew, because I didn't really understand them. These books contained various alphabets, codices of spirits to summon for a variety of purposes, and the consecration of ritual tools with bizarre and seemingly impractical ingredients. Most of them had a strong Christian slant to them. I didn't know why my witchcraft teachers had them or how they could be used. The whole topic of medieval magick seemed a little beyond me, yet it fascinated me. It was like a grammar school student picking up a college textbook, knowing there were important things in it but lacking the context to understand it. In witchcraft training, we learned bits and pieces of information associated with the Qabalah, tarot, Rosicrucian breathing exercises, and Hermetic philosophy, but we didn't understand the systems that wove them all together. I was told that they were "high magick" and that perhaps someday I would take an interest in the subject. At the time, I didn't think so. But eventually I did.

I got so interested in this form of high magick that I almost put my witchcraft practice on the back burner. I sought out a lot of the classic magickal texts and puzzled over them. Soon I met an amazing man who had much more information and practical experience with high magick, who explained to me the rituals of high magick, also known as *ceremonial magick*, in terms of my more traditional witchcraft. He introduced me to modern books that dissected the old texts and distilled their wisdom into a more digestible format. I soon noticed the similarities between the workings of the witch and those of the ceremonial magician. The circle, the four watchtowers, the summoning of spirits and angels, and the use of elemental and planetary correspondences are common to both. I could see the influence of high magick on my own tradition of witchcraft in the very structure and words of the rituals. I learned that some initiatory traditions of witchcraft train their students extensively in the arts of high magick. I never had this training, so I sought it out on my own. As I researched, I learned that many of the modern Craft founders had some knowledge of or involvement in high magick, and that the histories of both witchcraft and high magick were deeply interwoven. One might say that the modern forefathers of the Craft relied heavily on the knowledge preserved in the ceremonial manuscripts. It is only natural that one complements the other. Though seen as two separate traditions now, they most likely have a similar spiritual, if not historical, origin.

Older witchcraft books written in the twentieth century—not by New Age practitioners writing for practitioners but by those authors collecting folk history, charms, and esoteric pictures—never fail to include information on alchemy, Qabalah, spirit summoning, tarot, and many notable ceremonial magicians, including Cornelius Agrippa, John Dee, Eliphas Lévi, Aleister Crowley and the members of the Golden Dawn, in their descriptions of the history and practice of witchcraft. These books, not having practical instructions or modern spells, were less popular among new practitioners, but they point out a valuable part of our history that many modern witches ignore.

With this tutor's help, I began to integrate the practices of high magick into my own spiritual working. Knowledge of the Qabalah, and the Tree of Life, gave me a more detailed framework in which I could place my experiences, correspondences, and theology. This integral symbol of the Western magickal mysteries gave me a working model that detailed the universe with more depth than I had previously understood. It gave me a context for my own spiritual awakenings on the path. I found this new knowledge invaluable, and in the end, it only served to deepen my devotion to the Goddess and God and my practice of witchcraft as a tradition of spiritual evolution.

Ceremonial magick gave me a range of knowledge and understanding that expanded my worldview. The use of many cultural associations, from the mysteries of the East to alchemy and the ancient mysteries of Egypt and Greece, opened me up to a worldview of magick. Even the Judeo-Christian associations helped heal my division from my birth religion and allowed me to recognize and honor the mystic traditions in both of those mainstream faiths, even if they were not for me in this lifetime.

As I eventually took on students of my own and began teaching my traditions to others, I struggled to present this material to my circle of modern eclectic witches. The mysteries of ceremonial magick often frighten the witch. They are seen as too male, too intellectual, too complicated, formal, and stuffy. People want freedom and creativity, and I do too, but I found in my study of music and art that when you seriously pursue something and want to know all about it, you have to learn the rules first in order to know how to break them and still be effective. In music training, you learn all the theory, how the classical composers did things, and the evolution of music. In the modern era, we have the freedom to compose anything we want, in any manner we want, but some of the best modern compositions come from those who have studied and integrated the classics. You have to know, as a tradition, where you have been, where your roots are, in order to know where you are going. Then you have the freedom and knowledge to adapt things, and do so effectively. A lot of people do rituals with no rules, no structure, no theory, and then wonder why their spells don't work. Part of training in any art, if you hope to be a part of its present and future, is having enough respect for the tradition to know where it comes from and how it has evolved. I have studied art, music, and now magick, and have found this to be true of all three disciplines.

When I shared with my peers the books I was studying and working from, I got mostly blank stares or jokes. When I asked if they had read up on ceremonial magick, most had not. They didn't know what they were missing, even to find out that it wasn't for them. They didn't seek out new horizons and challenge their perceptions and understanding of magick. There will come a point in your magickal training when you will want to know about all forms of magick, even if you don't practice them. I wanted to be educated about magick. I wanted to know why my teachers had the medieval grimoires on their shelves. The wise witches I knew had an understanding of this brand of magick, even if they didn't practice ceremonial magick as their main tradition.

Many people would not consider ceremonial magick to be under the heading of witchcraft, but the more I studied, the more I realized, using my wide definition of witchcraft, that the ceremonial arts are one of the main branches of the Craft. We can see our ancestors in the ceremonial priestesses and priests of the ancient civilizations. In my own curriculum, I soon included high magick as the fourth branch of training and corresponded it to the element of air, the element of the magician, the Mercury archetype, for it's all about our thoughts, perceptions, and communication.

The first level, outlined in the first book in this series, *The Inner Temple of Witchcraft*, corresponds to the fire element and the inner spark of psychic development. The second level of training, found in *The Outer Temple of Witchcraft*, is associated with the earth element, focusing on the natural cycles, the four elements, spellcraft, and the magick circle ritual. The third level of training, encompassed in *The Temple of Shamanic Witchcraft*, covers the shamanic practices of the witch and focuses on the element of water, reflections, shadow work, and crossing the veil between the physical and spiritual worlds. The book in your hands, the fourth in the series, can be used on its own as a study of high magick in the context of witchcraft or as part of the continuing education in the Temple of Witchcraft series of books. There are some exercises in *The Temple of High Witchcraft* that require information from the previous texts or that refer to more information in those books for a deeper understanding and connection; these are abbreviated as *ITOW*, *OTOW*, and *TOSW*, respectively, with a chapter or exercise number listed.

The Temple of High Witchcraft is a distillation of my own experiences and explorations in ceremonial magick. It is a workbook for your own study, based on the course I offer my own students. It starts with four introductory chapters, to better understand the background of the lesson material. These four chapters are followed by twelve lessons, each with exercises, rituals, and homework, to be explored in a year and a day, as is traditional for witchcraft training. The thirteenth lesson culminates in a ritual initiation fusing the traditions of witchcraft and high magick through exploring your own views and understanding of the universe.

This fourth level is much like the graduate studies of witchcraft for my students. It exposes them to a larger worldview than what is offered in most witchcraft books, much like higher education exposes students to a diverse range of topics, cultures, and people. This course challenges students' beliefs, perceptions, and symbolism in their own magick and in their own life. One of the key words of the element of air is *life*, the breath of life, for it is through our air elemental energy that we perceive and seek to know the mysteries of life.

Each level of training presents a challenge. The Inner Temple's challenge is to awaken, to realize that life is magickal and you carry the spark of flame within you. The Outer Temple's challenge is to harmonize with the natural forces, usually through the cycles and seasons, to manifest the life you want. The Temple of Shamanic Witchcraft's challenge is emotional in nature, to find and face the shadow self and take responsibility for all that you have repressed. This fourth challenge is one of intellect, to stretch perceptions and step out of belief systems, and to find which thoughts and beliefs serve your spiritual evolution and which ones must be discarded or transformed. Ultimately, you will see your beliefs and models as tools rather than absolute truth.

The sword, blade, or athame is the tool of air, and in tarot cards, the suit of swords presents the most challenges, at least with only a casual observation. Most of the sword cards don't look happy. They present challenges, conflicts, and miscommunications. In the outer world, they are perceived as challenges involving other people. In the inner world, they represent the conflict of the mind, of all aspects of the mind—our beliefs, thoughts, images, and preconceived notions that are in conflict with each other. The swords present the most problems because the mind is the inner tool, the gift that presents us with so many challenges. The body, heart, and soul all have their challenges, but the mind can be the most problematic. We learn to quiet the mind through meditation and ritual, and to see things from a different perspective, but as human beings, we still get caught up in our beliefs, in the zones of comfort that our minds hold, and feel threatened and challenged by new ideas or points of view. The job of the sword is to cut to the truth. But your truth is not necessarily my truth. Your truth is only one aspect of universal truth.

It is the job of the guardians of the air element, the Mercurial archetypal beings who often manifest as trickster spirits, to "trick" us out of our minds and see things from a new point of view. We soon realize that a point of view is just that—one way of looking at things—and that there are many ways, all with merit, to look at the universe, magick, and spirituality. It's no coincidence that many of these trickster deities are also magicians. They are sages, scribes, and tutors in the magickal arts, but they are not always easy on us or kind. In the realm of Mercury we find the Egyptian Thoth; the Sumerian Nabu; the Norse Odin and his more maligned counterpart Loki; the Greek Hermes and the Roman Mercury; Merlin, the wild man magician; the African Legba, keeper of the doorways; and the Native American Coyote and Raven. Each reveals the mysteries, showing us that things are not always as they appear. They are the gods of magick, for the foundation of magick is a change in perception.

One of my favorite folk tales involves a trickster god. One version says this god is Odin, while others give credit to the Nigerian god Eshu. The god walks down the road that bisects the village wearing a special hat. The hat is colored red on one side and blue on the other. He turns his hat around and then walks back through the village. When people gather together and say, "Did you see the god in the blue hat?," his neighbor responds with, "No, no, he had a red hat on his head." Then they argue and fight. When two of the men who are brawling are taken before the king for judgment for their crime, the trickster god appears before them all and says, "It's my fault. I did it, and I meant to do it. Spreading strife is my greatest joy."

The two different views of god created two different paradigms, one based in blue and one in red. This is a metaphor for how many views we have of divinity. We each connect to the same source, the same power, yet come away with a different impression. Neither is completely correct. The trickster comes by and says, "You're both right. And you're both wrong." You can never have the whole picture of divinity while you are in this life. Spiritual traditions are just a point of view, a perspective on the whole. Our religions, and even our magickal systems, are just like looking at the god in the hat. They are just a model, a point of view, and not the ultimate truth. We have problems when anyone who believes that his or her perspective is *the* perspective and the only way. We then get into dogma and fundamentalism. Even in paganism, magick, and New Age traditions, we can find the same fundamentalism we see in the mainstream institutional religions. The trickster's role is to challenge us to get beyond it. His strife causes us to grow, change, and expand our point of view to include both colors of the hat. In witchcraft we have the model of the wheel of life, with forces rising and ascending, creating times of prosperity and peace and times of strife and blight, both of which are needed for the turning of the wheel. The wisdom is found in how we respond to the turning of the wheel.

If you are looking for a tradition to give you the "way," then witchcraft, or ceremonial magick, is probably not for you. In each, there are many permutations. We honor the trickster, and actively invite his revelations, even though they might come with strife, because it's in that challenge—to move beyond our comfort zones—that we grow. As for this book, if you are looking for traditional guidance on ceremonial magick in the style of the Golden Dawn, Thelema, or any of the numerous modern lodges, you've picked up the wrong book. If you are looking for one book to tell you *the* way to do a particular ritual, you will be disappointed. If, however, you are looking to understand the rituals of ceremonial magick and their potential relationship to witchcraft, and how you can integrate these practices into your life as a witch, then you are on the right path.

The Temple of High Witchcraft takes a deconstructionist approach to ceremonial magick. In each lesson, we will explore each level of the traditional Tree of Life through intellectual understanding of the correspondences, along with ritual and meditation. The traditional rituals of high magick will be explored in their more commonly accepted forms as practiced in the last century, but each ritual will be dissected, to understand each part and its purpose for the ritual. Then you will be given the option to learn the ritual in its original form, explore alternate versions of the ritual created by others, or reconstruct the ritual using symbolism, words, and images that work best for you. Many witches choose to rework the part of the ritual that contains Judeo-Christian imagery. I know I did. Through understanding the rituals, you will develop the skills to look at any grimoire or manuscript and take it apart and understand its objectives and techniques.

The final challenge of *The Temple of High Witchcraft* will be to create your own reality map. Magickal systems, cosmologies, and mandalas are all ways through which we try to describe the infinite, but each is only a map drawn from our limited perspective. We see the red hat or the blue hat, but not both. We don't know what's going on beneath the hat. The map is symbolic. It's not the actual terrain, just our best representation of it at this time. When we follow a map, we still get surprised and experience things not on the map. Reality maps, like the Qabalah, or Tree of Life, are helpful guides. Because the Tree of Life plays such a pivotal role in Western magick, we will explore it extensively, making it our primary teaching map. But then we will look at other points of view, other ways of mapping our magickal reality. You will be challenged to create your own map, your own version of reality that incorporates your thoughts, ideas, and perceptions, along with your experiences and creativity. You will be challenged to communicate your point of view to the world in a symbolic way.

Through understanding your own map, and the maps of others, traditional and modern, you will cease to be attached to your own way as being the only way, even for you. Your paradigm will become more fluid. Your mind will become more flexible, and you will be able to explore many possibilities. The intellectual study and expression will create a revelation. This mystery can never really be explained. The purpose of the ceremonial magician's "Great Work" is to find the balance and union of humanity with divinity through the nature of the universe. One identifies with divinity and the universe. Through attempting to explain the mysteries of the universe, and realizing that all words and symbols fall short of the actual mystery, you will begin to experience the mystery more deeply and come to a greater understanding of yourself and your own divinity.

The path set before you in this course is not an easy one to walk. I've had more students have difficulties on this level than any other. Unlike the emotional challenge of the third level, the intellectual challenge is often something we don't expect in witchcraft. It takes us by surprise, like the swords in a tarot reading. Among those who have completed this course work with me, the repeated sentiment at the last class, after the final project and ceremonies are done, is that in the end, all the hard work was worth it. They no longer feel intimidated by systems of magick that previously they knew little about. And they are more confident that their own point of view has as much validity as any other, yet they are not dogmatic in their approach to witchcraft. They are open to hearing new ideas and ways of doing things without feeling that their own truth is threatened.

In walking this path, you will come to understand that your truth is simply *a* truth, one of many. It's a reflection of the great truths told by the world's mystic traditions, each of which has its own voice, its own point of view. No one tradition has an exclusive claim to spiritual truth. *The Temple of High Witchcraft* will grant you a new sense of understanding, intellectual confidence, and the ability to express and articulate your truth with a broader spiritual vocabulary. In the end, communication, knowledge, and truth are the gifts of the element of air. Once you delve into this element's mysteries, you will embody its power.

Blessed be,
Christopher Penczak

The Magician and the Witch

When we look at images of the magician and the witch, we see that they are not so different. One of the first images of the magician that I remember from childhood was the wise old wizard. Wizards and witches have always gone together in the minds of our popular imagination. And there is a reason for this link beyond the alliteration of the letter *w*. The magician and witch have much in common.

Both magicians and witches have graying or white long hair, signifying a long life, during which knowledge and wisdom has been accumulated. Coming from a time and place where many die young due to illness, poverty, or war, survival into elderhood denotes a powerful person with a powerful will to live. They often wear a pointed hat that could be seen as a symbol of their place in society or their wisdom. Conical hats have been linked symbolically to the Cone of Power that magickal practitioners raise in a ritual circle and release out into the world to manifest their wishes. Both wear robes of a sort—cloaks, hoods, or capes reminiscent of religious garb, hinting at a religious status of some sort that was lost with the rise of Christianity. Both have a fondness for animals and plants and often will keep a special or unusual animal or grow unusual herbs. Both live on the edge of society. We see the hedge witch in her hut or cottage at the edge of the village, near the forest and the source of her wild herbs and medicines. We see images of the medieval wizard, real or fictitious, living in an isolated tower and surrounded by his books and laboratory. Both are sought after for advice. People visit the village cunning woman for cures, divination, and spells. In the old myths, magicians are the guides and tutors to the heroes and royal courts, pointing them in the right direction but letting them do the work.

Some practitioners think the roots of the words *wizard* and *witch* come from the same source, meaning "wise," though modern scholars would disagree. Even if the etymology doesn't support this theory, the image of each denotes the wise old one, with the witch more often depicted as female and the wizard as male. In the modern era, we know that a woman can be a magician and a man can be a witch, but archetypally they denote two similar but different paths. The hedge witch, with the intuitive feminine mysteries, keeps one path, while the magician, as the forerunner of the scientist, seeks to solve the mysteries of the universe through the study of texts and experimentation.

The division between the two might not be as clear in reality as it is in our mythical images. The magician is very much in tune with the forces of nature, the elements, and intuition. It would be impossible for him to have any mastery of magick without understanding the feminine mysteries. In turn, the witch must study and have knowledge to support intuition and instinct. Ritual books, symbolic charms, secret languages, and incantations are as much a part of the art of the witch as freeform, spontaneous workings. Both of these magickal paths balance and harmonize what we think of as masculine and feminine mysteries. One may be emphasized over the other, but both are paths of balance and recognize the need for both sets of skills.

When I began my study of witchcraft, I looked at a lot of disciplines and drew upon many different traditions, even sources that would not be considered traditional witchcraft. I drew upon the theories and terminology of Hermetic magick. The Hermetic principles (*ITOW*, Chapter 8) influenced me profoundly. They gave me a basis, as a rational, thinking person, to understand how magick could work. My first teachers approached witchcraft as a science, and the Hermetic philosophies were the means of conveying the ideas of the ancient world's scientists-philosophers-sorcerers. As a witch, I saw these ancient researchers into the mysteries as my ancestors. We all practice magick.

The word *magic* comes from the Middle English *magik*, and some prefer that spelling, or the spelling of *magick*, made most popular by Aleister Crowley's work, to differentiate stage show illusionists from spiritual practitioners. We can trace the word to the Old French *magique*, the Late Latin *magica*, and the Latin word *magice*. The Latin use of the word comes from the Greek term *magikos*, meaning "magical," and *magos*, meaning "magician." The history of the word goes back to the Old Persian term *magus*, usually translated as "magician" or "sorcerer" and possibly meaning "to have power." The term *magi*, the plural of *magus*, is identified most popularly with the three wise men from the East, who reportedly visited Jesus of Nazareth at his nativity. Many overlook the fact that these men were Eastern sorcerers or magicians who had far more in common with pagan priests and priestesses than modern-day Christians.

The term *sorcery* comes from the Old French *sorcerie* and from the Vulgar Latin term *sortianius*, meaning "one who influences fate and fortune." In modern times, the word sorcerer can mean vastly different things, depending on where you are in the world. Some people use the word sorcerer to refer to shamans and holy practitioners of the spiritual arts of healing. Others use the term for those who practice harmful magick. Interestingly enough, it is believed that the feminine sorceress has an older history than the male sorcerer. Throughout history, the terms *witch*, *sorcerer/sorceress*, *wizard*, and *magician* have been used somewhat interchangeably. By looking at all the languages and cultures that had terms for spiritual magick, and the practitioners of this art, we can see that the concept of magick, or working one's will through ritual and charm, was a part of the cultural landscape of many lands and time periods.

My teachers believed in a common spiritual ancestry for both the magus and the witch. This encouraged me to incorporate the ideas of the pagan magicians of the Middle East—of ancient Sumer and Babylon, Persia and Egypt—into the lore of the Europeans. I was taught that the two roles were not as different as they were seen before, and in many ages past, there was not much difference between them in the popular culture of the time. Our modern division between the witch and the mage is just that—a modern division. Differences between traditions grew over the last few thousand years. Some traditions remained wild and primal, and others became more intellectual, but magick was not divided neatly into two camps. The lines between witch, shaman, and magician were not clear-cut in the ancient world. During the Burning Times, the Inquisitors didn't see much of a difference between them. All were considered heretics and devil worshipers, even if the magician was working in a Judeo-Christian context. Those on a more intellectual path were able to hide in the upper echelons of society, while those on the primal paths attempted to blend in with the peasantry. Both continued their traditions in secret. Once the magickal practitioner was no longer a vital and open part of the community, the differences between the two became even more pronounced, but they still came from a similar root, and that common root is the force that continues to bring them together.

Through this holistic viewpoint, I was able to integrate the image of the magician into my identity as a witch. I described myself as a shamanic Hermetic witch, giving references to both the tribal ecstatic mysteries that became a part of my Craft as well as the intellectual and theoretical material of the Hermetics that influenced my way of viewing the work. I've found both to be invaluable to my own spirituality. I don't feel a schism between the study of ceremonial magick and the folk ways of the witch. I don't see a distinct line separating the two. When you compare the images of the magician and the witch, you find that they have far more common ground than most people would think.

THE POWERS OF THE MAGUS

One of the most popular images we have of the magician comes from the tarot deck. The classic image of the magician in the Rider-Waite deck gives us a lot of information about the magician and the magician's powers and teachings. It is also in this imagery that we find a lot of elements common to the witch.

The image on the Magician card, unlike the popular image of the wizard, is usually one of a fairly young man, a man in his prime, not elderhood (figure 1). Before him lies an altar, and on that altar are the four elemental tools of the four suits of the tarot deck. He has a wooden wand, metal blade, chalice, and pentacle, which usually stand for the elemental powers of fire, air, water, and earth, respectively. Here are the elemental "weapons" of ceremonial magick. They are also the ritual tools of the witch.

Figure 1: Magician Card

Skeptics would say that the modern witch's use of these tools is the result of the modern witchcraft founders borrowing from modern ceremonial magicians. I believe the tools to be more universal, showing up in many different forms and cultures associated with both witches and magicians. The witch's magick wand is a popular image from fairy tales, as is the witch's broom, an older version of the wand. The knife can be seen in old images of the witches' goddess Hecate. The cauldron is a popular witchcraft image from many cultures, transformed from the Celtic cauldron of immortality or inspiration into the image of the Holy Grail, the sacred chalice. The pentagram was drawn on the shields of the Celtic warriors devoted to the dark war goddess the Morrighan. The five-pointed star, the endless knot, is a classic symbol of witches and mages. We find similar groupings of ceremonial tools in the mysteries of the Cult of Mithras. They are not just tools, but four universal powers. Each tool not only represents one of these powers, because its form shares similar characteristics with the element's energy, but it also mediates that particular energy in ritual. Both the magician and witch perform ritual, thereby moving energy, with these instruments.

The magician often carries a fifth tool, a secondary wand that helps mediate the powers of the heavens and the Earth. With his right arm raised to the heavens and his left pointed to the land beneath him, the magician's body emphasizes the Hermetic wisdom "as above, so below." To create in one realm, you must create in both. To master one, you must master both. Some say he takes the heavenly power and makes it manifest his will in the world. Others say he takes his earthly life and raises it to the heavens. One of the lessons of the Magician card, when pulled in a divinatory reading, is of power and its appropriate use. Is the application of our power balanced in both worlds? If not, it will unbalance us. The four elements help us balance the powers of above and below.

The flowers decorating the card also emphasize the dual power. The red roses represent passion and vitality. Red is a color of life, of blood, and is associated with the physical and the sexual. Red is the color of will and power in the material world. In the Western tradition, the image of the rose, at its core a five-petaled flower, is a symbol of the energy centers and the unfolding of spirituality, much as the lotus is used in Egyptian and Asian traditions. Five is the number of the material world and the union of the elements. The white lilies, usually six-petaled flowers, are symbolic of the upper worlds, the macrocosm and the seven magickal planets—six bodies surrounding the Sun. The red outer robe and the white inner robe continue this theme of dual powers. The belt is fashioned as a snake devouring its own tail, an *ouroboros*—an ancient symbol of creation and rebirth, the magick circle between the worlds. The snake is a symbol of knowledge, awareness, and sexuality, strongly associated with witchcraft and the Goddess. Above the magician's head is the infinity loop, similar to the ouroboros but crossed over, showing the cycles between worlds and the infinite potential of magick. The center of the infinity loop is the point of balance between both worlds where anything is possible.

All of these symbols show a similarity between the two archetypal images of mage and witch, drawing them together closer. When we look at the role of the magician, we continue to find similarities to that of the witch.

THE EVOLUTION OF THE MAGI

Where did the image of the magician originate? Our first image of the magi, and the word itself, comes from the desert lands of the Middle East. The magi were said to be a caste or order of the ancient Persian society that organized society after the fall of Babylon and Assyria. After political setbacks in the Persian Empire, the magi were said to have spread from Persia to the Mediterranean, carrying the image of the sorcerer with them. The Persian magi most likely were involved in the Cult of Mithras, a mystery tradition influenced by Zoroastrianism that grew to power in the Roman Empire. First mentions of the magi refer to the Persians, but eventually the term evolved into a wider image of strange miracle workers, healers, and ritualists.

From where did this caste of magickal practitioners inherit their wisdom? The priests of the first civilizations, those of Sumer, Assyria, and Babylon, were well known for their star lore and knowledge of spirits. The Chaldeans were a part of Babylon and were known as sorcerers. The classical Roman writers used the term *Chaldeans* for the mathematicians and astrologers of Babylon, showing that they were versed in the sciences. Chaldean also has become a term to describe the mythology of Sumer, Babylon, and Assyria. The Babylonians drew their knowledge from the Sumerians. Many credit the Sumerians with the creation of the first real civilization on Earth. Though civilization can be defined in various ways, the early Sumerians did possess a technical knowledge and sophistication that marked a shift in human culture. In the practices of Sumer, we can find a foundation that profoundly affected all that came after it. Through the surviving accounts of Chaldean practice and mythology, we know of orders of priests and priestesses, versed in ritual and medicine, summoning spirits and making offerings to the gods. We also find a powerful tale involving the descent of the goddess Inanna to the Underworld, and this tale continues to influence modern witches in their initiation rites.

When we look at the inhabitants of many of the ancient cultures—from the Sumerians and Babylonians, to the Egyptian priests and scribes, to the Persian sorcerers and the keepers of the temples in Greece and Rome—we see a similar archetype. Parallel figures to the old priests of Sumer developed in all of these civilizations, along with similar rituals and myths of the descending deity. The Greeks and later Romans became the recipients of the wisdom traditions of not only ancient Iraq and Iran but also of the Egyptian mystery schools, whose ancient knowledge influenced the Greek philosophers who are renowned to this day for their wisdom and insight.

In the ancient temple clergy, we find the inheritors of the Stone Age shamanic traditions. As human culture developed from a hunter-gatherer society to a settled agrarian and urban society, the mystic traditions moved from a more shamanic tribal practice to temple practices, to suit the changing culture. Those who would have been the shamanic healers, the spirit workers and cunning ones, were trained in the temple as the priestesses and priests. Oral tradition was written down. Rituals became more codified. The mysteries of direct experience became religion and theology. The art and spirituality of the shaman was fused with more scientific pursuits, astrological patterns, and medical knowledge. The temple priestesses and priests acted as the wisdom keepers, guiding the religion of the society, creating a caste of those religiously and magickally inclined and allowing others in the society to focus on other pursuits.

These first magicians were both scholars and ministers. They acted as mediators for sacred energies through rituals, holidays, and rites of passage. These priestesses and priests acted as the storytellers and the record keepers, being some of the most literate members of society. The concepts of written language and magick were quite similar in the ancient world. Records were kept of medical knowledge, including anatomy, medicine, and even primitive forms of surgery. As these esoteric arts developed, they eventually lost more mystical leanings and became the foundations of our modern sciences. Astrology gave way to astronomy. Alchemy gave way to chemistry. Herbal medicine gave way to modern medicine.

The priestly caste often acted as advisers for royalty, from the pharaohs of Egypt, to the oracles of Greece counseling rulers, to the eventual image of the court magician advising kings and queens. Because of their unique perspective, standing between the worlds of matter and spirit, they offered unique advice to those in power. Their secret wisdom guided many cultures until magickal knowledge was no longer valued.

As history progressed, societally sanctioned magician-priests gave way to the priests of the Christian Church. The role of the magician became more internalized, with solitary mystics and small lodges of mystics seeking spiritual enlightenment. The temple priestesses and priests became the laboratory alchemists and medieval magicians. Many members of the upper class and royalty still valued the knowledge of the mage. Looking at the old grimoires, there is evidence to suggest that some magicians even pursued their magick under the cloak of the Church, as the Church has collected many occult manuscripts and the priests and brothers were more likely to be the literate members of society. The image of the magician as male grew, divorcing itself from the pagan priestesses, as at this time men were more likely to be literate, to be scholars with access to magickal texts.

When I look at the collective history of the magi and the witch, I don't see much of a difference. The common shamanic root links the two together. When I think of my spiritual ancestors as witches, I see their transformation from Stone Age healers to temple priestesses and even medieval scholars. In the ancient Greek world, there wasn't much of a distinction made between the magician and witch figures, as both were seen as practitioners of the night magick. As society settled in to an agricultural model, some of our mystics embraced temple life as ministers, while others remained on the outskirts as the folk magicians, without the temple scholar leanings. When I think of the priestesses and priests of Isis and Osiris, of Inanna, of Dionysus and Apollo, of Demeter and Persephone, spiritually, I see witches. But they are also magicians. When I look at those practicing traditions at the crossroads, with no temple but the bare earth, again I see the same figures, witches and magicians alike.

The Magician and the Priestess

In the tarot, the Priestess card is most likely to be associated with the witch (figure 2). It follows the Magician card and is number II in the major arcana. She is the priestess of the Moon and keeper of the mysteries. In a reading, this card can symbolize the need to listen to your intuition, perhaps over your reason and logic. It also signifies hidden things coming to light. The priestess holds the crescent Moon beneath her feet, symbolizing a mastery over emotions, over part of the celestial realm. Other than her Moon crown, she holds no real ritual tools. She has the equal-armed cross at her heart, the symbol of the Earth and a balance of the four elements within her. She does hold a scroll of knowledge and wisdom in her sleeve. She takes the writing of the magician and guards it. She is a guardian of the mysteries. Her throne sits between the two pillars of light and dark, mercy and severity. Beyond them is the gateway to the mysteries, where one can see the garden of pomegranates, the sacred fruit of Persephone, which kept this goddess in the Underworld. Rather than mediate the powers of above and below, as does the magician, she guards the gateway between the inner and outer worlds. The magician and priestess have similar themes and similar concepts, but different expressions. The magician appears more outwardly motivated, while the priestess is more inwardly motivated. They both move energy from one realm to another.

Many esotericists see the major arcana series as the development of the spiritual initiate, starting at birth, or awakening, as the Fool. We develop from this naiveté into the magician, learning our power—the power of our thoughts and words to manifest our will. Then we approach the priestess, and as we enter the mysteries, we become the mystery. The magician becomes the priestess. Because of this progression, and using the definition of a magician as anybody who does magick, many witches say that all witches are magicians, but not all magicians are witches. Though I understand the sentiment, this is not necessarily true. Many people practice the religion of witchcraft but never really understand or do magick effectively. Many magicians enter the mysteries but never claim the word witch or priest/ess as a part of their identity. And many people do magick but do not recognize its spiritual significance and perform it only for simple gain.

Another way of looking at the magician and the witch is through the lens of their inherent magickal nature. Some traditions believe that one is born into witchcraft, either by genetic lineage, by blood, or by past-life incarnation. Witches are related to the faery folk, or the angels or gods themselves. They are not quite human. Their ability to do magick is inherent, and training and rituals of initiation simply awaken the soul, or awaken the blood, to their magickal nature. Not only do witches walk the crossroads, their traditional meeting place, but in a spiritual sense they are the crossroads, a vortex of change and transformation between the worlds, which explains why many ordinary people not versed in the esoteric arts are uncomfortable around witches, even when they don't know the person is a witch.

Magicians, on the other hand, are fully human beings who, through knowledge, training, and dedication, unlock the mysteries of magick and thereby become some-

Figure 2: High Priestess Card

thing more than human. Through their own will and hard work, they awaken to the true nature of reality, to magick and divinity. Because of the witch's kinship with faeries, angels, and other spirits, witches are more likely to petition and request in ritual, with a view toward creating partnerships in the unseen realm. The unseen beings are their kith and kin, and doing magick is like calling on family. Some traditions of magicians identify solely with the Creator through ritual, and act as the Creator god manifest, taking the Judeo-Christian concept that humans are made in God's image and are sovereign over nature and the world, commanding and compelling the spirits and angels to do their bidding.

Though I understand the concepts behind these views, I'm not sure I agree with them. Though I had magickal experiences as a child, it still took a lot of hard work and training for me to become a qualified witch. I know many people who identify as magicians, who have an inherent magickal nature. They are not necessarily drawn to witchcraft. I know traditions of witchcraft that compel the spirits by sword or athame point, and mages who are very loving and reverent in their attitudes toward the spirits.

In the end, we all have a pagan ancestry of some sort, so we all have pagan blood and can awaken to the old magick.

I find it more helpful to see the common points between the magus and witch through our tarot imagery. Both are necessary parts of the human spiritual initiation. Ultimately, the tarot archetypes show us that both the image of the magician and that of the witch are linked together and a part of our overall spiritual evolution. The words, titles, and traditions we are drawn to in this life are our choice, and a part of that growth.

When we look at the images of the magician and the priestess through the lens of our collective history, we see similarities and differences. Both have been advisers and healers. Witches have focused more on the lower classes and the magicians on the higher classes, though the community role has fallen more heavily on the witch, being more accessible to more people as a healer and adviser and as the local wise one and herbalist, even in Christian times. Both have been known to do group work and solitary work. Both underwent a transformation from a practitioner honored in society to one who is feared, practicing in secret. Magicians appear outwardly to be less religiously inclined than witches. A key teaching of modern witchcraft is the celebration of the solar and agricultural holidays, as well as the Moons of the lunar year. The magician is practicing a spiritual tradition for self-mastery and enlightenment, to identify with the divine, yet the religious worship of the gods is not always emphasized. The witch appears to be oriented more toward practical and personal aims than a transcendent enlightenment, but the union with nature and the divine that comes with the practice of witchcraft leads to the similar state of enlightenment. The witch's practical aims are often community-oriented, giving them a semblance of altruism. Both the witch and the magician appear to be taking different paths, but they really are taking different approaches to the same place.

Theurgy and Thaumaturgy

One of the often-cited distinguishing characteristics that separate magicians and witches is said to be the type of magick they employ. Magicians are said to practice high magick, or *theurgy*, while witches practice low magick, or operative magick, also known as *thaumaturgy*.

High magick is the use of ritual to align with the divine. The high magick of ceremonial magicians is marked by complex rituals, precise instruments and tools, the inclusion of foreign languages, arcane substances, and either a piety to the divine or an identification of the self with the divine. Theurgy can be thought of as "god magick" and the pursuit of divinity. In its oldest, most primal forms, theurgy has been about asking, persuading, or bribing the gods to do or not do something for you. In a more modern context, it is about aligning your will with the divine will, in essence, seeking divine enlightenment while incarnated in a body. High magick is said to have a religious tone and to be a spiritual art. When looked at from a polarized view, high magick is considered white magick. While in our popular culture white magick is seen as "good" magick, magicians see white magick as the quest for divinity, to find enlightenment. Magick that causes change in another, or on the physical plane, even done with best of intentions, is considered gray magick.

Low magick is practical magick. It is working energy through simple ritual to create the conditions you want. Rituals can be intuitive and simple, using ordinary household tools and material found in nature. Herbcraft and stone magick are considered thaumaturgy as well as basic sympathetic magick. This is the magick of the local witch, the cunning one and wort curer or herbalist. Though there are basic concepts underlying this form of magick, as well as simple theories and ideas that guide it, there is no strict formula or "wrong" way of doing it. As long as your spell worked, and you manifested what you wanted, then you did it "right." If it didn't work, then some aspect of the spell was not in harmony with the basic theories, or your will was not strong enough to set the forces in motion. There is less of an emphasis on divinity, and more of an emphasis on simply shaping the natural forces and energies around us. Low magick, without the divine emphasis and the focus on producing results, is considered a form of gray magick when done with good or neutral intent, while it is potentially black magick when done with malice or to create harm.

The terms high and low magick are loaded, implying that one is better than the other. At a casual glance, they seem to indicate that high magicians are seeking something far more profound than lowly folk magicians, who simply want what they want for personal gain, having no higher cause. These styles of magick developed for many reasons, and the line dividing them is not as clear-cut as some people might like to make it. When you look up the definitions of both theurgy and thaumaturgy, both are associated with "miracles." Magicians were not always associated with theurgy. In the ancient Greek world, the witches and magicians often were equally scorned by the scholarly classes for practicing superstitions and taking advantage of people. Only later did the scholar's philosophy and ritual become linked with our concepts of theurgy.

A popular modern theory explains that these names were used because the peasants lived in the low land while the wealthier class lived on the higher ground. Others think of it strictly as a class issue and not a geographical one. Those in the lower lands were the lower classes and were more prone to illness and the passing of disease and vermin. They lived hard lives, with little time for leisure or higher education, and were intimately linked to the agricultural cycles. Their magick had to be practical—to cure the ill, keep the family together, and make the harvest grow. They didn't have the money for special temples, lodge buildings, or meeting houses. They practiced outdoors or in their homes. During the persecutions, they didn't have the space to secretly devote part of their dwelling to a magickal practice and go unnoticed, so their tools had to be hidden among common items. Rituals had to be completed quickly and quietly, without attracting a lot of attention. Their magickal practices were colored by the life they led.

Likewise, those of the higher lands were of the higher class, so they had greater access to education, time to ponder religious theology and learn foreign languages, and money to craft specialized tools. Compared to the lower classes, many of their basic needs were already taken care of. These magicians could devote their energy to personal evolution and the exploration of other cultures and states of reality. They were not as intimately linked to the forces of the land. They had more time to train with a tutor and learn the mysteries in a more formalized setting.

This image of low and high magick flips our previous associations of religion and magick with our witch and magician archetypes. It paints the magician as the religious scholar and the witch as simply being out for personal gain, yet we know a key component of witchcraft is the veneration of nature, along with the spirits and deities of nature. The religious aspect of the seasonal rites is a key component to bringing in the harvest and maintaining the balance. But now we have a more spiritual connotation to the scholarly magician image, though his religious impetus is based not necessarily in community but rather in the desire for personal enlightenment.

In truth, both the witch and magician practice theurgy and thaumaturgy. A good magician who is facing financial problems knows how to cast a spell for money. A good witch has her divine connection in her heart and mind when doing healing. Though we neatly put two different labels on these two forms of magick, they are intertwined, much like our magician and witch. I would argue that all the magick I do is a form of theurgy, even simple spells for money, curing a headache, or getting a parking space at the door. I see magick as a union of my will with divine will. As a priest of witchcraft, I always have divinity in mind when I do anything, but particularly when casting a spell. Magick is magick, regardless of the label you put on it. There will always be an aspect of personal will involved, because you have to personally decide to do the ritual. The power is in your hands, and is your responsibility. But there is always a divine connection, whether you realize it or not. Hopefully, most practitioners consciously recognize their divine connection to everything.

I would argue that the traditions taught in the Temple of Witchcraft series are all forms of theurgy, or divine magick. When you learn to enter a meditative state (*ITOW*, Chapter 6), you continually program yourself to work for the "highest good, harming none." With those words, you are requesting alignment with your higher, divine self and True Will. When you perform magick, you are encouraged to do your spells in a magick circle. Through the ritual of the circle, and in particular the act of the Great Rite, you are identifying with the Goddess and God through this ritual sacrament. When you then perform your seemingly low magick spell, you are aligned with the most profound divine forces. When you do any form of personal magick, expressing your will in the world, with this attitude of divinity, your conscious personal self gets to figure out which of your wishes are parts of your True Will (*OTOW*, Chapter 3) and which need to be transformed, cleared, or released. The theurgic aspects of magick are built right in to your practice.

Just as the polarized definitions of black and white magick do not fit a modern practice, neither does a clear-cut division of theurgy and thaumaturgy. I dislike the terms high and low magick, just as I reject the labels black and white magick. In a simplistic, naive approach, such divisions makes perfect sense, but as you delve more deeply into the practice of magick, such definitions are no longer relevant. We work with a whole spectrum of magick, black to white and all colors in between, as well as high and low with all points in between, depending on the goal of the working. Magick is powerful, and we must take responsibility for how we use it. Magick is both personal and transcendent, and can be used for practical results and transcendental awareness.

The Magick of Initiation

A better way of looking at this division between magick is looking at the differences between operant, or practical, magick and initiatory magick. Operant magick is what most people think of as spellcraft. It is doing magick with some form of tangible, real-world result. You work for something specific in the spell, and you get whatever you asked for. Sometimes you get what you asked for, but not exactly what you want, so the exploration of magick improves your communication skills with the powers of the universe. It helps you align your words with your will.

Initiatory magick has no clear-cut, tangible goal in mind, but focuses on the transformation of consciousness and the refinement of the soul. I've heard the two types of magick defined like this: operant magick is done to get you want you think you want, while initiatory magick is done to find out what you truly want. The rituals of initiatory magick reveal more of your true self, your divine self, and help you discover your True Will.

The rituals of high magick are really the rituals of initiation. We often think of initiation rituals as one person performing a ritual on another, inducting the second person into a magickal community or raising him or her a level or rank in that community. The priests and priestesses of the old religions, as well as our modern ministers, conduct rites of passage to integrate a person into the main community. Rites of magickal initiation often separate a person from the mainstream community, and integrate him or her into a special group, a brotherhood/sisterhood of fellow initiates.

Rituals from teacher to student, bringing one into the ranks of a mystical fraternity, are not the only rituals of initiation. Any experience that separates you from the
seemingly mundane life to gain a greater perspective, to elevate and transform your
consciousness, is a form of initiation. Life experiences can be very initiatory. Traumas and trials presented by life circumstances can bring the same benefits, if not even
greater ones, as traditional initiation, though you might lack the guidance of a teacher,
as you would have in a formal training group. The classic rituals of modern ceremonial magick are also initiatory in many ways. They are rituals that are designed to
expand consciousness and prepare the magician for a greater sense of divinity and enlightenment. They often are done as regular exercises, like certain forms of meditation
and yoga designed to prepare the practitioner for deeper states of consciousness. They
often have no clear-cut, real-world, tangible goal, yet their accumulated benefit can be
more profound than any simple spell to change your immediate material reality.

Conservative traditionalists will claim that initiatory magick cannot be done alone,
that one cannot have a personal union with the divine forces that results in a change
and transformation. They believe it can be done only by lineage holders. It is quite
beneficial to have the energetic "current" of a lineage running through your magick,
and even more so to have a mentor and teacher to guide you on the path, but the divine powers can reach out and claim any of us whom they seek to guide and transform
directly, without an earthly mediator for their energy. Often a magician can intend and
initiate this contact. One of the most famous magickal operations known to modern
magicians is the Abramelin Operation. Its aim is Knowledge and Conversation with
your Holy Guardian Angel. Setting aside the Hermetic mage's jargon, it means to
have communion with your higher self, the truest source of your divine will and the
best guidance possible for you. This communion transforms you by taking you out of
the morass of daily tribulations and framing your whole life in the perspective of your
divine purpose. There are several versions of this ritual, but they all involve solitary
actions initiated by the will and determination of the practitioner.

The ceremonial magician's rituals can have a twofold purpose, with both initiatory
effects and real-world results. One of the first rituals learned in modern ceremonial
magick is known as the Lesser Banishing Ritual of the Pentagram (LBRP). It typically
is done before and after all other workings. Regular use of the LBRP expands the aura

and thereby the magician's consciousness, establishes firm psychic boundaries, and clears the magician and temple of any unwanted influences. The Lesser Banishing Ritual of the Pentagram is considered the first step in high magick for most practitioners. It is defined as white magick. Yet the preparatory ritual can be used to clear a room of unwanted energies and even unwanted spirits. For those sensing malicious spirits or stagnant, sickly energy, this ritual has a very tangible, real-world result. It changes the environment. According to our previous definitions, that would make it a form of low magick or even gray magick. Yet most don't consider it to be such. After prolonged use of the LBRP, a real-world change takes place in the magician that others will notice. Even with the concepts of initiatory and operative magick, there is no clear line dividing the two. Our intentions are like a spectrum, and while our rituals might fall closer to the side of one end of the spectrum or the other, neither polarity can be divorced from the other.

The rituals of what most people would consider high magick are the cumulative rituals of initiation. We find the powers of initiation—both the traditional rituals of passing an energy from teacher to student and the rituals of the student making direct contact with the divine—in the mysteries of the modern witch. While most witchcraft books focus on the role of magick as operative magick, when we look at the rituals of high witchcraft, we are exploring a course of self-initiatory magick, drawing upon the traditions of both high magick and witchcraft to create a change in consciousness, a shift in awareness, and hopefully taking a step further along the path to divine enlightenment.

THE ENTWINED ROOTS

Looking at the history of Western magick, the spiritual family tree of witchcraft entwines many times and in many places with the family tree of the magi. The modern scholar's view is that ceremonial magick, particularly the traditions of the Golden Dawn, greatly influenced the reformation and reconstruction of Wicca in the twentieth century. There is less certainty as to how much witchcraft has influenced ceremonial magick. Scholars debate the historical age and practice of witchcraft, and whether the modern version has any links to ancient witchcraft. What was once considered fact by witchcraft practitioners has been put into doubt by modern scholars. Skeptics of Wicca's link to any past witchcraft tradition will say that Gerald Gardner made up the connection, but will still admit that, as a spiritual system, Wicca works quite well. Traditionalists will reference material, both scholarly and from family traditions and special lineages, to make their own case that what we do now in our magick is similar in form to what has been done in ages past, even if the context isn't entirely the same.

Such traditionalists believe the arts of the magician came out of the work of the tribal cunning folk and shamans, the witches. The information was said to survive in the forms of ceremonial magick because the magicians wrote things down, while many of the folk traditions were oral and were lost during the Burning Times. Even the famed and controversial alchemist Paracelsus, who popularized the Doctrine of Signatures, left academia to study with the gypsies and the wise ones of the woods to truly know the medicine of plants. The modern founders of both the ceremonial traditions and Wicca were involved in the practices of folk magick and of more formal ceremonial magick. Some current practitioners work with aspects of both traditions, and often don't know it or aren't aware of the rich history they share. I believe that in both the modern age and the past, the practices of witches and magicians have influenced each other. Like two different plants growing out of the same fertile soil, their roots are too similar not to share common ground and common origins. And like plants, they continue to cross-pollinate each other, adding to the richness and diversity of our spiritual garden.

The Ancient World of Magick

As our world moved away from the hunter-gatherer societies of the Stone Age and eventually toward the agrarian communities and the ancient cities marked by amazingly sophisticated developments in architecture, writing, temple traditions, politics, and philosophy, the mysteries of magick were not evenly divided between the witch and the mage. While some of the magickal workers remained in the rural areas, practicing what we would consider folk ways, and others were involved in more ecstatic and nonhierarchical cults of mystery, many practitioners became involved in the temple traditions of the ancient world. But the domain of the temples, and their more organized structures, was not exclusively the male mysteries. We find strong temple traditions devoted to both the goddesses and gods of the ancient societies.

The temple traditions held in highest regard by modern witches seeking to reclaim the mysteries of the ancient world are those of the Egyptian gods Isis and Osiris. Many witches use images of Isis and Osiris as the Goddess and God upon their altar. The story of this couple is used in many rites and classes to explore the themes of life, death, magick, and rebirth. Though some speculate that the origin of Isis is in an all-pervading mother goddess archetype from Predynastic Egypt and that she was absorbed into the later solar-dominant Egyptian pantheon, her worship spread in later eras to again become an all-encompassing mother goddess figure, beloved all over the ancient world.

From the tale of Isis and Osiris, witches take the themes of the eternal goddess's power to resurrect from death to life, but also the concept of the mysteries of death that forever change. The link between sex and death also is inferred, as sexual power always has been associated with the primal forces of life and death, as detailed in the mysteries of the zodiac sign Scorpio. When I look at the priestess and priest of Isis and Osiris, I see my ancestors, carrying the traditions of witchcraft, the cycles of the seasons in the exoteric outer world, and the mysteries of death, rebirth, magick, and the shadow in the esoteric inner world.

Believed to be older than the temple traditions of Egypt are those of Mesopotamia, including Sumer, Akkadia, and their spiritual descendants Babylon and Assyria. These cultures held rich mystery traditions of goddesses and gods. Many believe the arts of magick as we know them began in these lands. They are known for their abilities in tracking the heavens and interpreting their movements, in summoning spirits, in medicine and healing, and in petitioning the gods for blessings. Parts of the city-state territory known as Sumeria were later absorbed by the empires of Babylon, Assyria, and Persia. We find the origin of the term magi and the strong priest-magi archetype in links to the Persian traditions and religion. The Sumerian root influenced most mythologies of the Middle East.

Some of our most familiar divine images and archetypes in Western mythology find their origins in these Mesopotamian traditions, including the sky god Marduk, the scribe Nabu, the resurrection god Dumuzi, the Earth Mother goddess Ninhursag, the primal mother of watery chaos Tiamat, and the Sun god Shamash. The most important of these deities to modern witches is the goddess Inanna. Her mystery is much like that of Osiris, but this tale focuses exclusively on the goddess instead of a male figure descending to the depths. Modern mystics believe the mysteries of Inanna, a fertility and sexuality goddess, were reenacted in rituals of initiation. Inanna's priestesses maintained a temple tradition of sacred prostitution, initiating others into the ways of lovemaking and its magick.

Mesopotamian lore influenced the rise of the Persian religion, administered by the magi of the land we now call Iran. The Persian traditions evolved into a form of dualism, a philosophy of light and dark, spiritual and material, in conflict, which set the stage for the rise of Zoroastrianism. The prophet Zarathustra, known as Zoroaster to the Greeks, sought to reform the magician religion and traditions from a period of corruption. His religion and theology, emphasizing the light, became known as Zoroastrianism and had a profound influence on the world, particularly on Jewish, Christian, and Islamic worldviews. In this theology, the all-powerful and wise creator Ahura Mazda, or Ohrmazd, is in conflict with a being of destruction and impurity known as Angra Mainyu, or Ahriman. The righteous, or followers of Asha, the righteous light, ascend to heaven, while the evil and corrupt descend to hell to be purified. On the final day, all of the world and all souls will be purified and ascend to heaven.

Zoroaster's influence can be seen in certain forms of Gnostic Christianity. While in Zoroastrianism the world is not inherently evil, but a creation of Ohrmazd, it is implied that it needs to be purified from the influence of Ahriman. Gnostic tradition often looked at the world as inherently evil and taught that only through true and personal knowledge of the divine can one escape the material world and join the true god. The God of the Old Testament is considered to be the Demiurge, or the King of the World—not the true god, but rather the god of ego and form, keeping us in servitude and suffering. The material world, flesh, and pleasure are seen as traps to keep us away from the divine. In many ways, the Demiurge can be compared to the later Christian concept of the Devil. The dualism became more pronounced as the world became a battleground for the good and evil figures, with humanity caught in the middle. The *gnosis*, or knowledge of the Gnostics, is the direct ecstatic experience of the divine, and Gnostic philosophies and cosmologies are said to point the way to a true experience and eventual escape from the material world of suffering. It's important to note that not all forms of Gnostic Christianity held this worldview, as there was not one overarching Gnostic Church but rather a variety of independent sects until the rise of the Roman Catholic Church eradicated the independent Christians as it did the pagan traditions. Some forms of Gnostic worship were very feminine-reverent and had a lot in common with modern forms of magick and paganism.

Though most would not associate the traditions of the ancient Hebrew people with witchcraft and magick, there is a rich magickal tradition beneath the surface. With the associations the Hebrew people had with both captivities in Egypt and Babylon, some speculate that the Jewish mystics either influenced their captors or were influenced by these pagan cultures. There is probably a little truth to both. We know that in Old Testament accounts witchcraft might have been outlawed, but was being practiced in these territories. The account of the Witch of Endor links witchcraft practices to what today we would consider necromancy or spiritualism, the rituals to speak with the dead. Saul seeks a woman "with familiar spirit" to summon the spirit of Samuel for guidance. Many looking to folk traditions will point out that traditional witchcraft has always had more to do with the ancestors than with what most modern witches practice today.

Beyond the Witch of Endor, another link to the Hebraic tradition itself is the figure of King Solomon. Though one can debate whether this magician-king figure was an actual or mythical figure, he is described as a magician, with the ability to summon, bind, and control all manner of spirits, both good and evil, for the construction of the temple. He is attributed with writing a number of medieval grimoires on magick, though if there was a historical Solomon, his connection to these books is mythical and spiritual at best, and not literal. Yet as a figure he provides a tantalizing link between the image of priest and magician, and as a spirit worker he has seer or shamanic overtones. Most interesting to witches and magicians is his relationship with the Queen of Sheba. Some speculate that Solomon was actually a devotee of Astarte, the Phoenician goddess linked with Inanna and also known as Ashera. His famous Song of Songs is actually an invocation to her. It is further speculated that Solomon and the Queen were involved in forms of Phoenician fertility magick or tantra. Though these are all wonderful ideas in the mythical history linking the mage and the priestess-witch archetypes, there is no hard evidence that King Solomon actually existed, let alone was a practitioner of Phoenician sex magick. Yet his mythos continues to inspire magicians today.

The association of magicians with biblical lore also exists in the New Testament, as the infant Jesus is visited by three wise men, magi from the East, each bringing a gift of gold, frankincense, and myrrh. The figure of Jesus himself, often renounced by witches due to the persecution of the Christian Church against pagan ways, is embraced as a guiding principle in ritual magick. Some witches have a problem not with Jesus the teacher and healer, but with his subsequent followers. They echo a famous quote attributed to Gandhi: "I love your Christ. It's just that so many of you Christians are so unlike your Christ." Some even see Jesus as a witch figure, performing magick later viewed as miracles, traveling with a company of twelve and thus making thirteen in total like a coven, and venerating the feminine in his mother, Mary, and Mary Magdalene. Magicians see Jesus not as a witch, but as a magician, espousing many of the same principles that are found in magickal teachings across the world. Wild speculations as to how Jesus spent the time before his ministry place him in Egypt, India, or with the Druids in Europe, learning the ways of magick and the arts of life after death to prepare him for his work in the Middle East.

Witches and magicians find a familiar territory in the myths and traditions of the ancient Greeks and Romans. Many attribute the first true images of the witch to ancient Greece, through the traditions of the Thessalian witches and the images of Hecate and her priestesses. It is through the development of the Greek civilization that we have evidence of a split between the mysteries of the more rural, illicit religions and ecstatic cults meeting in the wilds and the more structured and formal temple traditions. Through their traditions, and due to interpretations and terms coined by the philosopher Nietzsche, we have the concept of Apollonian and Dionysian principles in culture, theater, and religion.

The Apollonian principle, named for the Sun god Apollo, refers to the processes that bring about greater individualization, form, and structure, including rational thought and logic. The Dionysian principle, named for the twice-born god of the vine Dionysus, embodies the process of union, breaking down individualization where the sense of self is absorbed by the greater whole, often through drunkenness or madness. Emotion, intuition, and chaos are the hallmarks of this path. At first glance, the Apollonian approach seems geared more for the ritual magician, while the Dionysian has more of a classic witch's sabbat feel to it. Greek society embraced both principles in varying degrees, just as today, the modern witchcraft mystery traditions embrace both principles. There is both learning and intuition in our traditions. Like Osiris and Inanna, Apollo and Dionysus have resurrection myths associated with them, from the cyclical return of the Sun to the dismemberment, death, and resurrection in the Underworld.

The Greek traditions lean to one side or the other. The mysteries associated with Orpheus, the Greek poet and musician born to the muse Calliope and the god Apollo, have a more Dionysian feel to them, particularly when compared to the later mystery schools.

These mysteries existed along with those of Eleusis, based upon the mythos of Demeter and Persephone. This is another story of descent and return. Persephone was abducted to the Underworld by the Underworld god Hades, then forced to eat the food of the dead (pomegranate seeds) and become Queen of the Dead. The rites of the Eleusinian mysteries were so secret that we don't really know what occurred, but speculations include ritual reenactment of the mythos, or even a hallucinogenic sacrament made from the ergot fungus that grows on grain.

The temple at Delphi is another bridge between the Apollonian and Dionysian currents. It was originally a temple to the mother goddess Gaia or the goddess Delphyne, and was later associated with the followers of Apollo. One would travel to the temple to consult Pythia, the oracle of Delphi. The historian Plutarch was a high priest at Delphi and recorded the process. The priestess would enter a small chamber and absorb fumes that inspired prophecy. Modern research suggests that a fault line beneath the temple actually released hydrocarbon gases capable of inducing trance and vision. For mystics, the famous quote "Know thyself" is from the archway of the temple, urging all to see the mysteries within. The temple at Delphi remained a major religious center until it was closed by the Christian emperor Theodosius.

The mystery teachings of a more Apollonian bent are found in the philosopher sages of Greece. The term *Hermetic*, applied to a wide body of Western mystery traditions, can be traced to Hermes, the god of travel, commerce, and messages. Hermes is free to travel the realms of Olympus, Earth, and the Underworld, with the sign of the caduceus as his mark of office. Hermes is also linked to the figure of Hermes Trismegistus, or "thrice greatest Hermes," and to the Egyptian scribe god Thoth, as the patron of alchemy and magick. Writings attributed to Hermes still influence modern magicians today. As a Mercurial archetype, he is associated with his Roman counterpart, Mercury, god of the mind, words, and communication. Myth links Hermes and Apollo together as brothers, and they traded gifts, the lyre from Hermes to Apollo and the caduceus from Apollo to Hermes.

Pythagoras established a secret mystery cult that was believed to be similar to the Orphic mysteries. Some say that either he trained with the Druids, or they, in turn, were trained or influenced by him during his travels of the world. Pythagoras studied in Egypt, Babylonia, and India and spent time with the Druids. He was said to have studied with the Thessalian witches, from whom he learned the arts of divination. Geometry, mathematics, music, and poetry played important roles in the teachings of Pythagoras. He was the first to create the theory of the "music of the spheres." Like magicians and witches of every era, he was reputed to have magickal powers, to converse with the animals, call eagles from the sky, and bilocate. Greek scholars continued the traditions of exploring the universe through philosophy, math, astrology, and art. They speculated about the nature of the soul and the otherworlds and also gave us the popular philosophies and concepts we still study at university today. The teachings of Socrates, Plato, and Aristotle laid a foundation for further metaphysical thought and subsequent traditions. Plato in particular influenced a third-century CE revival known as Neoplatonism, which would go on to influence Qabalah and Hermeticism for all future generations. Though we most often think of these philosophers as academics, their images and roles are not far from those of the village wise man or wizard, guiding the next generation's development and understanding of nature, the self, and the universe.

Though the mysteries and philosophies continued under Roman rule, a new mystery tradition gained notoriety—that of Mithras. Coming from Persia, Roman Mithraism probably differed greatly from its Eastern counterparts. It became a secret tradition exclusively for men and was very popular with the Roman military. Mithras was a deity who eventually was coopted into Zoroastrianism, turning into a divine intermediary between Ahura Mazda and the humans of the world. Mithras is identified with the Sun and the powers of light. He also is identified as a divine king and patron of rulers. Some myths have him incarnate in a physical body at one time, and today, many of us find parallels in his myth and symbolism with the figure of Jesus Christ. As with the Eleusinian mysteries, there is very little we know for certain about the Roman cult of Mithras, though today we believe its rites occurred in underground temples or caves, and involved the sacrifice of a bull and the bathing in its blood to be reborn again. Though we are not sure if the priests of this tradition considered themselves magicians or healers in the sense of operative magick, they share striking parallels to the initiatory magick of life, death, and rebirth found in all ancient civilizations. The stories of Mithras rose from Persia, the land fabled for its magi. Mithraism eventually lost its hold on Roman society due to the rise of Christianity, which borrowed aspects of Mithraism and opened its doors to anyone—men, women, and children—regardless of rank or status.

The Roman poet Virgil not only was a contributor to the world of literature, but also was known as an accomplished magician. One legend says that he was taught magick by demons that he accidentally released from a bottle he discovered while digging in a vineyard. Another legend, probably closer to the truth, says that he graduated from a magick school in Toledo, having been tutored in the arts by Moorish instructors. He may have created a similar school in Naples, where he was an instructor. Living in the first century BCE, Virgil was known for his ability to create remarkable healing baths, as well as use copper, gold, and iron for magickal purposes. His profession put him at odds with the less mystically inclined medical establishment of the day. Virgil was said to have died while performing a rejuvenation ceremony with his servant. The ritual required his servant to kill him and dismember the body, placing the pieces in a barrel and under a magick oil lamp for nine days. After that time, Virgil was supposed to be revived. His servant reluctantly did as asked by his master, but the emperor, looking for the poet, interrupted the ceremony, refusing to believe the ritual tale and instead believing the servant murdered Virgil. The emperor had the servant killed and then later saw a ghost of a small child running around the barrel and cursing him. The remains were buried in Naples.

We must remember that, as modern pagans, we look back fondly on the pagan scholars of antiquity as magician-philosophers who have contributed to our own magickal revolutions, but in their own times, they generally did not look kindly upon the magus image. Though the magi were well respected for a time as a priestly class in ancient Persia, the import of the magician image to ancient Greece and Rome did not come with the same stature. Though early figures such as Orpheus and Pythagoras included magickal and shamanic elements in their teachings, many later philosophers did not. Some of these ancient philosophers contributed to the world's poor view of both the magician and the witch, seeing little difference between the two and referring to them both with disdain. Such a development could occur only in a society that viewed magick as a skill separate from religion, medicine, and other crafts, and that viewed logic as superior to intuition. As the philosopher's world grew, the role of the priestess or priest of a little understood or respected religion was devalued, and the view of the magician as charlatan and deceiver, needing to be "debunked," flourished. Plato actually contributed greatly to a hostile view of magick in his work the *Laws*. Though many witches believe that Christians are solely responsible for the persecution of magickal practitioners, the laws against magick actually began in the Roman Empire and were adopted by the later Christian Empire to use against both Christian heretics and pagan practitioners.

Though these theories on life, the divine, and the soul help inform us as modern pagans, it is important to remember that many of these ancient philosophical teachings were based mostly on intellectual musings rather than on direct experience or contact with the Otherworld, or the transmission of teachings from the ancient mystery schools. Not until the Neoplatonists did we have the strong image of the theurgist, but that image is not often applied to those of the rural traditions of the mage and witch. These academics contributed a piece of wisdom to our modern pagan renaissance, but their teachings do not encompass all of our magickal experiences. Full esoteric teachings, coupling philosophy with direct experience, flourished in the traditions of alchemy and Hermetic magick.

The European Tribal Link

Another root of our ancient world magick comes from the Indo-European tribes. The traditions of witchcraft draw upon the Celtic and Teutonic traditions, which provide a very interesting connection to our image of the mage and wizard. These powerful tribes migrated out of the Indus Valley and had contact with ancient Greece and Rome, yet their civilizations were based on ideals and structures very different from the city-states and ancient empires. But still, there was magick in these societies, and these magicians bridge the gap between our image of the primal shamanic figure and the stately clergy of the temples.

Witches hark back to the Druids as spiritual ancestors, the wise ones of the Celtic society. The Druidic link is a convenient one for modern practitioners, because those in the tradition wrote down very little themselves, so our modern knowledge of Druidic wisdom is our best guess based on current evidence. A popular modern notion is that there were three levels of training and function in the Druid caste. The first was bard, a keeper of lore, knowledge, poetry, song, and history. The second was an ovate or judge, an arbiter of dispute. The third rank was the priest, the facilitator of seasonal rituals and the instruction of new Druids. Despite the popular image that modern people have of ancient Celtica as a unified nation of Celts, in reality the tribes were separate and often feuding. The only common link among them was respect for the Druid, who interpreted the words of the gods and whose judgment was final, for to be banished from Celtic religion was to be banished from Celtic society and have no place among the people.

With such a wide range of function, who were the Druids, really? Due to a revival of Druidism by English gentlemen in the eighteenth and nineteenth centuries, we have the image of the scholarly, wizardly old male Druid etched into our collective consciousness, fitting the archetypal wizard image. Though many portray Druidism as a male art, others cite that there were "Druidesses" as well as Druids. Though their intentions were good, these revivalists had no real link to or notion of actual Druidism beyond a love of nature. When contemplating the time period and culture of the Druids, it was far more likely that they wore animal skins rather than fine robes. Druids are more akin to our image of the shaman than that of the courtly magician, yet they fulfilled the function of the priest in their society. In fact, their caste is referred to as the priest caste of Celtic culture. They had no formal temples, but practiced in groves. Their training took at least nineteen years to complete and must have been as complex, if not more so, than the temple traditions of the ancient world, for the Druids were said to memorize everything they learned. In myth and story, they are considered to be great magicians, capable of summoning storms, healing the sick, cursing, and predicting the future.

The most famous image of the Druid is that of Merlin, known as a magician. As a practitioner of the magick of England, most likely he too was a Druid, if he was a living person at all. His archetype is that of the magician wearing a blue robe with yellow stars and a conical hat, but he was most likely an animal-skin wearer, with a feathered cloak, and more akin to the wild man of the forest than the court scholar. He has the role of prophet, and his advice is received like the trickster, forcing people to confront themselves and others. In some legends, he ultimately is tricked, and trapped in a tree or cave by his lover and student. Merlin is seen as a patron of both the Celtic shamanic traditions and the Hermetic magicians. Some believe that the name Merlin, or Myrrdin, is not a name at all, but rather is a title, given to the High Priest of Albion, of England, and encompasses a lineage of high priests stretching back to Atlantis. Merlin and the Druidic tradition give us the link to the Celtic Otherworld so strongly associated with witchcraft and the Goddess, as well as a link between the functions of priest, magician, and shaman.

The Teutonic tribes did not have the unifying force of the Druids in their society. However, most of these tribes did have magickal practitioners. Their practices are seen as very shamanic, without the same rigid caste system and division of ranks in their mystical orders. Practitioners often were devoted to the magick of a particular goddess or god, and would act as diviner or seer, as well as folk magician. One of the most powerful Norse influences on magick, both ancient and modern, is the figure of the all-father god Odin. Also known as Wotan, he is an archetypal Mercury magician figure. Called the star-cloaked wanderer, Odin travels the nine worlds of Norse mythology. He gives the gifts of inspiration and berserker fury, and has a strong association with language, a staple gift of the Mercurial god. Odin was said to experience a shamanic death while hanging from the World Tree, and received knowledge of the runes, a language of shapes and sounds that make magick. Each rune is not just a symbol, but is the actual embodiment of a power. Odin then gave the runes to humanity. Though not embraced by modern ceremonial magicians, the runes have become beloved by modern witches as a magickal alphabet and aid in spell casting. The runes are used to divine the future, receive guidance, and make powerful changes. Odin and his ancient rune magician followers are another bridge between the shamanic traditions of tribal people and the more systematic approaches of formal magicians.

Though not of Indo-European origin, but residing in a climate similar to that of the Northern tribes, are the traditions of Finnish practitioners. Väinämöinen, the primary figure of the mythical songs compiled in the Finnish national epic the Kalevala, is a divine being of even greater scope than Merlin. He is considered both a godlike divinity and a tribal figure, with similarities to both the shaman, traveling between the worlds of humanity and the divine, and the magician, as he uses song and poetry to make his magick, like the bards of Celtic tradition and the temple priests with their words of power and secret tongues. It is interesting how the mythical figures of Merlin, Odin, and Väinämöinen all possess an aspect of the wild man, poet, and magician.

Though most of us involved in neopaganism think of the Indus Valley traditions as those that migrated west through Europe, another branch settled in India, creating what we think of today as Hindu society. Hindu mystics form a bridge from the Stone Age wise ones, with their cave paintings of horned gods similar to those found in Europe, to a fully developed society with a formal priestly caste known as the Brahmins. In Vedic society, the Brahmins hold a similar status to that held by the Druids in Celtic traditions, yet unlike the Celts, their lore, mythos, and esoteric systems were recorded in a written format. The Brahmins experienced no persecution in the form of the Burning Times, so to this day, much of their lore survives. The oldest lore of ancient India contains cave paintings and images similar to the horned figures in European lore. There is a strong similarity between the dark goddesses of India and those of the European tradition. The knotwork in Indian art, though more angular in its features, likewise shares associations with the Celtic knot art.

Modern magicians wonder how many other similarities we might share with India, and whether we can reconstruct what was lost in the West from what was preserved in the East, with regard to knowledge of the forces of energy, both in the human body and in the cosmos. Many ceremonial magicians look to the Eastern teachings to compare and revive the Western traditions, as their tantric lore, and even their elemental tattva symbols show up in the modern Hermetic teachings. Even the Far East teachings of Taoism—Taoist alchemy and the use of the I Ching divination system—show up in Hermetic magick. The image of the Asian sages and wizards is not far off from that of the Western magician.

Magick Underground

Magick's decline from the public arena came about with the rise of Christianity as the dominant force in Europe and the suppression of the native religions. Even magicians who embraced a Christian framework were not always well received, as the suppression of magick had as much to do with politics and power as it did with theology. Magick embraced by the Church and priests were claimed as miracles, while magick from any other source was labeled Satanism. It is in this time that the split between the formerly complementary partnership of the intuitive feminine mysteries and the more direct male mysteries became pronounced. Magick was divided into the cunning traditions of the forest folk and peasantry, and the high magick of the courts and secret workshops.

The Hermetic magick that grew among the educated classes of European men incorporated a wide range of traditions into its fold. Alchemy from the East and Middle East, mixed with Egyptian and Greek symbolism, became entwined with the Jewish lore of the Kabbalah. The Hermetic texts made their way into the philosopher class, to the point where some saw Hermes as a Christ figure, or more appropriately, the first ancient pagan Christian. Christian mythos became an allegory for the personal salvation and resurrection of the magician. Exploration and experimentation of the ancient mysteries in this new context grew. Texts were copied and added to, increasing our magickal theories and understanding. Magickal alphabets were created to encode information. Though there were persecutions, and many did not escape them, the upper class endured a different type of Burning Times than did the hedge witches, midwives, and unfortunate victims of village hysteria.

In the first century BCE, a Jewish-Egyptian alchemist made a great contribution to the world of magick and alchemy. Named Maria and referred to as Maria Prophetissa, Maria the Jewess, or Miriam, she is considered by some to be the first alchemist and the inventor of several alchemical processes and pieces of equipment, including the balneum Maria, or bain-marie, a water bath similar to an early form of the double boiler. Very little is known of the historic details of her life, as she was confused with Moses's sister Miriam and later equated with Mary Magdalene.

Simon Magus is a controversial magician figure from the early Christian era. He was a magician and spiritual leader with quite a reputation in Samaria and Rome, and is given credit for the founding of the Simonian Gnostic tradition. He was known to perform magick, conjure spirits, brew potions, and advocate freedom in sexuality. The early Christian Church obviously saw Simon Magus as a rival to their figure of Jesus Christ, and our knowledge of him comes through their records. Simon and Peter entered into a conflict, and Simon allegedly died in a magickal duel with Peter, either flying and fatally falling when Peter canceled his power to fly, or failing to resurrect himself once he had entombed himself in the earth. His story is an example of how the early Christian Church sought converts by showing that its magick, or "miracles," were stronger than those of other magicians and more worthy of attention. Simon's Gnostic cult continued onward for a short time, sharing space with the early Christians, but eventually all his writings were destroyed and his cult died out with the rise of the mainstream Christian Church.

The work of the scholar known as Pseudo-Dionysius the Areopagite dates to the fifth century and includes the *Divine Names*, *Celestial Hierarchy*, *Mystical Theology*, *Ecclesiastical Hierarchy*, and many epistles. His work showed the influence of Neoplatonism, and he is credited with bringing the pagan traditions of Neoplatonism into a Christian framework, making it accessible to those in both the Eastern and Western churches. His work includes teachings on the names and nature of God, the celestial hierarchy along with the angelic realms and orders, and mystical theology. He provides a bridge to keep the pagan scholars' material alive and growing in the dominant Christian world.

Albertus Magnus held many titles, as master magician, Dominican bishop, alchemist, astrologer, count, and eventual saint. He is regarded as the founder of planetary magick and the use of plants and gems in magick. It is thought that his reputation as a magician might have held up his canonization. He died in 1280 and was canonized in 1932. The Vatican denied that he was the author of his alchemical manuscripts.

The life of Pietro d'Abano is an interesting one to note in the history of magick, as he lived during the transition from freedom to persecution. When he was young, the occult arts were practiced freely. He became a magician, astrologer, and physician, as well as an advocate for natural magick in healing, and divining the character of an individual by facial features, or physiognomy. By the end of his life, in 1316, the occult arts were highly suspect and the Inquisition was just around the corner. In the four-teenth century, his body was exhumed and publicly burned.

The French alchemist Nicholas Flamel allegedly discovered the Philosopher's Stone, the elixir of immortality, after being obsessed with a magickal text and eventu-ally traveling to Toledo, Spain, to consult the rabbis there. Some accounts say he is still alive and walking the Earth today with his beloved wife, Perenelle. He did, however, disappear from the history books by 1417 and left considerable wealth to many hos-pitals, churches, and chapels. As Flamel was a simple scribe, his legacy points to the potential transmutation of lead to gold to fund these endeavors.

Marsilio Ficino followed a path similar to that of Albertus Magnus, studying both natural and planetary magick. Like Magnus, Ficino had many different roles beside being a magician, including physician and priest. His system of Hermetic magick fo-cused on the planets and their influence on health. Due to his political and religious connections, as well as his doctrine that magick was completely compatible with Christianity, he was never persecuted. Both Agrippa and Paracelsus studied Ficino's work.

Giovanni Pico della Mirandola was a magician and Christian scholar in Italy in the 1400s. He studied at the Platonic Academy founded by Marsilio Ficino, under the pa-tronage of the Medici family. He became a notable scholar in the Hermetic tradition at an early age. He was at least partly responsible for bringing the Qabalah into the West-ern traditions. He is famous for the quote, "No science more effectively proves the di-vinity of Christ than magick and Cabala." His work made him quite controversial with the Catholic Church. In 1487, under the direction of Pope Innocent VIII, his work was condemned. He was forced to retract his writings and teachings and spent some time in jail. Later, Pope Alexander VI deemed his works free of any heresy.

Cornelius Agrippa was a renowned magician of the sixteenth century, and his *Three Books of Occult Philosophy*, still available in print today, is a staple in the modern West-ern esoteric lore. He traveled extensively and studied Kabbalah and Hermeticism, and was a leading force in the Christianized forms of Cabala. Thought not identified as a witch himself, he spoke about the superiority of the feminine gender and, while in Metz, acted as public advocate for a girl accused of witchcraft. Though he got her acquitted, he was then accused of witchcraft himself. He managed to stay ahead of witch hunters and print his book despite the Inquisition's attempts to stop him. He developed quite a sinister reputation undeservedly, and might have been the prototype for the Dr. Faust character.

Giordano Bruno was a Dominican, magician, and mnemonist, best known for his contributions to the Art of Memory, a system of memorization originating in Greece. His work fused the Art of Memory with Hermetic magick. He was charged with heresy and was forced to flee the order and Italy. He traveled extensively, and his "Giordanist" circles in Germany might have played a role in the development of the Rosicrucians. His teachings also eventually made their way into the Freemason teachings. Modern American witch Lori Bruno claims descent from Giordano and says that he was a practitioner of the Old Religion of witchcraft.

Pioneering work on angelic lore was done by Elizabethan magician and scholar John Dee, along with his psychic partner Edward Kelley, though the two barely got to use the intricate system of Enochian magick they received, including an entire language and alphabet. Records of it survived until the modern age, where it was used and built upon by magicians of the Golden Dawn and their successors. Both were surrounded in controversy, as Dee was Queen Elizabeth's court astrologer and adviser on occult matters and was possibly a spy. Kelley had a reputation for theft and lying, though Dee claimed that he was a gifted scryer, and that without his talents, the transmission of the Enochian teachings would not have been possible.

While some magicians remained in their intellectual towers and temples, some found their way into the natural world to continue their understanding of God. Paracelsus, famous and volatile alchemist and father of much of our modern medicine, gave up on academia to study with the gypsies and wise women of the woods who knew more of the world of nature and curing the ills of humankind than the growing community of medical practitioners. He also insisted, like Hippocrates before him, that knowledge of astrology was essential for any doctor. Paracelsus could be considered one of the fathers of modern "holistic" medicine, as he believed in treating both the body and the soul, and the imbalances in the relationship between the two. He looked at the effect of astrology and the weather on health, and believed in the power of magick and spirits as well as medicine. Reportedly, he had a crystal in his sword hilt that contained a spirit. Like Paracelsus, many of the pioneers in science and medicine, including Copernicus, Galileo, Kepler, and Newton, were also advocates of astrology, alchemy, and other esoteric arts. Modern biographies often whitewash such information to make these figures more "respectable" to the modern world.

The Comte de Saint Germain is an enigmatic figure in European magick and mysticism. Very little factual history is known of this man. Reports of his behavior are mixed and dubious at best, ranging from a wonderman alchemist capable of removing the flaws from gems to spy, braggart, womanizer, and con artist. After his death, lore about Saint Germain grew, portraying him as an adept of the mysteries, a mason, a Rosicrucian, and eventually a figure in Theosophy as a hidden master or ascended being, guiding the forces of magick and ceremonial orders from another plane of existence. His legend plays an important role for Theosophically inclined witches and magicians.

Francis Barrett was a major figure in jump-starting the revival of magick. The majority of the material in his book *The Magus* was composed mostly of large passages from Agrippa's *Three Books of Occult Philosophy*, which were not available at the time, and his book and students brought the occult arts to light in the early 1800s.

Eliphas Lévi was another clergyman fascinated with the occult. Ordained as a deacon, he was eventually expelled, most likely for studying or teaching doctrines contrary to the Church teachings. He is best known for developing associations between the tarot, the Qabalah, the Hebrew alphabet, and the elements. He died the day Aleister Crowley was born, and Crowley counted him as one of his past incarnations. Lévi greatly influenced the Golden Dawn system of magick.

Paschal Beverly Randolph was an occultist of many trades, from spiritualist and practitioner of high magick to hoodoo root doctor. He is best known for his contributions to mirror magick for use in developing conscious clairvoyance and practicing sex magick. He might have met Lévi in his travels, and he certainly influenced the next generation of mages, including Crowley and Blavatsky.

While the magicians plied their craft in the courts of Europe under the cosmology of Christianity, historians still argue as to what the witches were up to. Were they only scattered remnants of folk belief masquerading as witchcraft? Were there true cults educated and devoted to teaching the mysteries? It depends on whom you ask.

Many believe the witchcraft traditions continued in secret, hidden from the eyes of Christianity, at least for a time. These advocates envision an organized cult of the Goddess. Critics on the other end of the spectrum wonder what, if any, folk magick survived. As is so often the case, the truth is likely to be somewhere in between. There is enough anecdotal evidence to conclude that witchcraft, in some form or function, existed in Europe, though it was not likely a large organization. Much like paganism today, it was probably a loose collection of practitioners, some more serious and educated in the mysteries than others. Basic folk beliefs continued under Christianity, as well as the vocation of cunning men and women in the village. I'm sure that some of the keepers of the flame knew the old mysteries in one form or another, and kept them going for those who felt the call. It is in those mysteries that the roots of the witch and magician remained entwined during this dark period of history, although they were separated by class and culture.

The influence of the East on both the alchemist magicians and the witch cults is a point deserving of deep thought. Whereas the Eastern influences can be traced more overtly in ceremonial magick, with its written texts, many a traditional witch story will tell you that the office of the Man in Black in the coven structure, often cited as the Devil by Christian prosecutors, was not originally a symbol of anything, but was literally a black man who taught them the arts and mysteries, suggesting a Moorish connection. Black also became associated with the esoteric arts because of alchemy, coming from the land of Khem, Egypt, the black lands of rich Nile delta soil and the Arabic word for black (*khem*), which closely resembles the Arabic word for wisdom. The "chem" of alchemy and chemistry comes from this root. The Moorish kingdom in Spain lasted from 711 CE to 1492 and influenced Western occultism, art, and science. The Moors introduced many concepts and words to Europe, from Arabic numerals to the terms *zenith* and *nadir* in astrology. Arabic Qabalah, similar to the Hebrew version, delved deep into the study of numbers and words to find their true meanings. The city of Toledo, Spain, became synonymous with study of the occult arts. Christian Rosenkreutz, the mythical founder of the Rosicrucian Mysteries (which led to the modern movements of the Golden Dawn), was said to have studied in Fez, Morocco.

The rise of Islam in the East might have caused those in the Middle East who were devoted to older pagan faiths to move west to escape Islam. Through their migration, they eventually came to influence the Old Religion of Europe. Some might have hidden beneath the veneer of the Islamic tradition as they traveled. The formal structure of the coven, holidays, and ranks might have been aspects imported to the cults of the Goddess and family traditions from contact with the Saracens and Sufis. Gerald Gardner, who is believed to have been initiated into a Sufi order while traveling in the East, states in his book *Witchcraft Today* that witches say their cult comes from the East. The Eastern traditions could have influenced the West, or they could have come from a similar root, terrestrially, or the mystics of each culture could have found the same inner-world inspiration from the same symbols and actions. Teachers such as traditional witch Robert Cochrane, magician and occultist Rollo Ahmed, Sufi master Idries Shah, and the material of the Pickingill tradition brought to light by E. W. Liddell all point to Eastern influences predating Gerald Gardner.

Both Sufis and witches believe in a power that can be raised and transmitted, a power that is not symbolic but is an actual energy. They called it *baraka*, meaning "blessing" or "power." The Sufi saying "Baraka bashad" means "may the blessings be" and is strikingly similar to the "Blessed be" of witches. As in witchcraft, some Sufi practices have elements of sacred sexuality and the conference of blessing through sexual actions. In particular, there are traditions similar to the fivefold kiss, as outlined in the classic *The Jewel in the Lotus* by Allen Edwardes. The Aniza Bedouin were taught by the Sufi Abu el-Atahiyya (748–828 CE), and his disciples were known as Wise Ones and commemorated him with the image of the horns of a goat and a torch between them. A group of his disciples ended up in Spain under Moorish rule. The Dhulqarneni, or Two-Horned Ones, are a cult similar to the Aniza that flourished in Morocco and Spain despite the more orthodox Islamic authority's attempts to suppress it. The Dhulqarneni have many similarities to the image of witches, as they were associated with the Moon, danced in a circle to raise power, spoke Muslim prayers backwards, invoked the "Black Man" El Aswad, met at the crossroads, marked themselves with a small wound from a ritual knife at initiation, carried forked staffs (stangs), wore ritual robes, and met in groups of thirteen. Their meetings were called the Zabbat, "the Forceful or Powerful One," which sounds strikingly similar to the Sabbat of the witch.

The Templars were another point of contact between the West and East. Through a Christian order of knights, the Knights Templar were far from ordinary Christians, and their mysteries have never been fully explained to the satisfaction of all. Started in the aftermath of the first crusade, ostensibly to act as warrior monks to protect pilgrims to the Holy Land, the Templars did little protecting and spent most of their time in the Middle East, establishing themselves as an order, in the ruins of what was believed to be King Solomon's Temple. With rank and privileges afforded by the Church that no other group had, they soon became a force in the Christian world, starting modern banking. Occultists speculate that they found something in the ruins, from the Holy Grail to the Ark of the Covenant, to evidence that Judeo-Christian tradition was nothing more than myth, and not literal truth, as believed. After rising in power and prestige, they fell from grace in the eyes of the Church and royalty. Members of the order were arrested and tortured, ostensibly over a financial dispute with King Philip of France. Philip forced Pope Clement V to disband the order.

The Templars were accused of heresy, homosexuality, and witchcraft. They were particularly reviled for their worship of a being called Baphomet, and their image of this deity as a horned being with a goat head, beard, and hindquarters, and of mixed gender, with female breasts and erect phallus. A candle was often at the crown, as well as the inverted pentagram. Baphomet bore a resemblance to both the Christian Devil and the witch's image of the divine, and in particular to the witch's God, mixing male and female, human and animal characteristics. Idris Shah Sayid, as reported by Doreen Valiente in her *An ABC of Witchcraft*, suggested his name comes from the Arabic Abufihamat, or "Father of Understanding." Baphomet is much like the symbol of the Aniza Bedouins. Our modern image of the Devil from the tarot is drawn from the same image. The figure of Baphomet is also strikingly similar to that of the Greek god Pan, as occultist Eliphas Lévi equated Baphomet with Pan and the horned god found in medieval witchcraft lore. Though the androgynous nature does not seem very godlike to many, the old traditions often started with a bisexual androgynous figure.

Modern scholars suppose that the Knights might have been trained in the mysticism and philosophy of the East, though obviously not in the Islamic mysteries, as the keeping of idols would go against the core beliefs of Muslims. The Eastern mysteries in which the Knights were versed seemed much more pagan, yet were organized into orders and ranks within the larger organization. And what, if anything, did the Knights Templar tradition have to do with the magick attributed to King Solomon? No one knows for sure, but there are a few interesting parallels to what witches have been accused of, though none of the Templars are reported to have identified with witchcraft.

Though the Templars were disbanded, a full disclosure of their finances and membership was never discovered. Legends persist of the Templars who escaped persecution ending up in Scotland and starting the Masonic movement, another group with a mythical connection to Solomon and the ancient world. The Masons incorporated a lot of Templar mythical themes into their initiation rites. Others suppose that the mystics of the order either were absorbed into other Christian organizations or blended in with the rural folk and peasantry. Perhaps some put their mysticism to use as cunning men, and the existing cunning men and witches traded lore with the Masons, bringing the Eastern influence. With the expansion of Freemasonry, the cunning men of a community might have joined for the measure of secrecy it afforded them, both influencing the growth of Masonry and in turn being influenced by it. British Traditional Witchcraft degree systems bear a strong resemblance to the Masonic model, and one might debate which came first.

Through the Masonic connection we could have the additional link of Solomonic magick found in the Craft. During the Burning Times, folk witches were said to be caught with copies of the old grimoires, such as versions of the Key of Solomon. If there was simply a folk tradition of magick and not an organized tradition of some sort, it seems rather strange that pagan folk healers would want and keep Judeo-Christian manuals of magick unless there was some deeper connection and use. In Venice during the seventeenth century, Laura Malipero was caught with a copy of the Key of Solomon in her home, with a handwritten book that included excerpts of the key she transcribed. Though many critics will say that the witch's magickal journal is found only in the modern craft, and the term *Book of Shadows* appears only in the post-Gardner era, here we see at least some historical record of the practice of keeping a magickal book among witches. A woodcut dating from 1555, from the book *History of the Northern Peoples* by Bishop Olaus Magnus, depicts a witch using a knife and magickal herbs to control a demon she has conjured, reminiscent of the techniques found in the grimoires of Solomon, as an early version of the Key of Solomon is dated 1572. Though they are different systems of magick and different theologies all together, we still see a connection between the arts of high and low magick.

THE MODERN MAGICKAL REVIVAL

In the modern magickal revival of the late nineteenth and twentieth centuries, we saw a strange switch in the gender roles of magick. Many occultists believed that, on the subtle planes, those of the feminine gender mediate a more masculine, projective energy and those of a masculine gender mediate a more feminine, receptive energy. This seemed to prove true, at least in part, with the coming of the New Age. Some striking women played a strong role in the more intellectual mysteries and theorems of the New Age, while two men became associated with the traditions of witchcraft and the Goddess. Both phenomena made the image of the male witch and the female magician more common in our collective mind, though we still have plenty of examples of male magicians and female witches in this age of revival.

The tradition of Theosophy was an impetus for the New Age metaphysical movement in the West. Though not a tradition of magicians, it does have a magickal bent that often is overlooked. Theosophy, like the work of the Hermetic Qabalists, brought the strands of truth from many world traditions into a harmonious whole, though it is interesting that the Theosophical teachings tended to focus on the Eastern mysteries, Christianity, and those Western traditions of the pagan temple traditions, such as those of Egypt and Greece. The more ecstatic mysteries of the rural pagans, along with the Jewish mysticism, were not emphasized. The two most notable pioneers of the Theosophical movement were the founder of the society, Helena Blavatsky, who officially began the organization in 1875, and her spiritual successor Alice Bailey. Rather than have the image of the wise hedge witch, dispensing folk cures and conjuring magick, each woman wrote volumes of intellectually dense material, inspired by the hidden masters of the Theosophical tradition. Blavatsky's *Isis Unveiled* was much more magickal in nature than her later work *The Secret Doctrine*. One of Bailey's numerous works was entitled *A Treatise on White Magic*, emphasizing the spiritual components of magickal traditions.

While the archetype of the feminine intellectual and spiritual leader was on the rise in Theosophy, we had the more familiar image of the male magician in the Hermetic Order of the Golden Dawn and its various offshoots. Founded in 1888, the Hermetic Order of the Golden Dawn has a history rich with controversy and mystery. The root of much of the mystery is found in a document known as the Cipher Manuscript, and the speculations as to its veracity. In one popularly accepted history of the order, Rev. A.F.A. Woodford found the manuscript and believed it to be from antiquity. Woodford, a Mason and Hermetic Society member, consulted Dr. William Wynn Westcott and Dr. William Robert Woodman, both officers in the Rosicrucian Society of England, and then later Samuel Liddell MacGregor Mathers and his psychic wife, Moina Mathers. The Cipher contained the framework for a series of rituals. A document with the manuscript stated that anyone who deciphered it should contact "Fraulein Anna Sprengel" in Hanover, Germany. Westcott claimed to have done so, and further stated that Sprengel had given him permission to establish an order of magicians as a branch of the Rosicrucian Order of England. Together, his aspiring group of would-be magicians founded the Isis-Urania Temple of the Hermetic Order of the Golden Dawn and launched one of the most influential traditions of modern magick the world has ever known. At one time, members included figures such as William Butler Yeats, Arthur Edward Waite, and Florence Farr.

Of course, critics would argue that this unusual history only served to give the founders some sense of legitimacy and connection to the past through a mysterious German woman and that, in the end, her permission and authority had little influence on the triumphs and tragedies of the lodge.

The Order of the Golden Dawn had the intellectual bent that one would expect from the upper class of England. With their global view, they reconstructed rituals from the Cipher Manuscript with a foundation in Hermetic Qabalah, using the Tree of Life as their primary glyph and symbol system, but synthesizing Jewish, Christian, pagan, and Eastern elements to create a whole complicated cosmology and system of magickal theory. They drew heavily upon the scholarly work and research available at the time, and the work of previous magicians such as Eliphas Lévi, Cornelius Agrippa, Francis Barrett, and John Dee.

The group experienced a variety of internal conflicts and schisms. Samuel Mathers claimed psychic contact with the true rulers of the order, the "Secret Chiefs," which many assume to be a group of ascended beings guiding from the invisible planes of reality, similar to Theosophy's masters. These invisible rulers named Mathers the "Visible Head" of the order. His leadership eventually resulted in the dissolution of the group, yet the body of theory, ritual, and lore remained on the terrestrial planes and eventually was made available by others, most notably Israel Regardie. Modern magicians have used and adapted the Golden Dawn material in their quest for the completion of the Great Work—the enlightenment of the magician and the Philosopher's Stone of the alchemist.

Many attribute Mathers' relationship with the young and controversial figure of Aleister Crowley as a leading reason for the dissolution of the order. Though this certainly was a factor, not all the blame can be laid at Crowley's feet. Crowley joined the Golden Dawn in 1898 and became Mathers' protégé, much to the dismay of many of the other members. The two eventually had a falling-out marked by not only verbal assaults but also magickal ones. Crowley was a prolific and insightful author on the topics of magick and mysticism, but his greatest contribution to Western occultism was the transmission of *The Book of the Law* and the formation of his religion, Thelema. With the guidance of a spirit named Aiwass, thought to be Crowley's Holy Guardian Angel, or Higher Self, Crowley proclaimed himself the prophet of the next aeon, the Aeon of Horus. Thelema is Greek for "will," and the tradition is based on performing one's True Will over all other laws and creeds. Though it is erroneously believed by many to be a license to do whatever you want, Thelema refers not to the ego's will but to the soul's. According to Crowley, Thelema holds the pattern of spiritual development for the next age.

Though Crowley was a magician dedicated to the Great Work and the highest aims of magick, his life is often misunderstood, and even in life, Crowley promoted that misunderstanding. Reveling in the title of "the most wicked man in the world," and using a name his mother called him as a child, "the Beast," he did believe that the principles of Thelema would replace those of Judaism, Christianity, and Islam, and his apocalyptic ritual symbolism reflected that. His lifestyle and sense of self shook Victorian society, though many of the things he was ostracized for in his age, such as his bisexuality, would not be considered so scandalous today. Between reveling in his reputation and the fact that modern Satanists later drew upon some of his writings, he erroneously has been labeled a Satanist and thus is avoided by many seekers, even many witches.

In 1922, Crowley became the leader of the Ordo Templi Orientis, or O.T.O., a group of magicians working through sex magick. He also was involved in the Argenteum Astrum, the A∴A∴ or Order of the Silver Star, as an initiatory tradition, separate from, but harmonious with, the O.T.O. Conflicting reports state that Crowley was the founder of Argenteum Astrum and eventually abandoned it, while others state that the order is far older than and independent of Crowley, based on individual teacher-student relationships, and that he simply brought it to mainstream occult attention. As with so many topics in Crowley's life, and in the history of magick in general, we may never find an answer that satisfies both academics and devotees.

Crowley's teachings on magick were based heavily on the principles and structure of the Golden Dawn system, yet he interwove his own Thelemic cosmology to be the prominent element of the rituals. He reworked and rewrote many of the famous Golden Dawn rituals to suit his own purposes. Crowley is responsible for popularizing the spelling of magick with a *k*, to differentiate it from sideshow stage magic and illusions. He changed some Qabalistic and tarot correspondences, based on the inspired message of *The Book of the Law*. He encoded much of his own magickal teachings at the end of his life in the monumental *Thoth Tarot* and *The Book of Thoth* text in conjunction with the art of Lady Frieda Harris. Unlike the focus of the Golden Dawn, his workings had a much stronger sexual content and greater emphasis placed on the Goddess as an aspect of divinity, manifesting through the star goddess Nuit and the goddess Babylon. Like his magickal motto, Perdurabo, which literally means "I will endure till the end," his work has endured and continues to inspire and sometimes irritate magicians and witches of this aeon.

A lesser-known breakaway from the Golden Dawn, yet one who arguably has had as profound an effect on modern magick and Wicca, is Violet Firth, better known by her magickal name, Dion Fortune, short for "Deo, Non Fortuna," or "by God, not chance." Fortune left the Golden Dawn to form the Fraternity of the Inner Light, which eventually was renamed the Society of the Inner Light and is still in existence today. Here again we have an even stronger feminine magician archetype, both through her own persona and those of her characters. Fortune wrote several magickal texts, such as *The Mystical Qabalah*, but was best known for the deep wisdom teachings that influenced modern magick found in her magickal fiction, such as *The Sea Priestess*, *Demon Lover*, and *The Goat-Foot God*. Many feel that she openly expressed beliefs and theology in these novels and stories that she could not credibly present in more academic work, as she was writing before the repeal of the Witchcraft Act in England. She is famous for a line in *The Sea Priestess* that is quoted by magicians and witches today: "All the gods are one god, and all the goddesses are one goddess, and there is one initiator." Though Fortune was not considered a witch, much of the poetry in her novels has a very witchy feel to it, such as this passage from *The Sea Priestess*:

> *I am the soundless, boundless, bitter sea;*
> *All things in the end shall come to me.*
> *Mine is the kingdom of Persephone,*
> *The inner earth, where lead the pathways three.*
> *Who drinks the waters of that hidden well*
> *Shall see the things whereof he dare not tell—*
> *Shall tread the shadowy path that leads to me—*
> *Diana of the Ways and Hecate,*
> *Selene of the Moon, Persephone.*

Dion Fortune and her Sea Priestess character express the archetype of the witch as high priestess, regal and otherworldly, rather than cunning woman. Fortune's great contribution to the Western mysteries was the move away from sole reliance on the Qabalah and a quest to find the indigenous wisdom of the British Isles and the greenery of the land and the Goddess. She brought together the pagan and Christian mysteries of the Round Table and the Grail with the mysteries of Plato's Atlantis, forms of spiritualism and high magick. She died in 1946, but many claim that she is guiding the traditions she founded from the inner planes.

From the waves of the ceremonial revival in England came the witchcraft revival, with two very prominent and vocal men at the forefront, Gerald Gardner and Alex Sanders. Two active lineages in the modern craft, Gardnerian and Alexandrian witchcraft, still bear their names. Though many associate witchcraft with the Goddess, feminism, and the mysteries of women, these two prominent and controversial men left their stamp indelibly on the traditions and showed that the Craft has had a male side to it all along.

Gerald B. Gardner was a British civil servant who spent time traveling in the East and exploring the occult. He claimed initiation into a New Forest witch coven in England in 1939. After the repeal of the Witchcraft Act in 1951, Gardner started his own coven and brought the teachings of the Craft to public light. Critics would argue that his version of witchcraft was an amalgam of several different sources. He was influenced by his time in the East, as well as by the works of Margaret Murray and Theosophy. Gardner, like the founders of the Golden Dawn, was a Mason as well. It's hard to see what elements of these other traditions were a smoke screen for the New Forest coven, as members initially met in a Rosicrucian theater and possibly called themselves the Crotona Fellowship. The Fellowship was described as Rosicrucian, Masonic, or Theosophical, depending on the observer, and many believe it was a façade for the smaller group of witches to find appropriate new members. Few modern pagans realize that Gardner also was a member of the modern Druidic revival and held a charter for Crowley's O.T.O. organization. Gardner's version of the Craft seemed to embody all of these elements.

The strongest link to a line of modern ritual magick comes from Aleister Crowley. Gardner had a passing acquaintance with Crowley late in the magician's life. Author Francis King, among others, believes that it was Crowley who wrote the Gardnerian Book of Shadows. Though Crowley does not show up directly in his own works and personal accounts, there is speculation that he had a link to the witchcraft cult before his studies of ceremonial magick, to a line of witches potentially linked to the New Forest coven. George Pickingill, an infamous cunning man and witch of his time, was said to preside over nine covens in Norfolk, England, in the late 1800s. Crowley potentially was offered membership or even initiated into one of Pickingill's covens in his youth. Rumor has it that he was dismissed for his contemptuous attitude toward women in positions of power before he completed his training. The link of common initiatory traditions in the Craft might have been the foundation for Gardner's and Crowley's friendship.

Like Crowley, Pickingill was a controversial man, outwardly calling for the overthrow of Christianity, and was considered by some to be a Satanist. He advocated for witches and Satanists to band together to overthrow Christianity. He was known for his magickal powers, as it was said that he could command imps to pick the fields while he smoked his pipe and relaxed. He might have borrowed liberally from some academic and classical components of magickal texts, such as passages from Barrett's *The Magus*, to form his own tradition. He, too, might have influenced the rise of the Golden Dawn's generation of magicians. Doreen Valiente alleges, in *Witchcraft for Tomorrow*, that Pickingill might have had a hand, along with his Masonic students, in creating the Cipher Manuscript, which led to the formation of the Golden Dawn, though most researchers of the Golden Dawn's history would disagree. Moina Mathers, however, was said to have attended one of Pickingill's demonstrations of his magickal prowess for a group of Freemasons and Rosicrucians. The waters get murky when trying to determine who borrowed from whom and where a given teaching originated. How much of an influence Pickingill had on Crowley, Gardner, or anybody else is vastly debated.

Alex Sanders' line of witchcraft had the definitive flair of ceremonial magick to it. His witchcraft origin is not very clear, as various accounts exist of his initiation, from his grandmother to his uncle bringing him into the family tradition. Some even speculate that he was a failed Gardnerian initiate who began his own tradition based on the rituals he received, with some accidental miscopies from the Book of Shadows that slightly changed the theology and format, and then concocted his family history story as a cover. Maxine Sanders, Sanders' ex-wife and high priestess, paints a portrait of an established living tradition predating Alex's contact with any Gardnerians. In any case, the work he put forth to the world definitely was influenced by the world of high magick in terms of symbolism, ritual, and structure.

Sanders was inspired in particular by W. E. Butler, a member of the Society of the Inner Light and author of *The Magician: His Training and Work*, and Franz Bardon, author of *Initiation into Hermetics*. Author Janet Farrar, who is responsible for popularizing much of Alexandrian Wicca with her late husband, Stewart Farrar, and Gavin

Bone, speculates, in the book *Progressive Witchcraft*, that Sanders was trying to turn the folk magick of witchcraft into something more ceremonially oriented. Witches in the Alexandrian tradition often receive training in the arts of high magick, including fluid condensers, Enochian magick, Golden Dawn rituals, and planetary squares, which eventually made their way into other branches of Wicca.

The last major branch of magick to entwine magicians and witches is Chaos magick. Though this freeform, avant-garde, experimental movement of magick often is attributed to Peter J. Carroll and his books *Liber Null* and *Psychonaut* and even peripherally draws inspiration from the life of Aleister Crowley, the real grandfather of the Chaos magick movement and its practices is Austin Osman Spare. Spare had a brief association with Crowley as an artist for Crowley's publication, *The Equinox*, and was a member of the Silver Star. Though he is an inspiration to Chaos magicians everywhere, and Chaos magick is considered cutting-edge in the world of high magick, Spare himself identified truly as a witch and was initiated into the mysteries of witchcraft by a woman known to us only as Mrs. Paterson. She called herself his second mother, or witch mother, and gave him the craft name Zos.

Spare's form of magick was entwined with his art and sexuality. Though he met with a certain amount of critical and commercial success in England, he became disenchanted with the art scene and retired to obscurity. In the 1950s he met Gerald Gardner, who encouraged him to make sigils and talismans. Spare's magnum opus, *Zos Kia Cultus*, was unfinished at his death in 1956, though he published several books and works of art during his lifetime. His forms of sigilization and sexual magick became foundation stones in the traditions of Illuminates of Thanateros, or IOT, an organization that became equated with the Chaos magick movement, as it was founded by Peter Carroll and Ray Sherwin. Expanding upon many of the theories of Spare, Thanateros embodies the dual concepts of death (Thanatos) and love (Eros) in its cosmology.

The last of the major public witches of the twentieth century to proclaim potential influence from Crowley is author, astrologer, psychic, and numerologist Sybil Leek. This English witch claimed to have met with Crowley when she was nine, and he encouraged her poetry and magick, teaching her secret words and vibrations of power. She lived in the New Forest area and was initiated into several traditions, including a New Forest coven descended from George Pickingill. In the time of Gardner's and

Sanders' popularity, Leek, too, weighed in as a public voice of the Old Religion, and eventually moved to America to share her knowledge and writings with the world. Often at odds with the witchcraft community, she was against ritual nudity but advocated cursing in situations that warranted it, even writing a book of curses. She wrote many books on a variety of esoteric topics, and claimed that the spirit of Madame Blavatsky acted as her guide, urging her to write about reincarnation. Leek lived a colorful and adventuresome life, tying together many esoteric professions under the banner of "witch."

Modern authors continue to walk the paths of both the magician and the witch. Popular author Donald Michael Kraig has done for ceremonial magick what Scott Cunningham did for Wicca, making it accessible to those who truly seek and wish to live it. Few know that Kraig also is initiated in witchcraft traditions and was the onetime roommate of Cunningham, forming more than one bridge with the pagan community.

William Gray was a well-respected occultist of the twentieth century known for his work in the Hermetic tradition and ritual magick. He founded a magickal tradition known as the Sangreal Sodality, yet he had contact with traditional witch Robert Cochrane, and the two seemed to influence each other. Gray's Sangreal Prayer has made its way into traditions descended from Cochrane and can be found in the book *Witchcraft: A Tradition Renewed* by Doreen Valiente and Evan Jones:

> *Beloved Bloodmother of my especial breed,*
> *Welcome me at this moment with your willing womb.*
> *Let me learn to live in love with all you are,*
> *So my seeking spirit serves the Sangreal.*

Other practitioners who straddle the lines between witchcraft, paganism, and ceremonial magick include R. J. Stewart, Dolores Ashcroft-Nowicki, Herman Slater, Edmund Buczynski, John Michael Greer, Kala Trobe, and Jason Augustus Newcomb.

Though we'd like to believe that there exist secret and unbroken lineages of Gnostic magicians, reverent to the Goddess and the true mysteries behind Christianity and all religions, as suggested in the popular fiction of Dan Brown's *The Da Vinci Code*, few are stepping forward. Like most members of the family traditions of witchcraft, those who claim any lineage to pre-Golden Dawn magickal traditions are dismissed or put through an academic scrutiny that does not uphold their claims. I'd like to think the world is full of secret orders, working their magick behind closed doors for the evolution and healing of the planet, keeping the chains of the mysteries alive. Are these secret orders real? Perhaps, but perhaps not. We might never know for certain, and maybe it's best that way, as there is always a bit of mystery and mythos in the history of magick.

Though this history of the entwined roots of witches and magicians only scratches the surface, and a deeper study could reveal much more, it does begin to demonstrate to both sides that the traditions and beliefs we have in common are just as great as the divisions between us, and it is possible to claim identity and lineage with both sides of this magickal coin.

Hermetic Magick in Modern Witchcraft

During the time of the Witchcraft Renaissance of Gardner and Sanders, anything esoteric and occult generally was regarded as witchcraft, including Theosophy, Spiritualism, and forms of ceremonial magick, even if practitioners of such traditions would not regard them as such. Most witches don't realize what a strong influence a wide range of Hermetic and ceremonial teachings had upon the Craft during this revival.

The archetypal magician images of Merlin and Thoth were as much of a guide to those new to the faith as the triple goddess and the stag god. In many traditions of witchcraft, particularly forms of British Traditional Wicca lineages, the high priest is referred to as the *magus* in the Book of Shadows. In some Welsh traditions, the female witch is referred to as Gwiddon and the male Gwyddon, both closely related to the Welsh mage god Gwydion, brother to Arianrhod and often seen as a Merlin-esque figure.

My first exposure to Hermetic magick was through witchcraft and the key teachings found in *The Kybalion*, known as the Hermetic principles. These seven principles, which I emphasize with my own students in *The Inner Temple of Witchcraft* training (*ITOW*, Chapter 8), have guided my understanding of all magick and mysticism. In them we see the paradox of the divine consisting of one force, what is called the Divine Mind and what many witches call the Web of Life or the Great Wheel, yet the divine manifests in male and female, and has many forms and faces, including our own. There is the paradox of strict monotheism or polytheism found in mysticism. When one believes in immanent divinity, both possibilities are embraced. We all are connected and one, yet we all are individuals simultaneously. Roots of this theology can be found in the pagan priests and priestesses and scholars of Egypt and Greece, as well as in India. It is this brand of polytheism that most modern witches embrace, whether they articulate it or not.

What is known to many of us as the witches' pyramid—To Know, To Will, To Dare, and To Keep Silent—also is known as the Laws of the Magus or the Powers of the Sphinx. Its teaching can be found in the last section of the "official" history of the Golden Dawn lectures, as reprinted by Francis King in *Modern Ritual Magic*: "Be well assured, my Frater, that the Order of the G.D., of which you have now become a member, can show you the way to much secret Knowledge, and to much Spiritual progress, it can, we believe, lead true and patient students who can Will, Dare, Learn and be Silent to the Summum Bonum, True Wisdom and Perfect Happiness." The four precepts actually predate both Gardnerian Wicca and the Golden Dawn. Again, did the two traditions come to similar conclusions on parallel paths, or did one borrow from the other? And just because a paper trail might find its origin, as best as it can be traced, to the world of the magus, that doesn't necessarily mean the teaching itself originated there. These precepts most often are attributed to Lévi, but when dealing with a tradition in which little was written down, we may never know what lore the hedge witches and cunning folk taught those of their vocation. Hermetic tradition tells us the four laws of the magus go back to the sphinx, as the sphinx often is seen as an amalgamative creature consisting of the head of a human, the front of a lion, the hind of a bull, and the wings of an eagle—the totemic animals of the four fixed zodiac signs, Aquarius, Leo, Taurus, and Scorpio, which are emblems for the elements of air, fire, earth, and water, respectively. It is through the wisdom of the sphinx that a magician attains mastery. Through the wisdom of mythical Egypt, the witch priestess and mage are brought together again.

Many witches use a black and a white candle on their altar, for the Goddess and the God, respectively, with the black candle on the left side and the white candle on the right, when facing the altar. Those who look deeper into the symbolism will see the image of the Priestess card from the tarot. We "face" her, as she is flanked by the two pillars, and the candles are symbolic of opening the gates between this world and the next, as she is the guardian of the veil. Further investigation relates the two pillars to the pillars of Solomon's temple, as well as the two outer pillars of the Tree of Life glyph—the dark Pillar of Severity on the left as you face it, and the Pillar of Mercy on the right. An altar with these candles aligns us to the ancient temple traditions rooted in Qabalistic symbolism, even when we are not consciously aware of it.

In spellcraft, ceremonial overtones are found in the use of planetary days and hours, astrological calculations, magick squares, and sigils. It has been speculated that the British Traditional markings of the athame have a connection to the Solomonic magick of spirit summoning. Phrases used to consecrate the salt and water in ritual, such as the following, are also from Solomonic magick: "Blessings be upon thee, O Creature of Salt; let all malignity and hindrance be cast forth from thee, and let all good enter within. Wherefore do I bless and consecrate thee, that thou mayest aid me," and "I exorcise thee, O Creature of Water, that thou cast out from thee all the impurity and uncleanliness of the world of phantasm." Though at first glance this blessing of salt and water doesn't seem to fit a pagan folk magick tradition, in actuality it touches upon the animistic tendencies inherent in witchcraft and folk magick, seeing all things as having a conscious, animating spirit that can partner with us in magick. There is a spirit, a creature, animating all things—all people, animals, trees, herbs, and stones, and even salt, water, smoke, and fire.

The use of the Theban alphabet as code and script is reminiscent of codes in Hebrew, Enochian, or the Alphabet of the Magi. Many witches learn to clear the space of a ritual circle using some variation of the Golden Dawn's most famous ritual, the LBRP, or Lesser Banishing Ritual of the Pentagram, but they often don't understand the symbolism and meaning of this ritual. Those who do often have difficulty reconciling how the LBRP fits into the theology of witchcraft.

The beloved *Charge of the Goddess* poetry so often attributed solely to Doreen Valiente, Gerald Gardner's high priestess, has its roots in older material from Charles Leland's *Aradia, or the Gospel of the Witches*. Yet I found a primary concept from it almost word for word in an alchemical treatise known as *The Salt of Nature Regenerated*, originally written in Arabic and translated first to Dutch and then English in the late 1600s. This often-quoted line from the Charge, "And you who seek to know Me, know that your seeking and yearning will avail you not, unless you know the Mystery: for if that which you seek, you find not within yourself, you will never find it without," is very similar to this alchemical teaching found in the treatise: "If that which thou seekest though find not within thee, thou wilt never find it without thee." Did the two disciplines simply know the same mysteries, or did one influence the other? This shows a connection, if not a direct connection, between the core spiritual truths of two different yet fundamentally nature-oriented traditions.

Though most Wiccans favor a Goddess image that is triune in nature—Maiden, Mother, and Crone—the *Charge of the Goddess* depicts a dual Goddess—one of the Earth and the other of the stars. The starry Goddess is not far from the goddess Nuit of infinite space described in Crowley's Thelemic cosmology in *The Book of the Law*. In fact, one can't look at the teachings of Thelema and not at least see its parallels, as well as some direct contributions, to modern witchcraft. Out of all the male magicians of the Golden Dawn era, Crowley was by far the most "witchy" of the high magicians. He openly explored the shadow through sexuality and topics found too taboo, both profane and sacred, by the society around him. He was very much the wild man of the woods in spiritual, if not literal, location, exploring the frontiers of consciousness for himself and his community, bringing new teachings to the new age. It's no wonder he would be directly associated with witchcraft, even only anecdotally in his youth, with George Pickingill; in his prime, inspiring Sybil Leek; and in his elderhood, with Gerald Gardner. Many modern practitioners, both witch and magician, affectionately refer to Crowley as "Uncle Al" for his connection to our work. Some people believe that Wicca is nothing more than an outer-court organization of his O.T.O., designed to find those who are willing to explore sex magick and bring them into the mysteries of the Eastern order.

Many witches' first definition of magick is a variation of Crowley's famous one, "Magick is the art and science of causing change in conformity with Will." I like to add the word *spirituality* to "art and science," but basically this is the definition that I was taught and use. Many students of witchcraft learn it, and have other teachings and ritual phrases peppered with what arguably could be called "Crowley-isms," but are never aware of this. Though my first teachers rarely referenced Crowley or his work, the first tarot deck they showed me was the Thoth deck. Many witches are not great devotees of Crowley or Thelema, but his influence looms large, and often unconsciously, upon many strands of Western occultism. It's only when looking back upon my training now that I can see his influence on my formative years in magick.

Crowley's concept of Thelema, of True Will, profoundly influences how many modern witches interpret the Wiccan Rede. The lines most often quoted from *The Book of the Law* are "Do what thou will is the whole of the Law" and "Love is the law, love under will." They are not a far cry from "And it harm none, do what ye will" and the witch's teachings on Perfect Love and Perfect Trust. I learned that there are two meanings of the Wiccan Rede. The exoteric meaning is what most people look at—pursue whatever you want and desire as long as it does no harm. If you really think about it, this is a ridiculous teaching, because everything we do causes harm on some level. Witches know that, on a primal level, life feeds life. Even the most vegan, eco-friendly lifestyle causes harm on some level. If we walk across a field, we could kill an insect. Plant matter is alive, too, so if we eat something vegetative, that means the plant won't fulfill its normal life cycle. Fighting an illness kills microbes and bacteria. We then interpret the Rede as, do as little harm as possible, and be conscious of all actions. As we become more conscious of our actions, we begin to see the more esoteric meaning of the Rede. The "will" referred to is the True Will, where we are in alignment with our soul's purpose, and if we are in alignment at every moment, then we are consciously a force of nature and the universe. The harm we do is part of the cycles of destruction and creation. Being in our True Will requires great clarity and a transcendence of the personal ego and personal will that few achieve in every aspect of their lives. Yet both the witch and the magician strive for this goal as a path to enlightenment.

A beautiful line of poetry found in some versions of the Book of Shadows is, "I am the flame that burns in every man, and in the core of every star. I am Life and the Giver of Life, yet therefore is the knowledge of me the knowledge of Death. I am alone, the Lord within ourselves whose name is mystery of Mysteries." This bears a close resemblance to the other most-often-quoted part of *The Book of the Law*—"Every man and every woman is a star"—which speaks to the innate divinity at the core of every human being. Another line from the Book of Shadows is "Encourage our hearts, let thy light crystallize itself in our blood, fulfilling us of Resurrection, for there is no part of us that is not of the Gods." This bears a striking resemblance to the Gnostic Mass of Aleister Crowley, with the lines "Make open the path of creation and of intelligence between us and our minds. Enlighten our understanding. Encourage our hearts. Let thy light crystallize itself in our blood, fulfilling us of Resurrection," and the statement of each member when taking the Cake of Light, "There is no part of me that is not of the Gods."

Similarities in poetry and theology lend credence to the theory that Crowley wrote the Gardnerian Book of Shadows, or at least that Gardner borrowed liberally from Crowley in reworking the book and filling in the gaps of whatever traditional material he received from the New Forest coven. Our folk history tells us that Doreen Valiente is responsible for reworking and even removing much of the Crowley influence in the Gardnerian Book of Shadows, and that she brought a greater emphasis to the Goddess, who was not as prominent in the original material; yet these bits of Crowley's poetry have remained in publicly available versions of the Gardnerian Book of Shadows. Those who believe that the Gardnerian material can be traced to traditional witchcraft sources have an alternate suggestion for the source of the material, drawing upon Crowley's contact with George Pickingill and his possible initiation into a line of witchcraft earlier in his life. Such advocates suggest that Gardner consulted with Crowley to aid him in filling in the gaps in the traditional material by asking him to recall the rituals and experiences of his youth. Crowley's own Thelemic material also drew upon the witchcraft experiences of his youth, partially explaining the tone of Thelema and its resonance with witchcraft. The Gardnerian rituals and Thelemic inspirations were influenced by the same root traditions, and Crowley simply helped Gardner piece together all the material and use certain phrases to make it work. Consciously or unconsciously, Crowley possibly gave the traditional witchcraft lore a more Thelemic twist when remembering it in his elderhood to make sure his own magickal contributions lived on in Gardner's Wicca. One must remember that Crowley's work is far more widely available now after his death that it was in his own lifetime, and he probably did not foresee his profound impact on Western magick.

Though modern witches are not automatically followers of Thelema, we do have much in common with regard to finding our magickal will. Rather than following Crowley's religion, I suggest that we witches study it and use the reigning themes of Crowley's life, if not his particular employment of those themes, as inspiration. No one gave him permission to create magickal models. He simply did, using what worked for him. He didn't do it in a flippant way, without understanding what came before. He was a scholar, who learned and practiced traditional forms of magick before seeking his own inspiration. He was well grounded in traditions of the East and West, and his innovative teachings fit well into these frameworks. He didn't simply make them up from whole cloth, but he built upon the traditions before him, adapting them for this age.

Crowley's famous axiom, "Ever man and every woman is a star," suits the theme of this course. In this book, we will learn the art and science of deconstructing and reconstructing our own magickal models, our own reality maps. Thereby, we will become the center of our own system, our own star. Likewise, we will focus on the inner light and inner divine guidance, from our Holy Guardian Angel, or Higher Self, rather than dogma. Though Crowley laid a path in his rituals and teachings to follow, the lesson of his life is to be our own star, and follow the orbit and path of our own True Will, not those of our teachers. If we walk only in the footsteps of those who came before us and never venture any further, we, as a people, will not advance. We must take the steps to forge new paths in the wilderness and lead the way for those to come.

None of this is intended to imply that modern witchcraft has come solely from the traditions of Hermetic magick. We have quite a rich lore on the ancestors, the seasons, the fey, herbalism, and folk magick. But it does show that the teachings of both traditions have quite a bit in common with each other and are not in conflict. As the living traditions of witchcraft died out or went underground, later practitioners, raised in a modern intellectual society, sought to understand the wisdom of the Craft by looking at and drawing from its parallel spiritual tradition, the tradition of the magus. There was a healthy cross-pollination between mage and witch in the ancient days, when it may not have been easy to distinguish between the two, up until the times of the persecutions. We continue the traditions of using what works, learning from other wisdom traditions, and sharing what we know with those who have the eyes to see and the ears to hear.

One can't look at the history and lore of witches and magicians without seeing the potential conflicts, real and imagined, between the traditions. I know many a witch who wants nothing to do with the world of high magick. The Hermetic traditions are a trigger point for such witches, bringing up judgmental feelings. Many believe the "high" magicians look down on them in criticism or judgment. Many witches disdain the Judeo-Christian symbolism in high magick, or the intellectual, masculine approach to the mysteries. In their opinion, high magick is full of pomp and ceremony, with few practical results, and most witches favor practical results. Some magicians look at many witches as undereducated, misinformed, and concerned about controlling a situation with their will, to the point that they miss the spiritual orientation of magick and the fundamental understanding that all mysteries lead to the same place.

When we get past these stereotypes, we see that there are many things the magician and witch can teach each other. Qabalah can teach a witch how to see the truths of many cultures and traditions, looking through cultural symbolism to the core ideas. Practical magick can show the magician how to find the divine in the most mundane and ordinary places, spiritualizing every action. Practitioners of both traditions who truly understand the mysteries know that one must incorporate the intuitive and the rational, inspiration and discipline, to be truly effective and whole. A folk song known as "The Two Magicians," or "The Coal Black Smith," tells the tale of a blacksmith magus and a witch. Through a shapeshifting contest, the two rivals become lovers. I see a similar alchemy in play when there is rivalry or strife between magicians and witches, as the two are far more complementary than most people think.

REALITY MAPS

One of the core tools used to shape the progression of ceremonial magick is the reality map. *Reality map* is the term I use for any magickal model designed to help us understand both the nature of the universe and the nature of the individual. Such maps depict the relationship between the macrocosm and the microcosm, often in pictorial form. Magicians are served by their strong intellectual tradition, and seek to put the unknowable into form, to explain it to others. In their quest for enlightenment, magicians have encoded their spiritual experiences in the symbols, images, and ideas that have shaped their tradition. These symbolic tools became maps for others to follow and then to use to chart their own new territories, adding to the rich detail of the maps. To the aspiring magician, reality maps can be more valuable than the tools of our magickal craft, our blades and chalices, wands and pentacles, because the principles of our magickal tools are encoded right in the maps.

Medieval traditions and texts, particularly those relating to alchemy, are filled with reality maps, though they are never overtly called "maps." Particularly in the fancy picture books of witchcraft and magick of the modern age, we find reprints of woodcuts, engravings, and paintings that convey powerful spiritual information about the nature of the universe and humanity's role in it, as well as humanity's ability to transform

Figure 3: Alchemical Art—Engraving by Matthieu Merian for Johann Daniel Mylius's
Opus Medico-Chymicum, *1618*

and transcend the confines of the physical dimension (figure 3). They were created in artistic form as a way of sharing the information with those who "have eyes to see" yet concealing it from those who would persecute magicians and witches. A lot of information could be conveyed in a few works of art rather than being written out in a textbook or lesson. Decoding these medieval maps required a magickal way of looking at the world, as well as a basic understanding of the symbols of that tradition.

In addition to medieval European art, many things could be considered reality maps. We might view any mandala—from Eastern mandalas, which take a circular shape and divide it into parts and embellish it with divine figures, to Native American sand paintings—as a reality map. The Tree of Life glyph from the Qabalistic traditions is a reality map.

Other reality maps are encoded in teachings and mythology, and are not confined to a specific piece of art or design. The shaman's World Tree, depicting the Upper, Middle, and Lower Worlds, is a form of reality map. We see an even more detailed version of it in the shamanic mythology of the Norse, with their World Tree, Yggdrasil, detailing nine worlds. Other reality maps include the witch's circle, divided into four directions, as well as the Native American medicine wheel. Once you understand what reality maps are, you will find them everywhere in your magickal studies.

PICTURES AND WORDS

A few years back, I went to a wonderful magickal lecture that got me thinking about reality maps in a larger context. The lecturer was a mix of Celtic Reconstructionist and ceremonial magician. He talked about how, during the Stone Age, mythically seen as the Goddess Age, written communication was in the form of petroglyphs. Written on cave walls and stone works, these images evoked feelings and conjured magickal experiences. We only have to look at photos of cave art to get a glimpse into that level of consciousness. While some images are enigmatic, there are some common themes of the hunts, of animal gods, and of the stars. They are still powerful images to the witchcraft practitioner. The tribal shaman and healer was often the creator and keeper of these symbols, inspired by otherworldly journeys.

In the next major age, mythically seen as the God Age, petroglyphs evolved into more complex shapes, including alphabets, which led to our current modern systems of writing. Letters stand for sounds, which, when put together, create words. Words stand for concepts. Words strung together like beads on a necklace create complex ideas and can convey vast amounts of information. From Sumerian cuneiform and Egyptian hieroglyphics to Greek, Hebrew, and Arabic, language and writing evolved, as did our means of conveying them. From stone carvings to crude papers, parchment books to the printing press, and finally to the computer, our methods of making text developed, becoming more accessible to all. Originally, the written word was a mystery held by the scribes, priests, and magicians who held sway over the community.

Most of our language systems started out as sacred writings, much like our shaman's petroglyphs.

In the coming age, what many see as the Age of the Child, the Child of the Goddess and God, there will be a powerful amalgam of words and pictures. Our Internet is the first step in this process. A method of conveying information that uses both graphics and texts, pictures and words, will become the dominant, and balanced, form of communication. When I think of many of our reality maps from the past, fusing number, letter, word, and picture, I see how magicians have always been ahead of their time, intuitively seeking this balance. It is because of this clever method of communication that much of our esoteric lore was preserved, and is now worth, to many, scholarly attention. Because of the insight of age-old magicians, modern witches have a fount to draw upon that was not of a lost oral tradition, when reconstructing our own traditions and synthesizing new methods.

Modern witches study different systems of magick, mysticism, and these reality maps because previous mystics, our spiritual ancestors, put a great deal of thought, inspiration, and experience into them. These traditions can shed light on our own past and aid in the development of our future. Reality maps, like terrestrial maps, guide us on our way, though we might find the terrain is different now, when looked at through modern eyes. Still, the old teachings help us get there to survey the spiritual landscape for ourselves. Ultimately, they can inspire us to create our own version of the map, creating new systems and traditions. We stand on the shoulders of our ancestors, both blood ancestors and those of our spiritual lineage. Studying these traditions and mandalas is a way of honoring the past and making sure that, in our modern zeal, critical concepts, known to our magickal ancestors, are not escaping our attention. As in any art and science, we must know the foundation that is laid before us. Professional musicians study music from the ancient Greek times, through the classical periods, and to the modern era. Artists study art, knowing the trends that have come before them and learning the techniques of past masters. There is no need to reinvent the "wheel," particularly if we want to take magick to its next step in the coming age. A study of the wheel gives us a firm foundation to design our own vehicle.

As part of my level-four training in witchcraft and magick, I have my students study past reality maps, to understand how our ancestors have viewed the world, magick, and their place in the cosmos, and to revive the tradition of creating such maps in a modern context, by urging them to create their own. The creation of a reality map is the "initiation test" for level four, because it requires students to synthesize all the magickal knowledge they have learned before, into a new form. This synthesis challenges the students to really understand and integrate the past lessons. By creating a reality map, they are, in essence, teaching their worldview to others.

The best way to really know a subject is to teach it, to be able to present it to others, and to take questions and criticisms. This process can point out where you are strong in your knowledge and practice, as well as areas that you need to rethink, or reexperience, to fully integrate them into your worldview. Such mapmaking is a distillation process as well, as you winnow out the ideas, teachings, and tools that are not helpful for you, that are not a part of your magickal reality. And most importantly, by studying reality maps and conceptualizing your magickal point of view, you come to the realization that no one point of view, no one reality map, tradition, or philosophy, is the "right" one for everybody. We are taking on the impossible task of trying to put into form the formless, to explain the mysteries that really cannot be explained. Maps, terminology, and traditions give us a common language, and a way to come together in groups and as teachers and students, but once you see a wide selection of maps, and see that each, including yours, has its assets and drawbacks, then you realize there is room for many points of view that can be "right."

WHAT'S ON THE MAP?

Every reality map is different, for each creator, or each tradition using the map, has a different emphasis. Some things that are considered important by one tradition, and a pivotal theme of the map, are not considered important by others.

Each map is a paradigm, a way of looking at the world. A paradigm is simply a framework, a place where philosophers and scientists hang their ideas and see what views, theories, and laws are supported by the framework. Sometimes the frame is tossed out, sometimes it's reshaped, and sometimes it's given the stamp of approval and eventually accepted as reality by a large group of people. The paradigm is like a

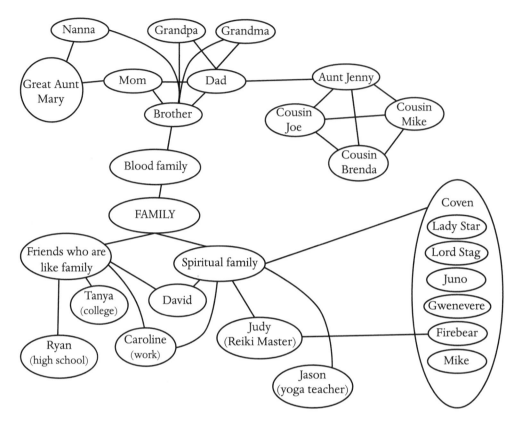

Figure 4: Mind Map

philosophical laboratory, in which the researchers can make generalizations and experiment, to see if reality conforms to the paradigm. Hermetically minded witches are much like scientists. One of the first definitions of witchcraft that I learned was "the art, science, and religion of the Craft." If we truly are scientists, then our paradigms, our reality maps, are like the living laboratories in which we run our experiments and refine our understanding of the universe and our place in it.

The concept of a reality map may be hard to swallow, particularly if you have little background in older occult texts and images. The idea of creating your own is probably even more daunting. I know that, when I teach it to new students, I often get a blank stare. My friend Olivette compared it to a popular learning technique called "mind mapping." When taking notes on a subject, we typically begin writing at the top left of the page and continue downward until the page is complete. With a mind map, we take concepts and arrange them in a geometric pattern, often connected with lines and text "balloons," to demonstrate the relationships between topics and subtopics (figure 4). The geometry is not precise, but it roughly demonstrates the relationships between the various concepts. The mind map might not make sense to anyone but the creator, but it is a symbolic way of using text to understand and remember key concepts. The result is similar to a more creative expression of a corporation's hierarchical flow chart.

A form of internal mind mapping using the mnemonic device known as the *memory tower* or *memory palace* is drawn from the teachings of the occultist Giordano Bruno. In his book *Ars Memoriae* (*The Art of Memory*), published in 1582, Bruno expanded upon the teachings known as the Art of Memory. Though he didn't invent the art, and was not the last contributor to it, Bruno's work played a major role in its development and gave the system an occult flavor.

A memory tower is a mental construct, an image you create through your visualization skills, into which you "put" various bits of information—ideas, past memories, fact sheets—that you don't want to forget. You imagine yourself putting a specific memory into a specific place, such as a drawer, box, or file folder, that you find in this constructed image. When you need to retrieve the information you've stored, you simply go back to that place and "open" the container of the memory, releasing it into your conscious mind. I use this technique a lot to remember book ideas when I'm not near a pen and paper. It also can be used to remember information for tests, assuming you can relax enough during the test to get into a meditative state to retrieve the information. Your instant magick trigger (*ITOW*, Exercise 12) can help you retrieve these memories during stressful situations.

I have incorporated the memory tower technique into the Visiting the Inner Temple meditation first given in *ITOW* and reviewed in *OTOW* and *TOSW*, as follows.

EXERCISE 1

Inner Temple and Memory Tower

1. Get into a comfortable position. If you are going into an inner meditative experience, make sure you are sitting comfortably, either feet flat on the floor or cross-legged on the floor. If you are getting into ritual consciousness, then simply stand with feet apart to give you balance and support.

2. Take a few deep breaths and relax your body. Bring your awareness to the top of your body, starting at your head, and give yourself permission to relax. As you breathe, release any tension. Move from your head and neck into your shoulders and arms. Relax and feel all the tension melt away. Relax your chest and back. Feel waves of relaxation move down your spine. Relax your abdomen, lower back, and hips. Relax your legs, down to your ankles and feet. Feel the waves of relaxation sweep all that doesn't serve your highest good out through your fingers and toes, grounding and neutralizing this unwanted energy into the Earth, transforming it like the earth turns fallen leaves into new soil.

3. Relax your mind. Release any unwanted thoughts and worries as you exhale. Relax your heart and open it to the love of the Goddess and God. Relax your soul, and follow your inner light, guidance, and protection.

4. Visualize a giant screen before you, like a blackboard or movie screen. This is the screen of your mind, or what is called your mind's eye. Whenever you visualize or recall anything, or remember a person's face or anything else, you project it onto this screen. Anything you desire will appear on the screen.

5. On the screen of your mind, visualize a series of numbers, counting down from twelve to one. With each number, you get into a deeper meditative state. The numbers can be any color you desire, drawn as if writing them or appearing whole.

6. You are at your ritual consciousness. Everything done at this level is for your highest good, harming none.

7. You are now counting down to a deeper, more focused meditative state. Count backward from thirteen to one, but do not visualize the numbers this time. Let the numbers gently take you down: 13, 12, 11, 10, 9, 8, 7, 6, 5, 4, 3, 2, and 1. You are now at your deepest meditative state, your magickal mindset, in complete control of your magickal abilities. Say to yourself:
   I ask the Goddess and God to protect and guide me in this meditation.

8. In your mind's eye, visualize the great World Tree, a gigantic tree reaching up to the heavens and deep below the earth, larger than any tree you have ever seen. It is a sacred tree, and you may recognize it as oak, ash, pine, willow, or any other tree that has meaning for you. If you don't visualize anything, then simply become aware of the tree using your other psychic senses. Hear the wind through its branches. Smell the earth where its roots dig in. Feel the texture of the bark. Simply know the tree is there and it will be. The tree is ever present and everywhere.

9. Imagine that the screen of your mind's eye is like a window or doorway, a portal you can easily pass through. Step through the screen and stand before the World Tree. Look up and feel its power. Touch the tree and place in it the intention of visiting your inner temple.

10. Look around the base of the giant tree, in the roots, and search for a passageway. It may be a hole or tunnel, or even a pool of water, that gives you entry into the tree. As you enter, you find yourself in a tunnel, winding and spiraling to your inner temple.

11. At the end of the tunnel you see a light, and you move toward that light and step out into your inner temple. Look around. Take stock of all you see. Notice all the fine details of your sacred space. Let the images come to you. The inner temple can be a place you have visited in the physical world, or an amalgam of sacred sites and shrines from your deepest inner knowing.

12. Look for a special place in your inner temple to be your memory tower. It already exists; it simply might not look like a tower. You might find a special building or tower if your image of the inner temple is like a temple

or castle. It might be a library with blank books and boxes. You might have an old-fashioned apothecary chest, with many different drawers, each able to contain a memory. It could be a laboratory with various colored liquids that record your mental patterns. It could be a garden of crystals, each with the ability to record your memories. You have many gateways in your inner temple, including a gateway of memories. When you go through the gateway of memories, you might find yourself in the perfect memory tower construct, something that will aid you in purposely storing your memories and in recollecting memories and ideas you thought were long lost.

13. Think of a memory, idea, or concept you want to store. Find the perfect container for it. Hold the memory in your mind and imagine "placing" it in the container and closing it, saving the memory until you go back to it. You, or your highest and best spirit guides, are the only ones able to retrieve these memories. They are completely safe and secure.

14. Once done, return through the World Tree tunnel that brought you to this place, and stand before the World Tree. Step back through the screen of your mind's eye, and let the World Tree gently fade from view.

15. Return back to normal consciousness, counting from one to thirteen and then one to twelve. You do not have to visualize the numbers. Gently wiggle your fingers and toes, and slowly move to bring your awareness back to the physical world.

16. Take both hands and raise them up over your head, palms facing your crown. Slowly bring them down over your forehead, face, throat, chest, abdomen, and groin, and then "push out" with your palms facing away from you. This gives you clearance and balance, releasing any harmful or unwanted energies you might have picked up during your magickal experiences. Tell yourself:

I give myself clearance and balance. I am in balance with myself. I am in balance with the universe. I release all that does not serve my highest good.

17. Ground yourself as needed. You can do this by pressing your hands down onto the floor and releasing excess energy into the earth. You also can visualize your feet and toes as roots digging deep into the earth. When all else fails, activating your digestive system by drinking a full glass of water or eating something can bring your energy back to your body.

At some point in the future, go back to the inner temple, to your memory construct, and retrieve the memory you placed there. Your experience of the memory should be as vivid and clear as when you "put" it there. Continue to practice this technique until you can easily and quickly store and retrieve information. You do not need to be in a deep state of meditation to store and retrieve such information. By using your instant magick trigger, you can enter a lighter meditative state in which you simply see the memory container, open it, and retrieve the memory.

Reality maps are much like mind maps and memory towers, except the mind they are mapping is the Divine Mind. Reality maps are symbolic representations of the user's understanding of the Divine Mind, of the universe and all things in it. They are a way to organize both otherworldly spiritual experiences and more practical ritual correspondences. Each position on the map, each zone, is like a container for a specific universal force or concept. When you understand the relationship between profound experiences and earthly correspondences, you can more easily induce those states of magickal consciousness through the use of ritual tools and correspondences. Though the process of pondering the divine and making designs in an attempt to understand it may seem like a form of intellectual masturbation, it ultimately is practical.

A reality map serves as a key code for organizing information. People ask me and, I'm sure, other experienced magickal practitioners, "How did you remember what that herb does? How did you remember the powers of that stone? How do you keep track of all these bits of information, from planets to pagan gods, to oils, herbs, stones, colors, and sounds?" The answer is easy. They all are on my reality map. Once you have a sense of your reality map, and a clear understanding of it, then the process of making it helps encode this information into your consciousness. These questions are as easy as asking, what is the first color of the rainbow or what direction is the sky? I have a hard time with raw memorization. I don't have a good memory for data such as names, dates, facts, and figures, and at first glance, magickal correspondences seem to be just that. But there are relationships between these various topics. Those that correspond to each other denote a single specific energy manifesting on many different levels—on the auditory level, the visual level, and the plant, animal, mineral, and divine levels. When I understand these relationships, I can more easily remember the facts.

Reality maps usually have some key concepts encoded within them. Such concepts include the following:

- **Powers of the Universe**—The primal powers of the universe, either embodied as divinities or without form, are demonstrated on the reality map. Sometimes these primary powers are further subdivided into more familiar categories, such as zodiac signs, planets, or the four elements.

- **Multiple Levels of Reality**—The reality map of any mystic shows that there is more than one dimension of consciousness. Some reflect simple binary views, with the physical and nonphysical worlds as the division, while others detail many subtle levels of reality.

- **Organization of Life**—Usually a reality map will outline various types of spiritual life, from physical humans to the ancestors, angels, elementals, faeries, and gods. They also will indicate humanity's place on the map.

- **Magickal Correspondences**—Along with the more esoteric concepts attached to each zone on the map, there should be a list of terrestrial tools that can be used to contact the energy of each zone. Modern correspondences include symbols such as runes, tarot, ogham, animals, herbs, oils, stones, and colors.

No one reality map is perfect or can perfectly relate all the systems known to the modern magician. Each map has its strengths and drawbacks, showing us that no one point of view can be completely correct. Some would argue that the Tree of Life is the closest to perfect of any reality map that humanity has ever used, as it has become the basis of many of the Western mystery traditions.

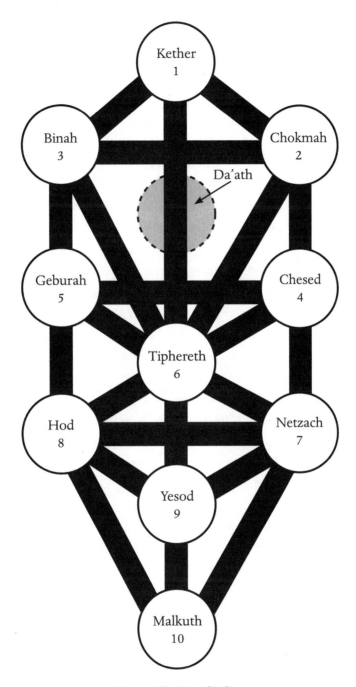

Figure 5: The Tree of Life

The Tree of Life

The Tree of Life has to be one of the most complex and complete spiritual and practical reality maps in the Western magick tradition. A glyph of ten circles and twenty-two lines connecting them, the Tree is the primary magickal symbol drawn out of the texts of the Jewish Kabbalah (figure 5). Kabbalah is a system of Hebrew mysticism traditionally reserved for married family men over the age of forty. The powers of this study are considered to be so intense that it is believed they could unground those who are not fully immersed in the responsibilities of family, home, and community.

Kabbalah is translated to mean "tradition," "oral tradition," or "received," based on the Hebrew word *QBLH*, and originally referred to an unwritten tradition. The Hebrew has been transliterated in many ways, and various "branches" of study are more strongly associated with certain spellings. Generally, references to strict Hebrew traditions usually spell it with a *K*, as Kaballah, Kabalah, or Kabbalah. Christian traditions use the Latin transliteration, Cabala. Hermetic traditions based on the Tree of Life usually use Qabalah, Qaballah, or even QBL. This is the branch that concerns witches and Western magicians the most. Distinguishing the traditions through these spellings is a relatively modern concept that is not adhered to by all people, so when reading a text, don't assume the author has followed these guidelines.

As Kabbalah is a Jewish tradition, its lore is rooted in the era of the Old Testament. Some claim the tradition was given to the first man, Adam, from either God or the angel Raziel, to aid humanity's redemption after the fall from grace and exile from the garden. In this, Raziel would have similar characteristics to the Greek Titan Prometheus, who brought fire to humankind. Adam then passed on the tradition to his son Seth, beginning the lineage of the wisdom that is "received" both from God and from a teacher. Here in the Garden of Eden, we have the image of the Tree of Knowledge and the Tree of Life. Though the Qabalistic Tree is said to be not a Tree in a physical garden but rather a model of creation, it's interesting that the term appears in the story of the Garden of Eden. The tradition possibly was lost and then received again. Noah was said to have received instruction in the mysteries of the Kabbalah after the flood. He passed it on to his sons, but it, too, was lost over time. Abraham was the next successor in the lineage, once again receiving the wisdom and passing it along, until it was forgotten in the enslavement of Egypt. Moses became the next successor to the reconstituted lineage, as God gave to Moses the teachings of the Kabbalah upon Mount Sinai, along with the written law of the Ten Commandments. The secret teachings then were passed on from master to student.

While this is a wonderful and rich mythical history, it doesn't tell us where Qabalah really came from historically. No one really knows for sure. Many occultists once thought that these teachings originated in the mysterious land of Egypt. When the Hebrews were enslaved in Egypt, Moses was said to study in the court of the Egyptian pharaoh. He received the core of this information from the Egyptian mysteries. In the context of Hermetic magick and alchemy, many secrets of magick passed through Egypt, but the alchemical images associated with Qabalah were later additions to the lore, as far as we know. Though we can find similarities to Egyptian lore, we also can find elements of the traditions in other pagan and magickal cultures, including those of the Chaldeans, the pre-Aryan Indians, the Greeks, and other Semetic people in the Middle East.

For the Jewish root of these texts, we have only to look to the Jewish merkabah mystics as the source of these teachings. Not much is known about the merkabah mystics, or the Ma'aseh Merkabah, the Work of the Chariot. The chariot is the chariot of God found in the Book of Ezekiel and is surmised to be a spiritual vehicle, for the mystic to not simply theorize about or meditate on the structure of heaven, but to travel there. One passes through various levels, or palaces, each with guards and passwords. The concept is very similar to those found in the Egyptian Book of the Dead. The ultimate purpose of the merkabah mystics is to see God upon his throne in heaven. We speculate that the ancient merkabah mystics were Hebrew shamans, so to speak, practicing journeying or astral travel. Their traditions were considered to be both very spiritual and very dangerous. The visions of these mystics could form the basis of understanding the various worlds of the Tree of Life.

It is said that a rabbi named Shimon bar Yochai and his son evaded the Romans after the destruction of the Second Temple in 70 CE. Hiding out in a cave, these two wrote the basis of the texts that would be known as the *Zohar*, or *Book of Splendor*, and the *Sepher Yetzirah*, or *Book of Formation*. As the Jews of the Middle East were exiled into the world as the Jewish Diaspora, they brought their mystical wisdom to other cultures and lands.

In the continuing current of Hebrew mysticism, a version of the Kabbalah appeared in the south of France during the eleventh century CE. Proponents of this system drew upon the merkabah mystics and the traditions of the Neoplatonists. The Neoplatonists interpreted the Greek teachings of Plato, a core idea of which is that emanations of energy are emitted from the divine creator. This branch of Kabbalah in France also obtained a text that eventually became known as the *Bahir*, one of the first major texts of Kabbalistic theory. The teachings spread throughout France and Spain. The city of Toledo, Spain, in particular, was a center of esoteric study, so much so that mention of it in Europe until almost the modern age was a code to indicate you were interested in the magickal arts and to see if the person you were conversing with was as well. Texts on the Kabbalah, such as the *Sepher Yetzirah* and *Zohar*, were made more readily available. Modern scholars now attribute the *Zohar* to Moses de Leon rather than Shimon bar Yochai, and believe he wrote it between 1270 and 1300 while living in Guadalajara, Spain. Authorship of the *Sepher Yetzirah*, also claimed by either Shimon mythically or even attributed to Abraham, also is disputed, but some think it dates to between 100 BCE to 900 CE. Eventually, as the lore became more popular and accepted in parts of the Jewish communities in Spain and France, the image of the Tree of Life, consisting of ten spheres and twenty-two paths, was formed in the fourteenth century. Even though the basic form was settled, variations on the pattern, and the correspondences, were still debated for many centuries afterward.

Before the expulsion of all Jews from Spain, the start of the Christian Cabala began, as Christians, seeking to convert Jews to Christianity, studied the Kabbalah not only to understand Jewish faith better but to "prove" that Jesus was the Messiah.

Many speculate that the exiled Jews from Spain found kinship with the pagans who also were being persecuted by the Church. Sometimes the rural folks would protect the Jews who did not want to convert or leave an area, and others times the Jews protected the pagans. They no doubt traded information, which explains how there can be such harmony between Jewish mysticism and pagan thought. Both pagans and Jews were feared for not being Christian and were seen as less than human in the eyes of many Christians, and both the wise ones and the Kabbalistic Jews were said to hold the secrets to magick. Though all this is interesting speculation on the part of those sympathetic to paganism, there's not a lot of historical evidence to back up these claims. Since Kabbalah is an oral tradition, there wouldn't be much written evidence, but let's not forget the far more likely influence of the ancient pagan scholars on the Kabbalah. We often forget that the classic works of the Greeks and Romans came from a pagan era.

Jewish and Christian branches of the traditions continued to develop, but it wasn't until the publication of the first of Cornelius Agrippa's *Three Books of Occult Philosophy* in 1931 that we saw the true Hermetic magickal Qabalah. Although the book was Christian on the surface, and most versions of non-Jewish Qabalistic lore had a Christian flavor, it was definitely a text for the magician.

The more orthodox branches of Christianity sought to disassociate themselves from all Cabalistic lore by the mid-1600s, as the Hermetic movement was closely allied with these teachings. Those who desired to explore the mysteries of the universe under the dominant Christian hierarchies soon found the esoteric lore going even further underground than before. Cabala became relegated to the arts of the court advisors and astrologers. They, in turn, compared their familiar arts with the Tree of Life. Alchemy, tarot, and Western magickal ideas were aligned with the teachings of the Tree during the Renaissance. This fusion of sources, seeing a commonality between cultures and traditions, is at the heart of modern Western magick to this day. Eliphas Lévi, credited as the founder of the modern occult movement, was the first to associate the path and Hebrew letters together with the major arcana of the tarot. Occultists in France and England built upon his work and trends, developing new themes on the Tree of Life. Few of them were versed in Hebrew, but many texts were available in Latin. The *Sepher Yetzirah* played an important role in this Hermetic version of the Tree, but the whole body of Jewish lore was not fully incorporated. Because there was a disassociation from some of the traditional Jewish sources, as well as an influx of magickal ideas not traditionally associated with the Kabbalah, images such as pagan gods and goddesses, which would be in disharmony with traditional Jewish Kabbalistic thought, were added to the lore.

By the end of the nineteenth century and the dawn of the twentieth, with the rise of the Golden Dawn, the concepts of many magickal books were added to the Tree of Life. Works from Lévi and Agrippa were revitalized. The various grimoires attributed to Solomon and the concepts of the text known as *The Sacred Magic of Abramelin the*

Mage all were put into the stew, along with ideas of Eastern mysticism, Egyptian mythology, and a quasi-Masonic structure of grades based on the Tree of Life. Through the popularization of this tradition and the publication of many works based upon it, the Tree of Life became a default basis of knowledge and understanding in the Western occult world. Eventually, traditions that had nothing to do with Christianity or Judaism sprung up, from the work of Aleister Crowley to the neopagan interpretations of Qabalistic lore. Now we see the Tree of Life undergoing a major revival in Western consciousness, as it is popularized on bookshelves and in the work of musicians and movie stars.

The modern magician's Tree of Life is really a system of philosophy, a tool for understanding. One need not be Jewish, Christian, or pagan to apply its wisdom. Because the prime cultural keepers of this wisdom, regardless of where it originated, have been the Jewish people, most of the teachings have a Jewish slant. Some controversial scholars look at the earliest roots of Judaism and see a polytheistic pagan culture that eventually grew into something monotheistic. So at its heart, the material is not contradictory for a modern pagan. We just have to keep the source and history of the Tree in mind when we learn about it.

The teachings of the Tree of Life can be divided into four categories, or four different Kabbalahs. Each one is important, though you might find yourself focusing on one particular aspect.

- **Dogmatic Kabbalah**—The study of Jewish scripture, such as the Torah, the *Sepher Yetzirah*, the *Zohar*, and the *Bahir*, along with many others.

- **Practical Kabbalah**—The making of charms, amulets, and talismans with methods based on the symbolism of the Tree of Life.

- **Literal Kabbalah**—The study of numbers and their relationship to Hebrew letters and words. Two words with the same numeric value have a relationship. The secret meanings of words reveal information about the scriptures, and everything else. Literal Kabbalah also includes the study of *notarikon*, a system of acronyms, and *Temurah*, a system of transposing letters similar to cryptography.

- **Unwritten Kabbalah**—The study of the Tree of Life and the correspondences of the Tree.

Many think of the Tree of Life teachings as divided into traditional Jewish Kabbalah and Gentile Cabala. Though the Tree is based on Jewish sources, in this book we will be studying the Gentile version because these teachings are aligned more closely with Western Hermetic magick.

What makes the Tree of Life system so useful is that almost any magickal or philosophical system can be mapped upon this glyph. Members of the Golden Dawn realized this, drawing upon the wisdom of previous magicians, and made it a foundation of their order, adapting the older material and adding to it immensely to make it a very complete and complex system. Modern practitioners now follow their lead and map all sorts of information on it that is not traditionally associated with Qabalistic magick, from Norse runes to Voodou lwa spirits and Aztec gods. All fit quite nicely upon the Tree in their own way.

The Tree of Life and the Hermetic Qabalistic traditions will be the foundation of this course for understanding the concept and application of reality maps. We also will look at the rituals of the Golden Dawn tradition, and its various offshoots, as the basis for our understanding of Western ceremonial magick. The two are interlinked. The words, sounds, and colors associated with the Tree of Life influence the rituals of modern ceremonial magick. As one of the most complete systems, and one that has influenced so many branches of Western magick, the Tree represents concepts that are important to know, even if you choose never to use them in your personal life beyond this year-and-a-day course.

Many witches dislike the structure of the Golden Dawn, or the Tree of Life in general, and choose not to work with it. I understand this. For a while, I felt the same way, but now I find that so much of the wisdom of the Qabalah has crept into my everyday life. Many witches are not exposed to Qabalah, but it underpins our traditions. Ceremonial magick was bound to find its way into modern witchcraft since both Gardner and Sanders had a strong understanding of it. It has been there since medieval times, and we cannot look at the collective history of Western occultism without seeing the cross-pollination between magicians and witches. Many modern witches get their understanding of and background on ceremonial magick from lineages tracing back to Alex Sanders, as the ceremonial component was more prevalent in some of his teachings. Others have drawn their witchy Qabalah from other sources.

We have seen the Qabalistic tradition go through many adaptations from its original sources. This trend continues today. The way the Tree of Life is used in *The Temple of High Witchcraft* will not always suit the traditionalist. I'm sure some Qabalistic magicians will cringe at the teachings in this book and encourage the use of the original Golden Dawn material as the best source for these teachings, in their proper context and not in witchcraft. I'm sure the Golden Dawn drew similar criticisms and far worse from the traditional Hebrew scholars and rabbis who saw magicians taking the teachings in a direction they did not feel was proper. Even well-respected magicians have adapted the teachings to fit their own systems of magick. Aleister Crowley adapted the tarot associations on the Tree. The Golden Dawn adapted the tarot associations from older sources. According to Francis King's *Modern Ritual Magic*, Florence Farr, a member of the Golden Dawn but also a member of a subsect of the Golden Dawn known as the Sphere, believed the Golden Dawn's traditional color scale correspondences to be wrong, so the members of the Sphere used their own color scales.

Magicians of many ages have seen fit to take license in working with traditional material, to create new traditions to suit their situation, culture, and temperament. As we align further and further with our higher self, our own genius, we more clearly understand what symbols and systems stimulate our connection to the universe and which parts don't work for us, while still recognizing that those different views work for other people. Some people are charged spiritually with preserving older traditions in their original forms. Others are charged in their life's work to synthesize, adapt, and make new ones. The Temple of Witchcraft tradition is one that encourages seekers to explore, experience, and adapt. Both those who hold on to the preserved traditions and those who create new ones can peacefully exist side by side, as each has something to contribute to the evolution of the world.

Is It Real?

One of the questions that always comes up when I teach about reality maps, and in particular the Qabalah, is, "Is this real?" My answer is yes and no. No map is the truth. I don't think "the" truth can be put on a piece of paper or written down in a book.

All maps are like good ideas. They are a good guess, a good metaphor for the words beyond shape and form. They are translations of these higher experiences into a language we can try to comprehend. A good reality map can continue to teach its mysteries over a lifetime.

Don't mistake the map for the terrain. The piece of paper you hold in your hands when on a hike is not the mountain. It is a symbol of the mountain, a tool to get you to the top. You wouldn't mistake the view from the top of the mountain for the map. They look nothing alike. Even a photo from the top of the mountain doesn't convey the entire experience of being on the top. You don't feel the wind, smell the air, hear the birds, or feel the energy when looking at a photo, no matter how good the photo is.

Paradox is part of the magickal mysteries. What is real on one level is unreal on the next. Trying to know for certain what is true and what isn't doesn't always lead to happiness, health, or a spiritual existence. If you act like a reality map is real, from the shaman's simple World Tree to the complex Qabalistic Tree of Life, or even if your own experiences match the reality map, then you have a tool for transformation. A reality map based on experience, tradition, and sound magickal theory will serve as that tool.

Our reality and experience are influenced by what I think of as our first "software." If we are each interfacing with the same divine force, yet each mystic interprets this force differently, then the various religions and traditions are like operating software for a computer. Each tradition, like operating software, fulfills the same basic functions, but each has its own specific view, quality, character, and complexity. The first way we learn something is the one that sticks with us the most and becomes part of our reality. It can be hard to break out of that box when shown ideas that do not conform to our own. We dismiss them outright as "wrong" because we didn't learn things that way, before becoming aware of their potential merits. The "new" ways that we are presented with obviously worked for somebody or they wouldn't have survived. We become attached to our own way, and can become dogmatic about it. The process of working with reality maps helps us break out of our self-created boxes and see that there are other ways of looking at reality.

For example, I learned from an early teacher the four points of the witches' pyramid and their elemental correspondences in a form that is different from what is considered to be the mainstream teaching. I kept the version I used and presented it in chapter 4 of *The Inner Temple of Witchcraft*. No sooner was the book out than I got mail from an individual telling me how I was blatantly wrong. Traditionally, "To Will" is for fire, "To Know" is for air, "To Dare" is for water, and "To Keep Silent" is for earth. I learned that "To Will" is for fire, "To Dare" is for Air, "To Keep Silent" is for water, and "To Know" is for earth. I learned that our knowledge was from the earth, that our intellect was also our cunning, our ability to push ourselves beyond our mental limits, and that silence was a virtue of the mysteries and of the dead, and the west and water represented the powers of the mysteries. The teachings hinged particularly on the earth associations, as the name of the elementals of earth, the gnomes, is said by some to come from the same root meaning of the word knowledge—*gnosis*. One of the archetypes associated with the earth element is the builder, the one who knows structure and creation. I later learned that the archangel of earth, Uriel, is also the archangel of the hidden sphere of Da'ath on the Tree of Life, the sphere of knowledge.

Most of the time the witches' pyramid is recited as "To Know, To Will, To Dare, and To Keep Silent" and corresponds with traditions that begin rituals by calling air in the east, fire in the south, water in the west, and ending with earth in the north. I learned to put fire in the east and begin ritual in the north, aligning the precepts around my circle and elements. Both methods work. My spellcraft and spiritual practice involved all four points of the pyramid and worked very effectively.

I corresponded with this individual, telling him the reasoning my teacher gave me. I acknowledged that he had a point, too, and conceded that, since I knew the traditional alignments, I should have included them as well as a side note, but really wanted to focus on my own traditions and teachings. The only response I got from this individual was that I was completely wrong. I found it interesting that, a few months later, I got another letter on the same topic from another person, but instead of offering the more traditional correspondences, the writer shared with me a totally different set of correspondences for the witch's pyramid that he had learned in his tradition. He associated "To Will" with earth, "To Dare" with fire, "To Know" with air, and "To Keep Silent" with water—correspondences that I later found in other traditions. It proved to me that there are many effective ways of corresponding ideas, and as long as they are rooted in a system that is coherent and makes sense, then they can work. Each "reason" we have for why something is "right" is a justification for why it works for us. Each magickal law is really a part of some magician's personal experience and ideas, passed on to others. As long as they are guidelines, they are very helpful. When they become absolute dogma, they hinder us. When we find other people with a magickal worldview that agrees with ours, we find validation, but the final authority of what is right for us rests with us. It was a few years later that I found validation through the teachings of Janet Farrar and Gavin Bone, on page 119 of their book *Progressive Witchcraft*: "One thing you will notice is that within the paths, the other Elements seem to exist within one another.... Knowledge is governed by air, but can be found in the Path of Earth."

Looking back now, my own understanding of the elements and the pyramid points have highly influenced my own Craft. If I didn't think of air as "To Dare," then I probably wouldn't be writing a book like this. Witches and magicians still fret about ritual points, such as wands being associated with fire or air, blades being associated with fire and air, which element goes in which direction, and in which direction to start a ritual. Deeper theological debates exist on the nature of faeries and angels, the necessity of tools and symbols, and the reality of the gods. Experts often disagree with one another. In these matters, we usually are highly influenced by our first teachers, our first impressions and understandings. These collected beliefs and experiences become our first operating software. Each is aesthetically different and might operate on different principles, codes, and symbols, but if you are an effective magician, your operating system is doing the same work as mine. In the end, there is little difference in word processing programs, though we each have our favorite ones, with our favorite custom configurations. Sometimes one will be more dominant in the market, and another will be a niche, but they all let us operate on the computer. That is why there is a saying that all religions are different roads to the same destination. I think that is true for all the mystic traditions, though I'm not entirely sure the institutional religions are going to the same place.

The founders of a tradition, whether a magickal tradition or an entire religion, simply pass on their software to more people, creating a trend in thought, action, and experience. Sometimes the copy of the software is almost exact, while other times the user will add to it, customize it, misinterpret it, or adapt it in new and exciting ways.

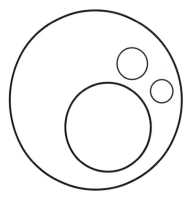

Figure 6: Worldview Circles

All reality maps basically are describing the same reality. Some are simple and some are complex, but they are the same reality, simply told from a different point of view.

Ultimately, studying and making a reality map expands your worldview. If your worldview is large, then it can encompass a more limited worldview and give you the vocabulary to talk to those who use that less expansive view. You can have several smaller worldviews incorporated into yours, and be able to switch between them like switching between computer programs, using the paradigm that suits you at the current time and in the current situation.

Worldviews are like looking at circles (figure 6). Your larger circle can encompass a smaller circle. Your own larger worldview might not fit into the smaller worldview without being distorted and misunderstood. I believe that is why there has been so much persecution of pagan traditions in the West, because the traditional institutional monotheistic worldview distorts that which it doesn't understand. We don't see the same degree of persecution in the East, because the Eastern religions have a more inclusive worldview and expanded consciousness, allowing for many potential truths. The purpose of any spiritual magickal system is to expand your consciousness to be one with the divine. Even as you find worldviews that do not suit you personally, to be able to understand them is a true asset of any initiate. If everybody tried to enlarge his or her own worldview, then we would all be in greater harmony and understanding with each other.

THE CEREMONIES OF HIGH MAGICK

When I think of the ceremonies of high magicians, I envision a solitary magician locked in a tower room, circle drawn on the floor in chalk and the atmosphere thick with incense and flickering candles. Shelves of books line the walls, with an alchemical laboratory of beakers and bottles. Rather than the shaman traveling in spirit to other worlds, I imagine the magician summoning the forces of the universe, the powers and spirits, to this workroom.

Though it's a romantic image, and some forms of magick do work that way, the foundation blocks of ceremonial magick are somewhat more like an exercise regimen. Ideally, they are daily rituals to build your psychic and magickal "muscles." As with lifting weights or doing aerobics, the more you perform these rituals—some of which may seem mundane or repetitive to the creative soul seeking to do everything intuitively and on the spur of the moment—the greater the benefits you will reap for your overall magickal health and strength. The element of air, and the tool of the blade, or sword, are most strongly associated with the path of the magician. Though we tend to associate the element of earth with (physical) discipline, air is the power of mental discipline needed to perform magick, particularly the traditions of ceremonial magick. This is a path of discipline. This is a path of mental structure and understanding. This is the path of the magician.

The Yoga of the West

Dion Fortune is well known for calling Qabalah "the yoga of the West." That can be interpreted in many ways. Much as yogic philosophy is a pivotal part of the Eastern spiritual landscape, Qabalah holds the same position, as the spiritual framework, the spiritual technology, geared to Western consciousness. Many Western seekers study the traditions of the East but discover that the programs, symbols, and traditions don't suit their Western world "software." Qabalah uses images that are more in harmony with the Western collective consciousness. While in our modern, multicultural world the traditions of the East and West are blending together in a more balanced manner than they were in Dion Fortune's time, she still has a valid point when she stresses that Westerners should be versed in Western esoteric systems rather than wholeheartedly abandoning the West and embracing the East. When I began my spiritual quest, I looked into Hinduism, Shintoism, and Buddhism, but nothing clicked with me, resonated with my soul, until I found witchcraft, as modern witchcraft, with its Qabalistic influences, is framed for a Western consciousness. Fortune feared that the cultural soul of Britain would be polluted by Eastern spiritual tradition, and sought to synthesize the European pagan traditions and Grail mysteries with Qabalistic traditions. Though she might not be in favor of a multicultural view of witchcraft and Qabalah, her work brings into focus the varying Western traditions in relationship to the Tree of Life.

Qabalistic ceremonial magick is like the yoga of the West, not only for the philosophical framework that it provides Westerners, with a framework as to how the universe is structured and the path of enlightenment, but also in its physical rituals. While ceremonial magick, like yoga, involves meditation, it also involves ritual movements. The familiar poses of yoga—bending, stretching, and taking on forms of animals, trees, mountains, and stars—are not so dissimilar to the rituals of ceremonial magick. The rituals of ceremonial magick involve techniques found in *ITOW*, *OTOW*, and *TOSW*, but fuse together these techniques, creating moving meditative rituals. In one ritual, a mage is simultaneously gesturing, chanting, visualizing, moving energy, and summoning spirits. A strange synergy occurs, where all these different disciplines become synchronized, and the magician becomes a finely tuned instrument for the divine will. As with a musician, there must be practice. There must be a relationship between the musician and the instrument, for the musician to be in the moment, to be in the flow where the divine truly plays through them both.

These rituals are much like yoga, or martial arts. Several small actions build to create larger rituals. One form builds upon another. The Western magick traditions either have a spiritual root similar to that of the Eastern traditions or have a literal influence from them, because each ritual includes the use of sound, sacred language, movement, geometry, visualization, ritual tools, and intention to create a change in consciousness and reality. As with martial arts and yogic postures, the first change happens in the practitioner, who is aligned with these divine forces, and then a change comes to the outer world, if necessary.

Upon first glance, the sequence of actions in ceremonial magick rituals is complicated and involved, but the sequence works well, and there is a clear pattern and intention behind each action, even if these are not obvious at first. Once the basics are mastered, more complicated rituals are developed from the foundation.

The differences between Qabalistic magick and yoga become clearer when we look at the actual practices of the two traditions. In the yogic traditions, much attention is focused on moving energy up the spine, the central axis, to make matter and consciousness ascend. The forces are embodied by Shakti, the Goddess, rising within us, from the base of the spine, to meet the celestial Shiva in the heavens. Much of the Qabalisitc rituals involve bringing down the light from the heavens at the top of the Tree, through the middle pillar of the body, the central axis, and into the kingdom of the material world.

The foundations of modern ceremonial magick come from the traditions of the Golden Dawn. Revealed to the world by initiates of the order, and adapted and varied by those in the tradition founding new orders with similar structure, the original Golden Dawn material is the foundation of modern magick. Though we'll be looking at that foundation, the rituals outlined in this material are not always true to the

Golden Dawn versions, though they are very similar. Many versions exist, from the various ceremonial orders to the strains of witchcraft that use and have adapted these rituals to make them more Craft-friendly, and from the descendents of Alexandrian Wicca to the Goddess- and Earth-reverent traditions of Dion Fortune.

The first foundational exercise of ceremonial magick is known as the Qabalistic Cross. Upon it, all other rituals are built. It is with this exercise that you align your personal self with the forces of the Tree of Life. You bring a cross of infinite light through the center of your being. In essence, you become a crossroads of light, where all things are possible.

While the Qabalistic Cross is simple and complete as it is described here, more detailed instructions on using words of power, ritual movement, and tools in ceremonial magick rituals will follow in the next section.

EXERCISE 2

Qabalistic Cross

1. Traditionally, one starts in the center of the room or on the west side of the altar, facing east. A ritual dagger or blade can be used to direct energy. Hermetic witches can use their athame, though some reserve a special banishing dagger for this ritual, as discussed in step 3. Many modern magicians simply use the fingertips of the right hand. I was taught to use the index and middle fingers together, with the rest of the fingers in a fist, but most traditions use only the index finger.

2. Visualize yourself growing larger and larger, to titanic proportions, as the Earth beneath your feet assumes the size of a soccer ball. Even though the Earth is small, you are firmly anchored to it and will not float away. You are extended into the heavens and among the stars in the cosmos. Visualize one bright star above your head. As it descends toward your crown, it grows in size, to become a ball of brilliant white light, emanating from the source. It is only a small portion of this source, but it still burns brighter than ten thousand Suns. Bring your knife or finger up to the ball of light, piercing it.

A beam of white light descends to your forehead as you guide it with your finger or blade. Touch your forehead with the tip of your finger or blade, and vibrate: **Ah-TAH**.

3. Bring your hand/blade down vertically across your body, until you are pointing at the ground, with your hand covering your groin area. Visualize the shaft of light descending through your body with the motion of your hand and then into the Earth, into the star in the center of the planet beneath your feet and onward through infinity. Vibrate: **Mahl-KOOT**.

    (Note: Some believe that a magickal dagger should never be pointed at the Earth, so instead you would point the handle of the dagger at the Earth. Others feel the blade points toward where you are directing energy, so if you are directing energy to the Earth, then the tip of the dagger must point that way. In the end, choose the position that works best for you.)

4. Bring your hand/blade up and touch your right shoulder. Imagine a star at your right shoulder. Visualize the vertical beam of light in your body extending a beam out from your heart area to the star in your right shoulder and out through infinity to your right. Focus on the beam of light. Vibrate: **Vih-G'boo-RAAH**.

5. Bring your hand/blade horizontally across your body, to your left shoulder. Imagine a star at your left shoulder. Visualize the horizontal beam of light now extending to the left star and infinitely to the left. Focus on the beam of light. Vibrate: **Vih-G'doo-LAH**.

6. Clasp your hands together over your chest in a prayer position. If you are using the dagger, hold it, point up, between your knuckles. Imagine beneath your hands, at the heart area, a golden glowing light. Vibrate: **Lih-Oh-LAHM, Ah-MEN**. Feel yourself in a cross of light, stretching infinitely through the universe.

When you are done, and if you are not continuing on to other rituals, bring your awareness back to the material world, resuming normal proportions and letting the cross of light fade. The words of this ritual basically translate to a prayer familiar to many: "For thine is the kingdom, the power, and the glory, now and forever. Amen." As you explore the sephiroth on the Tree of Life, you will learn how this prayer is really used as a code to ground the Tree of Life, through four main centers, in your body. The sephira at the top is the godhead, the "thine" of the prayer. The one at your feet translates to "kingdom," the one on your right to "power," and the one on your left to "glory," or "mercy." Though the Lord's Prayer was added to the Gospels, some believe it shows that the early Christians knew about the Tree of Life. Modern magicians will debate as to whether the prayer or the Qabalistic Cross came first.

PRONOUNCING THE WORDS OF POWER

One of the most common complaints of aspiring ceremonial magicians concerns the vibration, or toning, of the sacred sounds. Many books and lessons inspire fear in the practitioner, making the new mage question if the pronunciation is correct and/or if the way the words are intoned is correct. Not until I studied with a modern ceremonial magician did I realize that intention is the most important thing. This is the advice I give my own witchcraft students. It's better to do it, holding a strong intention, and let the practice evolve rather than not do it because you are afraid to do it wrong.

I've found that pronunciation is varied, depending on the tradition of ceremonial magick, the geographic location, and the cultural accent. I've heard a well-versed magician from Europe pronounce certain words one way, while American mages pronounce them slightly differently. I've studied some Hebrew with those in the Jewish tradition, but modern Hebrew and the Hebrew of ceremonial magicians are quite different. Hebrew, once a dead language, was resurrected recently as the language of modern Israel. The modern version of Hebrew is most likely quite different from the ancient version, even in meaning. Ancient Hebrew has broader and vaguer terms in the mystic traditions, showing the relationship between concepts, while modern Hebrew, like any modern language, has to be more precise. Even though ceremonial Hebrew is based on ancient magickal Hebrew, it is somewhat Anglicized. With the advent of popular books with phonetic spellings, we find that the Hebrew words have mutated yet again. We find pronunciations based on what the words look like in English rather than traditional Hebrew. We find variations of the terms Ches-sed versus Hess-ed and Bye-nah versus Bee-nah. Yet at the same time, all of these versions work. When I start to worry about getting it "right" or fearing that some aspect of my Qabalah studies and pronunciation is wrong, I'm consoled by the words of a very wise modern mystic and Qabalist, Lon Milo DuQuette. In *The Chicken Qabalah*, he writes:

> The first liberating secret Chicken Qabalists learn is that (as far as the Qabalah is concerned) there is no such thing as correct Hebrew Pronunciation. Yep. That's right. No matter how you pronounce the various words in the system, some snob is sure to pop up (especially in public) and correct you....I repeat, nobody knows for sure what the sacred language of the ancient Hebrews sounded like, or even if it was spoken at all! Pronunciation has less than nothing to do with the study and practice of the spiritual applications of the Qabalah.

Another enlightening folk tale on correct pronunciation comes from the East. A teacher of mantra meditation is traveling throughout the countryside, searching high and low for those in need of his teachings. He comes to a mountain where an old hermit is said to live. He crosses the lake near the bottom of the river, climbs the mountain, and comes to an cave, where he finds the old hermit, reciting the mantra but pronouncing it all wrong. He goes in, interrupts the hermit, and teaches him the correct pronunciation. The hermit thanks him profusely. The teacher thinks that at least this old man will get some benefit from practicing the correct method before he dies and will find himself in a better life in his next incarnation, though it's probably too late for him to reach enlightenment in this lifetime since he's been using a faulty mantra. The teacher continues on his travels and sees the hermit behind him, asking the correct pronunciation again, wanting to make sure he really got it. The teacher is a little annoyed, but instructs him again. The hermit thanks the disgruntled teacher and bounds back toward his mountain home, walking right across the surface of the lake as if it were solid land. The teacher is baffled. Perhaps his mantra, or more importantly the hermit's sincere effort and intention, are what led the hermit to enlightenment and gave him the miraculous ability to walk across water.

Intention is the key. We have the idea from our popular media that magick words press the secret buttons of the universe. We subconsciously think that, if a specific word is said, things will happen automatically. Yet from most traditions of witchcraft and magick we know that the power is really in the magician and the magician's connection to the universe. Words and symbols have a vibration, a resonance, but no matter how perfectly and technically they are executed, if the ritual is not a focus for intention, it won't be that effective. Even though we draw upon the "current" of those who have performed the ritual before us—using what witchcraft teacher and author Raven Grimassi calls the "momentum of the past," which adds power and provides a reason to follow traditional methods and ritual—if we have no will, then our momentum won't take us where we really want to go. In the end, even if we do something differently from other traditions or in a way that people might consider "wrong," if our ritual is filled with intention, then it will be successful. In this book, the foreign words will be spelled out phonetically, as I've learned them. You might find other pronunciations that work better for you in other texts, so feel free to use them.

The process of toning the various words of power also varies, depending on the tradition. The use of tones is called *vibrating, toning,* or *intoning.* Magicians also refer to it as a "vibratory formula." Basically, each word is said with force and power, in a manner similar to a drawn-out chant. Some people do it quite loudly, while others do it with less volume. Some draw out the syllables over a long period of time, while others finish phrases fairly quickly in comparison. Some feel a resonance in the upper palate and nasal cavities, which gives it that "vibration" sensation. Others don't. A long-enough vibration from your voice will result not only in other objects around you vibrating with this sound, but also parts of your energy bodies and the astral plane vibrating with this power.

I usually suggest that you take a full, deep breath and extend the phrase on the full breath, completing it as you run out of breath. It almost is shouted and often is pitched higher that your normal speaking voice, though some with low, resonant voices pitch it at the same level or lower. For example, "Ah-TAH" would be "AAAAHHHH-TA-AAAAAHHHHHHHH." If you are moving forces in your own body, as in the Qabalistic Cross, then your aim is for an inner resonance, particularly in your head. Lastly, as you learn to vibrate the names of the divine, you will aim to project the vibration, out into the world in front of you, to summon divine forces.

If you are in a living situation in which you cannot perform these tones out loud, then you can do it with a powerful inner voice, filled with magickal intent. Donald Michael Kraig refers to it as the "Great Voice." You can do it in a low voice, whisper, or even silently, but you must feel the vibration of the words in you. Again, it comes back to your intention, and using your voice as a vehicle for directing your will and intention. Find a place where you can practice it out loud, and then when you go to do it quietly, you will know how to conjure the same vibratory feeling within your body.

The Signs

Another component of ceremonial magick similar to that of the Eastern arts is the various ritual motions that act as the building blocks for the more complicated rituals. Many of the ritual gestures of the Golden Dawn are associated with the grade or level of initiation in its system of magick. Becoming thoroughly familiar with the various gestures will aid you later when you learn the rituals. Each gesture is not just a physical movement, but a gesture with occult significance. When you perform the gestures in the ritual correctly, you move energy and interact with the unseen worlds.

The Sign of the Enterer, also known as the Sign of Horus or the Attacking Sign, is used to direct magickal energy forward (figure 7). Start with your feet parallel and a shoulder's length apart. Imagine a star of light above you sending light down to a star beneath your feet. Inhale the energy down from the star above, and draw your elbows up and out, parallel to your shoulders. Bring your hands up to the level of your ears, bringing them parallel with the floor. Have your palms facing down and your fingers pointing forward. Step forward with your left foot, pushing your hands forward, lowering your head between your arms but gazing forward. Exhale and imagine the light coming back up and out through your arms and fingertips.

The Sign of Silence also is known as the Sign of Harpocrates or the Protecting Sign (figure 8). It stops attack and seals energy. It often follows the Sign of the Enterer. Start by making a fist with your left hand, and extend your left index finger. Bring your hand up to your mouth and press your index finger lightly upon your lips, as if

Figure 7: Sign of the Enterer

Figure 8: Sign of Silence

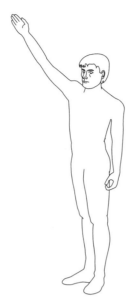

Figure 9: Sign of the Zelator Grade—Earth—Malkuth

saying "shhh." If your left foot is extended from the Sign of the Enterer, make sure you bring it back. In either case, stamp your left foot once forcefully. Together, the Sign of the Enterer and the Sign of Silence are the signs of the Neophyte grade in the Golden Dawn.

For the Sign of the Zelator Grade, you raise your right hand upward in front of you, at an angle of forty-five degrees, with the fingers extended and palm flat (figure 9). Your left arm is loose at your left side while you stand tall with your feet together. This is also a sign of elemental earth and the realm of Malkuth.

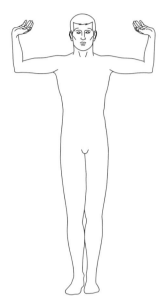

Figure 10: Sign of the Practicus Grade (Traditionally, the Theoricus Grade)—Air—Hod

The Sign of the Practicus Grade requires you to raise your arms upward, forming a *T* shape until you bend your elbows backward with your hands flat and upward, as if holding up the sky above your head (figure 10). Feet are together or a shoulder's length apart as you stand tall. This is the sign of air, also traditionally known as the Theoricus grade and assigned to the realm of Yesod and the rank of ②=⑨. In the symbolism of this text, the Practicus grade corresponds to air, the realm of Hod, and the rank of③=⑧, so we shall be calling this the Sign of the Practicus Grade, again differing from most traditional sources.

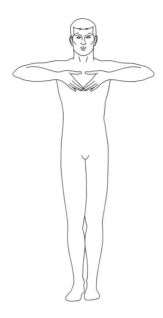

Figure 11: Sign of the Theoricus Grade (Traditionally, the Practicus Grade)—Water—Yesod

Like the previous sign, the Theoricus sign has you raise your arms until your elbows are parallel with the shoulders, but bring your hands in to your chest area, palms toward your body. With your thumbs and index fingers, make a triangle with the point facing downward (figure 11). This is the sign of water, also traditionally known as the Practicus grade and assigned to the realm of Hod and the rank of ③=⑧. In the symbolism of this text, the Theoricus grade corresponds to water, the realm of Yesod, and the rank of ②=⑨, so we shall be calling this the Sign of the Theoricus Grade, differing from most traditional sources.

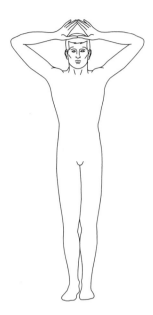

Figure 12: Sign of the Philosophus Grade—Fire—Netzach

The Sign of the Philosophus Grade mimics the previous sign, with a triangle formed with your index fingers and thumbs, but the triangle is now pointing upward, palms facing outward from the body, with the triangle up above the forehead (figure 12). This is also a sign of elemental fire and the realm of Netzach.

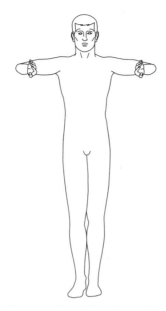

Figure 13: Sign of Rending the Veil

The two signs of the Portal grade are much like the magician's equivalent of cutting a door in a magick circle space (*OTOW*, Chapter 11). They are used to leave and enter a circle during a ritual. They should not be used if you are summoning any harmful force averse to you, but only during more benign rituals. To make the Sign of Rending the Veil, bring your hands up to your chest, clasped together as if in a prayer position. Thrust them forward and separate them, as if you are opening a curtain (figure 13). Step forward through the opening with your left foot. The Sign of Rending the Veil also is known as the Active Sign of the Portal.

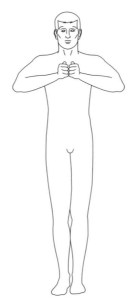

Figure 14: Sign of Closing the Veil

The Sign of Closing the Veil is done with almost the opposite motion as the previous sign, as you stand with your arms out like a cross, palms facing forward. Bring your hands together before you as if you are closing the curtain (figure 14). Step backward with your left foot, and let your arms fall to your sides. The Sign of Closing the Veil also is known as the Passive Sign of the Portal.

Figure 15: Sign of the Mourning of Isis

The four signs of the Adeptus Minor grade are some of the most magickal signs and are used in some of the most spiritual rituals of ceremonial magick. They are based on imagery of Egypt, like much of modern ritual magick. In particular, this grade focuses on the triple forces of Isis, Apophis-Typhon, and Osiris. The signs usually are performed in this sequence.

To make the Sign of the Mourning of Isis, or the *L* sign, place your right foot forward with your left foot at a right angle, slightly a shoulder's width apart from the right (figure 15). Raise your right hand upward to the sky, with your palm facing the left. Extend your left arm parallel with the floor, palm downward. Look to the left, along your arm, resting your chin on your left shoulder.

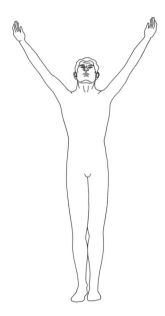

Figure 16: Sign of Apophis and Typhon

To make the Sign of Apophis and Typhon, bring your feet together, facing forward. Look up to the sky, and reach upward with both of your arms, forming a *V* (figure 16). Some feel this sign is similar to the Goddess position of Wicca (*OTOW*, Chapter 11) if the feet were spread wider apart.

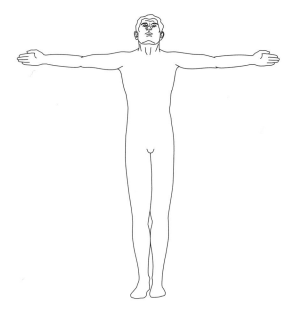

Figure 17: Sign of Osiris Slain

To make the Sign of Osiris Slain, continue looking up, but extend your arms parallel to the ground, forming a cross, palms facing forward (figure 17).

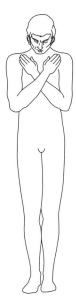

Figure 18: Sign of Osiris Risen

For the Sign of Osiris Risen, bow your head and cross your arms over your heart, traditionally right over left (figure 18). The Sign of Osiris Risen is also the God position of traditional Wicca (*OTOW*, Chapter 11).

Other gestures have been adapted from the occult arts to be used in ritual, such as the stance of the Magician, with the right hand extended to the heavens and the left hand pointing to the ground, symbolizing the macrocosm and microcosm connected through the magician. Other gestures from tarot cards, such as the Emperor, Hierophant, Hermit, and Temperance cards, have made their way into modern magickal rituals. A witchcraft stance that can be adapted to ritual magick is the pentagram position. Simply extend your arms straight out from your sides and spread your feet apart, holding your head high and forming a five-pointed star.

Witches have a variety of hand gestures that are similar to those of Eastern mudras and ceremonial stances. Strega, or Italian witches, use gestures known as *gettatura*. The traditional sign of blessing is the thumb, index finger, and middle finger extended upward and stiffly pressed together, with the ring finger and pinky folded downward toward the palm. Known as the *mano pantea*, it is used for blessing and protection from the evil eye and is quite similar to the ceremonial magician's hand position when performing ritual without a blade or wand. In the traditional Hierophant card of the tarot, the figure is forming this position with his right hand. If you spread your first two fingers and thumb apart while still holding the ring and pinky fingers down, you have another magickal gesture known as the *sign of the crossroads*. The three fingers of the crossroads position also are used for blessings and for witches to identify each other, like a secret wave. Another Strega gesture is the sign of the fig, or *fare la fica*, a feminine hex sign. Make a fist and place your thumb between your index and middle fingers, sticking out to resemble feminine genitalia. I know one witch who performs his Qabalistic Cross using this sign, to attune better to the Goddess, as the source of creation. The masculine hex sign is the *mano cornuta*, or sign of the horns. Tuck your thumb under your middle and ring fingers, and extend out the index finger and pinky, forming two horns.

The Magician's Tools

The magician's tools and altars are not so different from those of the witch. Though we all focus on the four elemental tools common to both—the blade, cup, wand, and pentacle—the magician's altar has quite a few different tools that should be familiar to the ceremonial witch.

Book of the Art

The Book of the Art, or a magickal grimoire, is much like a magician's version of a Book of Shadows. In fact, many believe that the concept of having such a book in witchcraft was borrowed from ceremonial magick, as any medieval witchcraft tradition most likely was oral, being practiced by those who didn't know how to read or write. Modern magicians often are meticulous in keeping magickal journals, following the example of Aleister Crowley. The traditional book was not just a journal with notes, but a magickal tool in itself. During summoning rituals, the seals and sigils of various spirits, angels, and demons would be written in the book, and the owner of the book was said to have knowledge of, and even control over, such spirits because the magickal book and symbols granted power over the spirits. Today, the Book of Shadows, often abbreviated as BOS, can be a similar working tool for the ceremonial witch. In fact, Gardner's name for his first Gardnerian BOS was *Ye Bok of Ye Art Magical*. I have a magickal journal that, though sacred, is different from my ritual book, which is a consecrated tool I use during circles.

Brass Vessel

A brass vessel or pot can be used as a container for seals of spirits, particularly a group of spirits known as the Goetia, as legend says the spirits themselves were contained in a brass vessel. Others use brass containers with a layer of sand at the bottom as censers for incense, used with charcoal. Many traditions of spirit summoning require a lot of smoke to summon the spirit to visible manifestation, and usually suggest burning Dittany of Crete incense for this purpose. Modern magicians attempting spirit summoning are advised to use charcoal with loose incense instead of commercial cones or sticks, because loose incense provides thicker smoke.

Chalk

Consecrated chalk is used for drawing the outline of a circle or triangle in certain rituals. It marks the physical boundary of where the energetic boundary is created through ritual. Names of divinity, angels, and spirits, along with magickal symbols, often are drawn in chalk in and around the circle where the magician will work. Others cast the outline of their circle in other powdery substances, from salt to powdered grain.

Cingulum

The cingulum, or cord, found in traditional witchcraft and often associated with the garter or belt, can be used for both measuring out circles or marking the boundary by laying the cord around the edge of the circle. Modern witches will improvise with this boundary and sometimes use masking tape, stones, coins, or candles to mark the boundary.

Cloth

Ritual tools often are wrapped in specially prepared and consecrated cloths to shield them from unwanted influences. Most favored are silks, coming from the living silkworm and said to be of a high vibration to both contain the tool's energy and reflect any unwanted vibrations attracted to it. Appropriate cloth colors include black, white, or the color of a specific sephira, depending on the tool, though white is often the default color because it naturally reflects energy.

Cubic Altar

The cubic altar consists of two cubes, one on top of the other, symbolizing the magician's concept of the macrocosm over the microcosm. In sacred geometry, the cube is a symbol of the element of earth, of manifestation. Performing your work on the upper cube shows that whatever change you manifest on your altar will occur in ritual on the macrocosmic level, the realm of forces. Then the result will manifest on the microcosmic level, or world of humanity. Though many traditions are stringent about the size, shape, and composition of this altar, I believe that most working witches know the altar is the embodiment of the macrocosm and microcosm in a magickal practice, and they don't necessarily need to abandon their altar to obtain a double cubic altar unless they feel personally motivated to do so.

Elemental Tools

The ceremonial magician's elemental tools are much like the witch's four main tools. Both use the wand, blade, cup, and pentacle, but the ceremonialist often will have these tools to work exclusively with the elemental forces, marking them with specific colors, Hebrew letters, and sigils relating to the elements. They can be referred to as the fire wand, air blade, water cup, and earth pentacle. Another wand is used for purposes not dealing directly with fire. Known as the *lotus wand*, it is tipped with a lotus shape and banded with fourteen colors—white for ultimate spirit, twelve chromatic colors for the zodiac signs, and then black for the material world. The magician holds it by the band representing the force he or she wishes to invoke. The air blade is used exclusively to direct the energies of air. Another blade, usually separate and distinct, is used for rituals that do not involve working specifically and solely with air, such as the

Lesser Banishing Ritual of the Pentagram, or LBRP for short, in which the banishing pentagrams of earth are used. A traditional Golden Dawn–style magician might have an elemental banishing dagger and a planetary banishing dagger.

A witch's tools often are more practical and, once consecrated, can embody the forces of several complementary concepts, and not be separate and distinct in physical form but still retain their effectiveness in function. Most ceremonial witches use their double-edged, black-handled knife—the athame—as both a tool for air and for the LBRP and associated rituals that require a blade. Many witches think the markings and use of the ceremonial magician's tools are overly complicated and unnecessary. But in his influential book *Mastering Witchcraft*, Paul Huson describes a tradition that claims to be unrelated to Gardnerian lines, that is highly influenced by ceremonial information, and the ritual tools are depicted with markings different from, yet just as complex as, those of the Golden Dawn. Many think the traditional witch's athame and its traditional markings actually are based on tools from the grimoire known as the *Key of Solomon*.

Ink

Since the arts of ceremonial magick involve sacred language in its spoken and written forms, many magicians and ceremonial witches go to painstaking lengths to create magickal inks to write out their spells and rituals, with ingredients ranging from herbal substances to mineral compounds. These inks often are aligned with astrological or Qabalistic forces.

Lamen

The lamen is usually a symbol designed in a piece of jewelry to be worn about the neck, falling at heart level. It is usually a disc in shape and made from a precious metal, such as silver or gold or any of the other planetary metals, depending on its use and purpose. The lamen suspends the concept it represents at the heart space of the magician, to become a focus for the magician. A lamen can be designed to be representative of a particular order or group. The Rose Cross of the Golden Dawn is an example of such a lamen, representing the center of the Tree of Life, Tiphereth. Sometimes the seal of a spirit is drawn on one side of the lamen, with an upright pentacle, for protection and to control the spirit on the other side. Modern magicians could use a plain, flat, solid disc, with a pentacle etched on the reverse side.

Lamp

The lamp is a symbol of spirit, used for the central flame of the Creator and the original spark of divinity. Other candles are lit from this central flame, as the oil also symbolizes the essence of life. Some traditions use colored glass or, for the modern practitioner, colored theatrical "gels" around the lamp, to color the light radiating in the ritual room to align with a specific ritual correspondence. Many witchcraft traditions do not use a specific oil lamp, but instead use a central pillar candle of white, gray, or an appropriate seasonal color.

Parchment

Just as the use of magickal inks is important to a magician, so is the proper paper also important. Various forms of parchment are used, from pretty colored modern paper to more traditional forms of velum or papyrus. Some magicians are of the mind that if a traditional spellbook calls for a sigil on goatskin, then no substitute will do. Though I love my collection of fancy paper for spells and rituals, and have used some handmade primitive papers, I don't have anything as exotic as animal skin.

Ring

A special ritual ring can be used in ceremonial magick. A ring often signals a rank. In some forms of witchcraft, a pentacle ring is used at first initiation. In ceremonial spirit summoning, a ring in the design of Solomon's Ring is used to bind and command spirits. Various versions of the ring have been used with Solomon's Seal as a pentagram or hexagram. Witches can consecrate a ring with the intention of commanding and binding spirits if the design of the ring is aligned with that intention.

Robes

Just as witches use robes and cloaks in ritual, so do magicians. Though many witches prefer to go skyclad in ritual, most magicians and magickal orders use specific vestments. Robe color or design often is indicative of rank within an order. The robe itself, cut in a *T* shape with a hood, is symbolic of the Egyptian ankh, favored by many ceremonialists. Robes often are worn doubled, with an inner robe, usually belted by a cingulum or other device, and an outer, open robe used somewhat like a cloak. The color of the robes can be in alignment with the correspondences of the elements, planets, or spheres on the Tree of Life. The robe, duly cleansed and consecrated, acts as a protective device for the magician, as well as being aesthetically pleasing.

Sandals

While it is quite possible to work barefoot, many magicians have special footwear for ritual. Sandals are sacred to the gods Hermes and Mercury, who as messenger gods are said to wear winged sandals. Some associate sandals magickally with the sphere of the Moon. Sandals can be trimmed in gold or silver, with magickal motifs.

Skrying Speculum

A speculum is a device into which a magician gazes during ritual to stimulate psychic vision. Traditional black mirrors and crystals balls can be used for skrying. Some magicians have ornate stones mounted on a frame, or highly decorated mirrors on a frame, designed to stand up at an angle, at a predetermined height, for ease of gazing in a specific ritual. I've noticed that many groups of witches prefer to spell scrying with a *c*, while magicians seem to prefer skrying with a *k*.

Sword

The sword is used in ritual work as an extension of the athame, often to cast a circle. Some covens have a sword belonging to the coven, as part of their group identity. In ceremonial magick, the sword is used in spirit summoning, to bind and threaten the spirit, as iron can disrupt the form of a spirit. This was true particularly in the medieval period. The sword has a longer reach than the dagger, so the magician can reach the spirit yet remain safely in the bounds of the circle. The sword also can be used to move things in and out of the circle, and into or out of the triangle, without the magician breaking the circle boundary.

Triangle

The triangle, also known as the Triangle of the Art or the Triangle of Manifestation, is used to contain a spirit being summoned before the practitioner. When upright, it's a symbol of fire and Archangel Michael, the protector. Some magicians have a wooden or cardboard triangle, consecrated and decorated with traditional symbols and names of power. Others use more temporary boundaries to mark the edge of the triangle, like chalk or cord. A skrying device can be placed inside the triangle.

Lodge Traditions

Magickal lodges are the formal groups that organize the teachings of ceremonial magick. Much like a coven in the initiatory witchcraft traditions, a lodge holds a body of teachings, with linear and logical aspects as well as intuitive and cultural ones, passed to an initiate through traditional teaching methods and rituals designed to transfer the energy, or "current," of the tradition to the initiate. With proper training, the initiate later will be able to pass that current on to others, adding to the energy and helping the tradition grow.

The term *current* is used in ceremonial magick to describe the cumulative living energy of the tradition, like a charge that moves in waves or bolts between current members, and even across time, to those of the past and future. The current can be thought of as an *egregore*. An egregore is a large, somewhat permanent thoughtform created by a group of people, a community, that survives over time as energy is added to it. Those connected to the egregore are able to draw upon its accumulated power, knowledge, and wisdom, like tapping into a vast reserve of energy. The egregore of a tradition carries its general "vibe," or persona, as each tradition has a different personality and presence. The magick of one tradition has a very different flavor from that of another tradition or solitary practitioner. The lodge or tradition egregore is said to "live" in the current of that tradition.

Currents are not exclusive to magickal orders. One could say that various cultural movements have created currents that moved through the greater society, with unconscious or unrecognized egregores. From punk musicians to yuppies, from hippie flower children to neo-Nazis, each has its own current. A visionary can be viewed in a historical context as the parent of a current. Aleister Crowley was decidedly a visionary, and his religion of Thelema, often described by the number 93, is said to

Modern Title	Golden Dawn Title	Rank	Sephira	Signs	Work
First Order					
Neophyte	Neophyte	0=0		Sign of the Enterer, Sign of Silence	Practical magickal practices, keep a detailed journal; neophyte means "newly planted"
Zealot	Zelator	1=10	Malkuth	Sign of the Zelator Grade	Greater mastery of the physical form; begin mastery of the astral
Theoricus	Theoricus	2=9	Yesod	Sign of the Theoricus Grade*	Successful regular meditation and ritual practice
Practitioner	Practicus	3=8	Hod	Sign of the Practicus Grade*	Complete intellectual training, particularly in the Qabalah
Philosopher	Philosophus	4=7	Netzach	Sign of the Philosophus Grade	Moral training; testing the initiate's devotion to the Order
			The Veil	Sign of Rending the Veil	The Portal Grade; crossing the veil to the next level of initiation
				Sign of Closing the Veil	
Second Order					
Adept	Adeptus Minor	5=6	Tiphereth	Sign of the Mourning of Isis	Perform the Great Work of Knowledge and Conversation of your Holy Guardian Angel
				Sign of Apophis and Typhon	
				Sign of Osiris Slain, Sign of Osiris Risen	
Advanced Adept	Adeptus Major	6=5	Geburah		Mastery of practical magick
Perfect Adept	Adeptus Exemptus	7=4	Chesed		Perfection of all matters

Modern Title	Golden Dawn Title	Rank	Sephira	Signs	Work
Third Order					
Master	Magister Templi	⑧=③	Binah		Tends to Disciples and is a master of Samadhi
Mage	Magus	⑨=②	Chokmah		Declares "Law" and is a master of all high magick
Ipsissimus	Ipsissimus	⑩=①	Kether		Beyond all comprehension; master of all consciousness; the very very self; his very own self

Chart 1: Initiation Levels of the Tree of Life

* For the purposes of *The Temple of High Witchcraft*, the Signs of Theoricus Grade and Practicus Grade have been reversed, to keep with the modern symbolism of assigning Hod to air and Yesod to water, rather than the traditional Golden Dawn assignments.

be the 93 Current. Though he initiated this move into the Aeon of Horus, with his own divine inspiration, others have added to the energies of Thelema, continuing the current after his death. Now, it is far more popular and well known than it ever was in his lifetime. We can look in a similar way at the traditions of the Golden Dawn or Gardnerian Wicca.

In lodge traditions, the current is disseminated to its members through various levels of initiation. Initiation replaces the genetic links of tribe and family of more primal forms of magickal traditions, and in larger populations, creates a spiritual brotherhood and sisterhood of initiates into the mysteries. The practice of lodge traditions is simply an extension of the various temples and cults in the ancient pagan world. Each has its own current and persona. The Temple of Isis is different from the Cult of Mithras. Isis groups in the ancient world were different in different locations, yet they all shared some similar components, uniting them as a tradition across space and time. The same can be said of those in the traditions of Mithras, or any other mystery school or temple.

Golden Dawn–based traditions use the Tree of Life as a model for their hierarchy and rankings, as various officers and initiation levels can be mapped on the Tree. The Golden Dawn has an Outer Order of five levels—a Neophyte level and four levels based on the lower spheres on the Tree of Life. This Outer training is the foundation of the elemental teachings. The Second Order comprises the more advanced teachings related to the Great Work. The members of the Second Order are also the earthly governors of the Order's terrestrial affairs. The Third Order, relating to the upper triangle on the Tree of Life, is represented by the Secret Chiefs, or inner-plane adepts that guide the Order spiritually and make their wishes known to the earthly heads of the lodge.

Many witches believe the initiations of high magick are similar in a spiritual nature to three traditional initiations in witchcraft. Both Alex Sanders and Gerald Gardner, with their links to ceremonial magick, equated various levels of spiritual initiation in Wicca with levels in the Golden Dawn or O.T.O.

Ultimately, one can follow the path from neophyte to inner-plane adept by climbing the Tree of Life. Each level is marked by two numbers: the initiation number, followed by the sphere on the Tree of Life associated with the level. The list in chart 1 shows my favorite, more modern names of the levels, followed by the traditional Golden Dawn names. Many different traditions using this scheme have broken away from the Golden Dawn titles.

The teachings of this book follow a lesson plan with a structure similar to that of the initiation levels. Just because you complete the last lesson in this book doesn't mean you have achieved that level of consciousness. This is simply a method of organizing the structure of spiritual teachings, based on the overall current of ceremonial magick. You might find the symbolism, particularly the lower elemental correspondences, modernized from traditional Golden Dawn associations to keep them more intuitively aligned with the previous witchcraft teachings of the Temple of Witchcraft series.

The old lodge paradigm, while still quite useful and educational, is more of the Piscean current, of hierarchy, of parent/child relationships. Critics will look to the imperfections of the founders, the visible head of the order, and in particular Mathers and Crowley, and dismiss the teachings of the entire tradition. Though imperfect, as are almost all human vessels, they were the ones to receive the teachings of these inner-plane masters and anchor the inner-plane schools in the material world. Perhaps at that time and level of consciousness we needed an outer head to disseminate the teachings. Even if Mathers and Crowley were not perfect, their connection to and interpretation of the teachings were clearer than those of an initiate who is just stepping on the path. They performed a great service, planting the seeds of the next age through their teachings. But as the consciousness current changes, so do our structures.

As we enter the Aquarian Age, our model of currents, disseminated to the world, might change. Aquarius is the Water Bearer, pouring out the cosmic currents to the world. Its glyph is the waves of water, but also of electricity, of light, thought, and energy on all levels. The Aquarian ocean, by its very nature of multiplicity, teaches us that there are many currents in the ocean. We each have our own individual magickal current, our frequency in the Aquarian waves. Each of us is called to be the visible "head" of our own order, becoming the captain of our own ship.

Though some would say that initiated witches of various traditions have an advantage over those who are not formally initiated but are brought to the Craft by the gods, those who follow the new paradigm set out in the Temple of Witchcraft series are connecting to a current, a modern egregore, that is in tune with the Aquarian current of individuality and community. These teachings have been guided by those on the inner planes to construct a platform for others to build their own ships for the Aquarian sea. Use your own individual Aquarian genius and your connection to your inner-plane adepts and guides to deconstruct and rebuild the lessons and rituals of this book. You will create your own new traditions and share them with others to inspire them to find their own path of spiritual evolution. Together, on different paths leading to the same place, we will find community and support while maintaining our individuality.

Deconstructionism

When modern witches delve into ceremonial magick, one of their first complaints is a sense of incompatibility with the symbolism. Though we know that much of our lore is intertwined with ceremonial magick, the Judeo-Christian imagery, use of Hebrew, and dogmatic approach are real turnoffs for continued study. When I first began, I felt these rituals were important to know as part of my magickal education, but I never thought I would make them part of my regular practice.

When we look at the modern traditions of ceremonial magick, from the Golden Dawn to the more avant-garde traditions with the ethos of Chaos magick, we find a rich history of creativity. One could even say the rituals are made up, with no true direct link to the ancient past. True, practitioners of the Golden Dawn based their rituals on the material of the fabled Cipher Manuscript, but there was a lot of creativity in the symbolism of their rituals and teachings. They merged many Western currents, from Jewish and Christian influences to Greek, Egyptian, and Hindu ones. We know that the magi of Persia, Greece, and Egypt were not performing Golden Dawn or Thelemic rituals, even though there might be some similarities. The modern lodge traditions are the product of modern magicians, inspired to synthesize world traditions for the initiates of their era. On the surface, some of the teachings are seemingly incompatible, yet they all form an amazing amalgam that works as a powerful and complete system of teachings for any inspired initiate to follow.

When I look at the teachings of ceremonial magick, and the main concept of this level of witchcraft training through the element of air, I realize that the ideas and concepts and the creativity are the most important aspects of the lessons. Once you fully understand the ideas, there is no law that says you can't change and adapt the execution of the ideas to suit your own personal tastes and needs. Well, perhaps a traditionalist would say there is an unwritten, or even written, law against it, but we know better. *Do what thou will is the whole of the Law.* Is it your will to adapt, create, and explore? If so, then, as a modern witch, you have the option of deconstructing and adapting the ceremonies of high magick to suit your own practice and tradition.

The traditional rituals, even though they are modern, are based on sound magickal principles and old roots. We need only look at the old medieval woodcuts to know that magicians and witches have been working with the ritual circle for quite a while. But how they cast it probably has never been as standardized as it is today. To deconstruct a ritual, you must intimately understand all the parts of the ritual, what they do, and how they do it. Many think such adaptation is a free license to cobble together anything that looks good at first glance, without an understanding of the forces involved. This is not at all what I'm advocating. If you're going to change something, then make sure you know what you are changing and why you are changing it. Yes, there is a measure of inspiration involved, but there also is a measure of intellectual understanding and magickal theory. In the end, the proof will be whether the change or adaptation works. I've had students who have adapted the rituals, yet complained of their failure and ineffectiveness. When I asked them for the reasons behind their ritual actions and words, they gave answers such as, "It felt right there" or "That's what my intuition told me." I'm a big believer in intuition and feeling, but if you find that a change in ritual doesn't work, then why not adapt it, or combine intuition and feeling with intellect? The traditional methods have been tested and proven to work. They became tradition only because others had found them to be effective. By following them, you can tap into that current of energy created by past users, and have even greater success. Why change a ritual if you don't have to?

But if the symbolism of a ritual isn't in tune with your own inner magickal landscape, and that symbolism prevents you from tapping into the current of a ritual, then adapt it to suit your purposes. Many times, the changes of the deconstruction/reconstruction

Figure 19: Awen

project are more cosmetic, changing words, cultural imagery, and style. These things do change a ritual significantly, but if you keep the overall pattern, theoretically it will still work. It's like having a computer with the same basic operating software and programs as another, but configuring the layout and interface so they are customized to your needs. The layout suits your own intuition and becomes more practical and easy to use. You also can think of it as saying the same thing to the universe but using a different "language," knowing the divine understands all tongues and dialects.

Other adaptations are more radical, altering steps or components of the ritual on a fundamental level. Remember, the traditional rituals were "new" at some point, and had to be tested and repeated, but they were created by those who had a great understanding of the forces of magick. Only with that understanding, with the coupling of intellect and art with inspiration, can you create working variations of a ritual.

The concept of *awen* is a form of divine inspiration associated with the Welsh bards, such as Taliesin. Awen is a form of power that fuels the magickal words of the bards. It grants the gifts of poetry and prophecy. Many think of it as descending like a beam of light, or fire, upon the bard. One could think of awen as being similar to the Judeo-Christian concept of "the Word," the sound of creation, or to the Hindu mantra OM, or AUM. Like AUM, awen is seen and often depicted as a triplicity of powers (*OTOW*, Chapter 6). Awen is depicted as three beams of light, sometimes with three dots on top, and surrounded by three circles, the three Celtic levels of creation, with this divinity in the center, radiating outward (figure 19). One Welsh proverb states that the three forces of awen are knowledge, thought, and inspiration. These truly are the three concepts needed for reconstruction of any magickal ritual. You must have knowledge of the ritual, clear thoughts about what works and what doesn't and how things should be changed, and inspiration to bring the ritual into form. The qualities necessary to master the element of air include an intellectual understanding of the theories, creativity and divine inspiration, and the ability to communicate these things to others and to the universe.

As you move through the exercises of this manual, keep in mind the following tips for deconstruction before attempting to adapt any ritual.

Learn the Original Ritual

Learn the traditional form of the ritual, even if it doesn't resonate with you at first glance. You might find you like the original tradition better than you thought you would. If you don't perform it, then you won't know what doesn't resonate with you, and why, so you won't know where to begin in the process of changing it. By knowing what has worked in the past, you can use that as a strong foundation on which to build your future ritual.

Define Your Goal

What is the purpose of the ritual? Once you fully understand that, look at how that goal is executed in the original version. Which steps can you keep, and which should you omit? If you are leaving something out, why? What does it do? It's probably in there for a reason, so what is that reason? Are you going to replace it with something that will fulfill the same purpose? If not, why not? If your ritual doesn't work, look first to the steps you omitted or changed greatly and see if the problem lies there.

Learn the Rules before You Break Them

If you wish to do something different in a ritual, understand what has come before. Though there is something to be said about being a blank slate, if you want to create something for the future, you have to know what was in the past, so you don't end-lessly re-create the same things that have come before you.

Don't Be Completely Averse to Cultural Symbols You Don't Like or Understand

Though the whole process is about creating rituals that resonate best with your own magickal self, seek to understand all the unfamiliar symbols that initially might make you cringe. The mystical teachings of Judaism and Christianity are quite different from the orthodox mainstream teachings, and you just might come to appreciate these traditions by looking at them through a pagan Qabalistic lens. The sacrifice of Christ isn't far from the pagan sacrificed gods. Most pagans, myself included, don't find particular resonance with the Hebrew, but I found it quite interesting to know that the Irish filid—the guild of seers similar to the British bards in stature and task, both of which are related to the Druidic traditions—were well versed in Hebrew, Greek, and Latin. Caesar made a commentary that the Druids knew Greek letters and writing, and used them when they needed to record something. So the languages of the ceremonial magicians, Hebrew and Greek, also are woven into the Celtic traditions. I always have looked to the Druids as my spiritual ancestors, so this was an important revelation for me. And I figured that, although the Hebrew came from a later period, perhaps the old ones saw a wisdom and power in it that I was missing. Western ceremonial magick can help us see the inherent wisdom in many mystery traditions that we normally would reject, yet without compromising our pagan roots and identity. When we can see the wisdom in another culture's symbols or teachings, we do not need to fear or ridicule it.

Mixing Cultural Symbols

For some traditionalists, there is still a great debate over the effectiveness and danger of mixing the symbolism and pantheons of various cultures in the same ritual, or even in your overall personal practice. On one hand, people think it's like mixing different software, where something is bound to break down in the process. Some even fear the wrath of the gods and spirits for disrespecting them. But when we look at the history of ceremonial magick, modern and ancient, we find a rich tradition of identifying similar currents of thought and similar godforms and borrowing liberally from neighboring and even conquering cultures. Roman soldiers in the cavalry in the Celtic territories worshipped the Celtic Epona, for she is a horse goddess. The Greek Apollo might have been "borrowed" from the concept of the Celtic solar figure Bel. The worship and art of Isis and Horus have been morphed into images of Mary and Jesus. The Greek Magical Papyri texts contain petitions to Greek, Egyptian, Sumerian, and Judeo-Christian figures, all in one spell.

The pattern continues today, and nothing horrible seems to happen. In many ways, new ideas and thoughts arise, while demonstrating the same age-old truths about magick. When we look at the modern rituals of ceremonial magick, we see they are amalgamations of Judeo-Christian symbolism and pagan elements from the Egyptians and Greeks. Not only do they work, but they work incredibly well for many practitioners. As we identify more and more with the entire globe rather than one land, we work in the images of our collective magickal identity from many lands. It all can work, but they are your rituals, so you must decide what symbols work for you. Are you a purist, seeking one culture? If so, that's great and can be very rewarding, and the depths of your experience and knowledge will grow greatly over the years. Are you an eclectic? I know I am, with a foundation in Celtic witchcraft but also a deep resonance with Greek, Egyptian, and Norse teachings. Only you can decide where you stand on this issue, but when creating a body of rituals to be used together, be consistent. Have the same cultural threads woven through each.

Don't Throw In Everything but the Kitchen Sink

At first, the rituals of ceremonial magick can seem rather overwhelming. There is a tendency to either minimize them so much that they are no longer artful and effective, or to throw in every symbol, technique, and teaching, making them clunky and unintelligible. Moderation is the key.

Seek Divine Guidance

The art of magick is not just you intellectually struggling to make a ritual work. It is a partnership with the divine. When you are working new rituals, check in with your gods and guides for advice and guidance. Many of my best reconstructed rituals were "given" to me in whole or part by my inner contacts. Through finding your awen, you will be guided to the proper balance and execution of your rituals.

With these points in mind, along with the many examples of reconstructed rituals, you will have a guide to help you work with the traditions of high magick and, if necessary, remake them in your own image. Reconstruction isn't anything new. It's been popularized with Chaos magick, and what I'm presenting here might be considered a more restrained take on the practice. Magicians have been innovators for thousands of years. We're simply continuing that long tradition.

When looking at the whole process of deconstruction and reconstruction of magickal ideas, the concept of reality mapping is a form of deconstruction. Many magicians take the reality map of their teachers and tradition and internalize it as their own reality. By making your own reality map, you are deconstructing an original, or several originals, and thinking outside the norms of your traditions, with your inspiration. This divine alchemy helps create the new systems of magick and enlightenment, flowing with the New Age.

THE MAGICIAN'S VOW

Most of us on the path of the witch draw our spiritual inspiration from those of the Old Religion, who were an intuitive and often illiterate people. So why should modern witches be concerned with the written language, symbol systems, and mathematics and geometry that are found in the Qabalah?

Though we already have explored our entwined roots, of magician and witch, and know that these traditions are part of our own cultural revival, we have, even more importantly, the example of our Stone Age ancestors. Though we think of them as illiterate and uncivilized by today's standards, they simply had their own civilization, which was, in many ways, far more complex than that of the medieval pagan peasants we know far more about. When we look to those in the Stone Age, the builders of stone circles and ancient monuments, we find a people highly versed in mathematics and measurement. We find a race deeply knowledgeable about the relationship of the stars and the Earth, of math and science, in relationship to their spiritual traditions. Though not directly linked to our Stone Age circle-building ancestors of spirit, the teachings of witchcraft and Qabalah grow from the same fertile grounds of Western consciousness.

As you explore these different forms of magick from the Western mind, keep in mind that this is a survey of different ideas designed to expose you to a new world and help you figure out what you can use at this time. Don't feel pressured to use it all, or master it all in a year and a day. You can repeat this work several times over. I know I have. Be gentle with yourself. When you come across something that appears too vast for you—for example, Enochian magick or summoning Goetic spirits—learn the material intellectually, and then, as you grow in experience and confidence, contemplate actually doing the exercises. I know I wasn't ready for Enochian when I first studied it, and it's something I still struggle with. I spent years reading about it and talking to people before attempting it, and eventually realized that, at this time, it's not for me and doesn't fit into my practice of the Craft. But knowledge and understanding of it is an important part of my magickal education, even if I choose not to use it.

This process of study can be daunting for the intuitive witch. Though quite different from the shadow work of *The Temple of Shamanic Witchcraft*, this exploration of the intellectual side of magick—how to be inspired and how to communicate your ideas and inspiration to others—can conjure a whole different side of the shadow, rooted in the air element.

Once you decide to embark on this course, I highly recommend that you commit to the year-and-a-day training with the intention vow given in exercise 3. The level-four teachings of this tradition are a process much like those of level three, and there are great rewards for those who experience the full process, even if the rewards are not quite clear in the middle. By the end, you will develop a great sense of intellectual and creative confidence and an ability to communicate your views to others, while not feeling threatened when others communicate their worldview to you. You will understand clearly and consciously how you see the world through your magickal eyes. And when that viewpoint no longer serves you, you will know how to adapt and reframe it for your highest good.

Exercise 3

Intention Vow

Obtain a yellow candle. Yellow is traditionally the color of air in Western ceremonial magick. It can be a taper or jar candle, as long as you can carve your name on it. You can use your most current witch name. You can even carve your name in a special language or code, such as the runes.

Use some magickal paper and a special pen or special ink and quill if you want to be very romantic about it. Write the following intention on it:

> *I, (state your name), ask in the name of the Goddess, God, and Great Spirit to walk the path of the magi, to bring the arts and sciences of the magician to my own Craft. I make this vow to the powers that I will learn the arts of old, but also find my own ways as I grow these seeds of knowledge within my being. I ask the magicians and witches of old to guide my path, guide my mind in the assimilation of this work, as I take what I need and want and find ways to transform the rest, uncovering the truly ageless wisdom written beneath it all. I ask that this occur with ease, grace, and gentleness, for the highest good, harming none. So mote it be!*

Next, cast a magick circle (*OTOW*, Chapter 11). If you desire, you can start with the Qabalistic Cross before you cast the circle. Hold your candle and think about your devotion to completing this work in the next year. Think about the mental mysteries, the mysteries of knowledge and communication. Light your candle. Bask in its light for a few minutes. Feel yourself in the center of your universe. Read your intention and ignite the paper, letting it burn in a flameproof cauldron. Take whatever time you'd like to meditate. Release the circle in the traditional way, and when cool, scatter the ashes to the winds.

HOMEWORK

- Perform Exercise 3: Intention Vow, and record your experiences in your Book of Shadows.

- Memorize the Qabalistic Cross (exercise 2).

- Become familiar with the various grade signs. They will form the building blocks of future rituals.

TIPS

- When working with the Qabalistic Cross exercise, keep in mind that there have been many variations to it. Some magicians imagine the horizontal beam of light starting in the left, from a point infinitely to the left, moving through the heart and out to the right infinitely. Many do not visualize stars or spheres of light at the shoulders, to simplify it. Alex Sanders, founder of the Alexandrian line of Wicca, was said to replace the word Ah-tah with the name of the top sphere, Kether. Many witches take out the Hebrew name of God associated with each sephira and simply use the sephira's name. Aleister Crowley added a step between drawing the light down from the above to the Earth below. He would point to the heart and vibrate *Aiwass*, the name of Crowley's Holy Guardian Angel, or higher self. Many of his followers either vibrate Aiwass as well, to be aligned with his current, or substitute their own Holy Guardian Angel's (HGA's) name, once they know it. Many also exchange the *Amen* at the end of the Qabalistic Cross with words such as Om, Aum, Aumgn, Aum-en, Amon, Ama, and Awen.

RECOMMENDED RESOURCES

- As you continue on your path in ceremonial magick and reality maps for the next thirteen lessons, you will find several books quite helpful. Some of these books are manuals of ceremonial magick that cover the material in greater detail and from a more traditional approach. The others are reference books of occult systems that will be invaluable when you start to research and explore reality maps and correspondence systems.

Modern Magick by Donald Michael Kraig

The Golden Dawn by Israel Regardie

The Ritual Magic Manual by David Griffin

The Magick of Aleister Crowley by Lon Milo DuQuette

The Magician's Companion by Bill Whitcomb

The Magician's Reflection by Bill Whitcomb

The Eastern Mysteries by David Allen Hulse (formerly, *The Key of It All, Book 1*)

The Western Mysteries by David Allen Hulse (formerly, *The Key of It All, Book 2*)

The Secret Teachings of All Ages by Manly P. Hall

The New Encyclopedia of the Occult by John Michael Greer

777 and Other Qabalistic Writings of Aleister Crowley by Aleister Crowley

Godwin's Cabalistic Encyclopedia by David Godwin

• Although not required of my students, I also highly suggest the comic book series *Promethea* by writer Alan Moore. The entire series is available in graphic novel trade paperbacks or hard covers. Through a visual medium, the comic teaches the reader about magick from a Western ceremonial perspective and spends quite a significant portion of the series on the Tree of Life. I find it to be one of the most effective teaching supplements I've ever used, making the highly intellectual ideas of Qabalah accessible to the general public. And it's fun, too!

• If you desire to make a set of ceremonial magick tools with the traditional colors and markings in accord with the Golden Dawn style, begin researching and collecting the necessary materials. I again suggest *Modern Magick* by Donald Michael Kraig for precise and clear instructions.

LESSON ONE
QABALAH BASICS

The fundamental image found in the Hermetic Qabalah is the glyph of the Tree of Life. The foundation of the tradition is encoded in this picture. The Tree becomes our reality map—a representation of the various levels of the universe, their associated levels of consciousness within us, and their relationships to us and each other. The Tree of Life also serves as a powerful mnemonic device to help us remember magickal symbolism, teachings, and practical correspondences. Many occultists consider the symbol to quite literally be the key to the Western mysteries.

THE SPHERES

The Tree of Life glyph is defined as ten sephiroth, sometimes referred to as *spheres* because three-dimensional models of the Tree depict the sephiroth as spheres, and each sephira is assigned a planet or other "sphere" of celestial consciousness. *Sephiroth*, the plural form of the word, means "numerations" or "numbers," as each sphere is assigned a numeric value, from one to ten. Sephira or sephirah is the singular form of the word. Beyond the assigned numerical value, each sephira is said to be an emanation of the divine, each producing the next more complex and dense divine manifestation. The map is based on ten divisions, as it is interwoven with mathematical teachings. Qabalists say that the number ten is an inherent part of the human perspective, as we each have ten fingers and toes on which to count, and the use of ten has contributed greatly to the evolution and understanding of mathematics.

The sephiroth can be considered "worlds" of consciousness, much like other models of reality that contain planes of existence such as the astral plane, emotional plane, and mental plane. Each of the sephiroth can be equated with such a descriptive quality. As each sephira is linked with a planet, each also is associated with the deities of the planet and their correspondences. As living energies, the sephiroth are both "places" and divine "beings" at the same time. The sephiroth also describe parts of human consciousness that magicians strive to activate and unite with through the enlightenment process.

The map begins with three levels of being known as the Three Veils of the Unmanifest or the Three Veils of Negative Existence (figure 20). As a witch, I've always found these to be interesting titles, for the negative polarity is associated with the Goddess and the number three is associated with the creative power of the triple goddess image, though such musings really have nothing to do with traditional Qabalah. The first veil is Ain, meaning "not" or "nothing," the highest realm of divinity totally incomprehensible to humanity. The second veil is Ain Soph, meaning "no limit" or "infinity," only slightly more comprehensible to humans as the concept of infinity. Lastly, the veil of Ain Soph Aur means "limitless light" or "infinite light," giving us one more descriptive term for infinity.

From the three veils emanate the ten sephiroth. The first sephira is Kether, seen as the Godhead and manifest form of divinity. Kether is beyond the astrological scheme and is associated classically with the center of the universe, what is known to Theosophists as the Great Central Sun. The second sephira is Chokmah, which is seen as a divine father figure and the generative force for the universe, while its partner, Binah, is the great mother figure and the receptive force of creation. Chokmah is linked to the stars of the zodiac, while Binah gives us our first true planetary correspondence, Saturn. The numbers on the Tree of Life move down to the right and read from right to left, just as traditional Hebrew is written from right to left. From this triad of Kether,

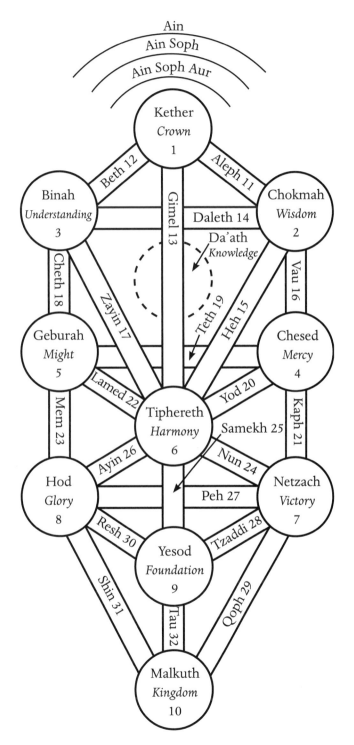

Figure 20: Tree of Life

Chokmah, and Binah, we descend to a world more manifest and understood by humanity, with Chesed, the sphere of divine mercy and embodied by a merciful king, and its pair, Geburah, the sphere of might and the warrior goddesses or gods. Jupiter is the planet of Chesed, while Geburah is aligned with Mars. Balance is struck in the central sphere with Tiphereth, the solar figure. From this sixth sphere we descend into the sphere of victory, Netzach, which is more like the sphere of passion and emotion, guided by the planetary figure of Venus. Netzach is balanced by the eighth sphere, known as Hod, the sphere of mind and intellect, embodied by Mercury. Netzach and Hod find balance in the manifestation of Yesod, the energetic foundation of the world akin to the astral plane and lunar realm. Finally, the Tree has physical manifestation of the world in Malkuth, the kingdom, or material plane, and quite literally the earthly sphere.

Another powerful analogy in understanding this reality map is that the sephiroth are like electrical transformers. Pure, unmanifested divinity is just too high of a current for humanity to understand and process. Each of these ten power stations "down-steps" the voltage to a more usable current, making it denser and more comprehensible for humanity.

THE PATHS

The ten spheres are connected by twenty-two paths (figure 20). While the spheres are like places and levels of consciousness and could be described as spiritual "cities," the paths are literally paths, roads that connect these spiritual places in creation. They are the circuits connecting each power station, allowing the current to change and be redirected. Each path is a process of change, of becoming or transformation, for it takes a change in consciousness to move from one sphere to the next. The movement from one sphere to the next is a specific process. Though the processes can be expressed differently in different cultures and symbol systems, the processes are fairly archetypal and universal. The Tree of Life is simply one of the most effective means of understanding each of these shifts in consciousness and provides ritual and meditative techniques to do so more effectively. The ten spheres with the twenty-two paths are collectively known as the *thirty-two paths of wisdom.*

The most popular path through the entire Tree is known as the Lightning Flash, Lightning Strike, or Flaming Sword (figure 21). It depicts the descent of unmanifest spirit through the ten stations and also shows the most complete path of return to join with the Godhead.

Each of the twenty-two paths on the Tree of Life is associated with one of the traditional twenty-two cards of the major arcana in the tarot (chart 2). More deeply embedded into Qabalah is the association of the paths with the twenty-two letters of the Hebrew alphabet. Each letter has a host of esoteric associations, including images and numbers that encode its hidden meaning. Much as the runes embody not only symbols but also mysteries—primal powers of creation—the Hebrew letters, too, are associated with the powers of creation. They are arranged in a Qabalistic diagram known as the *Cube of Space* (figure 22), a depiction of manifestation and a model for the powers of the universe, much like the Tree of Life itself.

On the Cube of Space, the Hebrew letters are grouped in three basic divisions. The first group comprises the three mother letters. Again, we have a strong mother-triple image for the start of creation. The three mother letters are associated with the elements of fire, water, and air. On the Cube of Space, they form the central axis of height, length, and width. Another group, known as the seven double letters, is associated with the seven magickal planets and thereby any of the other divisions of seven, such as the days of the week and the chakras. These letters are associated with the six primary directions (north, south, east, west, above, below) and the center. They are the faces of the cube. The final group of twelve single letters is associated with the twelve planets. These letters are the angles between the points, tracing the boundary of the cube.

More linguistic and mathematical mysteries are encoded in the Hebrew alphabet. One that is pointed out to link the Qabalah with circle magick is the fact that the alphabet is twenty-two letters with seven vowels. Twenty-two divided by seven gives us pi (π), which is the relationship of the diameter of the circle to its circumference.

Though at first glance many think that the Qabalah is an inherently male or sexist system of magick, we already see the feminine mysteries of creation encoded into it. Many will see a bias, as the first manifested gender sephira, Chokmah, is male, and the third sphere is the feminine Binah. Numerologically, three has a stronger resonance with the feminine principle, and while the counting may move from one, to two, and

Figure 21: Lightning Flash

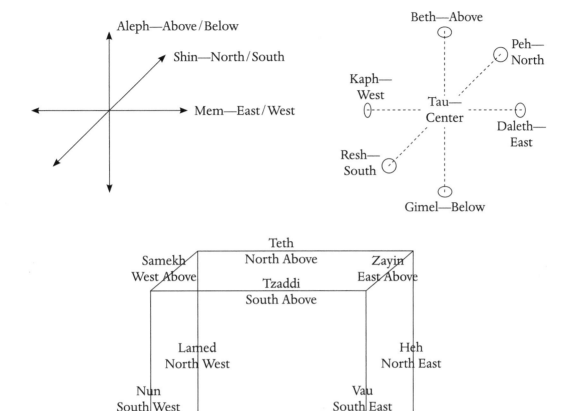

Figure 22: Cube of Space

then to three, there is a path connecting Binah directly to the uppermost sphere of Kether. Both principles are equally important in Qabalistic studies, as both the intellectual understanding and the direct experience are needed to truly climb the Tree. The number of each sphere is not chosen arbitrarily, but resonates with the energy and concept of the sphere. The paths are a continuation of the sephiroth. The numerical sequence of the twenty-two paths begins not at one but at eleven, as the first ten "paths" of wisdom are the ten sephiroth. Numerological associations with the Tree of Life and Hebrew alphabet are a big part of Qabalistic magick and understanding.

Letter	Latin Letter	Name	Meaning	Number	Type	Correspondence	Tarot Card	Astrology	Path
א	A	Aleph	Ox	1	Mother	Air	0 – Fool	Uranus	11 Chokmah to Kether
ב	B	Beth	House	2	Double	Mercury	I – Magician	Mercury	12 Binah to Kether
ג	G	Gimel	Camel	3	Double	Moon	II – Priestess	Moon	13 Tiphereth to Kether
ד	D	Daleth	Door	4	Double	Venus	III – Empress	Venus	14 Binah to Chokmah
ה	H, E	Heh	Window	5	Single	Aries	IV – Emperor	Mars	15 Tiphereth to Chokmah
ו	V, W, U	Vau (Vav)	Nail	6	Single	Taurus	V – Hierophant	Taurus	16 Chesed to Chokmah
ז	Z	Zayin	Sword	7	Single	Gemini	VI – Lovers	Gemini	17 Tiphereth to Binah
ח	Ch	Cheth	Fence	8	Single	Cancer	VII – Chariot	Cancer	18 Geburah to Binah
ט	T	Teth	Serpent	9	Single	Leo	VIII or XI – Strength/ Lust	Leo	19 Geburah to Chesed
י	Y, I, J	Yod	Hand	10	Single	Virgo	IX – Hermit	Virgo	20 Tiphereth to Chesed
כ	K	Kaph	Palm	11	Double	Jupiter	X – Fortune	Jupiter	21 Netzach to Chesed
ל	L	Lamed	Ox Goad	12	Single	Libra	XI or VIII – Justice	Libra	22 Tiphereth to Geburah
מ	M	Mem	Water	13	Mother	Water	XII – Hanged Man	Neptune	23 Hod to Geburah

Letter	Latin Letter	Name	Meaning	Number	Type	Correspondence	Tarot Card	Astrology	Path
נ	N	Nun	Fish	14	Single	Scorpio	XIII – Death	Scorpio	24 Netzach to Tiphereth
ס	S	Samekh	Prop Hand	15	Single	Sagittarius	XIV – Temperance / Art	Sagittarius	25 Yesod to Tiphereth
ע	AY, A'A, O, NG	Ayin	Eye	16	Single	Capricorn	XV – Devil	Capricorn	26 Hod to Tiphereth
פ	P, Ph, F	Peh	Mouth	17	Double	Mars	XVI – Tower	Mars	27 Hod to Netzach
צ	Tz	Tzaddi	Fish Hook	18	Single	Aquarius	XVII – Star	Aquarius	28 Yesod to Netzach
ק	Q	Qoph	Back of Head	19	Single	Pisces	XVIII – Moon	Pisces	29 Malkuth to Netzach
ר	R	Resh	Head	20	Double	Sun	XIX – Sun	Sun	30 Yesod to Hod
ש	Sh	Shin	Tooth	21	Mother	Fire	XX – Judgment / Aeon	Pluto	31 Malkuth to Hod
ת	T	Tau	Cross, Mark	22	Double	Saturn (Earth)	XXI – World/Universe	Saturn	32 Malkuth to Yesod

Chart 2: Hebrew Alphabet Correspondences

Divisions of Three

The Qabalah can be viewed in a number of ways, by subdividing the Tree of Life based on the different geometries contained within it. By studying the relationship of each sphere to another, and the patterns that several spheres make together, you can glean a deeper understanding about the Tree, yourself, and the universe. You will have a better understanding of how aspects of the universe, depicted by the spheres and paths, work together.

The spheres on the Tree can be divided into sets of triangles (figure 23). The first three spheres—Kether, Chokmah, and Binah—are known as the *Supernal Triangle* or *Supernal Triad*. They are the most elevated forces on the Tree. Just beneath them is said to be an Abyss with a false sephira called *Da'ath*, which technically separates them from the rest of the Tree. Kether is seen as the Great Spirit without form or gender, which then manifests as the great cosmic principle of the Father God and the Mother Goddess. All of creation results from the interaction of these three forces. When witches, myself included, call upon "the Goddess, God, and Great Spirit," these are the forces we are calling, as they flow into all other manifestations of divinity and, ultimately, all manifestations of reality. They are the perfect patterns of reality. While Kether is the source, the Godhead or fountain from which all energy flows, the God principle of Chokmah often is considered the seed of life, the cosmic star light filled with potential, while Binah is the Goddess principle of the great dark womb, which manifests that potential and gives it form. In the Thelemic cosmology of Aleister Crowley, Chokmah would be *Hadit*, an infinitely small, potent point in the center of *Nuit* (Binah), the star goddess of the infinitely vast space. Together, they generate the universe. To the more scientifically minded, one represents energy and the other matter. In any system, both of these forces are necessary for the manifestation of the rest of the universe.

The second triad, beneath the Abyss, is called the *Ethical Triangle*, *Moral Triangle*, or *Mental Triangle*. It encompasses the forces of the universe that are powerful and grand yet not as omnipresent as those represented by the first three spheres. The second triad is said to be the realm of mystical consciousness, whereas the upper triangle is spiritual consciousness without form, or at least any form that we in human consciousness can

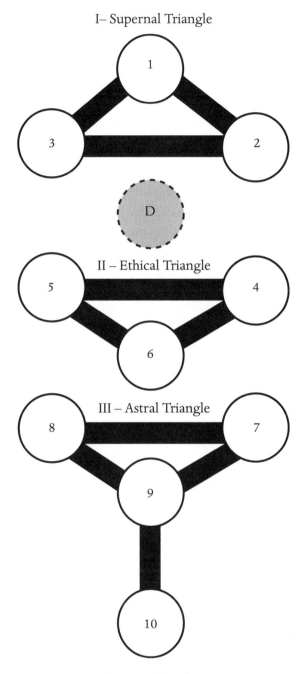

Figure 23: Triangles

recognize. The Ethical Triangle is really a reflection of the Supernal Triangle, reflected across the gulf of the Abyss. The powers are the embodiment of mercy, also defined as divine love, in the sphere of Chesed. Its counterbalance is Geburah, the sphere of force or might. The universe by its very nature is both gentle and harsh, giving and taking, forgiving and relentless. That paradox is the nature of things. Both creation and destruction are the forces that keep the wheels of the universe in motion, preventing stagnation. As humans, we often judge these forces as good or bad, depending on how they personally affect us. The balance point of this triad is the center of the Tree, Tiphereth, corresponding to the solar power, the Sun in the center of our solar system. It is only from a central point, the center of the wheels of life and death, that we can identify with the cycles and realize that creation and destruction are not personal forces, but powers of nature.

The last triad is known as the *Astral Triangle* or *Psychic Triangle*. This grouping of spheres represents the most material and human levels of consciousness. They are the spheres of creation to which we can most easily relate. Netzach is the realm of nature in the manifested universe, and the drives of nature within human consciousness— our passions, desires, and primal emotions. Hod is the realm of the mind, of language and ideas. The balance point of the triangle is the astral realm of Yesod, the energetic foundation on which all physical reality is based. It's our collective unconscious, the Dreamtime and Otherworld ruled by the Moon and intuition. The Astral Triangle is like a lower octave of the Ethical Triangle.

The first nine spheres are said to manifest the tenth sphere, the realm of Malkuth. Malkuth is the physical realm. Though it's not a part of any of the triangles, it's given the closest association with the Astral Triangle.

When the Tree of Life is used as a model for the individual, the Supernal Triangle is related to the spirit, the highest expression, while the Ethical Triangle is associated with the soul, the more individual expression of the spirit. The Astral Triangle relates most to the terrestrial personality of the individual in a specific lifetime, with the sphere of Malkuth, the tenth sphere, relating to the physical body, the vehicle for the personality and soul to express themselves in the world. A mirror to the Abyss, called the *veil*, is said to separate the first six spheres from the bottom four. The bottom four, the terrestrial self and terrestrial universe, appear to be cut off from higher forces to the casual observer. Once you pierce the veil, you find that the universe is vaster than most people believe.

The triangles demonstrate that personal evolution is not strictly a matter of climbing a ladder in a direct line toward some supernal enlightenment, but is a constant process of balancing polarities with a central fulcrum point, the tips of the triangles. We need a balance between our mind and feeling, Hod and Netzach, to find harmony within ourselves. Only through Yesod, where our thoughts and feelings take form and shape, granting us vision and ultimately magick on the astral tides, can we find that balance. Once we do, we are more prepared for the balance point of Tiphereth, a connection to our soul, or higher self, what is known to magicians as the Holy Guardian Angel. Once there is a connection to this central self, we can learn of both force, Geburah, and mercy, Chesed, and know when the application of either or both, and in what proportion, is appropriate. Lastly, we identify with the supreme divine feminine and masculine, yet realize that our true spiritual nature embodies both.

There is a reason that the bottom two triangles point downward toward manifestation while the Supernal Triangle points toward the Three Veils, toward what is beyond the Tree. Even though we desire to climb and expand our consciousness, our natural tendency is to descend when we are below the supernal world of the first triad; we seek to ascend once we have crossed the Abyss. The process of enlightenment and expansion constantly pulls us down to Malkuth, not to defeat us but to remind us that enlightenment is useless if we lose our footing in the material world and can't put our experience to use. One of the beings associated with Kether is called Metatron, and his crown is said to be in Kether, but his feet are in the realm of Malkuth. We all are called to awaken each of these parts yet not lose sight of the whole.

When looking at a properly proportioned image of the Tree of Life, we easily can find another division of three—the three pillars (figure 24). Each pillar represents a universal power. These powers sometimes are described in terms of yang, yin, and a mix between the two, as the colors commonly given are black, white, and gray, just like the Asian symbol of the Tao, known as the yin/yang. Other times they are described in terms of the three elements embodied by the three Hebrew mother letters, with the elements of water, fire, and air. Many mystic traditions give us a trinity division based on the powers of generation, destruction, and sustainment, as found in

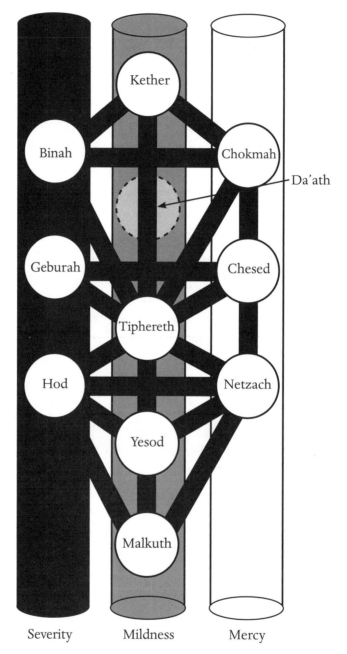

Figure 24: The Three Pillars

astrology with the qualities cardinal, mutable, and fixed. The correspondences of all these terms with the three pillars are not exact, but they give us a good starting point in understanding their power.

As we look at the Tree, the pillar on the left is colored black and is called the *Pillar of Severity*. Severity's pillar is the power of form and the destruction of that form, as all manifestations inherently have their own destruction within them. The pillar is considered feminine and relates to the water element. The three spheres on the pillar are like three octaves of the same force. Binah manifests the cosmic seed. It is the power of time and space. Geburah is the power to destroy and transform. Hod brings things into form and transforms them through language, ideas, and descriptions. Language and the mind itself are creative and destructive forces.

The right side of the Tree is the pillar of white, known as the *Pillar of Mercy*. This pillar is the movement of energy. It is considered more gentle than severity's pillar, as it warms and illuminates. It relates to the masculine principle and the energy of fire. Chokmah is the seed of life, of all potential creation. The lower octave of the supreme Father God is the benevolent father of mercy, Chesed, the wise and just force of compassion and goodness. The lowest note on the pillar, Netzach, is the passion of life, or personal love and drive. Each sphere on this pillar directs energy outward in some way, be it the energy of life, compassion, or passion.

The middle pillar is colored gray, standing between the Pillars of Severity and Mercy. This is the middle way, the path of balance between polarities, and is known as the *Pillar of Equilibrium* or *Pillar of Mildness*. This is where both extremes are tempered, and the best can be brought out and the worst mitigated. The element of air corresponds to this pillar, though the last sphere, Malkuth, is assigned to the earth element. Kether is the primal light that is neither male or female. Tiphereth is the solar light, the personal creative energy in our solar system, and the giver of life. Yesod is the reflected light of Tiphereth, the moonlight of imagination, where all potentials exist. Malkuth is the ultimate manifestation of these forces in an ever-changing balance, for Malkuth is immersed in space and time. As Hermeticists and Hermetic witches say, "As above, so below." Qabalists are fond of saying that "Kether is in Malkuth and Malkuth is in Kether." The Supernal Triangle is the ultimate macrocosm, with everything else being a manifestation of a microcosm.

Notice how the three pillars run through each of the triangles. The sphere on the middle pillar is always the balance point on the triangle, with the two extremes to either side.

When looking at the Tree as a model for the human body and energy systems, the three pillars are very similar to the three channels of energy described in Vedic lore. The middle pillar is the central core channel of energy known as the *sushumna*. The pillars on either side correspond roughly to the male and female nadis, called the *Pingala* and *Ida*, or Sun and Moon channels. The spheres on the middle pillar, as well as the lines that balance the two spheres crossing the middle pillar, are very similar to the Hindu chakra points.

Some Qabalists notice a weaving of polarities down the two outer pillars, reminiscent of the double helix formed by the Ida and Pingala in the human body. Though we broadly assign all the spheres on the left pillar to the dark polarity of the feminine nature and those on the right to the light polarity of the masculine nature, the archetypal energies of each sephira are not that clear-cut.

The powers of each pillar seem to change as we cross over the Abyss and the veil. On the Pillar of Severity, the classic feminine force, the second sphere, below Binah, is that of Geburah. While Binah is the Great Mother, Geburah is associated with the warrior and, specifically, the Mars archetype. Many practitioners assign to Geburah feminine figures, such as the Greek warrior goddess Pallas Athena and the Celtic war goddess the Morrighan. Though war can be seen as a feminine art as well as a masculine one, the concept of the receptive Mother in Binah is transformed into a more projective force. On the other side, the projective seed power of Chokmah is transformed once it moves down the Pillar of Mercy, into the sephira of Chesed, becoming the force of compassion. The receptive and compassionate force of Chesed naturally complements the forceful power of Geburah.

Beneath the veil, there is a further transformation of complementary energies. While the Pillar of Mercy is seen as masculine, its bottom sephira, Netzach, is embodied by Venus, a goddess figure, and the Pillar of Severity, the godform of Hod, is aligned with the androgynous yet still male figure of Mercury. Just like the yin/yang, the two pillars show how each force contains the seed of its opposite.

Four Worlds

The spheres on the Tree of Life can be categorized in a few different ways, showing the relationships between different sections of the glyph. One of the most popular methods of division is known as the *four worlds*. The concepts of the four worlds are familiar to the witch, as the associations are with the four elements. While most witches think of the four elements in what the magician would call the microcosm, or the manifested world, on this level the elements are operating on a grand scale, known as the macrocosm. In these four Qabalistic worlds, they are operating at their highest functions on a cosmic level, not just a terrestrial level. One concept that is repeated in Qabalistic study is that of octaves. Patterns repeat on a variety of levels, much as a musical scale on a piano repeats over and over again in a higher and higher register. Here, the elements are manifesting in a higher register.

Unlike other systems of elemental ordering, the Qabalistic model uses the pattern of fire, water, air, and earth, pairing the primal elements at the top of the hierarchy and the more complex elements at the bottom, with a male-female pattern in their classic gender correspondences. Other esoteric traditions usually assign the order according to what is perceived as least dense to most dense, such as fire, air, water, and earth. The associations also are different from what many learn in other traditions, such as the seasonal correspondences.

The first world, the world of fire, is named *Atziluth* (figure 25 and chart 3). It is the realm of divinity. Atziluth means "nearness," as it is closest to the unmanifest divinity. Pagan magicians would associate this with the true home of the gods, the deities who manifest the unmanifest divinity. Though the gods exist in all worlds, in all octaves, this is the level that resonates the most with their true nature. More monotheistic mages would not see the pagan deities at this level of being, but would look to a more unmanifest form of divinity. This is the realm corresponding to divine will, the will of divinity. Atziluth is most strongly associated with the Supernal Triangle of Kether, Chokmah, and Binah, though some would associate it only with Kether.

Briah is the second world. Linked to the element of water, it is the realm of creation, though alchemical traditions would assign it to the element of air. Briah means "creation," as it is on this level that the divine impetus takes form to create. Briah

World	Element	Function	Beings	Season	Letter
Atziluth	Fire	Divine/ Archetypes	Deity	Winter	Y
Briah	Water	Creation	Archangel	Spring	H
Yetzirah	Air	Formation	Angel	Summer	V
Assiah	Earth	Manifestation/ Action	Elemental	Fall	H

Chart 3: Four Worlds and Their Correspondences

corresponds to the heart, or love, of deity, in the most divine sense. It is the creative power. The beings associated with this realm are the archangels, the divine directors who guide the manifestation of creation. Briah is aligned with the spheres of Chesed, Geburah, and Tiphereth, though some traditions give Briah rulership over Chokmah and Binah.

The world of formation, or *Yetzirah*, corresponds to the element of air, though alchemical traditions align Yetzirah with water. This is the mind of the divine, though many Hermeticists who talk about the Divine Mind from *The Kybalion* (*ITOW*, Chapter 8) might be referring to all four worlds collectively rather than just Yetzirah. The beings of Yetzirah are the angels, divided into ten orders in Qabalistic lore, each headed by an archangel. While the archangel guides and directs, the angelic orders manage the task of manifesting the results in their various levels of reality. The spheres of the Astral Triangle—Netzach, Hod, and Yesod—correspond with Yetzirah, though other traditions give Yetzirah rulership over the intermediary spheres of Chesed, Geburah, and Tiphereth, along with Netzach, Hod, and Yesod.

The last of the four worlds is *Assiah*, the world of manifestation, form, and action. All traditions agree that the sphere of Malkuth, the most physical of all the spheres, is linked to Assiah. The beings of Assiah are known as the elementals, beings whose consciousness embodies one of the four classic elements—fire, water, air, and earth. In Malkuth/Assiah we have a smaller, microcosmic octave of the four elements. All spirits, planetary intelligences, and people manifest in the realm of Assiah.

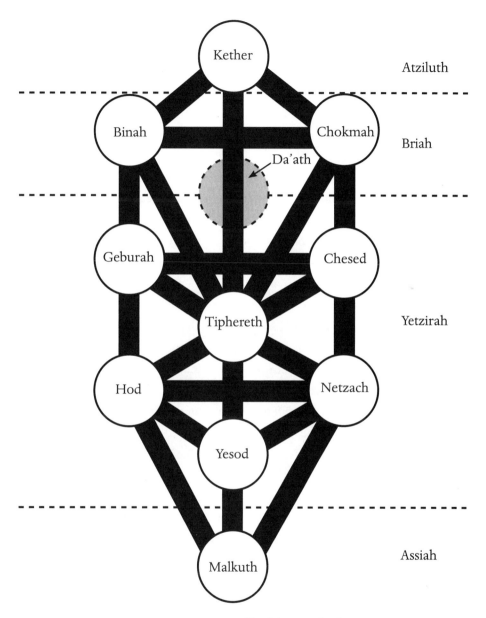

Figure 25: Four Worlds of the Tree of Life

The spheres are divided among these four worlds, yet not all traditions agree as to where the divisions fall. The ones described are most commonly accepted in modern magick.

In reality, all ten spheres exist in all four worlds simultaneously. Each has a fiery aspect, watery aspect, airy aspect, and earthy aspect, even if that's not their primary nature. One can refer to the Chesed of Briah and the Chesed of Assiah. Both are the sphere of Chesed, but each has slightly different associations. In fact, the spheres are said to have different color associations in each of the four worlds. Each color spectrum, known as a *scale*, is referred to as the King Scale, Queen Scale, Prince Scale, or Page or Princess Scale, associating each world with one of the four court cards in the tarot. The generally accepted color of a sphere comes from the Queen Scale.

To reflect this interconnection of four Trees, some magicians use the Tree of Life figure known as *Jacob's Ladder*, named after the vision of the ladder ascending to heaven (figure 26). There are two major versions of the image, each with a full Tree existing in all four worlds. The difference between the two images is that one has the four Trees stacked vertically on top of each other, and the other has them overlapping. Both represent the same concept, yet the two are related. The one with the overlapping Trees gives us further correspondences to meditate on when thinking about how a sephira or path in one world is a different sephira or path in another world.

Though Jacob's Ladder can be an interesting image to meditate on when you have further Qabalistic knowledge, for now, focus on the basic Tree of Life glyph, and simply know that it exists in all four worlds, just as you exist in all four worlds, with your divine, emotional, mental, and physical components.

Most importantly to Qabalists, the four worlds and their elements each are associated with one of the four letters in the Tetragrammaton. *Tetragrammaton*, which is Greek for a four-lettered word, refers to the most holy name of God in Qabalistic traditions. It's often with the Hebrew teachings that the modern witch loses interest in Qabalah, and that's understandable. When I first looked at the Hebrew names of God in this magick, I wanted nothing to do with the god of the Bible. All the images were patriarchal, stern, and unforgiving. Even in the more lenient New Testament, I wasn't a fan. Why would I do magick with this god? My magick predated this, at least in concept. Yet there was something mysterious about it, and once I looked beyond

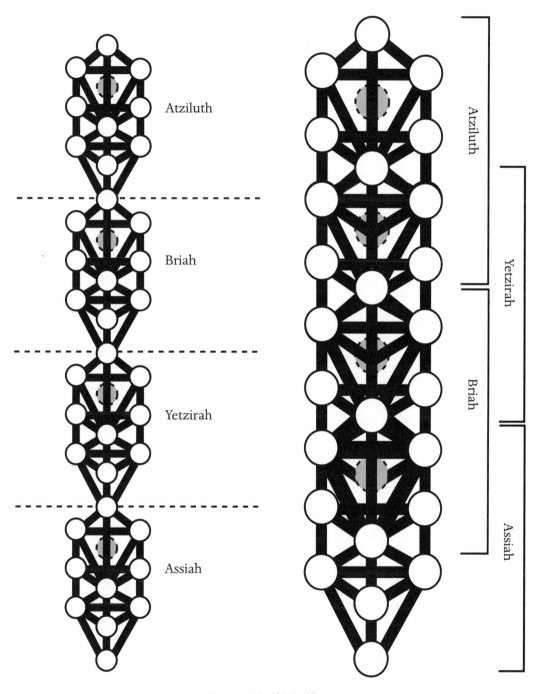

Figure 26: Jacob's Ladder

the surface, I realized that the Jewish mystics recognized God not only as Father but as Mother and everything in between. The image of the patriarch was for the exoteric religion, while the esoteric practitioners knew that God was both male and female and neither, what I would call the Divine Mind or Great Spirit.

The Tetragrammaton puts the name of that Great Spirit into form. The name is considered unpronounceable and is marked as YHVH, or Yod, Heh, Vau, Heh. Readers make it into "Yahweh" or "Jehovah." Ritual magicians simply chant the four Hebrew letters. The phonetic sequence, images, and intentions are said to be a key to creation, as the name exists and reverberates in all four worlds. This power to create through language is the true concept behind the "Word of God" or the modern idea of the Logos. It is not the name of a patriarchal god, but a name that embodies four principles, male-female-male-female, and embodies all the elements and all the planes of existence, from divine, to archangelic, angelic, elemental, and human. The letters stand for God the Father, Mother, Son, and Daughter.

The magickal group known as the Ordo Templi Astartes, or O.T.A., uses a different formula for the Tetragrammaton, feeling YHVH has too much of a patriarchal association. Instead of YHVH, they use either *AMShO*, with the three Hebrew mother letters and the Greek letter omega (Ω) for earth, or *ShMAT*, for fire, water, air, and T (Tau) for Saturn/earth.

Witches of the Robert Cochrane tradition use the numbers 1734 as a code similar to the Tetragrammaton, representing a numeric cryptogram for the witch goddess of creation. In a letter to Joe Wilson, dated 12th Night, 1966, Cochrane wrote:

> ... the order of 1734 is not a date or an event but a grouping of numerals that mean something to a witch. One that becomes seven states of wisdom—the Goddess of the Cauldron. Three that are Queens of the Elements—fire belonging alone to Man, and the Blacksmith God. Four that are Queens of the Wind Gods. The Jewish orthodoxy believe that whomever knows the Holy and Unspeakable name of God has absolute power over the world of form. Very briefly, the name of God spoken as Tetragrammaton ... breaks down in Hebrew to the letters YHVH, or the Adam Kadmon (The Heavenly Man). Adam Kadmon is a composite of all Archangels—in other words a poetic

statement of the names of the Elements. So what the Jew and the Witch believe alike, is that the man who discovers the secret of the Elements controls the physical world. 1734 is the witch way of saying YHVH.

Though I don't subscribe to Cochrane's specific mythology, it's easy to see how the Divine Mind is associated with the seven powers seen in the seven magickal planets, days of the week, colors, and chakras, as well as the three forces embodied by the triple goddess of fate (generating, organizing, and destruction) along with the four elemental powers and directions. So 1734 quite nicely sums up the witch's view of the powers of creation.

A fifth letter, Shin, for spirit, is added to the Tetragrammaton to make the Pentagrammaton, signifying the enlightened or ascended human who has integrated all four elements and spirit. Many magicians have placed the five letters around the pentagram as part of the star's magickal correspondences. Shin appears in the center of the Tetragrammaton—Yod, Heh, Shin, Vau, Heh. To Christian Cabalists, this combination of five letters usually symbolizes the figure of Jesus Christ. It is pronounced "Yeh hah-shu-ah," or "Joshua," which eventually became "Jesus" in English when translated from the Greek.

Here is another point at which we lose a lot of witches in their study of Qabalah. If the God of the Old Testament wasn't enough, here we go bringing in Jesus. Well, like it or not, Christianity greatly influenced the world, including esoterics and magick, during the last two thousand years. When looking over the history of magick, it's hard to completely separate the magickal Qabalah from the Christian Cabala, as many magicians were practicing Christians, at least nominally, to placate the Church, or in the esoteric sense of the highest Christ principle. Christ often was seen as an allegory for the alchemist's Philosopher's Stone, turning lead into gold and curing all diseases. Many Qabalists saw Christ as a magician himself. Strict Jewish Kabbalists will look at the Pentagrammaton and not necessarily relate it to the historical figure of Jesus. The Pentagrammaton is the realization of the Adam Kadmon, the perfected and enlightened human.

Though I don't particularly work with Christ as a spiritual entity, I do think it's important for modern pagans and witches to not fear or dislike the figure automatically.

I have no problem with Buddha, and I don't work with him directly either. I admire both figures for what they stand for at their core, even if I am not a practitioner of their traditions. Whenever I encounter a witch who is dead set against acknowledging Christ on any level, I think of Alex Sanders, the founder of the Alexandrian tradition of Wicca, who had a huge influence on the Craft and its popularity. Toward the end of his life, he had a statue of Jesus on his altar right next to a statue of Pan. If Pan can get along with Jesus, then I can be okay with him, too.

The four elements have a macrocosmic expression in the four Qabalistic worlds and a microcosmic manifestation in the four elemental planes of Malkuth, but they also have an intermediary manifestation, in the four bottom sephiroth. Malkuth, Yesod, Hod, and Netzach each represent a level of elemental learning in magickal tradition. Most modern traditions, including the ones in this book, see Malkuth as earth, Yesod as water, Hod as air, and Netzach as fire, although, like everything Qabalistic, not everyone agrees on these correspondences. Slightly older traditions reverse Yesod and Hod, matching the elemental order found in the larger Qabalistic worlds and maintaining the pairing of fire/water and air/earth. Each of these sephira can be associated with an element and one of the elemental "weapons" of both ceremonial magick and witchcraft, bearing a strong resemblance to the four gifts of the Tuatha de Danann in Celtic mythology. The use and eventual mastery of the four tools and the four elements open the veil to the higher spheres of the Qabalah.

Magickal Correspondences

With only a basic understanding of the Tree of Life, you already can see how this one symbol encodes a vast amount of magickal information. Through a survey of the triangles, pillars, and four worlds, you can find esoteric lore that you've already experienced in ritual and meditation. The Tree is a map of the spiritual dimensions of the universe and of the dimensions of human consciousness. The map of the universe is really a map of the self. Each of the correspondence sets on the Tree of Life is like an octave to the other sets, each being a reflection of the other, and the study of one set deepens the understanding of the other. Not only does the Tree map the inner worlds and subtle planes, but it also acts as a map of the physical solar system and universe and functions like a universal memory tower, available to anybody who chooses to walk in and look around.

The Tree of Life is a vast storehouse of magickal concepts and information. Almost any spiritual system can be mapped on its branches. Each sphere of the Tree contains the highest ideals of the cosmos. Each sphere has associations with physical objects, tools, and symbols that help a magician relate to those high ideals. The correspondences encoded on the Tree can be used in ritual, meditation, and magickal formulas. The Tree is a method that allows magicians or witches to store a lot of information in their personal memory, and if something escapes it, the Tree provides an easy system to look up the needed information. Israel Regardie described the Tree of Life as a file cabinet, with each sephira like a folder containing a variety of ideas and information. Here are just some of the correspondences found on the Tree of Life.

Chakras

As the middle pillar is analogous to the spine of the Tree of Life, with the two outer pillars as the Ida and Pingala, we can see the three horizontal "paired" spheres together as a power center, along with the four spheres of the middle pillar, making seven levels in all. Though magicians differ in their associations, Kether, meaning "crown," generally is associated with the crown chakra (figure 27). The pair of Chokmah and Binah aligns with the third eye. The throat and heart are where things get murkier. The mysteries of Da'ath, this "non-sephira" and the Abyss, are aligned with the throat chakra. Other systems simply use Geburah and Chesed for the throat chakra level. The heart is aligned with Tiphereth, again sometimes in a triad with Geburah and Chesed and sometimes not. The pair of Netzach and Hod align with the solar plexus. Yesod corresponds to the belly chakra and Malkuth to the root chakra.

It is through Qabalistic symbolism that we see one of the interesting discrepancies in Eastern and Western lore. Most Eastern traditions see the last power center at the base of the spine, as many exercises are done on the ground, with the spine contacting the Earth. Western magickal lore puts the last center, Malkuth, at the feet or slightly below the feet, in alignment with the spine. Most Western magick rituals are done standing up, with the feet, and not the spine, touching the ground. I feel the energy center is in the base of the spine, yet when we stand, its energy extends downward to ground us to the Earth.

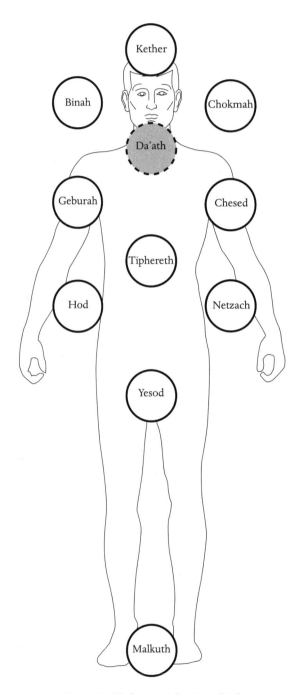

Figure 27: Chakras and the Tree of Life

Author John Michael Greer, in his book *Circles of Power*, makes an interesting point when comparing the chakras, Qabalistic centers, and Chinese energy centers, each of which has a reality that works for its practitioners. Greer compares the human energy system to a string on a musical instrument, like a guitar. You can press down on various points on the string and get different tones, yet they all work. The differences between various cultural energy systems are like pressing down on different places on the string. Each is valid but slightly different, describing a similar yet subtly different "note" in the human body's energy system.

Planets

Each of the spheres on the Tree of Life is associated with a planet and that planet's archetype (figure 28). When we look at the glyph, it's really a map of our solar system from the perspective of the Earth at the bottom. All the planets are neatly represented

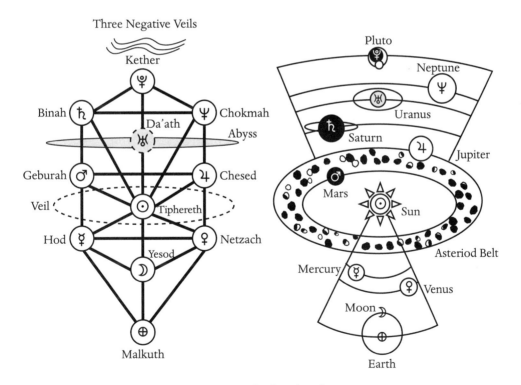

Figure 28: Tree of Life as the Solar System

in symbolic proportions, if not scientific ones. The recent change in the scientific status of Pluto does not alter its Qabalistic or astrological associations.

Traditionally, the seven magickal planets of the ancients are associated with spheres three through nine; and the planet Earth and the realm of the four terrestrial elements, the elemental powers called in the witch's circle, are associated with the tenth sphere, Malkuth, which often is symbolized with an X dividing it into four equal parts. It's interesting to note that X is the Roman numeral for ten. The second sphere, Chokmah, usually is identified with the stars of the zodiac and, primarily, the fixed signs of Taurus, Leo, Scorpio, and Aquarius, our four totems of the Sphinx. Kether is seen as beyond the stars, as the center of the cosmos. Modern Qabalists have attempted to associate the outer planets with the upper spheres, though they don't always agree.

From a witchcraft point of view, the planets are paired on the horizontal bars in an interesting manner. Most witches look at the planets in terms of polarities and complements, particularly male and female. The Sun and Moon make a natural pair, yet they are on the middle pillar vertically, rather than on the two sides of polarity. Venus and Mars are seen as a pair—the modern symbols of female and male, love and aggression—yet they are diagonal from each other, not on the same level, with Tiphereth between them. Jupiter and Saturn are another pair—symbolizing expansion and contraction, the generous king and the harsh taskmaster/taskmistress—yet they are also diagonal. This seeming imbalance of diagonal movement creates a dynamic tension along the lightning flash. Each planet reaches out to its mate. This tension helps the energy of the Tree ascend and descend rather than remain stagnant at any one level. Nothing remains static with this force of attraction. Interestingly enough, the orbs most strongly associated with the witch—the Earth, Moon, and Sun, or Malkuth, Yesod, and Tiphereth—are on the middle pillar, the most direct path yet one of the most perilous, heading across the Abyss and to the Godhead of Kether.

Deities

As each sephira corresponds to a planet, it also corresponds to the godforms of the planet. Each planetary archetype manifests in a variety of cultures. You can map the gods of almost any pantheon and find their places on the sephiroth. I believe these deities are the manifestations of each sphere in the realm of divinity, of Atziluth, but some would see them in one of the other three worlds, seeing the only manifestation of the divine in Atziluth as the sacred Hebrew names of God associated with each sphere. As creation has its Tetragrammaton, each sphere has a special name that encapsulates its own creative power. Chanting this name in ritual aligns you with the energy of that sephira.

Angels

In Hebrew magick, creation is ministered to by the angelic realm, which includes the messengers and enforcers of divine will on the various planes of existence. Though some modern pagan magicians shy away from angelic magick, the concept of angels is universal and predates strict Judeo-Christian lore. Many believe that the knowledge of such spirits comes from Sumer, Babylon, and Egypt. Shamanic cultures see the angelic figures in terms of divine messengers and "sky heroes" of tribal legend. In Qabalah, each sephira is ruled by an archangel, a primal power anchored in the formative world of Briah. Each archangel rules an angelic order, also known as a choir, a distinct class of angels associated with a specific function or purpose in harmony with the sphere's power. The angelic orders are rooted in Yetzirah. Some magicians describe the angels within an order as the cells within the body of the archangel. Thus, when an archangel is summoned to do work, the angels are present throughout the universe, with their "body" stretching from one end of the cosmos to the other. They respond by directing the attention of one or more of their "cells," which take on their likeness in manifestation.

Natural Magick

The Qabalah manifests in the last of the four worlds, Assiah, as the magickal correspondences familiar to so many of us in magick. Qabalists assign stones and gems to each of the ten spheres based on astrological associations. The alchemical metals are assigned to the spheres as well. Herbs also have astrological and Qabalistic associations. Scents, particularly those of incense and oils, are associated with the sephiroth. Scent plays a key role in unlocking the powers of the Tree of Life.

Symbolic Magick

Beyond the physical manifestations of the energies of the sephiroth in nature, the Qabalah maps ideas and languages. The first symbol encoded in each sephira is numerological. Each sephira has a number, and numerologists tell us that each number has a vibration, an energy, that affects those who naturally resonate with it or specifically invoke it. Qabalah has a rich history of numerology, though mainstream numerology and Qabalistic numerology are quite different even though they share certain principles. A Qabalistic ritual to work with the powers of the ninth sphere, Yesod, might call for the practitioner to do things nine times—to speak evocations nine times, ring a bell or knock nine times, or light nine candles. Aligning the symbolic associations with the natural magickal correspondences of both the ritual and the sephira increases the resonance between the two. This can be done by lighting nine silver/purple candles or using nine silver coins, the colors and metal of Yesod. Languages can be charted on the Tree, such as the Hebrew alphabet, with all of its symbolic and mythical associations. Others have put various magickal languages on the Tree quite effectively. Beyond the formal languages and symbols, other images, including totemic animals, have been used to describe the spheres.

Tarot

Tarot cards have become a modern mainstay of wisdom on the Tree of Life, pictorially describing the energies of each path and sphere in a way that those uninitiated into the mysteries of Qabalah can understand and recognize. The major arcana are assigned to the pathways, for these cards represent the powers of change and transformation, making shifts from one level to another (figure 29). The suits are assigned to the sephiroth. Each numbered card resonates with the sphere of the same number. All aces, or ones, belong to Kether. All twos belong to Chokmah. All threes resonate with Binah, and so on. The elemental associations of the suits—fire/wands, air/swords, water/cups, and earth/pentacles (discs)—show the power of each sphere in one of the four worlds. The Four of Cups shows the power of Chesed, the fourth sphere, in the realm of Briah, the water world. The Four of Swords shows the power of Chesed in Yetzirah, the air world. The court cards also are assigned to the spheres, with all the adult male figures (usually kings, though they are referred to as knights in some

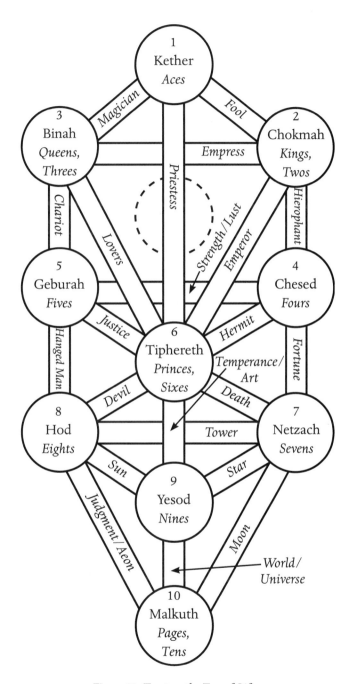

Figure 29: Tarot on the Tree of Life

decks) in Chokmah, and the queens in Binah. The young male figures, either knights or princes, are assigned to Tiphereth. Lastly, the young female or androgynous figures, the pages or princesses, are assigned to Malkuth.

Visions, Virtues, and Vices

The highest spiritual ideals of the Tree of Life are encoded in the sephiroth. As the Tree is a map of the soul, each realm has a *vision* associated with it, a spiritual concept that can manifest in magickal work as an epiphany, revelation, or actual vision. This vision is the key to understanding and integrating the wisdom of the sphere. By reading about each of the visions and interpreting your life and personal initiatory path using this symbolism—which might not always follow the numerical order of the return path of the Lightning Flash, from ten to one—you will gain an understanding of the work you have done and what you have yet to do. Even if you do not work specifically with the Qabalah, these visions are very much like universal benchmarks that mystics from a variety of traditions experience and simply describe with different symbols. Each sephira also is assigned a *virtue*, or a quality that one who has integrated the vision should display in some manner, as well as a *vice*, or a quality displayed when one is challenged by the energy of the sephira. Though these terms have a Judeo-Christian flavor to them that makes the average Wiccan wince, I nonetheless have found them very helpful. Simply think of the virtue as a quality to manifest, the vice as a quality to diminish, and the vision as the inspiration we receive when working with this sphere successfully. Having the vision lets us know we are truly in touch with the forces of the sephira, and gives us the awarness to integrate its lesson into our daily lives.

When studying a correspondence system like the Qabalah, it's important to not equate the correspondences with the power they resonate with. All the correspondences go into the file folder but are not the file folder itself. Though frankincense, gold, the Sun, the lion, and the Greek god Apollo all are attributed to Tiphereth, they are not all the same thing, and the nature of Tiphereth encompasses them all yet contains even more. They simply are ways of connecting with the divine energy of Tiphereth.

As the glyph can represent various octaves of energy, corresponding symbols and items can have more than one place on the Tree. For example, the image of Thoth or

Hermes, the gods of wisdom and magick, usually is assigned to the eighth sphere of Hod, ruled by Mercury, but some put Thoth/Hermes in the second realm of Chokmah, as a father of civilization and creation. He appears again in the path connecting Chokmah to Binah, as the path ruled by the tarot card the Magician, also influenced by the planet Mercury. Which is right? They all are. Hod represents the more personal and terrestrial function of Thoth/Hermes, while Chokmah represents his supernal function. The Magician is the power of Thoth/Hermes in action. Just as people are more complex than their zodiac Sun sign attributes, gods, animals, and even plants and stones can have more than one strict attribute. They are multifaceted and truly exist in the entire Tree, but assigning them to specific spheres makes the process of understanding them more helpful for those of us operating at human consciousness.

It's also important to remember that the "traditional" correspondences seem to change over time, as perspectives change. What is most popular today is due to the work of the Golden Dawn and Aleister Crowley. They based their work on that of earlier magicians. Magicians often have their own personal correspondences and don't agree with each other. A variety of new adaptations have been created to suit the magician and his or her own tradition. As this text is intended to adapt modern Qabalah for witchcraft students, I'll be using a lot of my own personal correspondences, based on my own experiences and those of my friends, covenmates and students, to add to the living lore of this versatile magickal system. I will emphasize some of the correspondences that are more helpful to a witch.

No one system is absolute or final, no matter what its proponents say. To be a living tradition, it must evolve and grow or it will wither away. Secure and self-realized magicians know there is always room for interpretation, variation, and change. No one way works for everybody all the time. No one system can completely encompass all correspondences and all traditions without some dissonance. This is the Law of Divine Inconsistencies. Nothing is perfect, at least from a human perspective. It is because of that seeming imperfection that we seek to understand and work and play until the pieces make sense to us. Without that bit of tension, we wouldn't strive forward. A study of the variations of symbols and ideas will help you grow, understand, and ultimately find what works for you. You might find that the ideas are more complementary than you thought at first. Don't expect your own reality maps to be perfect and harmonious.

When I first was studying the Qabalah, one discrepancy really stuck out to me. I had learned that the number five was a Goddess number, associated with Venus. Five-petaled flowers are associated with love and female genitals. Our mystical associations with pentacles and five-petaled roses are symbols of Goddess reverence and feminine wisdom. Then, in the Qabalah, I learned that Venus is associated with the number seven, and Geburah, the sphere of Mars, is associated with five. At first it didn't make sense. I was stuck on the idea that five was Venus's number. Later study showed how the seven sisters of the stars share some attributes with Venusian energy. Geburah is martial but is often seen as a war goddess, not always a god. The pentacle is a gateway to both life and death, and could be shared by these two powers. I soon realized that Mars and Venus were exactly in the right place on the Tree of Life, and it all made sense to me in the overall system.

In the end, all ideas can have validity if they have meaning for you. If something works, magickally or otherwise, it works, and often the philosophy we create to explain it can be a matter of semantics. In magick, salt cleanses and purifies, but how does it do these things? As a dense earth substance, does salt attract heavy, unwanted energies and trap them in the crystals? Does it clear away things because it is white and clear and pure, neutralizing unhealthy energies? Does it attract pure, clear energy to displace the unwanted, harmful energy? Any of these explanations, these magickal theories, can be valid, depending on your own magickal ideas. Yet the practical witch and the philosophical magician both will tell you that salt works for these purposes.

Alternate Forms of the Tree

The current Tree of Life and its associations are simply the most modern and widely accepted form. There have been many variations throughout history and other ways, including many modern ways, to understand the ten powers.

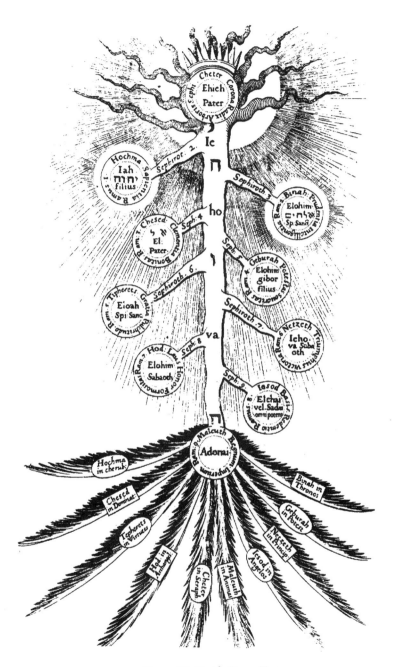

Figure 30: Upside-Down Tree

Plate XXI. Arber Sephirotheca, from *Utriusque Cosmi* by Robert Fludd, 1621, Vol. II.

The Upside-Down Tree

When a modern witch looks at the strange Tree of Life glyph of ten circles and twenty-two lines and tries to see a tree, the usual assumption is that the branches are in the first three sephiroth, while the trunk is the middle pillar and the base of the tree is Malkuth. Though this would be a very good assumption, and most do view the Tree this way, the original thought was of a Tree with its roots in the heavens (figure 30). Kether is actually its root base, and the roots extend into the three veils. The rest of the Tree consists of the branches, and Malkuth is considered to be the "fruit" of the Tree, it's ultimate expression, with the "seeds" or patterns of the Tree within it.

Emanations

As each sphere is said to emanate from the last, a valid model for the Tree that ignores the twenty-two paths is a series of ten concentric rings (figure 31). From Kether comes Chokmah and then Binah, radiated outward, with Malkuth as the outer ring. Others reverse it, seeing the entire physical universe imbedded in the spiritual powers, and have Kether on the outside, with the rings becoming ever more dense as they emanate inward, culminating with Malkuth in the center.

Fractal Tree

A fractal is a shape in which part of the image is similar in shape to a given larger or smaller piece of the shape when magnified or reduced. Fractals are commonly generated through mathematical graphics programs on computers, and graphically demonstrate many of the scientific thoughts about the holographic nature of reality and patterns repeating themselves, as in the Principle of Correspondence (*ITOW*, Chapter 8). With this idea in mind, it is said that not only is there a complete Tree of Life in each of the four worlds, forming Jacob's Ladder, as demonstrated in figure 26, but there also is a full Tree inside each of the sephiroth, as shown in figure 32. If you're looking at Malkuth, there is a Kether aspect to Malkuth, a reflection of Kether in Malkuth. There is also a Chokmah aspect to Malkuth, a Binah aspect, and so on. Some might describe them in terms of fractions with a common denominator, the Kether/Malkuth, Chokmah/Malkuth, and Binah/Malkuth, respectively. Many say the upper states of the Tree are unattainable by humans, at least while in a human body, yet people meditate and

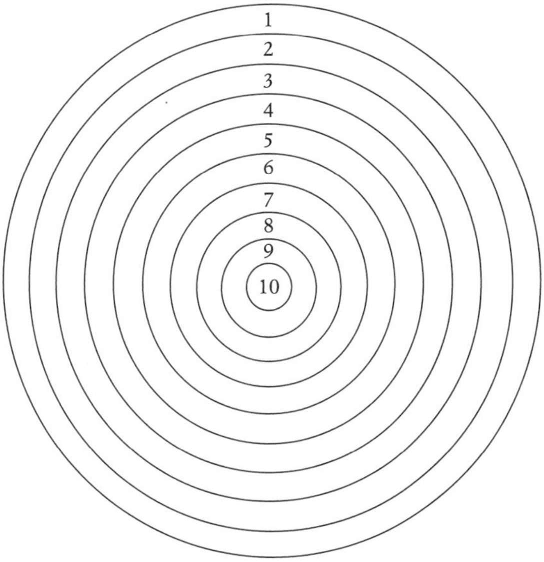

Figure 31: Emanations

rise on the spheres, and appear to connect to these planes. Either these people are de-lusional, or they are reaching that level within the highest sphere they have personally attained. For example, if someone is anchored in the consciousness of Yesod, then he or she can experience the Kether of Yesod but not the ultimate union with the divine in the "true" Kether. If we take this theory to its logical conclusion, then each of the spheres within these smaller Trees has a Tree, and so on, making the level of subtlety infinite. We can zoom in and out for more or less complexity and detail. But for all practical pur-poses, we need only contemplate the Tree within each sephira at this first level.

If you have been following the Temple of Witchcraft series, you might be wonder-ing how the shaman's World Tree fits into this complicated Tree of Life map. Both seem to fulfill the same function, as a road map to the otherworlds and the beings we can meet there, but the shaman's Tree seems more primal and intuitive.

I believe the World Tree and the Tree of Life are simply two different ways of looking at the same thing. The Qabalah maps areas of consciousness well known to the shaman. Some shamans had more complex systems than the simple three-world model. Norse

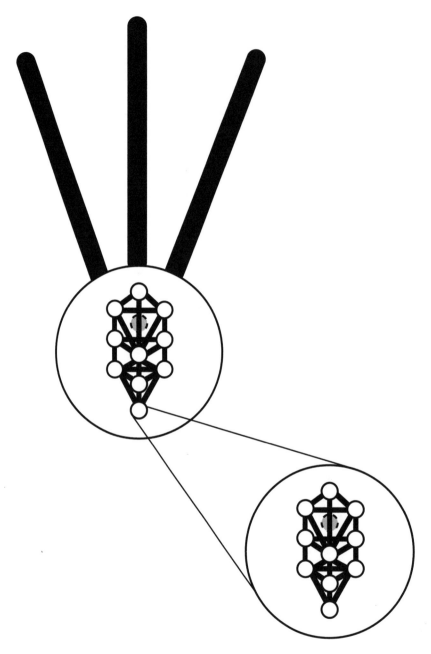

Figure 32: Fractal Tree

mythology details a nine-world system. The Celts may have had as many as twelve realms. The Qabalah simply draws the lines on the map in a different way.

Some look at Malkuth and see it divided into four, with a black triangular "pie" piece on the bottom. They see that as the Underworld, with the rest of Malkuth as the Middle World and the remaining sephiroth, nine through one, as the Upper World. Though that image can work, I don't necessarily agree with it. It gives the Underworld very little importance, and as a witch, I know the Underworld is pretty important.

Other Qabalistic teachings say that each sphere has a healthy, or Qabalistic, expression and an unhealthy shadow expression, known as its Qlippothic expression. They call this dark side of the Tree the *Tree of Death* or the reverse of the Tree of Life. Sometimes it is depicted behind the Tree in shadow, with Da'ath as its gateway. Others see it as a reverse Tree, a mirror reflection coming out of Malkuth and descending. It is said to be devoid of divinity. Though I think an understanding of the Qlippothic Tree is important, it doesn't quite fit my idea of the Underworld, which is quite divine and oftentimes very loving.

Others divide the ten spheres and rearrange them according to their nature (figure 33). Malkuth is the Middle World. The Lower World starts with Yesod and descends in the order of Netzach, Geburah, Da'ath, and Binah. Yesod holds a special place as the gateway to the other worlds, so I see it rotating around the Middle World, like the rising and setting Moon. The Upper World includes Hod, Tiphereth, Chesed, and Chokmah. Tiphereth, like Yesod, has a special relationship with the Tree, as sometimes the brightest light of Tiphereth is found in the heart of the Underworld, what some call the "sun at midnight" spiritual experience. Kether is either assigned to the Upper World or seen to encompass the entire Tree. By following the numerology, we make an almost perfect spiral around the World Tree, descending and ascending alternately.

All of these Qabalah basics can seem quite complicated and intimidating. This is simply an overview of the system, to give you a framework with which to work. Believe it or not, Qabalah is purposefully complex. As an "air" path of the mind and philosophy, the various correspondences and complexities are designed to overwhelm you, until you begin to see everything reduced to nothing, to the same basic patterns. These patterns are found in everything and everyone. A Zen koan is meant to be contemplated by a student, with the solving of the riddle resulting in an epiphany and an understanding

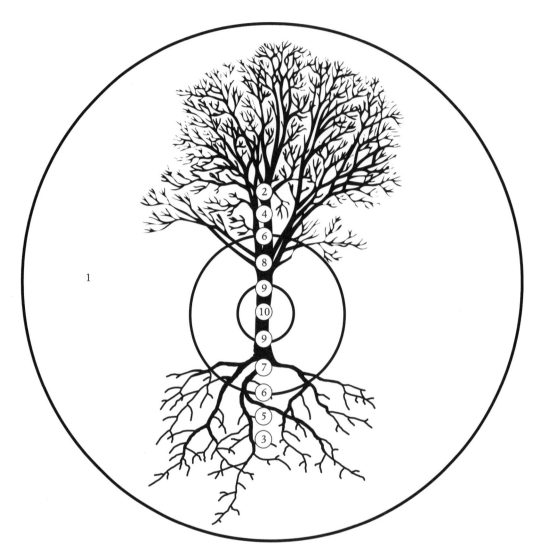

Figure 33: Map of the Three Worlds of the Shaman and the Tree of Life

of how consciousness works. The Qabalah is like a vast koan of magickal inconsistencies, meant to be contemplated to bring a greater sense of enlightenment. From this purer state of consciousness, you see how everything works together and then truly understand that the glyph of the Tree is only a two-dimensional map, which does not reflect the beauty of the multidimensional universe. This map is only one of many tools.

Think of the work you do in this chapter as planting a seed. You are planting a seed of understanding within yourself. Through the lessons and rituals, you will nourish and water that seed, and it will take root within you, helping you understand and travel anywhere in the universe you desire.

One of the best ways to plant this new seed is to personally touch these levels of being through an exercise known as "rising on the planes." If you have performed the previous training in *The Inner Temple of Witchcraft*, then you will have no problem or worry when briefly touching upon these ten levels of existence. Each subsequent lesson in this book will focus on a particular sephira, helping you integrate its lessons.

EXERCISE 4

Rising on the Planes

1. To get into a meditative state, do exercise 1 through step 7 (page 76).

2. Be aware of your physical body and the physical world around you. This is Malkuth, the kingdom or garden of creation. This is the realm of the four directions and elements, of the seasons and time. Here is the wheel of time and space guiding birth, life, death, and rebirth in the physical world. This is the realm of the earth goddesses and grain mothers. This is the realm of the fertility gods. Feel the physical world. Notice your breath and body. Feel your pulse as the blood travels in your veins. Feel the clothes on your skin. Smell the air and any meditation incense you have burning. Hear the sounds around you.

3. Once you feel fully immersed in the garden of Malkuth, feel your sense of self grow lighter and lighter, rising out of your body. Be aware of a sphere of light above you, purple flecked with silver. This is the sphere of Yesod, the astral foundation of Malkuth. Enter the realm of purple light. Feel yourself

and the power of your emotions. Feel as if you have entered a dream realm, where the light reflects and morphs to reflect your thoughts and feelings. This is the realm of the moon priestesses, fertility gods, and sacred timekeepers. While in this realm, feel your magick, your intuition, grow and wax, like the waxing of the moon.

4. Your buoyant self-image rises out of Yesod and into an orange sphere of light above you. You enter the realm of Hod, the realm of Mercury, the mind, and language. Your perceptions immediately change, becoming quick, clear, and sharp. Logic, reason, and communication are the powers at work here in Hod. This is the realm of the messenger gods and magicians. This is the realm of the tricksters and scientists. The very realm seems to be made of language and information, coalesced into a form that your mind can comprehend.

5. Above Hod is the emerald green of Netzach. Feel yourself magnetically pulled, attracted into the realm of the Venusian love goddess. This is the realm of nature, of primal passion and fiery attractions. This is the realm of verdant life, often linked with the devas, the architects of nature, and with the faery races. This is the realm of love, from the love of nature to the love of romance and passion.

6. In the clear blue skies of Netzach, you see the golden-yellow orb of the Sun, of Tiphereth. You automatically are drawn up into the golden light. This is the realm of unconditional, illuminating love, that love associated with the sacrificed gods and healing sun kings. This is spiritual illumination, inspiration, and a connection to your own personal divinity. Feel yourself soaking up the golden rays of light, like a plant absorbing sunlight, to be converted into your spiritual fuel.

7. The yellow of Tiphereth gives way to the red fire and light of Geburah. As you enter Geburah, feel the fire and power build within you. Feel the aggression and judgment of the warrior gods and goddesses. Only by passing through Tiphereth can you effectively use this power. The fires of Geburah burn away all that does not serve you, tempering and honing you, like a blacksmith with a blade, to your true purpose and divine will.

8. The fire red is consumed by the descent of peaceful blue all around you. Though it seems to envelop you, you know that you have risen to the sphere of Chesed, of compassion. Chesed, the realm of Jupiter, is expansive and inclusive. It is the power of benevolence and gentleness. This is the realm of the ascended masters, inner teachers, and enlightened beings. This is the realm of the sky gods and wise kings.

9. Imagine rising out of the blue light and leaping across a chasm, passing over the Abyss and landing in the dark fertile sphere of Binah. Like the rich earth embodied by Saturn and the deep ocean all at once, the Great Mother in Binah receives you. You are floating in an ocean of all potentials, the primordial ocean of creation and deep space.

10. From Binah, you float upward into the fountains of light in the gray sphere of Chokmah. Chokmah is like the trident of Neptune, in his form as the cosmic sea god. Chokmah's energy is like the spurting of cosmic oceans and geysers. This is the realm of the Great Father and starry king.

11. The spurting stars urge you upward to the zenith of the Tree, the crown, Kether. Immerse yourself in the brilliant prismatic white light of the crown. This is the purest state of consciousness humans can conceive of, beyond male and female. This is the Godhead, the Great Spirit, the Divine Mind. Feel yourself meld with the light.

12. Soon you find yourself slipping from the light of Kether. You slowly descend down the spheres, through the gray light of Chokmah to the darkness of Binah. You move across the Abyss through Chesed's blue light and the ruby red of Geburah. The golden light of Tiphereth eases you back into the personal sphere, bringing you through green Netzach, orange Hod, purple Yesod, and finally to the material realm of Malkuth and your body.

13. To return to normal waking consciousness, perform steps 15–17 from exercise 1 (page 78).

By the end of this chapter, you should have some idea of what you were doing in Exercise 2: Qabalistic Cross (page 96). You were envisioning the Tree of Life in your energy field, with Kether at your crown and Malkuth at your feet. At your right shoulder is anchored Geburah, and at your left shoulder is Chesed, which also is known as *Gedula*. The words of the prayer from that ritual all are associated with the sephiroth: *thine* for the divine Godhead at Kether, *kingdom* for Malkuth, *power* for Geburah, and *glory* for Chesed.

HOMEWORK

- Perform Exercise 4: Rising on the Planes, and record your experience.

- Keep a traditional journal as part of your magickal work. Record both your magickal experiences and the events of your day-to-day life. Watch for the effects of your magick in your daily life. This journal can be a part of your Book of Shadows (BOS) or completely separate, depending on your needs.

- Practice any of your basic skills from *ITOW* and *OTOW*.

- Practice Exercise 2: Qabalistic Cross.

TIPS

- Memorizing unfamiliar words can help plant the Tree of Life within you. Seek to memorize all ten names of the spheres and their numbers.

- Many students find it helpful to make a drawing of the Tree of Life glyph. You can color it or write in words, symbols, and all sorts of information, as a form of artistic learning and magick. Some even hang it behind or near their altar as a focus for meditation and contemplation. The simple act of drawing with precision and intention can imbed the Tree in your mind and help the seed within you grow. For now, draw a large but empty Tree of Life, and fill in the correspondences as you go through each subsequent lesson. You can add both traditional information and your personal experiences to the diagram, making it uniquely yours.

- You can use a separate notebook for your Qabalistic studies, devoting a section or a few pages to each sphere and path. Some use Regardie's idea literally, and make a Qabalistic file folder for each sephira.

Lesson Two
Malkuth

The last sphere to manifest on the Tree of Life is actually the first one that concerns the aspiring witch and magician. It is the realm of Malkuth, the proverbial garden of paradise where so many creation myths begin. The true lesson of Malkuth is to understand that we never left the garden, that it's been all around us the entire time. The only thing that changes is our perspective of it.

Though many see the magick of the Qabalah as inherently nonpagan, Malkuth encodes one of the primal teachings of modern witchcraft and paganism in its very nature—that of immanent divinity. As witches, we believe that everything is divine. We believe the material world is the Earth Mother and we are like cells in her body. If we truly believe in the Principle of Correspondence, then we know that Mother Earth is but a cell within the vast universal body. Not only is everything interconnected, but everything is a manifestation of the divine. In the Tree of Life, the divine emanates outward from the primal source in ever more complex and dense forms, resulting in the material universe. The material universe is not separate from the divine, but is one aspect, one-tenth, of creation. That means everything in the material world is a manifestation of the divine, from the natural world of trees, plants, animals, rivers, clouds, and stones to our own human bodies, homes, machines, and computers. Nothing is unnatural because everything is divine.

The true key to Malkuth is understanding that the divine is everything and everything is the divine. Once we look beyond the veneer of the mundane world, we realize that everything has a sacred aspect. Divinity is inside, around, and interpenetrating everything. Nothing is mundane because everything is sacred.

Malkuth

Meanings: Kingdom, Garden

Level of Reality: Physical Reality, Manifestation

Parts of the Self: Guph, Physical Body, Sensation, Feet

Experience: Knowledge and Conversation of the Holy Guardian Angel

Obligation: Discipline

Illusion: Materialism

Virtue: Discrimination

Vices: Inertia, Laziness

Name of God: Adonai ha-Aretz (Lord of the Earth)

King Scale Color: Clear Yellow

Queen Scale Colors: Russet, Olive, Citrine, Black

Prince Scale Color: Same as the Queen colors, but flecked with Gold

Princess Scale Color: Black rayed with Yellow

Element: Earth

Planet: Earth

Image: Young Queen, crowned on a throne

Archetypes: Earth Mother, Grain Goddess

Greek/Roman Deities: Gaia, Demeter, Persephone

Egyptian Deities: Osiris, Geb, Seb, Isis

Middle Eastern Deity: Kishar

Celtic Deity: Danu

Norse Deities: Freya, Audumla, Nerthus

Hindu Deity: Lakshmi

Archangel: Sandalphon (Angel of Prayer)

Angelic Order: Ashim (Humanity)
Choirs: Order of Blessed Souls, Ascended Masters, Secret Chiefs, Hidden Company
Grade of Initiation: ①=⑩ Zelator
Animal: The Sphinx
Musical Note: F
Tool: Circle
Incense: Dittany of Crete
Tarot: All Princesses/Pages (young female/child)
      Ten of Wands, Swords, Cups, and Pentacles
      Judgment/Aeon—to Hod
      World/Universe—to Yesod
      Moon—to Netzach
Metal: None
Stones: Rock Crystal, Tiger's-Eye
Plants: Lily, Ivy, Willow

I suggest that you use the correspondences of Malkuth to decorate your altar for this month of study, or build a secondary altar for your Qabalistic studies. When teaching this course to my students, we take the round classroom altar and decorate it as if it were this sephira, angling the major arcana tarot cards corresponding with the paths outward in the appropriate path directions. For Malkuth, we have Judgment/Aeon in the upper left, the World/Universe in the middle, and the Moon in the upper right (figure 29). The tens are in the center, to the four directions, along with the four princess/page cards. The altar cloth is colored in the sephira's color with the appropriate number of candles on it. In this case, we use ten candles in earthen tones, with rock crystal scattered around. We use the appropriate incense in the incense burner, though Dittany of Crete is not always on hand, so sometimes I substitute another earthy scent, such as patchouli incense. These Qabalistic correspondences on the altar provide a sensory focus for the lesson, stimulating touch, sight, and smell. Then we change the altar correspondences for the next lesson. Explore using a redecorated primary altar, or secondary altar dedicated to your Qabalistic studies, as a tool for your own understanding of the Tree of Life.

Entities of Malkuth

In some mythologies, the realm of Malkuth is considered to be the Kingdom of God, and once you know you *are* the Kingdom, nothing can take you out of it. In other, more feminine-focused mythologies, Malkuth is seen as the Garden of the Goddess. The divine image of Malkuth is a young queen, crowned upon her throne. She is on the throne, signifying her rulership, her dominion and sovereignty over the land, for she is one with the land. In the myths of the sacred king, he is sovereign only because he is wed to the goddess of the land. From her, he gains his power to command. Without her consent, he has nothing.

An important image is that of the Bride of the Earth enthroned, or the Shekinah, or feminine incarnation of the divine in Jewish myth. The bride or young queen is the symbol of Malkuth, but the throne itself is an image of the first form, a symbol of the third sephira, Binah. The image mimics the Egyptian Sitting Pose meditation position suggested in *The Inner Temple of Witchcraft* (Chapter 6) and *The Temple of Shamanic Witchcraft* (Chapter 5). This is the meditation pose favored by many ceremonial magicians, as it grounds you in the two aspects of the Goddess—highest and lowest, stars and Earth.

The goddesses of Malkuth are all deities associated with the land itself, from all of physical reality to, specifically, our planet Earth and the fertility, the bounty, of the Earth. All Earth Mother figures and grain goddesses are the embodiment of Malkuth, of the sacred garden. Most common are the images of Gaia, the Greek Earth Mother, or Demeter, the grain goddess. Some assign Demeter's daughter, Kore, as the flower maiden, to the sphere of Malkuth, because all of the princesses or pages of the tarot deck also are assigned to Malkuth, so the young maidens as well as the mothers are the goddesses of Malkuth. The maidens, or princesses/pages, represent the Goddess in her terrestrial form, the Goddess of the Earth found in the Charge of the Goddess, while the queens are the Goddess in her supernal or starry cosmic form, encompassing everything. The Earth Mother and grain goddesses are not just the rulers of Malkuth; they, in essence, *are* Malkuth. They are the manifestations of the physical world. They are the consciousness of the physical universe. We are all part of their body, so we are all a part of the Kingdom of God, or the Goddess's Garden of Paradise.

This primal garden signifies the time in our consciousness when we were not separate from our creator, when we saw ourselves as one. Many in the Goddess-oriented traditions see this as the Stone Age civilizations, potentially matriarchies of some sort, before written language and agrarian technology, when our very lives were much more interwoven with the realm of nature and the body of the Goddess. This is the true meaning of the stories about the Garden of Eden, and in many ways, it was our knowledge that separated us from this sense of union. Yet it is still there; we just need to recognize it again. We never left the garden, for we are the garden. This sense of separation served our evolution for a while, but it is now time, as individuals and as a global society, to reunite with the garden, to fully recognize that we are part of the greater whole, and bring what we have learned from our time of seeming separation to enrich the entire world. It is only through a connection to the Goddess of this garden that we can do this. I believe that is why so many modern movements of spirituality are emphasizing the Goddess force, to spark that reconnection, so we can then in turn recognize both Goddess and God, and the force beyond shape and gender that illuminates them both.

The sacred Hebrew god name that embodies the power of Malkuth is Adonai ha-Aretz, meaning "Lord of the Earth." Toning this name of God will align you with the power of Malkuth. You can chant it ten times to further manifest its power. The challenge of Malkuth is to bring out this divine quality within the initiate, so he or she can be a "Lord of the Earth." For us witches with a sensitivity to gender terms and divinity, I think of *Lord* and *Lady* as equivalents. On the mystical level, Adonai ha-Aretz really signifies sovereignty on the material plane and should not emphasize one gender over the other. If any one gender is emphasized, for the Qabalistic witch, the true force of rulership over the Earth is the Lady.

The angelic forces aligned with Malkuth vary, depending on the mythology. Sandalphon is the archangel most often named as the guardian of Malkuth. He shares a strange history with the archangel Metatron, the only other angelic being that was said to have been human before being raised to angelic status. Some believe Sandalphon to be Elijah, while others see him as the current manifestation of John the Baptist. Angelic lore is not an exact science, and there are many variations of the names and categories of angels, differing among Jewish, Christian, and Islamic lore and among Qabalistic magicians.

In Hebraic lore, the order of angels under the command of Sandalphon is the Cherubim, or the Strong Ones, who help lay the foundation of the material universe. In some more modern mystical lore, the angels associated with Malkuth are not traditional angels at all, but a group of ascended or enlightened humans, who have merged their own personal will with divine will, merging with their angelic nature. In this angelic lore, they are known as the Order of Blessed Souls, or the Withdrawn Order. It's appropriate that their leader is the archangel that is associated with transformed humanity. The Cherubim are what are known as *bodhisattvas* in the Eastern traditions or true saints in the Christian tradition. In ceremonial magick, there is the concept of the Secret Chiefs, or the inner-plane adepts, to match the Theosophists' ascended masters. Most witchcraft traditions don't have the same concept. The closest concept we have is the Mighty Dead, or enlightened ancestors. Traditional Craft groups, such as those of the 1734 Tradition descended from Robert Cochrane, have coined the term *the Hidden Company* for a similar concept, and I must admit I like this term the best. They are the "enlightened" master witches of ages past gathering at the edge of our circles and guiding our magick, visions, and covens.

The Vision of Malkuth

The profound experience, the "vision," of this sephira is the Knowledge and Conversation of the Holy Guardian Angel. The Holy Guardian Angel, or HGA, is considered to be the higher self, or true self, of the magician, and what classically is considered "white" magick is magick done for the contact, communication, and eventual union with this aspect of the self. But what exactly is "knowledge and conversation" with this being? Magicians disagree on the specifics, but generally it means to have not only an intellectual understanding of the HGA but also a direct experience with it. Once that direct contact is made (the "knowledge"), then the next step is to have regular communication with the HGA as a primary guide in life (the "conversation") to guide the developing soul into spiritual alignment and eventual enlightenment, to become one of the Hidden Company. For now, the higher self becomes part of the spiritual "team" that a magickal practitioner gathers from the various realms of the Otherworld. Witches often have a "contact" in each of the realms of the faeries, ancestors, and angels, plus a primary patron deity. The higher self guides and directs the witch's interface with this team of spirit allies. A higher sphere of the Tree, Tiphereth, is reserved for the active identification and greater union with the Holy Guardian Angel.

How do you receive the vision of Malkuth, or any vision in the Tree? It's different for everybody. It might be an intuitive experience. I know quite a few people who are very developed spiritually but are not necessarily from a witchcraft or ceremonial magick background, and I would say, based on my conversations and experiences with them, that these friends have all had knowledge and conversation with their Holy Guardian Angel, yet they probably wouldn't. They haven't done any arcane rituals or had a profound vision, but they have developed a sense of their personal divinity and learned how to communicate with it, often quite intuitively. Through this connection, they have demonstrated a greater mastery over the material realm of Malkuth. They just wouldn't use those terms.

The rituals and magick of the Qabalah provide us with triggers for the visions, tools to acquire the skills to manifest those levels of consciousness, and benchmarks to understand when we have met the requirements of each level. The first tool is the *obligation* of the sphere. The obligation is the skill necessary to master the realm. For Malkuth, the obligation is discipline. A person needs to have a measure of discipline to continue any spiritual practice. The more formal traditions based on the Golden Dawn system required an initiate to perform the its most basic ritual, the Lesser Banishing Ritual of the Pentagram, or LBRP, daily for a year before learning other magick. Without discipline, you could not go forward. Whether the spiritual program is one of prayer, yoga, martial arts, exercise, chanting, meditation, or circle magick, it can transform you only if you do it regularly. We easily get distracted in the material world. Without discipline, we would accomplish nothing, spiritual or material.

The *virtue* is the trait demonstrated when one has gained a certain understanding of and mastery over the sphere. The virtue of Malkuth is discrimination. People hear this and often think it has something to with having a prejudice against someone different, but it's more appropriately *discernment*. This discrimination is to determine what is good for you and your world and what is harmful. It is the power to draw boundaries between you and the world, and knowing when to let down those boundaries. Boundaries are energetic, but they are also physical. They involve staking out personal and energetic space.

The *illusion* of a sephira is what might appear to the initiate as a virtue, but in the end is simply untrue, and leads the magician astray. Malkuth's illusion is materialism. In an effort to master the material world, many begin to identify with material things, rather than discerning what aspects of the material to integrate and what aspects to disassociate from. In this identification with Malkuth, there is a desire to accumulate—material goods, wealth, and power. The concept of mastering the terrestrial world transforms from a mastery of the self, body, health, and material life to a mastery of the world around the magician, and the people and resources around the individual. Materialism has seduced many in our world, not realizing that it's simply the first pitfall of the first sphere.

If discrimination is the virtue of Malkuth, then the *vice* is inertia or laziness. While one pitfall is to overidentify with the material world, seeking to control and amass terrestrial power, the other end of the spectrum is to do nothing. Lack of discipline and direction leads a potential seeker into a state of immobility. The overwhelming possibilities, the daunting challenges, and the long road ahead immobilize rather than inspire the person. Nothing is done. No path or tradition is taken. The aspiring magician sinks into inertia and does not progress. There must be a balance between drive and inertia. There is a time to work and a time to rest, and we can get caught at one end of the spectrum.

When you properly apply discipline in the spiritual practice of the realm of Malkuth and find stability and balance, then you can open to the Knowledge and Conversation of the Holy Guardian Angel and demonstrate the virtue of true discrimination. The mystery of Malkuth is to lay the foundation for all the subsequent work. If you cannot master the basic skills of life, of taking care of yourself, your home, and your material needs, then you will not have the solid foundation you need to truly reach for the heavens and descend into the depths. Mastering Malkuth gives you the necessary skills and grounding to take the lessons of the other spheres and manifest the heavens on Earth in the next age.

MALKUTH MAGICK

While each of the lower four spheres on the Tree of Life has a primary element associated with it, Malkuth is special. Its primary element is earth, as it's the plane of manifestation and the material world. Its astrological association is the planet Earth. But the material world is the culmination of all four elements, and the realm of Malkuth is associated with all four elements. It's divided into four equal segments, colored russet (red), olive (green), citrine (yellow), and black. The colors are associated with the four elements and the four seasons, for this is the world where all the elements come together and move through time and space in cycles, like the Wheel of the Year.

The totemic figure of Malkuth is no terrestrial animal, but the sphinx. The sphinx is a combination of the four elements, just as Malkuth is. This animal is a combination of the four animals of the fixed zodiac signs—the bull of Taurus, the lion of Leo, the eagle of Scorpio, and the human of Aquarius. The powers of the sphinx are identified with the witches' pyramid and the Laws of the Magus—To Know, To Will, To Dare, and To Keep Silent. All four of these points are needed to master the magick of Malkuth and ascend to the next sphere.

The four powers also are embodied by four aspects of the Goddess, as in the four princesses. The Princesses of Wands, Swords, Cups, and Pentacles are like the elemental queens of the fire, air, water, and earth. Yet princesses/pages, by their very nature in ceremonial magick tarot systems, all have an earthy aspect. They represent the daughter principle, the manifestation of the Goddess in the material world. As pages, they are known as messengers in a tarot reading, but they are not simply the force of communication, as signified by the air element. They are the force in the reading and the querent's life that tells it like it is, the reality of the situation, the fundamental physical reality of the events. They do not present what we want to hear or see things through rose-colored glasses. They simply tell us what is, whether we want to hear it or not. The court cards of the tarot are described in terms of fractions, with the numerator, or top half of the fraction, being the element assigned to the court card. Princesses are aligned with earth. The denominator, or bottom half of the fraction, is the element of the suit. So the Princess of Wands is the earthy aspect of fire, or earth/fire. The Princess of Swords is the earth/air. The Princess of Cups is the earth/water.

The Princess of Discs, or Pentacles, as the earth/earth principle, is particularly important. She is the seed within the fruit of Malkuth, and within this Goddess figure lies
the potential for all of creation. She is the mother of the next Tree of Life to evolve
from our fruit, continuing the cycle.

The four powers also are pursued in the four tens of the tarot. Ten is the last number of the cycle, signifying completion. The four tens are quite intense. Each has a
classical name associated with it. The Ten of Wands is Oppression. The Ten of Swords
is Ruin. The Ten of Cups is Satiety or Happiness, depending on the deck, and the Ten
of Pentacles is Success. Two of these cards, the fire and air suits, imply difficulties on
a mundane level, while the remaining two, the water and earth suits, imply more of
a "good" completion. This shows that the very nature of Malkuth resonates with the
two more feminine elements and can conflict with the two more masculine elements.
Each demonstrates, regardless of our labels of "good" or "bad" based on personal pleas-
antness, a necessary step in understanding the power of that element in the tenth sphere.
Each suit in the tarot is a journey, and each must be brought to completion so the cycle
can begin again, in a more aware and refined manner. On a mystical level, the suits are
not good or bad, but demonstrate a secret on the four sacred quests of the elements.
The wands and swords help us surrender to the forces around us, so that we may release
and be reborn. The cups and discs help us understand the true secrets to happiness and
success, not just what we think will make us happy or successful.

Ten-based numerology also plays a part in the sacred geometry associated with
Malkuth. A primary figure in the teachings of Pythagoras is known as the *tetraktys*
(figure 34), a pattern of ten dots, showing the importance of the first ten numbers unfolding in the archetypal creation pattern of the universe. Each level of creation from
the top point adds complexity to creation, until the last level of manifestation has four
points, like the four classic elements.

The decagram is a ten-pointed star (figure 35). Though there are several different ways to draw it, the most popular among magicians is two pentagrams, or five-
pointed stars, drawn over each other, one with a point upright and the second with
a point downward. Together, they create a decagram. Though not used as popularly
as the pentagram, the decagram does have its own mysteries. As both an upright and
a downward star, it is symbolic of the microcosm and the macrocosm, the shaman's

Figure 34: Tetraktys

Middle World, where all forces converge and all things are possible. Above and below are displayed visually in the decagram. Modern magicians have taken the traditional correspondences of the pentagram and applied them to the decagram, giving two points to each element, as well as one point to each planet, dividing the ten planets into two groups of personal planets (Sun, Moon, Mercury, Venus, and Mars) and their "higher-octave" equivalents (Jupiter, Saturn, Uranus, Neptune, and Pluto). A clever magician can adapt variations of the pentagram and hexagram rituals of the Golden Dawn tradition with the image of the decagram.

Though the decagram corresponds numerologically with Malkuth, the starting place for the aspiring ceremonial magician is really the first ritual of the pentagram, known as the Lesser Banishing Ritual of the Pentagram. Most traditions use the upright image of the pentagram, symbolizing your feet being anchored in Malkuth. Some traditions' rituals, such as Thelema's Star Ruby pentagram ritual, use an inverted star and a widdershins motion, imagining themselves upside down, to symbolize being anchored in the Sun or stars.

The Lesser Banishing Ritual of the Pentagram has many purposes. The most immediate one is that it banishes all terrestrial forces that do not serve your highest good, clearing your aura and clearing the environment of the space where it is performed. Though the ritual creates a sacred space, the space is not the same type of container that is created with the witch's circle. The ritual simply clears the space and makes it

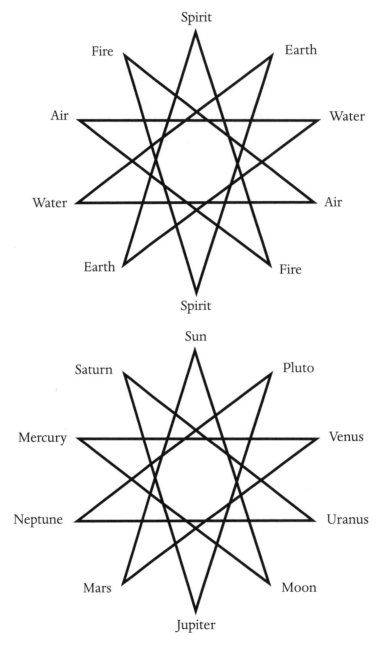

Figure 35: Elemental and Planetary Decagrams

relatively neutral territory for whatever work you desire. The LBRP usually is done at the start and end of every ritual in modern ceremonial magick.

Over a long period of time, the LBRP aids in anchoring the Tree of Life within your aura consciously, and helps to awaken and balance the power center within you. It also calls upon divine entities—in this case, the archangels—and strengthens your connection to them and their realm. The LBRP is considered a basic exercise to physically and psychically condition you for deeper magick and more complicated rituals. Regular use of it, or a variation of it, will clear, strengthen, and expand your aura, just as regular exercise will heal and strengthen your physical body.

EXERCISE 5

Lesser Banishing Ritual of the Pentagram (LBRP)

1. Start by performing the Qabalistic Cross (exercise 2).

2. Facing east, draw a banishing pentagram in flaming blue light with your blade in your right hand or with your extended right index finger, starting outside of your left hip, up to a height above your head, down and outside the right hip, across and up to a point outside your left shoulder, straight across to a symmetrical point outside your right shoulder, and then back down to where you began (figure 36).

3. Inhale and assume the starting pose of the Sign of the Enterer (page 102). Exhale and make the Sign of the Enterer, directing energy from your hands (or blade, if you are using one, still in the right hand, pointing forward, matching the extended fingers on the left hand) into the blue pentagram you just drew. On the exhale, vibrate the name of God for the eastern quarter: **Yud-Heh-Vahv-Heh** (YHVH).

4. Make the Sign of Silence (page 102). Point your finger/blade in the center of the pentagram and then trace one-quarter of the circle in the air with a line of light (usually white), bringing you to the south.

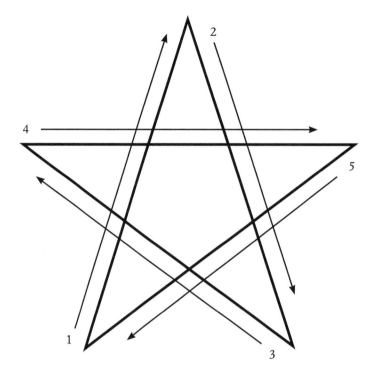

Figure 36: Banishing Pentagram

5. Facing south, draw a banishing pentagram, just as you did in the east in step 2. Energize this pentagram with the Sign of the Enterer, and vibrate the divine name for the southern quarter: **Ah-doh-nye** ("my Lord"). Make the Sign of Silence and then trace one-quarter of the circle with a line of light, bringing you to the west.

6. Facing west, draw a banishing pentagram, just as you did before. Energize this pentagram with the Sign of the Enterer, and vibrate the divine name for the western quarter: **Eh-heh-yeh** ("I am" or "I shall be"). Make the Sign of Silence and then trace one-quarter of the circle with a line of light, bringing you to the north.

7. Facing north, draw a banishing pentagram, just as you did before. Energize this pentagram with the Sign of the Enterer, and vibrate the divine name

for the northern quarter: **Ah-glah** (AGLA, an abbreviation for the phrase *Ah-Tah Gee-Boor Lih-Oh-Lahm Ah-Doh-Nye*, meaning, "Thou art great forever, my Lord"). Make the Sign of Silence and then trace one-quarter of the circle with a line of light, bringing you to the east, completing the circle.

8. Stand in the center of the circle, facing east. Feel yourself in a circle of light marked by the four blue pentagrams. Feel your space become a sphere of energy, clear of unwanted influences and filled with divine power.

9. Evoke the four archangels of the quarters. Start by standing tall, feet together and arms outstretched, like a cross representing the four quarters. If you are using a blade, it should be pointed up, in your right hand. Without moving to face the directions, speak the angelic evocation:

> **Before me, Raphael.**
> **Behind me, Gabriel.**
> **On my right hand, Michael.**
> **And on my left hand, Uriel.**
> **For about me flames the pentagram.**
> **And within me shines the six-rayed star.**

The evocation is meant to be said with authority, and the angelic names can be vibrated like the divine names. Each angelic name traditionally has three syllables: Rah-fay-EL, Gahb-ray-EL, Mee-chai-EL, and Ohr-ree-EL The six-rayed star refers to the hexagram, the star shape associated with the heart of the Tree, Tiphereth.

10. Repeat the Qabalistic Cross (exercise 2).

The banishing pentagram can be done at arm's length, to clear your aura, or at the four walls of each room, to clear the entire temple space. If you are clearing the entire room, always move in a clockwise direction while moving from the center of the room, traditionally behind the altar, and out to the four directions, starting in the east and returning to the center of the room when the circle is closed in the east.

This is the more traditional version of the LBRP. Many witches simplify it, omitting the Signs of the Enterer and Silence, and are not as formal and measured in their movements, though part of the ritual's purpose is to teach discipline and precision in all actions, synchronizing your thoughts, words, visualizations, movement, and will. I have used a "baby" version of it that is quite effective. You can find this version in my book *The Witch's Shield* (Chapter 6).

When you are thoroughly familiar with the LBRP, deconstruct it. Meditate and contemplate on each of the parts and what each one does. What do you feel when you do each part? How does the energy change? What effect does each part have?

If you, like many witches, dislike the LBRP, then reconstruct it, using images and symbols that fit better into your personal mythology. That might seem like sacrilege to some, but all the great magicians have taken liberties with classic rituals. The LBRP, while powerful, really originated in this form with the Golden Dawn, so you are not messing with an ancient ritual passed down from generations, but are adapting a modern construction. Aleister Crowley did the same thing when adapting the LBRP into his Star Ruby ritual, with its Thelemic imagery and flair. It fit his personal worldview and the tradition he created. Rituals evolve over time. The following angelic evocation, in an older form, was from a child's prayer and used different angelic directions than what we find in modern traditions.

> *In the name of the Lord God of Israel,*
> *May Michael, the protection of God, be at my right hand;*
> *And Gabriel, the power of God, at my left;*
> *Before me Uriel, the light of God;*
> *Behind me Raphael, the healing of God;*
> *And above my head Shekinah El, the presence of God.*

This next prayer was probably based on the older Babylonian evocation, a lorica prayer. This prayer acts like a spiritual breastplate, protecting the speaker.

> *Shamash before me,*
> *Behind me Sin.*
> *Nergal at my right,*
> *Ninib at my left.*

See appendix II for examples of more "witchy" LBRPs to inspire your reconstruction efforts.

The components of natural magick used for Malkuth are all those that are traditionally assigned to both the planet Earth and the element of earth. They are the dense, woody, and terrestrial scents, stones, and herbs. Raw rock crystal, rather than polished or pointed quartz, is the favorite stone. I also like to use rough granite or any stone found in my garden. Tiger's-eye is the gem of Malkuth. The incense known as Dittany of Crete is preferred for its powers of manifestation. It's an herb that smokes profusely when burned, and its smoke is used in spirit-summoning magick, to provide a smoky "body" for the spirit to physically manifest and take shape in the ritual.

One of the core tools used in ritual magick is holy water. Now, water doesn't seem like a fitting tool to learn about in Malkuth, but the water of witches and magicians has a strong earth component to it, being salt water. The salt added to the water is used to purify a physical space before ritual, purify the magician, and cleanse tools that are anointed with it. The water is asperged with a branch, usually pine, shaking out the water drops on the ground of the ritual space. Very modern witches will use a spray bottle to fill the air with the holy water. Others simply have the water in a bowl and either pour it out gently or flick it with their fingers.

Traditional blessing water is created simply by mixing together a small amount of salt with the water, and blessing it with the intention to purify, consecrating it. Some traditions formally evoke the spirits, or creatures, of the salt and the water, to aid in that purification. Many witches will use their athame or wand to direct the energy to catalyze the cleansing properties of the salt and water. Variations on this theme include mixing other substances into the water, to give it new properties. Sometimes a sprinkle of a particular herb or a drop or two of essential oil is mixed into the water. Rue is popular for its protective and purifying properties, though it can cause a skin rash and pregnant women should never be around it. I tend not to use rue unless I have a specific reason to do so. Flower essences and gem elixirs can be safely added to the mix without worrying about medicinal interactions or allergic reactions.

I like using a holy water that is aligned with Malkuth by incorporating all four elements. Water is mixed with sea or kosher salt for the earth element. A lit match is submerged in the water, adding its fiery essence to the mix. Sacred ash, from a sacred fire, the same substance that is released in the smoke of the fire, is used for air. For many witches, the ash of a Beltane fire would be most appropriate. Saving the ash of specially prepared fires used in other rituals, such as ash from an oak, ash, or hawthorn tree, is also powerful. I like to use a pinch of ashes from my ash pot (*OTOW*, Chapter 9) that contains my spell ashes. I also put in a sprinkle of a flower, usually rose, for the element of spirit, though the strong floral scent also has air-element qualities to it.

Exercise 6

Making Holy Water

1. Make sure you have all the necessary ingredients: water (preferably well or spring water), sea salt or kosher salt in a dish, matches, sacred ash and rose petals, a ritual bowl to mix them in, and a bottle to save the water if you choose to use it again at a later date. Traditionally, do this at your altar space.

2. Center and align yourself, either by doing Exercise 2: Qabalistic Cross; Exercise 5: Lesser Banishing Ritual of the Pentagram; or exercise 1, through step 6, to enter a light meditative state of ritual consciousness. If you would like to do this as part of the magick circle, simply cast a magick circle and perform this consecration as part of the ritual.

3. Place the bowl of water upon the peyton, the altar pentacle. Plunge your athame into the water, and direct your intention to purify this water. Imagine the water filling with a light, usually a bluish or blue-purple light, and say:

   I exorcise and bless thee, O Creature of Water, casting out all impurities and discordant energies. May you ever be blessed as a vessel for healing and love.

4. Remove the water bowl and place it on the left side of the altar. Place the dish of salt upon the peyton. Touch the salt with the tip of the athame. Direct your intention to cleanse and consecrate this salt for your working. Imagine the salt glowing with a bluish or blue-purple light, coming from the tip of your blade, and say:

I exorcise and bless thee, O Creature of Salt, casting out all impurities and discordant energies. May you ever be blessed as a vessel for strength and purity.

5. Place the water bowl back onto the altar peyton. Mix the salt into the water and, while stirring at least three times clockwise with your athame, say:

May the salt and water conjoin as one in the love of the Goddess.

6. Take a pinch of ash between your fingers and say:

I exorcise and bless thee, O Creature of Ash, casting out all impurities and discordant energies. May you ever be blessed as a vessel for wisdom and sight.

Add the pinch of ash to the water.

7. Hold the match, strike it, and say:

I bless and thank you, O Creature of Flame, for you are the power of transformation and transmutation. Please add your spark of life to this holy water.

Submerge the flame into the water, but once it's out, remove the matchstick from the water.

8. Hold the rose petals in your fingers. Sprinkle the petals into the water and say:

I ask for your blessing, O Creature of the Living Green. May your blessings of spirit be upon this water. May you and the spirits of the four elements aid me in sanctifying myself and this space, to know that we are always in the garden and grove of the Goddess and all is sacred. So mote it be.

9. Hold your hands or point your athame over the mixture and fill it with light and energy. Stir the mixture ten times clockwise with your athame. Your holy water is complete. You can use it to bless your temple or ritual space, to anoint yourself before ritual or meditation, to use in healing magick, or to ritually cleanse tools and objects. If there is water left from the ritual and you wish to keep it over time, store it in a cool, dark place, away from direct sunlight. If you opened a magick circle, then close the circle. If you started with the LBRP, traditionally you would repeat it to close the space. If you simply entered a meditative and clear space, then ground yourself as needed.

Malkuth Pathworkings

The term *pathworking* for a guided-imagery meditation more than likely comes from Qabalistic symbolism, as the twenty-two paths are used to shift your consciousness from one realm to another. Technically, all the paths are connected to each other, but the most conscious pathways in our collective intelligence are outlined by the formal paths on the Tree. The imagery of the paths and sephiroth is focused upon to connect with that energy and experience the shift in consciousness.

Tarot cards have become the main correspondents to the paths, and each card is used like a gateway. One can "step" through the doorway, the frame of a card, and interact with the magickal beings depicted in the cards. The interaction can give you valuable insight to shift your experience and awareness. Those based in more traditional ceremonial magick will suggest working with a traditional deck, one encoded with Qabalistic symbolism, such as the Rider-Waite, the Golden Dawn, or the less traditional Thoth deck of Aleister Crowley. Though those decks can be helpful, ultimately you must resonate with the deck, and any tarot deck with the traditional arcana, suits, and court cards, as opposed to an oracle deck based on a different system, can be a focus for pathworking.

No path needs to be taken to Malkuth. It is all around us. All we have to do to experience it is simply tune in to it, remembering the sacred garden all around us. Malkuth does have three paths leading out of it, and an understanding of those three paths helps you better understand Malkuth and its relationship to the rest of the Tree of Life.

Each path represents a key experience to look "beyond" Malkuth and realize there are worlds broader than just the material one. On the right side of the Tree, we have the path of the Moon tarot card, leading up to Netzach, while on the left side, we have the path of Judgment, also known as the Aeon, leading up to Hod (figure 29). Both represent two very different kinds of epiphanies, often following a traumatic experience. Judgment is the intellectual epiphany, in which we realize mentally that the world is not as it appears, and climb into the realm of Hod. The Moon is an emotional epiphany, usually an emotional crisis, trauma, or breakdown, the classic "if it doesn't kill you, it will make you strong" experience, in which intuition and the unseen must be relied upon to survive. This leads to the more primal revelations of Netzach. The middle path, embodied by the World, also known as the Universe, is literally the middle path between these two extremes. It is the easier epiphany experienced through observing nature, and finding the next step of enlightenment through the seasons, the cycle of nature, plants, animals, and even science. All three of these awakenings lead out of the garden of Malkuth and help us understand Malkuth better. But for the following exercise, we will remain in the kingdom, and explore the mysteries right here all around us.

EXERCISE 7

Malkuth Pathworking

1. Perform the Lesser Banishing Ritual of the Pentagram (exercise 5) to clear your energy field and the space where you are doing this working.

2. While in this space, call upon the divine forces of Malkuth. There are many ways to align yourself with Malkuth. You can knock ten times on your Malkuth altar. You can light ten earth-toned candles, or four candles in the colors of black, russet (red brown), citrine (yellow), and olive (green). You can chant the divine name of Malkuth, **Ah-doh-nye ha-ah-retz** (Adonai ha-Aretz), ten times. Make a prayer to any of the godforms associated with Mother Earth or the grain goddesses. Call upon Sandalphon to open the way. Any and all of these actions would be an appropriate way to connect with the forces of Malkuth. Light Dittany of Crete as incense if available, or another appropriate earth incense.

3. To count down into a meditative state, do exercise 1 through step 7 (page 76).

4. Let the familiar world around you fall away, as if the material reality you know is only the façade, and beneath it lies the beautiful garden of the Goddess, a veritable paradise surrounding you. The land around you becomes a vast primordial garden, more beautiful than you can believe, filled with all

manner of exotic plants, flowers, and trees. It is both wonderful and frightening in its primal power.

5. Wander the garden, taking notice of everything around you. Animals might cross your path. Particular plants could catch your eye. Be alert for the messages of Malkuth.

6. In the distance, you see a temple. The Temple of Malkuth might be an open-air shrine rather than a closed-off building. Perhaps it is a circle of ten standing stones. As you count, you notice ten stones to mark the boundary, just as Malkuth's number is ten. You notice four distinct paths leading out from this garden temple, the paths of the four elements. There might be goddess or sphinx statues adorning the shrine.

7. In the center of this shrine is a throne, and a regal woman sits upon it. You feel compelled to approach her, for she is the Queen on the Throne, the goddess ruling the sphere of Malkuth. Introduce yourself. Ask this goddess her name. Commune with this goddess, asking her to teach you the mysteries of Malkuth. If you are ready, she will, or she will introduce you to beings who can aid your journey and lessons at this time, for the beings of the first garden want to be in relationship, in conscious communion, with the humans of Earth, and they welcome you as an emissary to their world. Perhaps you will gain insight into the duty and obligation of the sphere and how to avoid the vice and illusion. You might even gain the vision of the sphere of Malkuth, a glimpse of your own higher self, your Holy Guardian Angel, or have the opportunity to deepen your relationship with it. This process may begin with a stronger sense of intuition and psychic knowing, and develop into a relationship with this part of yourself, like a spirit guide relationship.

8. When done, thank all the beings who have communicated with you. They might offer you a gift, a token of their goodwill. If you accept, it is polite to reach within your being and offer them a gift of your goodwill. Be sure

that what you give reflects the energy and intention you plan to put into the sphere's lessons.

9. Once you have said your farewells, leave the shrine and return to where you began. Focus on the waking world you know, and feel it return around the garden.

10. To return to normal waking consciousness and end your journey, perform steps 15–17 from exercise 1 (page 78). You can close the temple by repeating the LBRP.

Initiation of Malkuth

The initiatory challenge of Malkuth is the elemental grade of elemental earth. In ceremonial magick traditions, this rank is known as the Initiate or Zelator. The Sign of the Zelator is the sign associated with this grade. The requirement is having greater mastery of your physical body and gaining the discipline to walk the path of the magician. For the witch following this series of books, you already have worked with the four elements. You already should be familiar with the element of earth, which was the basis of the second book in this series, *The Outer Temple of Witchcraft*. In this system, earth is the element ruling the second grade. This fourth level is an advancement, a higher octave, of the second grade. Both grades deal with the rituals, correspondences, and techniques that people consider to be "magick." In *The Outer Temple of Witchcraft*, you were introduced to the elemental powers to build a working relationship with these forces in ritual. In this book, you are challenged to gain a greater mastery of the principles in yourself and your life. We never can truly "master" any spiritual force while incarnated in human consciousness. Our relationship with these forces grows, expands, evolves, and is refined over time, creating an intimate bond with the Otherworld, but when we have grasped the foundation of each mystery and successfully applied it in our life to fulfill our True Will, then we can say we've attained a level of mastery.

Each of the four elements represents a type of quest that humans undergo in life. Though our myths paint a portrait of the quests as seeking things outside ourselves, as the quests are manifested in the four sacred tools, they really are about seeking and mastering qualities inside ourselves. For both the witch and the magician, the four sacred tools are the four tools of the elements, the four weapons of the art of magick—the wand, blade, cup, and pentacle. The four tools have congruent images in the mythologies of the Celts, with the four treasures of Ireland, the four gifts brought by the Tuatha de Danann from the four mythical cities of the corners of the globe. Scholar R. J. Stewart credits the work of visionary poet Fiona MacLeod for bringing the elemental correspondences to the four treasures and influencing the modern occult movements such as the Golden Dawn and modern Wicca.

Earth

Spiritual Lesson: Sovereignty
Spiritual Tool: Stone of Sovereignty, Stone of Fal
Fears and Challenges: Irresponsibility, Giving Our Power to Others
Virtue: Vitality
Psychological Function: Sensation
Stage of Learning: Ignorance
State of Matter: Solid
Environmental Sphere: Geosphere
Scientific Force: Gravity
Periodic Element: Carbon
Humor: Black Bile—Melancholic
Body System: Digestive
Sacred River: Water
Sacred Geometry: Cube
Celtic City: Falias
Qabalistic World: Assiah
Classical Age: Iron
Caste: Laborer
Sufi Breath: In Nose / Out Nose
Mudra: Thumb and Middle Finger
Planets: Earth, Venus, Saturn, Pluto
Fixed Sign and Animal: Taurus—Bull

Egyptian Animal: Beetle
Metal: Lead
Chakra: Root
Time of Day: Midnight
Season: Winter
Vowel Sound: A
Egyptian Syllable: Ta
Hindi Syllable: Lam
Tibetan Syllable: A
Modern Syllable: El
Obstruent Sounds: g, gh, k, kh
Time Signature: 4/4
Hebrew God Name: Adonai ha-Aretz or AGLA
Archangel: Uriel/Auriel
Angel: Photlakh
Ruler: Kerub
Elemental King and Queen: King Ghob and Queen Tanu
Goetic Ruler: Ziminiar
Enochian King: MORDIAIHKTGA
Stones: Garnet, Jasper, Obsidian, Smoky Quartz
Herbs: Comfrey, Mandrake, Mushroom, Patchouli, Solomon's Seal

The treasure associated with the earth element is the Stone of Fal, or Lia Fáil, known as the Stone of Destiny. Though there are two physical stones that are identified with the Stone of Destiny, the mythical treasure of the Irish gods is said to be a magickal stone that cries out in a roar of joy when the rightful king puts his feet upon it. It is said to rejuvenate the ruler and give long reign.

Even though this treasure is called the Stone of Destiny, I learned from my inner-world contacts that the concept of sovereignty is the essence of the stone's teachings. Sovereignty is used to describe the royalty, as rulers of the land, but one who is sovereign is autonomous and free from external control, whether it be a king, nation, or individual on the path. Equated with the pentacle or the disc in ritual magick, it is both the first step and the last step, as it implies a mastery over the physical world through our spiritual powers, as the top point of the pentagram rules the other four. In mastering the element of earth, we must master our physical life, take charge, control, and responsibility for our life, our own "kingdom" in the world. We each have a kingdom in our own lives, but the trick is to not let anybody else rule our kingdom, nor seek to rule anyone else's. We often give away our sovereignty, or try to rule another's, thinking we know what is best. What is best is for every individual is to rule his or her own life. The end of line 59 in chapter 2 of *The Book of the Law* says, "If he be a King, thou canst not hurt him." There is a power and regality in those who achieve this level of wisdom, despite their earthly status.

In certain forms of witchcraft, a high priest is given the title *Lord* and the high priestess is called *Lady*, not just for the circle, but as a part of their Craft name. I first thought this pretentious, as the traditions I trained in didn't emphasize it, but the true understanding of the titles is that one who truly has reached that level of initiation must have his or her own sovereignty and, being charged with a tradition, share the sovereignty of that tradition with the other high priestesses and priests of the tradition. But in the end, all of us on the path aspire to be Ladies and Lords, Queens and Kings, sovereign over the nation of ourselves.

To gain a greater understanding of our sovereignty, and to collect our own Stone of Sovereignty and learn its lessons, we must go to the guardians and caretakers of the element of earth. We must visit the realm of elemental earth. We must visit with the elementals of earth, the gnomes. But we must go beyond basic contacts in the realm of earth and find wise teachers and guides, who have mastered the principle of sovereignty themselves. We must find the elemental rulers, the classic elemental "kings" of the elements, each ruling their own kingdom. In some modern lore, the more traditional kings are associated with their matching queens, though these associations were given to me by a student as she received them and are not used in most magickal systems. I offer them for those who want to work with more feminine images. You also can call upon the archangel associated with the element, as you already are building a relationship with the archangels if you are regularly performing the traditional LBRP. Many witches prefer to find pagan gods and goddesses that resonate with the nature of the element. For the element of earth, the Earth Mothers, grain goddesses, and young queens would be appropriate.

Finding the elemental realms on the Tree of Life can be confusing. They are the four cosmic worlds, each based on the symbolism of one of the four elements. But when we cast a circle, we are calling upon more terrestrial powers for the elements. Some think the four elemental realms all are anchored in Malkuth entirely, as Malkuth is divided into four sections and, as the physical realm, needs all four elements for manifestation. This is one way to look at it. Others see the elemental realm associated with the corresponding sephira. Some see the elemental realm anchored in Malkuth, while the teaching spirits, such as the elemental rulers or angels, are rooted in higher spheres. Any of these models could be correct. Though they might resonate with a particular level on the Tree, they too, each have their own Tree of Life, as their evolutionary scale in their realm. It is only our arrogance that makes us see them as limited rather than simply different, and we assign these artificial conditions of being upon them smaller than ours. If we expect them only in one place, we find them only in one place, but they are really a part of the whole Tree.

In the end, "where" you find the elemental realms is unimportant. Knowing you can connect to them from your inner temple (*OTOW*, Exercises 13, 17, 21, and 25) and going there to learn more about them are the important aspects of the work. If you have yet to visit the elemental realms, you might want to do the exercises just listed to get your feet wet, before you seek to master the elements in the exercises in this book.

EXERCISE 8

Elemental Earth Journey Seeking the Stone of Sovereignty

1. This exercise is an expansion of the experiences in Exercise 25: Journeying to the Realm of Earth from *The Outer Temple of Witchcraft*. You can start by performing the LBRP before this journey to prepare yourself. Then perform exercise 1, steps 1–11, to go to your inner temple.

2. Orient yourself in the center of your inner temple. Look for the four doorways to the elemental planes. You might find that your guides bring you to the garden of Malkuth, with its four paths to the four elemental planes. In either case, orient yourself to the direction of elemental earth. Hold the intention

to journey to the realm of earth and seek out the Stone of Sovereignty. You know you might not receive it, but the journey will give you teachings to better master the element in your life so you can come back and claim it. Open the doorway of earth, perhaps using the invoking pentagram of earth as a magickal "key" (*OTOW*, Chapter 6). Enter the path or tunnel that leads to the elemental plane of earth.

3. When you are fully in the realm of earth, seek out the primal powers of the plane. Hold the intention to go to the heart of the realm, to seek out the elemental ruler, king, queen, archangel, or a deity of elemental earth. Perhaps a guide will take you there directly, or you will have to search, and the searching will be part of your lesson.

4. When you reach the heart of the elemental plane, state your request to receive the Stone of Sovereignty. The keepers of the stone might ask you why you think you are worthy, and you might have to tell them or demonstrate your skill. You could be challenged. Meet the challenges to the best of your ability. If you are ready to receive the stone, the elemental teachers will give it to you. If not, they will instruct you in what you have to accomplish to be able to receive the stone in the future. They may offer to tutor you in the ways of the earth element.

5. Travel back from the realm of elemental earth, back the way you came unless guided by the teachers to take another route. Go back to the inner temple. Close the gateway of elemental earth in a manner similar to the way you opened it. If you used an invoking pentagram, then use a banishing pentagram now.

6. To return to normal waking consciousness and end your journey, perform steps 15–17 from exercise 1 (page 78). Close with the LBRP if you opened with it.

This is but the first of four journeys that will help you pierce the veil and expand your consciousness to achieve a greater level of mastery of the elements.

The ritual tool on your altar that anchors you to the Stone of Sovereignty is your earth element tool. For some witches, it is a stone or crystal in the north of the altar. Traditionally, the peyton, or paten, the ritual pentacle, can be a symbol of both spirit and earth specifically. The Golden Dawn–style pentacle is based on the imagery of Malkuth but really is a "hexacle," as Donald Michael Kraig says, because it uses the six-pointed star even though ritual magicians call it a pentacle or pantacle (figure 37). For some traditions of magick, the magician's personal reality map glyph becomes the pentacle. John Dee's septagram was etched onto his wax disc. Traditional witches use a metal or wood pentacle, with more ritualistic symbols than their more eclectic cousins.

HOMEWORK

- Do Exercises 5–8 and record your experiences in your Book of Shadows.

- Practice the LBRP, the original version or your personally reconstructed version.

TIPS

- Fill in the Malkuth correspondences and colors on your own Tree of Life drawing. Contemplate them as you add them to the image. Start memorizing these correspondences.

- To gain greater mastery over Malkuth and the element of earth, bring your physicality into your spirituality. Make exercise, yoga, or martial arts a bigger part of your spiritual "work." View nutrition, rest, and exercise as part of caring for the divine essence of you that resides in Malkuth.

- Study appendix II to deconstruct and reconstruct the LBRP to your liking. You might decide that your magick is more traditional and, at least for now, not alter the ceremonial magick rituals at all. That's a wonderful choice, and studying other variations will deepen your understanding and appreciation of the original. Don't rush into creating your own unless you fully understand

Personal implement of Chic Cicero

Figure 37: Golden Dawn Pentacle and Traditional Witchcraft Pentacle

the original. You can opt to learn the original version for this year-and-a-day program and then go back at a later date to make your own variations.

- Pick one other reality map from appendix I to contemplate. Understanding a variety of worldviews will help you when you construct your own world map.

- When pathworking, many people worry about whether the spirit they meet is the spirit associated with the pathway/sephira or is something else, such as a figment of their imagination, a mischievous trickster, or even a harmful spirit. My favorite spirit-verification technique is to ask the spirit three times its true name, and if you get the same name, then it is true. Others ask for the name and a "wave of love" to be sent to them, to know it's not a harmful spirit. In ceremonial magick, one might challenge the spirit to give the signs of the grade associated with the sphere, and the name of God and angel associated with it.

- Don't feel as though you need to master your Stone of Sovereignty before going on to the next lessons. These are tools you can be using throughout the entire year-and-a-day course and beyond. Keep visiting the realm of earth, and integrate these lessons into your daily life. We continually work with these four principles, but you should have a solid relationship with them before going on to the fifth book of this training, *The Living Temple of Witchcraft*.

• When you do feel that you have received the Stone of Sovereignty from the inner-world teacher of the earth element, be sure to reconsecrate the earth tools you have on your altar (particularly if you have a stone) and/or your ritual peyton. If it isn't already, the peyton will become more and more a foundation for your magick. I place on my peyton whatever spells, intentions, and tokens of meditative workings that I have going on for a long time, to keep focus. At the end of this course, you may decide to make a new peyton, and on it inscribe your own personal reality map or mandala. If you work with several different sets of tools, you might find your inner Stone of Sovereignty extending out from your hands to empower a peyton or tool and then retracting back within you when the rite is concluded.

• Practitioners of some traditions of ceremonial magick believe that the banishing pentagrams will "deconsecrate" elemental tools when done with those tools around. The remedy is to wrap elemental tools in white silk, which has a vibration that blocks out magickal forces and psychic vibrations, and to put the tools away until after the banishing. That is why specific tools are used for banishing rituals, and why there are many wands and blades used in the tradition. As a witch, I disagree with this premise. I haven't found that any of my tools have been banished or deconsecrated because I've done the LBRP. I think the intention is the most important aspect of the ritual, and my intention with the LBRP is to banish harm and unwanted influences. The elemental and planetary rituals can be only so effective. They are not 100 percent effective. We each have an earthy component to our being—our physicality, our practicality, our groundedness. The LBRP does not banish those things from us. I'm still physical. In the ritual, I'm still practical and focused on my goal. I have not become unearthed or ungrounded at all. So the LBRP didn't banish all earth energy, but simply removed the unwanted forces. If there is anything unhealthy and unwanted in my tools, the ritual might banish those forces, but the rest of the "good" intentions remain.

• You might wonder why the Lesser Banishing Ritual of the Pentagram has both the words *lesser* and *banishing* in the title. Are there invoking rituals of the pentagram? Are there greater rituals? The answer to both is yes. A wide variety of rituals have been based on the pentagram, and not all magicians use the same format for these rituals or agree on their structure. In this lesson, you have learned the format of the Lesser Ritual of the Pentagram. It can be adapted to be a banishing ritual with the use of the banishing earth pentagram, as taught in the lesson, or an invoking ritual with the invoking earth pentagram. Generally, the Lesser Ritual of the Pentagram, both banishing and invoking, uses the earth pentagram. Some magicians believe that it is wisest to use the invoking version of this ritual at the start of your day, to bring beneficial forces to you, and to use the banishing version at sunset or the end of your day, to clear your energy field before bed or for other magickal workings.

Technically, you have learned the Lesser Banishing Ritual of the Pentagram of Earth, for we used the earth banishing pentagram, with the idea that it will aid in the protection and cleansing of all dense and unwanted forces. The earth is a compound element, containing aspects of all other elements, just as the symbol of earth, the pentacle, has points for all five elements. You can, however, adapt the ritual elementally. If you desire to invoke or banish a particular elemental force from your space while leaving other elemental forces untouched, you can make specific elemental Lesser Banishing Rituals of the Pentagram. If you want to invoke a specific element for a working, you can adapt the rite to be the Lesser Invoking Ritual of the Pentagram of the desired element. This can be very helpful when doing elemental meditations and other magick focusing on a specific element. Do a general LBRP and then invoke a specific element. Or, if you are in a situation in which one element is overwhelming you, you can banish it for a time. For example, let's say a severe family situation is overwhelming you emotionally. You have to make a hard decision about something, but your feelings are clouding your reason. You could do a LBRP of water to clear yourself of these influences partially, if not completely, and do a reading asking for guidance. For now, master the basic LBRP before you attempt to work with these other rituals. The greater and supreme rituals of the pentagram will be discussed later in this book.

• Some teachers believe in altering the colors of the pentagrams envisioned in the LBRP. Technically, since these are banishing earth pentagrams, such teachers would advocate envisioning pentagrams in the corresponding green color. If doing a LBRP of fire, air, or water, the pentagrams would be red, yellow, or blue, respectively. I tend to use blue in the LBRP because that's the way I first learned it.

LESSON THREE
YESOD

The ninth sphere on the Tree of Life is a realm familiar to most witches and magicians. It's called Yesod, though most don't know it by such an esoteric name. Most of us know it by its more familiar name, the *astral plane*. Yesod translates to "foundation," as the astral plane is the energetic or spiritual foundation of the material world. Early on, occultists learn that everything physical has a counterpart on the astral plane, but not everything astral has a physical counterpart. To be created, an object, situation, or magickal effect must first occur on the astral plane. Without this astral foundation, nothing can occur.

Yesod is the plane of magick, for it is reactive to the imagination, thoughts, and will of a magick worker. Here, we can shape the foundation of reality, and if we empower our creations with enough energy, they can pass through the veil into manifestation in the material realm of Malkuth. Our imagination, through our words, images, ideas, and symbols, shapes the proto-matter of Yesod, the astral light, and through our creative efforts we make our magick. Ritual is simply the language of creation, using symbolic actions and words to shape this realm and infuse our creations with energy.

The Moon, Yesod's ruling planet, is associated with both magick and psychic ability. It opens the inner visions. Through this ability, we visualize and create, but we also receive intuitions and impressions. The Moon resonates with both the belly, our gut-level consciousness, and the brow, the third eye of psychic vision, where we see the past, present, and future.

In psychological terms, Yesod is described as the collective consciousness. It's the collective unconsciousness for most of humanity, while magicians seek to make this realm conscious and aware, not unconscious and unknown, diving deep into this Moon-ruled ocean of consciousness to explore all secrets lurking below the surface. Yesod is not just the plane of creation and magickal imagination but also the lens through which we see the other realms. Witches look past the physical reality to the energetic patterns that support reality, and with this vision, we see things not as they appear but as they really are. This realm of consciousness, of collective archetypal imagery, gives us a vast library of symbols to interface with it and with the higher levels of creation. The higher we climb on the Tree, the more abstract our experience becomes, yet our consciousness, anchored in Malkuth, looks through the filter of Yesod to "translate" the energies into images and feelings we can understand. Some images will be part of the collective human consciousness, archetypal in nature, while others will be part of the personal consciousness, our own little grotto within Yesod, and will be meaningful only to ourselves. Because of its ability to give shape and form to abstract energies, Yesod also is considered the realm of dreams, the "place" we travel to when we sleep and experience both global and personal symbolism, and it often reveals something about our inner nature. Yesod is the magick mirror on the Tree of Life. On one hand, it's reflective, and gazing into it reveals things previously unknown. On the other, it's the reflective surface from which the magician and witch conjure forth their new reality, and the gateway to enter and leave the nonphysical worlds.

Yesod

Meanings: Foundation, Treasure House of Images, House of Illusions

Level of Reality: Astral World, Collective Consciousness

Parts of the Self: Nephesch, Astral Body, Automatic Consciousness, Subconsciousness, Unconsciousness, Intuition, Genitals

Experience: Vision of the Machinery of the Universe

Obligation: Trust

Illusion: Security

Virtue: Independence

Vices: Dependence, Idleness

Name of God: Shaddai El Chai (Almighty Living God or Living Mother God)

King Scale Color: Indigo

Queen Scale Color: Purple or Violet

Prince Scale Color: Dark Purple

Princess Scale Color: Citrine flecked with Azure

Element: Water

Planet: Moon

Image: Beautiful, Erect Naked Man

Archetypes: Moon Goddess and Fertility Gods

Greek/Roman Deities: Selene, Artemis, Diana, Endymion

Egyptian Deities: Bast, Isis, Osiris, Anubis, Nepthys, Thoth, Khonshu

Middle Eastern Deities: Adonis, Tammuz

Celtic Deity: Arianrhod

Norse Deities: Frey, Freya, Mani

Hindu Deity: Ganesha

Archangel: Gabriel (Archangel of Truth, Angel of Water/West, Messenger)

Angelic Order: Cherubim (Strong Ones)

Choir: Angels

Grade of Initiation: ②=⑨ Theoricus

Animals: Elephant, Turtle, Toad

Planetary Vowel Sound: A (ah)

Resonant Letter: l

Musical Mode: Aeolian (Natural Minor)

Muscial Note: C

Tools: Sandals, Perfumes

Incense: Jasmine

Tarot: Nine of Wands, Swords, Cups, and Pentacles

      World/Universe—to Malkuth

      Sun—to Hod

>   Star—to Netzach
>   Temperance/Art—to Tiphereth
> **Metal:** Silver
> **Stones:** Quartz, Moonstone, Pearl
> **Plant:** Comfrey

For this month's lesson on Yesod, set up a Yesodic altar, using the colors of purple and silver and the appropriate tarot cards: the nine of each suit, as well as the major arcana—the World/Universe, the Sun, the Star, and Temperance/Art—leading to and from Yesod in their appropriate places on the altar (figure 29). No court cards are associated with Yesod. When doing a Yesod working, burn jasmine to align with this sphere. If jasmine is unavailable, mugwort makes a fine and more affordable lunar incense. Wearing silver and carrying moonstone, quartz, or pearl also aid in the alignment with Yesod.

Entities of Yesod

As Yesod is the lunar realm, the being most strongly resonating with it is the lunar goddess, crescent crowned and shining in her silver light. She is the Goddess of the Witches, identified with Artemis and Selene, Diana and Luna, Hecate, Isis, Bast, and Hathor, Inanna, Astarte, and Ishtar, Arianrhod, Ceridwen, and Morrighan. In Greek gemetria, Hecate's name adds to 334, what Michael S. Schneider, author of *A Beginner's Guide to Constructing the Universe*, calls "a permissible single unit from 333," which connects her to Yesod (3 + 3 + 3 = 9) and Binah. As the figure of the Moon, the lunar goddess has many faces, as does the Moon, yet a part of her is always hidden, just as a part of Yesod is always hidden, veiled and unclear. There is always something new to be discovered within its depths.

The lunar goddess is the keeper of the mysteries. As the first realm beyond Earth, she is the gatekeeper to the more expanded states of consciousness. Though the High Priestess card of the tarot is associated with another path, and spheres that connect it. Astrologically, the card is ruled by the Moon and depicts the Moon goddess, often more in alignment with a virginal Mother Mary figure, yet as the third card in the major arcana sequence after the Fool and Magician, she sits at the gates, between the two pillars of consciousness, guarding the sacred fruit of pomegranates beyond her. Hers is the secret knowledge she shares with initiates. Only those who pass through her moongate move on to the mysteries. If you cannot navigate the oceans of her astral plane, and thereby a level of your own emotional mastery, then you cannot pass.

Strangely enough, the common archetypal image of Yesod is not feminine at all, but usually a young male figure. Usually described as a beautiful naked and erect man, and sometimes described as being in an eternal slumber, this image confuses most of us at first. Shouldn't the Moon's sphere be solely a Moon goddess? Yes and no. It's the Moon goddess and a fertility god. The generative organs, both male and female, are associated with Yesod and the belly chakra that corresponds with it. Yesod is the generative, creative force that is both goddess and god.

The fertility god is the link between Malkuth, the Earth, and Yesod, the Moon. The cyclical life drive, such as that found in the harvest, the vegetation, embodied in many traditions as the God force, is the connective tissue between Moon goddess and Earth goddess. The Moon has a direct and magickal link to fertility, from the better known Moon cycles in the bodies of women to the growth and success of the harvest. The Moon pulls on emotions and affects the sex drive in both men and women. The erect phallus is the power of the physical realm reaching upward for the higher realms, and is emulated in sacred art, from the lingam stones to obelisks, towers, and temples reaching for the heavens. Even the fluid that issues forth from it is pearlescent white, and lunar in nature.

In mythology, the Goddess's consort often is the fertility god of vegetation, powerful yet temporary, and often is put into stasis or the land of the dead. The one that best embodies the common image of Yesod is Selene's lover Endymion. He was cursed by Zeus to sleep forever, dreaming of his lovely goddess Selene. She visited him regularly, and her lack of diligence to the chariot of the Moon caused the cycle of darkness from the sky. Their connection created the cycle of the Moon and fertility upon Earth. Other cultures relate the Moon to masculine deities. To the Egyptians, both Thoth and Khonshu have lunar associations. The Sumerian Sin and Norse Mani are also Moon deities. Though many pagans fail to see lunar attributes in male energies, the Moon was the most precise and exact timekeeper known in the ancient world, even if its cycles were not as readily visible as the Sun's.

The divine god name associated with Yesod is Shaddai El Chai, usually translated as "Almighty Living God" or "Almighty God Living Forever." The words *almighty* and *forever* reflect the sense of power and permanence implied in the name of Yesod as a foundation, since a foundation must be solid. Yesod also is known as the Treasure House of Images, as the astral plane is our collective consciousness and all its images, as well as the House of Illusions, for the Moon illuminates but doesn't reveal the truth. Shaddai El Chai can hide other images within its name. Another translation of the term relates it to the mother goddess, seeing Shaddai's association with breasts or mountains. Those looking through a feminine prism translate Shaddai El Chai as "Living Mother God," showing us again that there is both male and female in Yesod and nothing is quite what it seems.

The archangel of Yesod is Gabriel, who is also the classic angel of the western quarter and the element of water. Gabriel's name usually translates to "God is my strength," and he is known primarily as God's messenger. While classic Wiccan symbolism automatically puts water associations with Yesod, and I usually maintain that correspondence, some Golden Dawn associations assign Yesod to the element of air, giving it more in common with the messenger principle of Gabriel, and assign Hod to the element of water, to keep the elemental order of the Tetragrammaton—fire, water, air, and earth for Netzach, Hod, Yesod, and Malkuth. As each sphere has associations with all the elements, contemplation on the relationship of both water and air with Yesod can be quite illuminating.

In one system of angelic magick, the order known as the Cherubim or Kerubim, the Strong Ones, are the angels of this realm. The Strong Ones are laborers of the universe, helping lay the foundation of the material universe. Some Theosophical theories relate the devas to this realm, giving Yesod a further connection to nature and fertility. Modern lore refers to the devas as nature spirits, but they are more like the oversouls of nature spirits, the divine architects, directors, and pattern keepers of the material world. They hold the shapes or blueprints of everything in the material world, while the spirits of Malkuth actually manifest them. In other angelic systems, the choir associated with this sphere is known simply as the angels, the lowest-ranking choir and the one closest to humans. These are the companion angels to humanity, acting as guides, friends, teachers, healers, and guardians. This would match the New Age concept that our "spirit guides" reside on the astral plane, working with us in dreams and awaiting our conscious attention during meditation.

THE VISION OF YESOD

The experience of Yesod is the Vision of the Machinery of the Universe. This is such a strange term, popularized by our European alchemical mandalas, illustrated by images of clockwork machines guided by the hand of the god, moving the planets, stars, elements, and people all in their place. Though some witches find this imagery to be too cold and mechanical, the vision refers to an understanding of the mechanisms of the universe. Through it, you both understand and, on a deep wisdom level, know how the universe works. Everything has a purpose. Everything has a place. There is a pattern to the design of creation. Nothing happens randomly.

As Yesod is the sphere of magick, this vision is perfect for it. The key to attaining this vision on the path of witchcraft is to do magick. The Vision of the Machinery of the Universe is really a true integration of magickal theory. Be it through the Hermetic principles or any other magickal system that seeks to explain the universe and how one can participate consciously in the universe, once the knowledge is grounded into consciousness, you are never the same. Through this pivotal experience, brought on through both magick and intuition, you know there is no such thing as random chance or accident. Synchronicity becomes your teacher. Through the application of lunar forces, you soon grow to know that you are connected to all things, and all things are connected to you. We all become like cogs in the machine of the universe, and if even one was missing, then the machine would not run as smoothly. Everything is necessary and has a function to fulfill. Perhaps a better image for witches is that we all are cells within the body of the universe, and each cell is necessary for the full functioning of the body of the universe.

You learn of both personal will and higher will, and the merger of the two for the win-win fulfillment of both yourself and the universe, by enacting your functions to their highest potential. You reach this highest potential through taking action—doing magick and following it up with real-world work, and listening to intuition, inner guidance, and inspiration.

The obligation to fulfill in order to receive this vision or experience is trust. When we start in magick, we trust the system, the teacher or tradition. On an intellectual and rational level, our first impression will be that this is nonsense and cannot work. How can we affect something else through the power of subtle magickal energy? But we have a calling to magick, and if we trust even for a moment that magick has been done before, then we know we can do it too. We also must trust in the universe, and see the larger pattern and understand there is a purpose for everything. Those who don't perform ritual magick still can experience this vision. They might see it as divine will or God's plan, and have to have trust that there is a purpose, and that everyone and everything has a place.

The illusion partnered with trust is security. Just because we trust that magick is possible, and that everything does fit in the machine, it doesn't mean that our place within the machine will conform to what our ego desires. We might not get what we want, but learn that we get what we need. Trust doesn't bring security. Life still can be difficult, especially so when we live from a need to satisfy our personal insecurity. A very good student of mine studied with a traditional Kabbalistic teacher who told her that once you know the machinery of the universe, you will never have sadness again. When earthquakes and disasters hit, you will never question why. You will know it's a part of God's plan and have unending peace. From a Qabalistic witch's perspective, that is only partially right. We believe that we are still on the wheel of life, with ups and downs in emotions while we strive to identify with the center. We know a part of us experiences joy when there is a blessing or sadness when there is tragedy.. A knowledge of the Machinery of the Universe doesn't necessarily grant eternal peace, but does provide the tools to find peace in the midst of difficult situations. We are always on the line of paradox, reconciling the personal and divine, and that is a healthy part of the human experience. The security of eternal peace is an illusion.

The virtue of Yesod is independence. Knowing that everything has a place within the greater pattern is very liberating. You then are encouraged to follow your bliss to find your optimum place in the machine, knowing that your search is part of the pattern. The vices of Yesod are dependence and idleness. In magick and in life, you cannot wait for something to happen. You have to follow up your intentions with action.

YESOD MAGICK

Yesod magick is magick itself, though certain forms of magick are more complementary to this realm. Magick that shapes and forms the astral plane, through visionary work in trance or subtle affirmations and magick words, corresponds the most with this power. Any ritual to call down the waxing or waning power of the Moon is Yesod magick. Magick that brings out the hidden, invisible virtues of herbs and stones through the light of the Moon falls under this sphere. Sea magick—working with the literal tides rather than the psychic ones—is also a part of Yesod. Opening the gates of intuition, or the gates of the astral plane, to confer with spirits, gods, and angels through a reflective pool, mirror, or the inner vision is also Yesodic. In fact, one might say all of traditional witchcraft falls under this sephira.

All water magick can be related to the Moon and Yesod, including physical and emotional healing, psychic development, dream work, and divination. Water magick is appropriate, as two of the totems of Yesod, the frog and the turtle, are related to water, yet both show an ability to adapt, and come onto land, showing the power of Yesod to move things from the astral ocean into the physical world of manifestation. The nonwater totem is the elephant. Elephants have long been associated in magick with bringing luck and good fortune, though the elephant-headed god Ganesh might be more appropriately a Hod godform. Though not classically associated with Yesod, animals such as wolves, dogs, shellfish, moths, and cats also could be associated with this realm.

Liquids—perfumes or scented oils, in particular—are tools of Yesod. The modern availability of essential oils makes working with Yesod much easier for the magician. An essential oil is the volatile fluid, the potent magick, of a plant substance. Scent is a method of harnessing our automatic consciousness tied to Yesod, and the right scent or combination of scents can release deep power within us. Scent is found throughout the Qabalah, but the art of perfumery, which is very intuitive, resonates particularly with Yesod. A great book on Qabalistic correspondences and blending techniques is *The Magical and Ritual Use of Perfumes* by Richard Alan Miller and Iona Miller.

One of the most popular oils used in ceremonial magick traditions and favored by Thelemites is Abramelin Oil. This recipe is mentioned in the Abramelin Operation for communing with your Holy Guardian Angel. The oil also is said to be in resonance with the Aeon of Horus, the next age.

Abramelin Oil

   8 parts cinnamon oil

   4 parts myrrh

   2 parts galangal oil

   7 parts olive oil (or other base oil)

A medicinal aromatherapist would caution you about the use of cinnamon oil and its potential to severely irritate the skin, though a magician might say that's half the magick, as the irritation brings a fiery energy to where the oil has been applied. If irritation is a concern, then add more base oil, or dilute the cinnamon oil with base oil before adding it to the mixture. In one variation of the recipe, instead of using essential oils, you macerate the dry herbs in a base of olive oil in a sealed jar in a warm room (such as near a water heater) for at least a month. Strain out the plant matter and bottle the oil. It won't have as strong a scent, but magickally it will be potent.

Sandals are another ritual tool associated with Yesod. At first this appears to be another nod to the water-air connection between Yesod and Hod, as sandals seem to be the tool of Mercurial figures, like Hermes and his winged sandals. Sandals are a symbol of travel and are demonstrative of the travel through the upper planes to which Yesod opens the magician. Rising on the planes can be considered a form of Yesod magick.

In tarot, all the nines are associated with Yesod. In each of the four suits, the nine represents the penultimate step toward completion. The nines manifest favorably in the suits of earth and water, with titles such as Gain and Happiness in many deck systems, while the more masculine elements manifest less favorably in Yesod, with fire and air manifesting as Strength and Cruelty. The title Strength, not to be confused with the major arcana card, doesn't sound so bad, but some decks depict a battered and bruised wand holder gathering strength and anticipating the final conflict. Cruelty is the card depicting what happens when our emotions of Yesod get mixed in with our mind in adverse ways, creating worry and obsessive thinking about forces we have no control over, events in the past or worries of the future.

The geometry of the ninth sphere is the nine-pointed star, or *enneagram* (figure 38). A variant enneagram, also pictured in figure 38, was used by the esoteric philosopher G. I. Gurdjieff to describe the basic geometry of the universe, and later was used as a symbol of a nine-point personality system. Nine was an important number in Egyptian mythology, as the group of nine primary gods was known as the Ennead. Though there were many groupings, or enneads, the Heliopolis Ennead is one of the most important to modern pagans, depicting a series of gods in one version of the creation mythos of Egypt.

As Yesod is on the middle pillar and resonates with the creative energy, an appropriate ritual for learning the lessons of Yesod is the standard exercise known as the Middle Pillar. In this exercise, you circulate life force from the heavens through your own middle pillar, what others see as the central column of the chakra system, and then through the aura, or body of light.

In the Middle Pillar exercise, you move energy by visualizing it moving through each sephira rooted in your body and energizing each center by chanting the Hebrew divine name for each of the five centers on the pillar—Kether, Da'ath, Tiphereth, Yesod, and Malkuth. This exercise, with its five points, is similar to the Fivefold Kiss found in some initiation traditions of witchcraft. Each opens the energy centers, though the kiss has different locations and uses the aid of another person to open these points. One can think of the Fivefold Kiss as a modified Middle Pillar done by a couple for initiatory purposes.

EXERCISE 9

Middle Pillar

1. Prepare yourself and the space with the LBRP (exercise 5). Remain standing if possible, aligning the middle pillar physically within your body with straight body posture.

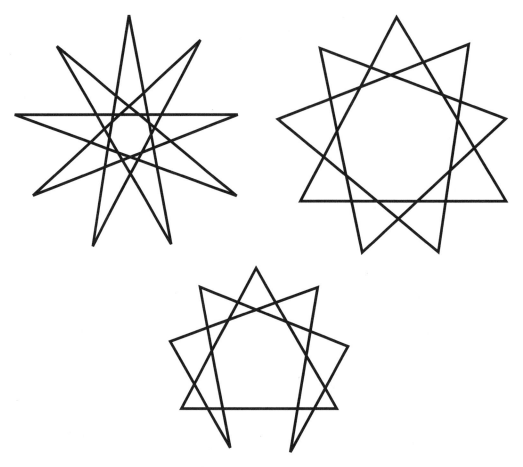

Figure 38: Traditional Enneagrams and the Enneagram of Personality

2. Bring your attention to the top of your head. Imagine a sphere of brilliant light above it—Kether in your own personal Tree of Life. Contemplate this light as your own indivisible divine self. Vibrate the divine name of Kether, **Eh-heh-yeh** (Eheieh), three to four times as you feel the energy align with the crown of your head.

3. Visualize a beam of light from the sphere at the crown of your head descend into your neck, forming a second sphere of light at your throat, in the Da'ath position in your own personal Tree of Life. Vibrate the divine

name of Da'ath, **Yud-Heh-Vahv-Heh El-oh-heem** (YHVH Elohim), three
to four times, feeling the two spheres and the connecting path and awakening the power of creation.

4. Visualize a beam of light from your throat descending into the space between your heart and solar plexus. For some magicians it will be slightly
   higher or lower. Feel a sphere form in the Tiphereth position in your own
   personal Tree of Life. Vibrate the divine name of Tiphereth, **Yud-Heh-
   Vahv-Heh El-oh-ah V-dah-aht** (YHVH Eloah va-Da'ath), three to four
   times, while feeling all three spheres and the connecting lines, as well as
   the warmth of the internal Sun with your chest radiating outward.

5. Visualize a beam of light descending from the third sphere into the lower
   body or genital region, forming a fourth sphere, the Yesod position in your
   own personal Tree of Life. Feel the generative and creative power in this
   position. Vibrate the divine name of Yesod, **Sha-dai El Chai** (Shaddai El
   Chai), three to four times, and while keeping all four spheres and their connecting lines in mind, focus on the mastery of your lower creative self.

6. Visualize a beam of light from your belly area down to your feet, forming
   a sphere of light half above the floor and half below the floor. Focus on
   your connection to the world, as it fills the space of Malkuth in your own
   personal Tree of Life. Vibrate the divine name of Malkuth, **Ah-doh-nye
   ha-ah-retz** (Adonai ha-Aretz), three to four times.

7. Feel the energy flow from your crown down to your feet along your middle
   pillar. Remain in this meditative state for as long as you'd like.

8. When done, close with the LBRP.

Variations of the Middle Pillar have you intone the divine names a different number
of times. Three to four times usually is deemed sufficient to flow with the appropriate
divine energy through the body. Some try to align the names numerologically, vibrating Kether's name one or ten times, Da'ath's name eleven times, Tiphereth's six times,
Yesod's nine times, and Malkuth's ten times.

You can continue the exercise by moving the energy through your aura or subtle bodies, for your own healing, clearing, and energizing. This is known as the Circulation of the Body of Light and helps build a strong, clear aura. To do it, skip the last step (the repetition of the LBRP) and move directly from the Middle Pillar to the Circulation.

EXERCISE 10

Circulation of the Body of Light

1. Start with the Middle Pillar (exercise 9).

2. Imagine the light of Kether descending into your crown and overflowing, like a cup filled with too much wine, but the overflowing white-light energy moves down the left side of your body. It moves down your head to your left shoulder. It moves down your left side and beneath your feet. It moves up your right leg and right side, up your right shoulder, and back up to your crown.

3. The flow of energy continues like this, down your left side and up your right side. Notice that with your will, you can make it flow tightly to your body, invigorating your physical self with primal energy.

4. You could feel the energy move down your left shoulder and your outside left arm and then upward, toward your left armpit. The energy then moves down your trunk, left hip, and the outside of your left leg. The energy moves beneath your left foot and up your inner left leg, touching the base of your spine. Then it moves down your inner right leg, under your right foot, and up the outside of your right leg. Then the power flows from your right hip and trunk up to your right armpit, down your inner arm, and around your right hand and fingers, moving up the outside of your right arm. Finally, it moves up your right shoulder, neck, the right side of your head, and to your crown.

5. You also can make the energy flow in wider loops, with much broader strokes, to fill your entire aura. Feel the flow widen, and notice how it feels in your aura.

6. While the energy flow from left to right continues, be aware of a second flow of energy. Again starting at your crown, feel the energy flow down the front of your body, beneath your feet, and up the back of your legs and back, toward your crown again. As with the first loop, notice that you can make the flow cling tightly to your physical body, or move in wide loops to fill your entire aura.

7. Keeping both the left-to-right flow and the front-to-back flow in mind, feel the light of your crown move down the middle pillar. When it reaches the final sphere of Malkuth at your feet, two trails of energy spiral up like DNA around you. Like the first two flows of energy, the DNA-like spirals can be tight to your body, but eventually they feel like they are surrounding your aura, spiraling back up to your crown area, to descend again through the middle pillar.

8. Your entire energy body is filled with circulating light, which is healing, reconstructing, and reinforcing your aura. Like exercise, this helps build energetic "muscles" to increase your capacity to both direct and hold more magickal energy.

9. When this feels complete, you can stop the energy circulation, or simply let your awareness of it fade. Let your body naturally absorb any remaining energy that does not flow back up to your crown.

10. Perform the LBRP. If you need to ground yourself, do so now, though most people do not need to ground, but simply need to adjust to the new level of energy.

The Middle Pillar and Circulation of the Body of Light can be used in ritual to generate the energy and raise the power for the working of the ritual, be it an inner working of transformation and enlightenment, clearing the pathways, or a working in which you fill the ritual space to empower an object, talisman, or spell to manifest in the outer world. See appendix III for variations of the Middle Pillar exercise.

Empowered energy can shape the astral plane in many ways. One of the most effective ritual methods for working with both individuals and groups is through the use of magickal storytelling. Language shapes the energy we raise, and through language and the images it evokes, we create new patterns on the astral plane.

The storytelling tradition goes back as far as we've had language and stories to share. The first magickal and mythical stories were most likely the shaman's adventures in the Otherworld, related around the fire to those in the tribe. The tradition grew to the philosopher-teachers in the ancient world using parable and drama both to express their intellectual points of view and to shift consciousness to open the student or initiate to new levels of awareness where such points could be made and absorbed. We see similar workings in the bards of the Druidic tradition, and the poets and myth keepers who later inherited their tradition, detailing the deeds of heroes and the magick, history, and genealogy of the culture, all through song and story. *Galdr* (Old Norse) and *Galdor* (Old English) are both terms used in Teutonic magick for spoken magickal charms. Rune Galdr, specifically, involves the chanting of the runes, while other forms of Galdr consist of charms that are spoken or sung, told like stories, describing what the magician wants to achieve through magick. Anglo-Saxon Galdor charms for protection, healing, blessings, and cursing were common. Spirits and even inanimate objects were addressed in the story, instructed by the magician. This spoken-word magick is the basis for our idea of a "spell." Older versions used alliteration and poetic repetition with slight variations, while a more modern trend is rhyming in verse. Today, we might see the same tools used in hypnotherapy and ritual induction, as well as modern revivals of storytelling, to keep folk tales alive. Storytelling has always been a form of hypnosis, creating change in both the speaker and the listener.

From a Yesod perspective, stories are not just tools and teaching methods, but living entities. Once created on the astral plane, potentially they are in existence forever. They become thoughtforms, which grow in power as more energy is put into them. Clever storytellers can tweak and change a thoughtform, transforming it into whatever serves them best. Stories shape our society, culture, and values, our interface with the higher realms, just as Yesod is an interface with the worlds beyond. Such thoughtforms may never actually leave the astral realm and manifest in the physical, but they shape the ideas of the physical world, and how people relate to the supernal, through imagination.

Though seen by trained magicians as folk magick at best, the arts of the Druids or the Greek philosophers, including their myths and songs, were certainly forms of high magick. The same dangers inherent in all magick also exist in storytelling. The entity created from story and image can take on a life of its own and go in directions in which the story creator, and reteller, doesn't want it to go, yet its hold on popular consciousness gives it a life of its own.

Stories come in many forms. They can be of daily life, the actions of the world and culture, detailing and organizing the information of the society of the storyteller. Teaching stories are those told specifically to pass on information, be it religious or secular, mundane or philosophical. Teaching stories pass on history, codes, values, folklore, medicine, and ritual. These stories and songs are mnemonic devices to keep the information in living memory and easily pass it on to others. The last kind of story is the true magickal story, the stories of wonder working. The very telling of the story is a charm. The words create a shift in energy, in consciousness, and ultimately in reality, both inner and outer reality.

Working stories and songs can be used to invoke either a specific entity (by reciting its name and qualities to manifest it in the consciousness of the listeners and/or speaker) or particular qualities in the listener. Certain stories might be told on the eve of battle, to invoke and inspire victory. Others are used during rituals of fertility, of both the land and humans, to make sure there is health and abundance. Magickal stories can alter the mood of the listener and invoke a particular emotion. The Irish tales, particularly the Song of Amergin, involve shapeshifting. The poet is comparing himself, his consciousness, with a variety of animals and natural phenomena, not just for poetry's sake but also to shift his shape like a god and become one with these things.

Stories can be told to bless anything from food to homes. They can be told in ritual to bless people, such as a tale of true love told to bless a newlywed couple. Stories also can be told to cure or to reveal things that need to come to the surface, yet listeners of such stories might not want their past actions to come to light. Some teaching stories are really wonder workings, for they are not passing on information but are forcing the listeners to change their perspective and thereby change their consciousness and grow spiritually. The most popular wonder-working stories are healing stories.

Stories can be a form of healing therapy on all levels. They can be told to inspire convalescence and recovery in the face of grave illness, to distract from physical or mental pain, or even to get us in touch with the more unconscious and disconnected parts of ourselves. Stories can be used to diagnose, making the story more participatory, like the popular Choose Your Own Adventure novels of the 1980s. The listener guides the story through choices, which provide the healer with greater insight. More can be revealed in such stories than in a direct counseling session in which one is forced to confront life directly. Those who are confused can find solutions to their problems by stepping out of their personal self and into the character of the story. Open-ended stories where the listener has to figure out the answer or "moral," rather than having it be told, can be amazingly helpful in healing counsel.

Like magick, storytelling is both an art and a science, and both inspiration and technique are needed to effectively evoke a change in consciousness. Stories are like rituals, and those who have good ritual skills as a priestess or priest are often good storytellers as well.

Determining the setting of the story is the first step in the technique. Like a ritual setting, it sets the tone. What is the lighting, the time of day, the space of the participants, scents, and temperature? All of these things contribute to the experience. Teaching and initiation stories can be told most effectively in dark isolation, helping to induce trance in the listeners, rather than having participants passively look at pictures in the story. Who is your audience? The telling of the story often is adjusted for those who will be listening, to be most effective for the group.

The more ritualized a story is, the more capable it is of working wonders. Ritualized telling is important. When involved in ritual, we all recognize certain actions that signal the start of ritual and begin to induce an altered perception. For witches, the casting of the circle and the calling of the quarters become the bookends for the ritual. The ritual starts and ends with symmetry, but what occurs in the middle might be different each time. When you begin a story with a familiar phrase such as "Once upon a time" or even "A long time ago in a galaxy far, far away," listeners know that a tale is coming next and prepare themselves for it. You can use your voice to mimic the emotions you want to evoke—loud and excited to induce energy, or soft and subtle to take the listener deeper. As in hypnotherapy, the style of vocal induction, including rhythms, repetitions, pauses, and strong images, can make all the difference.

The language of the story itself can be artfully undefined. When you use words such as *freedom* or *love*, each listener has to determine what these concepts mean, personally or culturally, and possibly redefine them in the context of the story. Magickal tales with the theme of "be careful what you wish for, for you just might get it" teach us how to be precise in our use of words. Think of the stories of a genie granting three wishes. The genie gives you exactly what you ask for, not what you thought you asked for or what you really wanted. It follows only your words. Stories about magick wishes and genies are really teaching stories for a magician.

In your own magickal stories, you can use hidden analogies to get a point across, such as using themes similar to current events, but in a different setting. With the new setting, people can detach from their usual perspective and entertain new possibilities, not realizing the lesson of the story actually applies to them. With this storytelling technique, you can comment on current political or religious debates without overtly referring to current events, and the different setting can get people to see the situation in a new way.

Although the next exercise is written in a format in which one person tells a story to a live audience, as that is the oldest tradition of magickal storytelling, all of the ideas can be adapted for small groups as well as modern forms of media. Some of the most magickal storytelling today can be found in comic books, novels, television, movies, and popular music. If you keep in mind, when telling a story, that you are creating a living creature on the astral plane and investing it with energy, then you will recognize that all acts of creation are magickal, even those we don't necessarily intend to be magickal. All stories get their start in this realm of dreams and imagination, and that is the essence of magick.

Exercise 11

Magickal Storytelling

For those going through this course with me in person, the next assignment is to tell a magickal story to the class. This can be the retelling of an old myth, as you've heard it or with a new twist based on your intention, or an entirely new story. But there must be a magickal intention behind the story. Some students retell a popular Greek or Celtic myth, but often tell it from the perspective of one of the characters. Others make up a new story or song. Some students read their story word for word, while others are inspired in the moment. Some even memorize their story line by line. Some students tell their story in dramatic fashion, while others find the purpose was the great act of magickal courage to get up in front of a group of people and tell a story.

If you are studying this material with a partner or small group, or have any magickal group you work with, then the assignment is to tell a magickal story to the group, just as my in-person students do. If you don't have a group, you can look for an opportunity, however informal as you'd like, to tell a magickal story. If you are camping outdoors, do it around the campfire. Find a way to work it into a social party. Grab a friend for a trusted audience of one and tell him or her you need to complete a homework assignment. If this is not possible for you, then I want you to write, illustrate, or compose a magickal story for future use. The idea of this fourth level of training is to synchronize your words, or vocalizations, with the image of the world you wish to manifest, and truly discover the power of the word in everything you do. Ideally, you will share this story with others at some point, but if that's not possible at this juncture, then do what you can.

To get guidance and inspiration for your story, I suggest that you visit the gateway of creativity (*ITOW*, Chapter 14) in your inner temple.

YESOD PATHWORKINGS

You already have learned that the main pathway into Yesod is from Malkuth, the path ruled by the World/Universe tarot card. It is through the middle path of Malkuth that we get to Yesod, following the magician's orderly path from ten to nine up the Tree. Yesod has three more paths, leading higher up the Tree. Though you won't be climbing them in this lesson, understanding the relationship between Yesod and the higher spheres can help illuminate your understanding of Yesod itself.

From Yesod we can take a step higher through the path of Temperance / Art, undergoing the alchemical transformation to ascend to Tiphereth and find the first stage of enlightenment. The path of Temperance is the magickal conjunction of the Sun and the Moon, leading to expanded consciousness. The path of the Star card links Yesod to Netzach. Through exploring the True Will of this Aquarius-ruled card, the Star helps us ignite our true passions and talents, where we shine, leading to the fire elemental grade of Netzach. Its opposite path, linking to Hod, is ruled by the solar light of the Sun card. Through the individual awareness presented in the Sun card, we discover the mysteries of intellect found in Hod.

EXERCISE 12

Yesod Pathworking

1. Perform the Lesser Banishing Ritual of the Pentagram (exercise 5) to clear your energy field and the space where you are doing this working. You also can do the Middle Pillar and the Circulation of the Body of Light (exercise 10), if you so choose, to open the middle path within you and energize you for the work.

2. While in this space, call upon the divine forces of Yesod. Burn your purple and / or silver candles and Moon incense. Try knocking on your altar nine times. Vibrate the divine name of Yesod, **Shaddai El Chai**, nine times. Call upon any of the Moon and fertility deities of the sphere, or Archangel Gabriel.

3. To count down into a meditative state, do exercise 1 through step 7 (page 76).

4. Let the familiar world around you fall away, as if the material reality you know is only a façade and beneath it lies the beautiful garden of the Goddess, a veritable paradise surrounding you. The land around you becomes a vast primordial garden, the garden of Malkuth, the familiar garden of the four paths.

5. Some feel the call of Yesod from above, the shining universe all around us, pulling upward toward the lunar sphere, while others feel the pull of the Earth, and find that within the land is the silvery light of the lunar sphere. Both the goddess of the Earth, the World, and the goddess of the material Universe lead to the same place. You might have to go to the heart of Malkuth, to the Temple of Malkuth, to find your path to Yesod. But when you are ready, focusing your thoughts upon the World/Universe card as your key, you will find either an opening within the earth, where a spiraling staircase appears, or the silvery light of a Moon path that descends from the heavens. Follow the path that appears to you.

6. While on the path, you are flooded with images of life and of the world—images from a biological, chemical, and physics perspective to images of the four esoteric elements that are the underpinnings of the universe. You feel the presence of the Goddess of life leading you to the next world, and contemplate if you are in the right place and at the right time doing the work of your True Will in the world. If not, how can you be?

7. The path leads you to a sphere of purple and silver light, magnetically drawing you into it. To enter the Moon gates of Yesod, you might have to draw the crescent moon glyph or give a key word or symbol, such as the divine name of the sephira, Shaddai El Chai. But once you align yourself with Yesod, the gate opens and you enter the Moon realm.

8. Everything appears as it does on the night of the full Moon, bathed in a silvery white light, a luminal twilight in which things are not as they seem. Everything appears to have a truly visible aura to it, or at least an energetic outline of the etheric body. The place is primal and wild, somewhat like Malkuth, but peaceful and cool in the realm of perpetual night. You hear, and might even see, the flow of water, the churning of the tides, and the movement of rivers. Creatures of the night roam Yesod, in particular frogs, turtles, and, yes, even elephants. The creatures of Diana's wild hunt also abound in the silver land. Be aware of the messengers of Yesod.

9. You make your way to the temple of Yesod. The lunar temple is white, silver, and purple. Like Malkuth, it may be an outdoor shrine of stones and statues or an indoor temple. In either case, nine sides will set its boundary.

10. Within the temple are the powers of Yesod. You might gaze upon the slumbering and erect man of fertility, his lover the generative Moon goddess or Archangel Gabriel. Commune with one or all of the beings of Yesod. Ask to learn the mysteries of Yesod in a manner that is correct for your highest good at this time. Perhaps they will teach you the sphere's virtue, vices, and obligation and even give you a glimpse into the vision, the Machinery of the Universe, to better consciously understand your place within the universe.

11. When done, thank all the beings who have communicated with you. They might offer you a gift, a token of their goodwill. If you accept, it is polite to reach within your being and offer them a gift of your goodwill in return. Be sure that what you give reflects the energy and intention you plan to put into the sphere's lessons.

12. Once you have said your farewells, leave the shrine and follow the path back. Return through Yesod and the World/Universe, back to Malkuth where you began. Focus on the waking world you know, and feel it return around the garden.

13. To return to normal waking consciousness and end your journey, perform steps 15–17 from exercise 1 (page 78). You can close the temple by repeating the LBRP.

ÏNITIATION OF ¥ESOD

The grade of Yesod is alternately thought of as the elemental grade of water or air, depending on the tradition, with the rank known as either the Theoricus or Zealot, again depending on the tradition. But the work is clear. The initiate must keep a regular meditation and ritual practice.

For witches following the Temple of Witchcraft system, in this lesson we follow the classic Wiccan symbolism of relating the Moon to water. The quest for Yesod and the water element is the legendary quest for the grail.

Water

Spiritual Lesson: Compassion

Spiritual Tool: Cup of Compassion, Undry, Holy Grail

Fears and Challenges: Fear of Loneliness, Rejection, or Commitment; Projection

Virtue: Generosity

Psychological Function: Feeling

Stage of Learning: Opinion

State of Matter: Liquid

Environmental Sphere: Hydrosphere

Scientific Force: Weak Force

Periodic Element: Hydrogen

Humor: Phlegm—Phlegmatic

Body System: Circulatory

Sacred River: Wine / Blood

Sacred Geometry: Icosahedron

Celtic City: Murias

Qabalistic World: Briah

Classical Age: Bronze

Caste: Merchant / Craftsman

Sufi Breath: In Nose / Out Mouth

Mudra: Thumb and Index Finger

Planets: Moon, Venus, Jupiter, Neptune

Fixed Sign and Animal: Scorpio—Eagle

Egyptian Animal: Crocodile

Metal: Silver

Chakras: Belly, Heart, Brow

Time of Day: Sunset

Season: Fall

Vowel Sound: O

Egyptian Syllable: Nu

Hindi Syllable: Vam
Tibetan Syllable: Va
Modern Syllable: Om
Obstruent Sounds: z, zh, s, sh
Time Signature: 6/8
Hebrew God Name: Elohim of Eheieh
Archangel: Gabriel
Angel: Taliahad
Ruler: Tharsis
Elemental King and Queen: King Niksa and Queen Mara
Goetic Ruler: Corson
Enochian King: MPHARSLGAIOL
Stones: Moonstone, Amethyst, Aquamarine, Pearl
Herbs: Camphor, Jasmine, Lemon Balm, Lotus, Mugwort

Grail legends abound, mixing pagan and Christian symbolism. It's hard to know exactly what the grail is, with its rise in popular media, linking it to the Knights Templar and a variety of conspiracy theories. Here, we are talking about the regenerative force of elemental water in its purest state—perfect love and compassion. Many traces of the grail can be seen in pagan history.

In the stories of the Irish treasures, the grail is the Cauldron of the Dagda, the *Undry*. As it's seen as a cauldron of abundance, no one goes away hungry from it, though some tellings of the tale state that you got what you deserved from the cauldron, be it meager morsels for those unworthy or feasts for greater heroes and sages. At first it appears to be an earth symbol, but it's not just the food of the body, but also spiritual sustenance.

In the Welsh tales of Ceridwen, we have her sacred cauldron dedicated to brewing greal, a potion to give her ugly son all the knowledge and wisdom of the world. Modern pagans think of greal as the root of the word grail in later myths. Ceridwen's servant, Gwion Bach, burns himself while stirring the cauldron and accidentally imbibes a drop of the potion, getting all the magick. In this initiatory tale, he eventually is transformed into the great bard Taliesin. The cauldron of knowledge and inspiration again seems to lack the water symbolism, being more air, yet Gwion Bach learns to shift his shape fluidly through magick, which is as much an intuitive process as an intellectual one. The inspiration of the bard must come from the head through the heart to be effective.

In Arthurian myths, the Holy Grail is linked with the Christian concept of the cup of Jesus, but it still retains Goddess associations as the power that will restore the wasteland from its ailment and bring the fertility of the land, and thereby the Goddess, back to the people. The Holy Grail's power restores balance to the relationship between the sacred king and the goddess of the land. Only those who are pure of heart can find the Holy Grail, so the king must send his noblest knights on the quest. Some myths link it to an emerald, which is a strong stone ally for heart healing. Some occultists who use the mixed Christian and pagan imagery in the Arthurian legend hope to bring together Christians and pagans peacefully under one mythos that accommodates both worldviews.

I think of the grail as the Cup of Compassion. We each seek the compassionate well of the inner worlds, and of our inner heart, that can heal all wounds, redeem all who have fallen, and elevate all relationships. It is this living stream of compassion that truly connects our hearts to the Goddess of the Heart. With the grail, we have the gifts of abundance from the Undry of the Dagda, the inspiration of Ceridwen's cauldron, and the sacred drink of the Arthurian Grail that makes the wasteland bloom with roses.

To find our inner compassion, we must seek the grail on the elemental plane of water. If we already embody compassion, then the guardians of the element of water—the undines, the elemental rulers, Gabriel, and the sea gods and goddesses—will release our grail and unlock its powers to flow from our heart. If we are not ready to receive the Cup of Compassion, then they will point us in the direction of more heart learning.

Exercise 13

Elemental Water Journey Seeking the Cup of Compassion

1. This exercise is an expansion of the experiences in Exercise 17: Journeying to the Realm of Water from *The Outer Temple of Witchcraft*. You can start by performing the LBRP before this journey to prepare yourself. Then perform exercise 1, steps 1–11, to go to your inner temple.

2. Orient yourself in the center of your inner temple. Look for the four doorways to the elemental planes. You might find that your guides bring you to the garden of Malkuth, with its four paths to the four elemental planes. In either case, orient yourself to the direction of elemental water. Hold your intention to journey to the realm of water and seek out the Cup of Compassion. You know you might not receive it, but the journey will give you teachings to better master the element in your life so you can come back and claim it. Open the doorway of water, perhaps using the invoking pentagram of water as a magickal "key" (*OTOW*, Chapter 6). Enter the path or tunnel that leads to the elemental plane of water.

3. When you are fully in the realm of water, seek out the primal powers of the plane. Hold the intention to go to the heart of the realm, to seek out the elemental ruler, king, queen, archangel, or a deity of elemental water. Perhaps a guide will take you there directly, or you will have to search, and the searching will be part of your lesson.

4. When you reach the heart of the elemental plane, state your request to receive the Cup of Compassion. The keepers of the cup might ask you why you think you are worthy, and you might have to convince them that you are ready to do so. You could be challenged. Meet the challenges to the best of your ability. If you are ready to receive the cup, the elemental teachers will give it to you, often embedding it in your heart, or in your nondominant, or receptive, hand. If not, they will instruct you in what you have to accomplish to be able to receive the cup in the future. They may offer to tutor you in the ways of the water element, giving you an assignment to complete before you return.

5. Travel back from the realm of elemental water, back the way you came unless guided by the teachers to take another route. Go back to the inner temple. Close the gateway of elemental water in a manner similar to the way you opened it. If you used an invoking pentagram, then use the banishing pentagram now.

6. To return to normal waking consciousness and end your journey, perform steps 15–17 from exercise 1 (page 78). Close with the LBRP if you opened with it.

This is the second of four journeys that will help you gain greater mastery of the elements for deeper workings.

The ritual tool of the cup anchors your Cup of Compassion in the world. Ritual magicians sometimes etch on the bottom of the chalice the numerological value of their "true" name, converting the letters to digits and adding them in the style of modern or Qabalistic numerology.

HOMEWORK

- Do Exercises 9–13 and record your experiences in your Book of Shadows.

- Learn and practice the Middle Pillar and Circulation of the Body of Light rituals, either the traditional versions or your own personally reconstructed versions.

- Continue to practice the LBRP.

TIPS

- Fill in the Yesod correspondences and colors on your own Tree of Life drawing. Contemplate them as you add them to the image. Start memorizing these correspondences.

- To gain greater mastery over the realm of Yesod and the element of water, be keenly aware of the energetic and spiritual aspects of all your relationships and interactions with people. Also be aware of the power of your thoughts and images to shape your reality. Practice neutralization (*ITOW*, Chapter 8) to prevent unwanted daydreams and thoughts from manifesting.

- Study appendix III to deconstruct and reconstruct the Middle Pillar exercise to your liking and worldview, if you so choose.

- Pick one other reality map from appendix I to contemplate. Understanding a variety of worldviews will help you when you construct your own reality map.

- Don't feel as though you need to master your Cup of Compassion before going on to the next lessons. These are tools you can be using throughout the entire year-and-a-day course and beyond. Keep visiting the realm of water, and integrate these lessons into your daily life.

- When you do feel that you have received the Cup of Compassion from the inner-world teacher of the water element, be sure to reconsecrate the chalice that you have on your altar. If you work with several different sets of tools, you might find your inner Cup of Compassion extending out from your hands to empower a chalice and then retracting back within you when the rite is concluded.

Lesson Four
Hod

Hod is the eighth sphere on the Tree of Life, and many would consider it, above all others, to embody the spirit of the magician, for it is the sphere associated with the intellect, with language and thought processes, and these are all the tools of the ceremonial magician. The realm of Hod is aligned with what occultists would call the *mental plane*, for it is said that here, all things are made from language. The translation of Hod is usually "glory" or "splendor," and refers to the glory or splendor of the mind, and the mind's ability to create and communicate. The mind is a glorious part of ourselves and of the universe. Though in science many think of the mind as a byproduct of the brain and nervous system, we still don't understand from a scientific perspective what the mind is or how it interfaces with the brain, let alone how to work with it fully. It is a splendid mystery that can never be fully understood.

The occultist would say that the mind is not just in the brain, but permeates the entire body, surrounding it. The entire body listens to our thoughts, and responds to them. That is why a magician is so careful in thought and word, as those are the keys to change health, well-being, and all of reality, for our mind touches and is a part of the cosmic mind. It's no wonder that, in the Hermetic view, the Creator is seen as the Divine Mind, and what we have in common with the Creator is our mind, our ability to think and thereby bring something into existence, if we so choose.

The symbol of the magician, as the trickster, is slyly the symbol of Hod as well. In the diagram of the Tree of Life, Hod is depicted as a circle with the number eight in it. If you turn the number eight on its side, you have the infinity loop or Mobius strip associated with the magician. If you look at the traditional images of the Magician card in the tarot, an infinity loop is over the Magician's head. Part of the glory of the mental plane is its infinite power and possibilities. Anything you can put a thought to, put into an idea or words, that can be conveyed to the universe or to another, is possible. The power of the mental plane is limitless in terms of magick.

Hod

Meanings: Glory, Splendor
Level of Reality: Mental Realm
Parts of the Self: Ruach, Mind, Reason, Intellect, Right Hip
Experience: Vision of Splendor
Obligation: Learning
Illusion: Order
Virtue: Truthfulness
Vices: Dishonesty, Falsehood
Name of God: Elohim Tzabaoth (God of Hosts)
King Scale Color: Violet Purple
Queen Scale Color: Orange
Prince Scale Color: Reddish Russet
Princess Scale Color: Yellowish Brown flecked with White
Element: Air
Planet: Mercury
Image: Hermaphrodite
Archetypes: Magician, Messenger, Trickster
Greek/Roman Deities: Hermes, Mercury
Egyptian Deities: Thoth, Anubis
Middle Eastern Deity: Nabu

Celtic Deities: Gywdion, Lugh, Math, Merlin

Norse Deities: Odin, Loki, Heimdel, Hermod

Hindu Deity: Hanuman

Archangel: Raphael (Archangel of Healing / East / Air)

Angelic Order: Beni Elohim (Sons of Gods)

Choir: Archangels

Grade of Initiation: ③=⑧ Practitioner

Animals: Jackal, Two-Headed Snake

Planetary Vowel Sound: E (eh)

Resonant Letter: R

Musical Mode: Locrian

Musical Note: D

Tools: Words and Names of Power, Apron

Incense: Storax

Tarot: Eight of Wands, Swords, Cups, and Pentacles

> Judgment / Aeon—to Malkuth
>
> Sun—to Yesod
>
> Tower—to Netzach
>
> Devil—to Tiphereth
>
> Hanged Man—to Geburah

Metal: Quicksilver

Stones: Opal, Agate, Hematite, Sapphire

Plant: Orchid

For the following month, decorate your altar with Hod correspondences. Use an orange altar cloth, with eight candles and other orange items. Quicksilver is the metal for this sphere, but due to its toxic nature, few magicians have access to it, so aluminum is a proper substitution. Storax is the traditional incense, but substitutions of lavender, sandalwood, or peppermint can be used as incense or in oil form to evoke the power of Hod. Arrange the major arcana tarot cards on the altar in a semicircle arc to represent the paths from the sphere of Hod, starting with Judgment at the bottom to Malkuth, then the Sun to Yesod, the Tower across horizontally to Netzach, the Devil to Tiphereth, and the Hanged Man up to Geburah.

ENTITIES OF HOD

Hod is the realm of magicians, from the courtly magician in our Merlin fantasies to the tricksters and messengers between the worlds. Thoth-Hermes is a great primal image of Hod, the two gods of the ancient world identified so strongly with each other, as each contains a face of the Hod magick. Thoth, also known as Tehuti from the Egyptian pantheon, is the powerful scribe god who brought mathematics and the magickal arts to humanity. Though depicted as wiser and more powerful than the other gods, and in some cases credited with creation of the universe, Thoth usually takes a back seat in the stories, preferring to guide, aid, and advise the gods of Egypt. Thoth is associated with Hermes, who also is credited with giving certain arts to humanity. In the Roman traditions, Hermes is linked to Mercury, and both are seen as fleet-footed messenger gods who travel to all the realms yet are not anchored in any one realm. Mercury is both messenger and psychopomp, a guide to souls between worlds. He is a patron of magicians, but also of businesspeople, gamblers, and thieves. Like the quicksilver metal that is his namesake, Mercury is hard to pin down to any one shape or form and easily flows into another. He is a patron of the arts, medicine, and philosophy, yet is an irreverent trickster. There is not just one side to him.

In other mythologies, the image of the Mercurial trickster is conveyed, and Thoth-Hermes finds his cognates among the magicians of the world. In Norse mythology we have two sides of the same trickster force in the blood brothers of Odin (or Wotan) and Loki. Odin is harsh and stern at times, but inspires both poetry and berserker madness. He is the all-father and wandering guide to the Norse gods. Loki, on the other hand, is credited with the destruction of the gods, and as his myth develops, he becomes a darker and more difficult figure to understand. In Sumer, the figure of Nabu, the scribe god, has more in common with the scholarly pursuits of Thoth. In Celtic myth, many of the figures are magicians or wizards as well as warriors. The Welsh Gwydion has similarities with the Merlin archetype, schooling his nephew Lleu in the arts and crafts to claim his name and power. His aid to Lleu is not always easy or clear. Gwydion uses deception to further his aims, yet does so for noble reasons. Native traditions have trickster spirits such as Coyote and Raven filling similar roles as teachers with a twist.

Hod is embodied by the image of the hermaphrodite. In myth, Hermaphrodite was the child of Hermes and Aphrodite, having both sets of sexual organs and a mix of male and female traits. The image has been used in magick and alchemy to show the perfected blending of male and female energies in harmony. In Hod, it also shows that the mind is androgynous, and the power of our thoughts and words are neither male nor female. Still, in the lore, the realm of the magician takes a slightly more masculine image, as some see the devotion to the intellectual mysteries over the primal mysteries as the way of the male magician over the primal witch. But, in essence, each contains the other. One must balance both genders to be a true adept on the path.

Hod, like Mercury, is fluid and reflects many concepts. It absorbs knowledge, which makes it difficult to assign specific correspondences to this realm. Though by all accounts Hod's lessons are of the intellect, classical Qabalists assign to this sphere the element of water, not air, for Hod is on the water pillar headed by Binah. Quicksilver is a liquid metal and does contain some water qualities, but language definitely correspondends with air. Because of this, the correspondences between Hod and Yesod can be unclear. Likewise, the elements of fire and air are interchanged, with the tools of wands and swords. Great debate among magicians still exists as to the proper correspondences, and that has grown to include the archangelic correspondences of Hod and then Tiphereth.

I personally align the archangel of air, Raphael, the healer, with the sphere of Hod, and keep Michael, the archangel of fire, yet a solar fire, with Tiphereth. Other traditions insist that Michael is the archangel of Hod, while Raphael is of Tiphereth. Some systems have compromised and stated that one archangel rules the sphere while the other assists, and the reverse is true for the second sephira. As a witch, corresponding Raphael and air with Hod makes the most sense to me, and works most effectively for me in meditation and ritual, so that is the correspondence I choose to use. Raphael means "God heals" or "healed by God." Healing is really the art and science of getting the various parts of the body and consciousness to speak to each other in a harmonious fashion. Raphael is depicted carrying the caduceus associated with modern medicine and Hermes, or a blade or scalpel-like tool that modern healers say he uses for psychic surgery. In myth, his knowledge was not limited to healing, but encompassed all of magick. Raphael gave Noah a book of medicine after the flood and reportedly gave King Solomon his magick ring to command the spirits to build his temple. Raphael is an archangel of magickal knowledge.

In Hebrew angelic magick, the order associated with this realm is the Beni Elohim, the "Sons of Gods," or perhaps more appropriately, the "Sons of Gods and Goddesses." The term is somewhat confusing and carries some mixed meanings. *Sons of God* is a term used for angels in general, though when it is linked to the somewhat controversial Elohim, as a plural form, some believe it refers to the children of the ancient gods. Mythically, this is seen as an order of beings not entirely angelic or human, but a mating of the two. Sometimes they are linked to or equated with a race of beings known as the Nephilim, the giants of the Old Testament. Generally, they are said to hold the qualities of Hod, of mind and memory and the powers of magick. This ancient race of giants was said to be the teachers of the arts and sciences who jump-started civilization. In that sense, they sound much like the godforms of Hod, and their reputation is mixed. Some sources see them as heroes, while most orthodox sources see them as demons. Such angels were sometimes known as the Watchers, and certain traditions of witchcraft and magick believe they are the forces that are called upon when we invoke the "watchtowers" of the four elements.

In a Christian version of angelic magick, the choir associated with Hod is simply referred to as the archangels. In this system, the archangels are the order of angels assigned to Hod, rather than being the princes of the sephiroth, each ruling over one sephira, as they are in most Qabalistic magick.

The divine name of Hod, Elohim Tzabaoth, means "God(s) of Hosts" or "God(s) of Armies," though the name might resonate more with Michael's martial attributes when thought of solely in military terms. Hod is the bottom sphere on the Pillar of Severity and does has some severe qualities to it, as the mind is cold in its logic. But a magician sees that the hosts or armies refer to more than just military might. A host or army is a large and diverse group that finds structure, purpose, and unity together. Logic is the process of searching through diversity of form and shape to see the patterns that bring things together or separate them.

The Vision of Hod

The Vision of Splendor is the experience of Hod. Quite literally, it is a direct experience of Hod, of the mental reality, and understanding the beauty and complexity of the mind. As the divine name Elohim Tzabaoth conveys, the vision of Hod is an experience of unity through diversity, and awakens the initiate to the infinite diversity of the universe and of the mind, both the personal mind and the Divine Mind—to know that, quite literally, anything is possible. Each of us comes to that awareness in a different way, and the vision might not be a "vision" at all, but a deep understanding that cannot really be put into words, for the expression of language in Malkuth is but a pale reflection of the true language in Hod.

To reach this level of awareness, the obligation is learning. One must seek to study, to understand, all aspects of creation. This is not just the study of magick, but the study of the world, the study of the self—including art, psychology, chemistry, astronomy, and, yes, magick. The ancient philosophers were not specialists focusing only on ritual. They knew the worlds around them, for all things are connected. The study of one topic, no matter how seemingly mundane, can bring great awareness of another realm of life, including spiritual development. In Theosophical terms, Hod is the orange ray, associated with science and technology, as many Theosophists believe that both modern and ancient technologies can usher in spiritual evolution.

The illusion paired with this obligation is order. For in study, we realize that there is pattern, there is unity, but there is no absolute order, at least not that we can perceive. As soon as we think we have things figured out, a new piece of information comes along to show us how wrong we are and that the universe doesn't always behave in the manner we think it will. When you study, you realize that no matter how much you know, there is always more to learn. That is part of the splendor, the infinity symbolized by the magician's loop, that is embodied by this sphere.

The virtue exemplified by one who has attained this level of consciousness is truthfulness. A Hod initiate understands the power of the word and will not use words falsely. One on this level will not betray the power of words or the power of the truth. On a practical level, the magician knows that as we gain power, each of our words gains power, and if we say something we don't intend, our magickal power can make those words a reality even when such changes were not our intention. One of the reasons witches learn the technique of neutralization (*ITOW*, Chapter 8) is to prevent this from happening as the power within them grows. One who is patently dishonest doesn't hold the power of Hod, and this is obvious in word and action. An interesting thing to note is that the tricksters in the sphere of Hod almost never lie. They are true to the letter of the word, yet often trick us out of seeing and hearing things the way we want to see and hear them or force us to step out of our assumptions.

Hod Magick

Like Yesod, Hod is inherently magickal, as so many of us link language to our magickal intentions. Hod helps teach us that all our thoughts and words are potential acts of magick, and we must master them in order to rise on the Tree. Its totems and images stimulate the mind and are linked to knowledge and the magician tricksters. The jackal has associations with Anubis, the Egyptian god who shares some psychopomp characteristics with other figures, as he is a guide to the dead and holds the knowledge of the afterworld. The two-headed snake is reminiscent of the serpent in the Garden of Eden. Though portrayed as the villain of the story, like Eve, some traditions see the snake as the hero, the one who presents us with knowledge. Hod magick is magick of knowledge, esoteric and arcane knowledge, as well as mundane common sense and good judgment. Magick that uses symbol, words, writing, and alphabets is completely in alignment with Hod.

Some witches write out their petition spells (*OTOW*, Chapter 12) in magickal scripts, translating basic English into an arcane-looking spell. Not only does this practice have power psychologically, but the alphabets themselves are said to be divinely received, and carry their own power inherent in their shape. To use them is to align yourself with magick.

A popular script among witches is known as the Witch's Alphabet, but is more appropriately called Theban script (figure 39). Attributed to Honorius the Theban, it has been used by witches as a code in spells and Books of Shadow, both as a magickal tool to confer power and to prevent uninitiated eyes from reading the rituals. In the

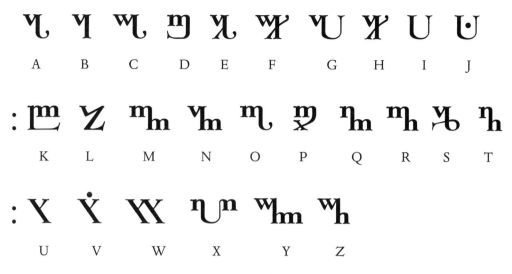

Figure 39: Theban Script

1980s and 1990s it fell out of popularity among modern witches in favor of the runes and ogham, but still is used quite frequently by those following older traditions. Each symbol has been equated with a Latin letter, making translation quite easy once you memorize the code. In his book *The Sacred Magic of the Angels*, ritual magician David Goddard states that Theban is a lunar-based angelic language, so it's no wonder that witches traditionally resonate with it.

As the eighth sphere, Hod is linked to the witch's image of the eightfold Wheel of the Year, the symbol of continual change. What is magick, if not change? Yet it is an understanding of the eternal and infinite, beneath the changes of life and the world's cycles, that is embodied by the infinity loop of the magician. The geometry of eight, the octagon and octagram, also are part of the yearly eightfold cycle of death, regeneration, and rebirth (figure 40).

In ceremonial magick, there is a ritual, akin to the Native tradition, in which one honors the four directions at four different times of day with Egyptian symbolism. It attunes the magician to the four elements, their elemental gateways, and the cycles of life in a daily flow. Traditionally, the ritual is done at sunrise, noon, sunset, and midnight, though modern magicians will use waking, midday, sunset, and bedtime as the

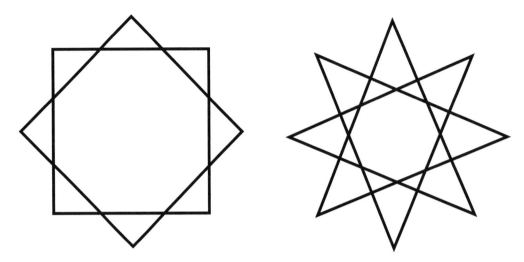

Figure 40: Octagrams

four personal boundaries of the day. These are liminal times, between day and night, light and dark, which in all traditions are considered times of power and alignment.

The traditional ceremonial magick version of this ritual is known as the Four Adorations and can be found in Aleister Crowley's *Liber Resh vel Helios*. It is based strongly on Egyptian symbolism and the traditions of Thelema. I first learned it as a part of Donald Michael Kraig's *Modern Magick* course and since then have adapted it to suit my own cosmology (see appendix IV). I encourage my students to do the same.

Exercise 14

Four Adorations

1. At sunrise, face east.—AIR

   Stand with your arms upright, as if you were supporting a heavy pole above your head.

   Make the Sign of the Practicus Grade—Air—Hod (traditionally, the Theoricus Grade). Say:

   Hail to Thee who art Ra in Thy rising, even unto Thee who art Ra in Thy strength.
   Who travelest over the heavens in Thy bark at the uprising of the Sun. Tahuti

standeth in His splendor at the prow and Ra-Hoor abideth at the helm. Hail unto Thee from the abodes of the night.

Make the Sign of Silence.

2. At noon, face south.—FIRE

Make the Sign of the Philosophus Grade—Fire—Netzach or the Triangle of Manifestation above your head. Say:

Hail unto Thee who art Hathoor in Thy triumphing, even to Thee who art Hathoor in Thy beauty, who travelest over the heavens in Thy bark at the midcourse of the Sun. Tahuti standeth in His splendor at the prow and Ra-Hoor abideth at the helm. Hail unto Thee from the abodes of the morning.

Make the Sign of Silence.

3. At sunset, face west.—WATER

Make the Sign of the Theoricus Grade—Water—Yesod (traditionally, the Practicus Grade), with the triangle over your belly, point down. Say:

Hail to Thee who are Tum in Thy setting, even unto Thee who art Tum in Thy Joy. Who travelest over the heavens in Thy bark at the downgoing of the Sun. Tahuti standeth in His splendor at the prow and Ra-Hoor abideth at the helm. Hail unto Thee from the abodes of the day.

Make the Sign of Silence.

4. At midnight, face north.—EARTH

Step forward with left foot. Make the Sign of the Zelator Grade—Earth — Malkuth. Say:

Hail unto Thee who are Khephera in Thy hiding, even unto Three who art Khephera in Thy silence. Who travelest over the heavens in Thy bark at the hour of the Sun. Tahuti standeth in His splendor at the prow and Ra-Hoor abideth at the helm. Hail unto Thee from the abodes of the evening.

Make the Sign of Silence.

Hod Pathworkings

Two paths already have led you to Hod: the intellectual judgment, and often the breakdown of the rational, that leads directly from Malkuth to Hod via the path of the Judgment/Aeon card; and the more gentle path of the Sun card from Yesod to Hod. The magician's lightning flash up and down the Tree doesn't always offer the easiest path, but some would argue that it's more holistic and therefore somewhat easier to process because no sephira is skipped, so no critical point of consciousness is missed when rising on the planes. Yet all paths need to be integrated to fully ascend in consciousness and embrace the godhead of Kether.

With those two paths embraced, there are three remaining paths that lead out of Hod and into the higher spheres on the Tree of Life. Hod and Netzach are balanced through the martial Tower card. The Tower is the destruction of what the mind and ego have created, to get back to the fundamental foundation that can be found in the primal Netzach. The path of the Devil connects Hod to Tiphereth. The misunderstood Devil is the gatekeeper, requiring us to renounce our self-made shackles and chains, created by our mind, to reach the higher self of Tiphereth. Hod also touches Geburah, its higher octave on the Pillar of Severity, through the path of the Hanged Man. You will have access to the power of Mars only through surrender to the higher will. Only through sacrificing the mental ego, redeeming it through the higher powers, will you have the full might of Geburah.

EXERCISE 15

Hod Pathworking

1. Perform the Lesser Banishing Ritual of the Pentagram (exercise 5) to clear your energy field and the space where you are doing this working. You also can do the Middle Pillar and the Circulation of the Body of Light (exercise 10), if you so choose, to open the middle path within you and energize you for the work.

2. While in this space, call upon the divine forces of Hod. Burn your eight orange candles and Mercury incense. Try knocking on your altar eight times. Vibrate the divine name of Hod, **Elohim Tzabaoth**, eight times. Call upon any of the Mercurial deities of the sphere, or Archangel Raphael.

3. To count down into a meditative state, do exercise 1 through step 7 (page 76).

4. Let the familiar world around you fall away, as if the material reality you know is only a façade and beneath it lies the beautiful garden of the Goddess, a veritable paradise surrounding you. The land around you becomes a vast primordial garden, the garden of Malkuth, the familiar garden of the four paths.

5. Go to the heart of Malkuth, to the Temple of Malkuth. Decide which path you wish to take to Hod. Will you travel via Yesod? If so, follow the path back to Yesod, as you did in exercise 12, and journey to the Temple of Yesod. Look for the gateway of the Sun to lead you to Hod. Will you travel directly to Hod, through the Judgment/Aeon card? If so, look in the Temple of Malkuth for the gateway of Judgment/Aeon, and enter it.

6. While on your path, reflect on the symbolism of the path. Let the images of the associated tarot card and path come to you. Let your thoughts and feelings be guided by the power of the path. Learn what you can of the path, and of your process, to expand your consciousness to Hod.

7. Feel the call of the orange sphere from your path. The orange light, glistening with quicksilver, calls to you. You are bidden to enter the gates of Hod. To enter, you might have to give a symbol of Hod, such as the divine name (Elohim Tzabaoth), the glyph of Mercury, or the name of a Mercurial god. Enter the orange light and feel your mind immediately sharpen and quicken. Your thoughts become like quicksilver, racing back and forth, yet your mind feels clear. You wander the world of the orange light and explore the realm of language and magick. Everything seems quick, full of energy and information. You may encounter some of the beings of Hod, such as the totems of the jackal or two-headed serpent or the figures of the four eights in the tarot.

8. Make your way to the Temple of Hod. You enter an eight-sided chamber that looks like a vast library or college, a place of learning. It appears to be made of language, and you perceive this information right in its very structure. You begin to realize that everything you perceive is just that—a perception, made of thought and language. You see gateways for all the paths in and out of Hod.

9. The figures of Hod are there waiting for you—perhaps the great Hermaphrodite, both male and female in his/her splendor. The Mercurial gods—Thoth, Hermes, Mercury, Odin, Loki, Nabu—could be there as well, together or separately. Archangel Raphael oversees the proceeding and may be available to converse with you. Ask to learn the mysteries of Hod in a manner that is correct and for your highest good at this time. They will teach you of the sphere's virtue, vice, and obligation, and perhaps give you a glimpse of the vision, the Vision of Splendor.

10. When done, thank all the beings who have communicated with you. They might offer you a gift, a token of their goodwill. If you accept, it is polite to reach within your being and offer them a gift of your goodwill in return. Be sure that what you give reflects the energy and intention you plan to put into the sphere's lessons.

11. Once you have said your farewells, leave the shrine and follow the path back. Return the way you came unless you feel guided to return via a different pathway and know the pathway back well. Now is not the time for further exploring, but is the time to go back and integrate these experiences. Return to the garden of Malkuth. Focus on the waking world you know, and feel it return around the garden.

12. To return to normal waking consciousness and end your journey, perform steps 15–17 from exercise 1 (page 78). You can close the temple by repeating the LBRP.

İNITIATION OF HOD

In our system of witchcraft and Qabalah, Hod is assigned to the air grade. In ceremonial traditions, it is given the rank of ③=⑧, the Practicus or Practitioner level, and the student is assigned to complete all of her or her intellectual studies, including a basic working knowledge of the Qabalah. An understanding of the theories and ideas of magick is required at this stage of initiation, but more importantly, an understanding of the truth is required.

Air

Spiritual Lesson: Truth

Spiritual Tools: Sword of Truth, Excalibur, Sword in the Stone, Fragarach

Fears and Challenges: Fear of Being Wrong, Insanity, Lying

Virtue: Honor

Psychological Function: Thinking

Stage of Learning: Knowledge

State of Matter: Vapor

Environmental Sphere: Atmosphere

Scientific Force: Electromagnetism

Periodic Element: Oxygen

Humor: Blood—Sanguine

Body System: Respiratory

Sacred River: Milk

Sacred Geometry: Octahedron

Celtic City: Finias

Qabalistic World: Yetzirah

Classical Age: Silver

Caste: Military/Ruler

Sufi Breath: In Mouth/Out Mouth

Mudra: Thumb and Pinky Finger

Planets: Venus, Mercury, Uranus

Fixed Sign and Animal: Aquarius—Human

Egyptian Animal: Hawk

Metal: Quicksilver

Chakras: Heart, Throat
Time of Day: Dawn
Season: Spring
Vowel Sound: E
Egyptian Syllable: As
Hindi Syllable: Pam
Tibetan Syllable: Ha
Modern Syllable: Leem
Obstruent Sounds: d, dh, t, th
Time Signature: 3/4
Hebrew God Name: Elohim Tzabaoth or YHVH
Archangel: Raphael
Angel: Chassan
Ruler: Ariel
Elemental King and Queen: King Paralda and Queen Eostar
Goetic Ruler: Amaymon
Enochian King: OROIBAHAOZPI
Stones: Agate, Calcite, Carnelian, Turquoise
Herbs: Hazel, Lavender, Peppermint, Sage, Skullcap

In mysticism, truth means many things. It is both absolute and subjective, which seems contradictory to the uninitiated. Living with paradox is the role of the initiate, and we have to reconcile many seemingly contradictory truths within us. There is an absolute divinity. That is the truth. Yet we learn that truth is not an absolute when it's personal. We can each have our own truth, or own view of the absolute divinity, creating the variety of spiritual traditions, religions, and philosophies. We know what resonates with us as truth, but it is not always what resonates with our friends, family, or community. The quest for truth is the quest for spirituality.

The quest for truth is double-edged, and appropriately the symbol of air, and of truth, is the sword. The desire to know the absolute and universal truth can lead to fanaticism. All our dogmatic, radical, and fanatical institutions usually are started with the best of intentions, yet when people cannot discern personal truth from universal truth, such groups attempt to force their own view of truth on others. No truth really can be forced on another. The flip side to the sword is falsehood—the fear of not finding the truth, the fear of being wrong, the fear of being insane, and the fear of speaking your truth and being judged by others. Fear, though seen as an emotion, has roots in the mind, in the realm of air. Fear is the paralyzing force that prevents us from finding and effectively speaking our truth.

The double-edged blade is found in many powerful legends, most often as Excalibur, the sword of King Arthur. The myths of the sacred sword often are tangled, as some see the Sword in the Stone and Excalibur as one and the same, while others see them as two separate swords. The Sword in the Stone was proof of Arthur's lineage and right to be king, for only he could draw it out of the stone of the Earth. Excalibur was a gift from the Lady of the Lake. Though potentially two separate swords, each is carried by the king, the sovereign defender of truth, of what is right in the land. Each is associated with a feminine element and figure—the Goddess of the Land and the Lady of the Lake—showing that the sword bearer is an intermediary between the goddess of the mysteries and the people. One who wore the scabbard was said to never die from wounds inflicted, so the truth will always have a defender.

In Celtic myth, a similar sword, the Sword of Nuada, or Sword of Light, is one of the four sacred treasures of Ireland. Some relate it to the mythical sword Fragarach, meaning "the answerer," giving it air associations, or "the retaliator." The sword also was said to be wielded by Manannan mac Lir and Lugh. Lugh later gave it to the hero Cuchulain. The sword is said to cut enemies in half, and no armor can stop it. All these figures are heroes, yet Nuada was the ruler of the Irish gods, the Tuatha de Danann. He went through a wounding, in some ways similar to Arthur's experience, and lost his hand in battle. He had to abdicate his throne, for the king must be perfect in body as well as spirit. Through magickal medicine, Nuada's hand was replaced by a silver hand and then later flesh and blood, and he was restored to the throne.

We must find our own inner truths, our own "answerer" sword. I envision the inner tool of the air element as the Sword of Truth. Armed with our own personal truth, along with the three other weapons of the elements, we easily can discern truth from falsehood in our lives, especially when we seek to fool ourselves into falsehood. The sword is the tool that lets us dissect our ego, then keep the parts that serve us and transform those that do not. Seek out the Sword of Truth on the elemental plane of air. For now, your "sword" might manifest only as a short blade and will grow with time and further training in the ways of the High Priest/ess.

EXERCISE 16

Elemental Air Journey Seeking the Sword of Truth

1. This exercise is an expansion of the experiences in Exercise 21: Journeying to the Realm of Air from *The Outer Temple of Witchcraft*. You can start by performing the LBRP before this journey to prepare yourself. Then perform exercise 1, steps 1–11, to go to your inner temple.

2. Orient yourself in the center of your inner temple. Look for the four doorways to the elemental planes. You might find that your guides bring you to the garden of Malkuth, with its four paths to the four elemental planes. In either case, orient yourself to the direction of elemental air. Hold your intention to journey to the realm of air and seek out the Sword of Truth. You know you might not receive it, but the journey will give you teachings to better master the element in your life so you can come back and claim it. Open the doorway of air, perhaps using the invoking pentagram of air as a magickal "key" (*OTOW*, Chapter 6). Enter the path or tunnel that leads to the elemental plane of air.

3. When you are fully in the realm of air, seek out the primal powers of the plane. Hold the intention to go to the heart of the realm, to seek out the elemental ruler, king, queen, archangel, or a deity of elemental air. Perhaps a guide will take you there directly, or you will have to search, and the searching will be part of your lesson.

4. When you reach the heart of the elemental plane, state your request to receive the Sword of Truth. The keepers of the sword might ask you why you think you are worthy, and you might have to convince them that you are

ready to do so. You could be challenged to demonstrate that you speak your truth. Meet the challenges to the best of your ability. If you are ready to receive the sword, then the elemental teachers will give it to you, often embedding it in your heart, or in your dominant, or projective, hand. If not, they will instruct you in what you have to accomplish to be able to receive the sword in the future. They may offer to tutor you in the ways of the air element, giving you an assignment to complete before you return.

5. Travel back from the realm of elemental air, back the way you came unless guided by the teachers to take another route. Go back to the inner temple. Close the gateway of elemental air in a manner similar to the way you opened it. If you used an invoking pentagram, then use a banishing pentagram now.

6. To return to normal waking consciousness and end your journey, perform steps 15–17 from exercise 1 (page 78). Close with the LBRP if you opened with it.

The ritual tool of the athame anchors your Sword of Truth in the world. British Traditional Wiccans often paint or carve specific markings into their athame, such as those shown in figure 41. Not being from a Gardnerian or Alexandrian line, I prefer the markings in figure 42. If you choose, mark your blade when you reconsecrate it after receiving the Sword of Truth.

HOMEWORK

- Do Exercises 14–16 and record your experiences in your Book of Shadows.

- Learn and practice the Four Adorations exercise, the traditional version or your own personally reconstructed version.

- Continue to practice the LBRP, Middle Pillar, and Circulation of the Body of Light rituals, traditional or personal versions.

First Side

The Horned God; Life; the Kiss; the Scourge; the Moon Goddess; and Scorpio, the sign of life, death, and resurrection.

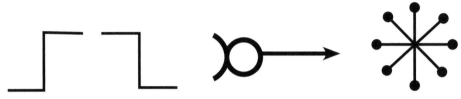

Second Side

The Goddess and God as a perfect couple; the sign for directing the power; the eightfold path and the Wheel of the Year.

Figure 41: Athame Markings, Traditional

TIPS

- Fill in the Hod correspondences and colors on your own Tree of Life drawing. Contemplate them as you add them to the image. Start memorizing these correspondences.

- To gain greater mastery over the realm of Hod and the element of air, be keenly aware of your thoughts and words, and in particular your conversations with others, to perceive truth and falsehood in your own words and those of others.

- Study appendix IV to deconstruct and reconstruct the Four Adorations to your liking and worldview, if you so choose.

- Pick one other reality map from appendix I to contemplate. Understanding a variety of worldviews will help you when you construct your own reality map.

First Side

On the far left is Libra, the sign of justice, balance, and the double-edged blade; and on the far right is Scorpio, the sign of life, death, and resurrection. Your own name, witch name, or motto should go in a magickal script between the two. Note that my nontraditional markings are drawn vertically, from top to bottom, rather than horizontally.

Second Side

The Triangle of the Triune Powers—Goddess, God, and Great Spirit; the five elements; the Moon Goddess; the sign for directing the power; and the Wheel of the Year, the cycles of life.

Figure 42: Athame Markings, Nontraditional

- Don't feel as though you need to master your Sword of Truth before going on to the next lessons. These are tools you can be using throughout the entire year-and-a-day course and beyond. Keep visiting the realm of air, and integrate these lessons into your daily life.

- When you do feel that you have received the Sword of Truth from the inner-world teacher of the air element, make sure to reconsecrate the blade that you have on your altar. If you have not already made markings on the handle, you can use the traditional or my nontraditional markings. If you work with several different sets of tools, you might find your inner Sword of Truth extending out from your hands to empower a blade and then retracting back within you when the rite is concluded.

LESSON FIVE
NETZACH

The seventh sphere on the Tree of Life is Netzach. Paired with Hod, it is the opposite of Hod in terms of temperament and process. Netzach is the realm of feeling, emotion, and sensuality. It is primal, bypassing language and words and getting right into feelings. Netzach is what occultists would call the *emotional plane*, but it also has a very strong physical component. Netzach is not nature manifest, but the drive of nature to survive, to procreate, to flourish and diversify. It is the green sap of the world flowing, but also the blood and passion within us. Some relate it to the green world of faeries, of nature spirits and primal beings, viewing it like a paradisiacal Arcadia. It is the realm of nature magick, and what would be called folk witchcraft, when compared to the scholarly temple traditions on the side of Hod.

In Theosophical material, Netzach would align with the force known as the *green ray*, an energy inherent in witchcraft and nature, but also the arts, including visual arts, music, and dance. It is the sensuality of creation and the enjoyment of such creations. A gregarious nature, along with the primal power of emotion, are found in Netzach. This realm is all about feelings and instinct, but its highest expression, what some would say is our highest natural instinct, is love. The name Netzach translates to "victory," and it is the victory of emotion over thought. It is really the victory or triumph of the beautiful primal emotions that many of us are out of touch with in our effort to be civilized. This victory is embodied by the experience of this plane, the Vision of Beauty Triumphant. When used appropriately, Netzach is the powerful balance to Hod. Both thought and feeling are needed in a truly realized individual.

Netzach

Meaning: Victory
Level of Reality: Emotional Realm
Parts of the Self: Desire, Left Hip
Experience: Vision of Beauty Triumphant
Obligation: Responsibility
Illusion: Projection
Virtue: Unselfishness
Vices: Selfishness, Impurity, Unchastity
Name of God: YHVH Tzabaoth (Lord of Hosts)
King Scale Color: Amber
Queen Scale Color: Emerald Green
Prince Scale Color: Bright Yellowish Green
Princess Scale Color: Olive flecked with Gold
Element: Fire
Planet: Venus
Image: Beautiful Naked Young Woman
Archetype: Love and Fertility Goddesses
Greek/Roman Deities: Aphrodite, Venus
Egyptian Deity: Hathor
Middle Eastern Deities: Inanna, Ishtar, Astarte
Celtic Deities: Branwen, Aine, Gwynhwyfar
Norse Deity: Freya
Hindu Deities: Lalita, Lakshmi
Archangel: Haniel (Archangel of Venus)
Angelic Order: Elohim (Creative Gods and Goddesses)

Choir: Principalities
Grade of Initiation: ④=⑦ Philosopher
Animal: Lynx
Planetary Vowel Sound: A (ay)
Resonant Letter: w
Musical Mode: Phyrgian
Musical Note: E
Tools: Lamp, Girdle, Rose
Incense: Rose, Red Sandalwood
Tarot: Seven of Wands, Swords, Cups, and Pentacles
> Moon—to Malkuth
> Star—to Yesod
> Tower—to Hod
> Death—to Tiphereth
> Fortune—to Chesed

Metal: Copper
Stones: Emerald, Rose Quartz, Tourmaline
Plant: Rose

The correspondences of Netzach are all Venusian and usually very appropriate for those on the witch's path. The altar should be decorated in groups of seven. The color scheme is green and sometimes pink. Green and pink stones, particularly emerald, green tourmaline, peridot, and rose quartz, resonate strongly with Netzach. Copper is its metal. The incense to be burned during these workings is rose or red sandalwood. Either can be worn in an oil or potion to align with the sphere. All the sevens of the four tarot suits resonate with this sphere. The paths leading to and from Netzach are associated with the Moon, the Star, the Tower, Death, and Fortune in the tarot. These cards can be arranged appropriately on the altar's edges to mimic the sphere's alignment on the Tree.

Entities of Netzach

The spirits of Netzach are intimately linked to the green world. The archetypal image of the spirit of Netzach is a beautiful naked young woman, the epitome of the love and fertility goddess. The planet associated with Netzach is Venus, and all the goddesses of love, pleasure, sensuality, sexuality, and fertility can be found in the domain of Venus. There is an error in thinking that Venus is simply "just" a love goddess, when the archetypal energy of Venus contains so much more. To the practitioners of the ancient world, love, fertility, and the land are intimately tied together. The fertility of humans, and their ability to attract one another to propagate the species, is directly linked to the fertility of the land and its ability to bring abundance. When Aphrodite rose from the foam of the ocean and stepped onto land, flowers grew in her wake as she brought fertility and beauty wherever she stepped. Aphrodite is also the patron of the arts, which fall in the realm of all things luxurious, sensual, and creative. There are images and tales of dark Aphrodite, and it must be remembered that the event of her birth, the spilling of Uranus's blood and genitals, also led to the creation of the Furies. There is a similar root to the words *Venus* (the Roman name for Aphrodite and the planet's name), *venereal*, and *venom*, all of which have links to the term *venifica*, a Roman term for *witch*.

The images of the Middle Eastern Venusian goddess have a broader range than what most pagans think of as Venus. Starting with Inanna, the Sumerian Queen of Heaven and Earth, we have a tale of a goddess linked with the great mysteries themselves, of descent to the Underworld, death, and rebirth. Similarly, the figures of Astarte and Ishtar teach the mysteries. The temple "prostitutes" of these Middle Eastern goddesses were purveyors not simply of sex but also of the mysteries of union, of Goddess and God.

In the northern European myths, we have the cultures of the Norse and the Celts with strong earth fertility goddesses. Freya, the Norse goddess associated with love, from whom we get our planetary name of Venus's day, *Friday*, for "Freya's day," is a goddess who encompasses far more than just romantic love. Speak to a Norse practitioner and equate Venus with Freya, and you will get a wonderful lesson. Freya is a goddess of magick, of seership and visions, of love, yes, but also of sexual power and, as a member of the race of gods known as the Vanir, of the land. She is master of the elements and keeper of powerful magick that even Odin has envied.

In the Celtic myths, the goddess we would associate with Venus is even harder to find, as almost all Celtic goddesses have a link to the land, and the fertility of the land, along with all their other associations. One could look to the goddess Aine. Others see the figure quite strongly in Branwen, divine sister to Bran the Blessed. Some modern pagans would see the story image of the goddess of love and fertility as Queen Gwynhwyfar from the Arthurian myth cycle. The Celtic Faery Queen also might appear in this realm. Some see the passionate side of the fey embodied in this realm.

In Egyptian magick, Isis has absorbed almost every goddess form, and many see her as the beautiful queen of heaven, associated with love, as she strives so hard, for love's sake, to help her husband in his trials against their brother Set. Hathor, as the nourishing cow mother, also can be associated with Netzach and Venusian principles.

The whole gamut of emotions, drives, and desires that go in to the need for fertility, be it land, human, or personal fertility, is the domain of the Venusian sphere. Looking at the deities associated with the morning and evening star, it is clear that they embody far more than simple romantic and sentimental love. Creativity and imagination are as much a part of this sphere as sex and relationships, for these qualities fall into the personal fertility of the artist and magician. The passions of artistic people are ruled by this sphere, as well as the desire of the mystic to evolve. The love one must have for the divine is almost like sexual love. Many traditions sublimate sexual passion in celibate orders, to direct the energy toward divinity. The nun is said to be a "bride of Christ," and priests are considered "married" to the Church. In their quest for divine union, most witches and magicians use sexual energy directly rather than sublimating it. All emotions lead higher up the Tree, and specifically higher up the Pillar of Mercy, to a higher octave of unconditional love. That is really where our drive and passion eventually lead us.

Venus and Netzach also have an association with Athena. Venus rules both Taurus and Libra, and with Libra, the sign of the scales, Athena is given a nod, being associated with wisdom, law, and the scales of justice. In magickal numerology, the number seven is associated with virginity, and thereby the virgin goddess Athena. Since no number below seven can enter into it without creating a decimal, it is considered a "virgin" number. Also, seven does not reproduce any of the numbers between one and ten through multiplication, so, having no children of the primary ten digits, it still is considered a virgin. In Greek gematria, the name of Athena adds to 77. Her other name, Pallas, adds to 343, or 7 x 7 x 7, also indicating volume. Her title Parthenos adds to 515, and 51.4 is very close to the angle of a regular heptagon, the seven-sided shape of Netzach. In fact, when you connect the lines of a seven-pointed star, you are said to be creating Athena's Web (figure 43).

The archangel of Netzach is a confusing correspondence. The name of the archangel changes with different sources and teachers, making its identity hard to know for certain. In an effort to make the four archangels of the quarters match the lower spheres (Gabriel—Yesod, Raphael—Hod, and Michael—Tiphereth), many assign Uriel, the archangel of the north and elemental earth, to Netzach. Netzach's nature and green associations make this connection plausible. Uriel's name is sometimes spelled Auriel, adding to the confusion, as certain practitioners see Uriel and Auriel as two separate beings and not simply two different spellings. Uriel is more appropriately assigned to the sphere of Da'ath and the planet Uranus. More often, the archangel attributed to Netzach is Haniel, the archangel of Venus. Haniel means "grace of God," and classically this angel is associated with fertility, love, herbalism, and the secrets of beauty and makeup.

The angelic order of Netzach in Hebrew magick is the Elohim. The Elohim is a term used to refer to God, yet controversially many of a pagan persuasion refer to a translation meaning "gods," both male and female. Those who follow this interpretation believe that the story of Genesis doesn't say that God created the world, but that the gods created the world. Putting the Elohim as a class of angels in the seventh sphere provides some interesting food for thought for Qabalistic magicians and witches alike. Those with a monotheistic view would put the various gods of the pagan pantheons in the sphere of Netzach, as the gods of nature. The divine name of Netzach, *YHVH Tzabaoth*, or "Lord of Hosts," refers to the divine in groupings, and Netzach is said to take the divine brilliant light of Tiphereth and refract it into the rainbow of nature, revealing many faces of divinity. The separation that occurs through the prism of Netzach is all of nature—not just the invisible spirits and gods but also their immanent manifested forms in nature. This sphere separates divine energy into everything—spirits, gods, people, rocks, trees, plants, animals, planets, stars, atoms, and molecules. Some translate the divine name as "Out of the One, Many," yet magicians still ascribe individual gods to the upper spheres. Both Netzach and Hod have associations with "hosts," with the divine expressed as a multitude of beings, or a pantheon.

To the witch and pagan magician, the Elohim are the "little gods," what might be referred to by some as the devas, the bright and shining spirits that guide nature on the terrestrial level but are not necessarily the prime moving celestial forces. In Netzach, the Elohim manifest so that each being guides an aspect of divine manifestation. They guide the drives and passions of creation, be it the Elohim that helps inspire the artist or musician, or the one that inspires attraction and lust, or the one that drives a nature spirit to bloom a flower in its domain.

In a version of Christian angelic magick, the choir ruling this realm is known as the Principalities. They are the angels of large collective groups, particularly nations. The Principalities are less personal than the archangels and angels, but are still involved in the affairs of humans and the guiding of civilization.

THE VISION OF NETZACH

The experience of Netzach is a tough one, for it is called the Vision of Beauty Triumphant. When a student first hears the name, it conjures up images of war, of battle, which are not what most of us think of when envisioning Venusian spirituality. The triumph isn't achieved through violence, but is a triumph that occurs within the soul. The initiate sees the beauty of nature, of the arts, of relationship, and in that inherent beauty, the divinity pervading all things shines through. Divine beauty becomes the dominant motivating force, rather than the difficulties and woes of life. They are still there. Netzach doesn't make problems magickally disappear. But the beauty, and the optimism that beauty brings, shine through the drabness and darkness, until the beauty of everything, even things aesthetically considered ugly, shines through. Those who endure harsh conditions of isolation or imprisonment need to experience this vision, and if they do, they can survive, because despite their conditions, they can find the beauty, and thereby the divinity, of the situation, regardless of the personal hardship. While Netzach's purpose upon descent is to divide the one light into many, to manifest nature, its vision granted to us as we ascend is to see that all things visible and invisible are connected, are one. Love and beauty are the redeeming factors of this sephira, because it is either through pure love or through seeing the beautiful patterns of connection that we find this union. The mystic with a profound sense of universal love can move through this sphere, but so can the quantum scientist, seeing the beautiful symmetry and patterns of connection in all things. One of the reasons so many religions encourage the initiate to be in nature, to study and observe nature, is to find this beauty, love, connection, and ultimately the sense of union that helps us gain greater mastery of this sphere and its creative impulses.

The obligation of Netzach is responsibility. The energy of this sphere is powerful, capable of doing as much harm as good. This is why passion, drive, and sexuality have been so demonized. They open us quickly to the other worlds and divinity, but they also are fraught with dangers. It's easy to use this power to manipulate others, to seduce without caring or get what you want for your own pleasure, or to create so obsessively that other aspects of life and relationships break down. The energy, though wild and filled with abandon, must be used measuredly and with discipline by the initiate. There is a time to be filled with passion and creativity, and there is a time to pay the bills. Knowing what time you are in is a mark of the initiate.

The illusion of Netzach is projection, which is found in every culture and community. It is where we see our own ideas, traits, feelings, or attitudes in other people. This occurs particularly when we externalize either "good" qualities in ourselves that we refuse to see in ourselves, or more commonly when we project blame, guilt, and responsibility onto others in an effort to ease our own feelings and defend ourselves against anxiety. When we don't want to take responsibility for these powerful drives, we project them onto another. Suddenly we are not the one to blame, so we then can direct all our powerful feelings onto another person. Those who have found the responsibility of Netzach tend not to be blame-oriented or project their own emotions onto others. When they do, they quickly realize it and take responsibility for their feelings and the situations they have created with their projection.

The virtue of Netzach is unselfishness. The initiate of Netzach and the Vision of Beauty Triumphant knows that this power is not ours to own, but is of nature. We are stewards, wards, and mediators of it, as humans and even more deeply as priestesses and priests of the nature religions. We do not own the gods, nor do they really own us, but we are in cooperation and partnership. In a strong and divine partnership, each side gives to the other unselfishly. In certain sexual tantra teachings, each partner is encouraged not to focus on his or her own pleasure but to unselfishly serve the partner. If both do this, their lovemaking will be exquisitely divine. The lover, priestess, and artist know the most powerful and creative moments flow through us. We become a channel for the energy, be it sexual power, magickal power, or even true creative power. The moment we try to control, hoard, or own the energy, the flow diminishes and we lose our inspiration.

The vice of Netzach is selfishness, the opposite of its virtue. Also described as impurity or unchastity, it conjures up an image of a moral code condemning sexual behavior, which isn't the case at all. Any specific behavior is permitted if it's guided by responsibility and unselfishness, even if it's not embraced by traditional society. Cora Anderson, co-founder of the Feri Tradition, speaking specifically on the Feri Tradition but with a sentiment that I think should apply to all witchcraft and magick traditions, says in *Fifty Years in the Feri Tradition*, "The Craft as we know it has a code of honor and sexual morality which is as tough and demanding as the Bushido of Japan and of Shinto…" When we act upon lust and desire without a sense of honor, a sense of integrity and most importantly divinity, then we enter the vice of Netzach. It also can be described as a lust for power rather than the lust for the divine, for spirit. Lusting after power simply for power's sake stops the flow of this energy, or corrupts and poisons it within us. Many magickal, sexual, and romantic relationships become toxic when one seeks to control this powerful flow to take charge and command of others. Many who enter the realm of the vice then use projection to justify their actions. This vice is not a prohibition on how you should relate to others sexually, romantically, artistically, or magickally, but a call to maintain our integrity in all these things. With integrity, we can do anything our will and desires call us to do. Without it, we sow the seeds of our own fiery destruction.

Netzach Magick

The ways of magick for the realm of Netzach are considered more primal and natural than those of the realm on the opposite side of the Tree. The key word of this sphere's message is beauty, on all levels, and we go to the realm of nature, of blooming and natural beauty, to find our tools and allies.

Netzach encompasses folk magick and fertility magick and charms. Much of the magick from *The Outer Temple of Witchcraft* would fall in the sphere of Netzach, the sphere of nature and fertility mysteries. But Qabalistic witches then take this magick to the next level, and traditionally it is developed through the teachings of the alchemist.

As Netzach is a sephira of fire, the lamp is one of its magickal tools. It's the lamp of awareness, for this terrestrial fire then leads to the fire of spirit, to the next sphere of Tiphereth. It's the fire of passion and burning for the divine at its highest level. On a more mundane level, it's the fire of illumination and magick, like a candle. In days past, lamp magick was cheaper and more common than candle magick. Oils can be infused with herbs, sprinkled with powders, or imparted with color to enhance the magick. Lamp and candle magick are similar in nature.

Along with the lamp, the girdle is another tool of Venus. Matching the apron of the worker of the temple, found in Hod and in Masonic tradition, the girdle is the working tool of the beauty goddess. Legends tell of Aphrodite lending her girdle to Hera to again attract Zeus. In the story of Inanna, it is her breastplate that she gives up at the fourth gate to the Underworld. The girdle is both protective of the chest/torso area and enhancing, embracing the feminine beauty. Like many tools of the priestess, the girdle has fallen out of fashion in many magickal circles in actual practice, but for our purposes here, the idea of the girdle of the goddess is what's important.

Lynx is the totem of Netzach. One might guess it's for its exotic look and luxurious coat. But the lynx is also traditionally known as a guardian of the mysteries, a guardian of the veil, and those who carry Lynx medicine are said to be keepers of the mysteries, just as temple priestesses were keepers of the mysteries.

Seven is the number of Netzach, and the geometries of Netzach are powerful. In modern Qabalistic magick, the seven-pointed star, or *septagram*, is associated with the Venusian goddesses, particularly Inanna, Ishtar, and Astarte (figure 43). Modern magi-

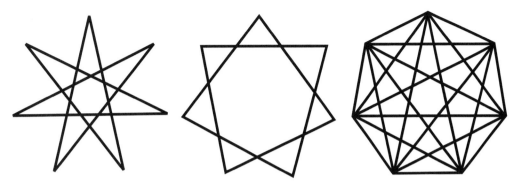

Figure 43: Septagram or Faery Star, Ceremonial Septagram, Athena's Web

cians have assigned one of the seven magickal planets to each point, though there are some disputes as to which point goes with which planet. Generally, the pattern of the star follows the pattern of the planetary days of the week. The symbol is used in rituals much like the pentagram and hexagram rituals of more traditional Qabalah. The seven ancient planets, and their corresponding Qabalistic spheres, are referred to as the Seven Heavens, for they are seven realms beyond and around the material world of Malkuth.

The septagram also is known to some as the Faery Star or Elven Star, aligning the user with the realm of the fey, of nature. It acts as a gateway between our world and the faery realm. I really like what author Francesca De Grandis says, in her book *Goddess Initiation*, about the Faery Star: "It symbolizes the secrets unique to you, the star you follow, a special star that is yours alone. The faery star reflects the secret mysteries that only you know. They can be found only in your own heart and deep within the cells of your body." Strangely enough, as often as patterns of seven repeat in our myths, the septagon and septagram are notoriously difficult to draw perfectly, as the angles are not exact degrees (the center angle is 51.428571, as opposed to a pentagon's 72), making the seven-sided figures as elusive as the faeries.

The symbol of Venus, popularly known as the feminine symbol, is the only planetary glyph on which we can encode the entire Qabalah (figure 44). The symbol divides the cross of the material world with the circle of the heavens, and shows how Tiphereth, the Sun, is the linking point between the cross and the circle. Venus and the Sun have always shared some golden associations and attributes, and this diagram helps illustrate the

Figure 44: Venus Symbol and the Tree of Life

special solar-Venusian relationship. Love is the foundation of the Tree of Life. Venus is the planet that most reflects the light of the Sun, and is described as a light bearer as well as a beautiful goddess.

The rose is one of the most perfect symbols of Netzach, as it is a symbol of beauty, love, and the mysteries on a variety of levels. Even those with no magickal background know there is something powerful about the rose. No wonder it has held sway in Western culture for so long as a symbol of romance, love, and spirit. As the lotus is the flower of the East and is visualized in the body's chakras, the image of the rose often is used by the Western magician for each of the power centers. Its complex but beautiful symmetry really demonstrates the powers of Netzach. Though the core of the rose is seen as a five-petaled flower, it still resonates with Netzach and Venus.

One of the best known, but often the least practiced or understood, rituals of modern ceremonial magick is the Ritual of the Rosy Cross. The rosy cross is a symbol with great meaning (figure 45). It is the sign of the Philosopher's Stone, the product of the alchemical marriage of our two natures. In a similar vein, it is the union of the female, the rose, with the phallic male, the cross. Some see the union of the two more in alignment with the image of the ankh than with that of the traditional cross. The rosy cross is the symbol of the Great Work. The image is found in the traditions of the Rosicrucians, Freemasons, Golden Dawn, Thelema, and O.T.O. The lamen of the Golden Dawn is the Rose Cross, and according to Israel Regardie, it combines all the attributes and correspondences used in the Golden Dawn.

Some see the Ritual of the Rosy Cross as gently evoking the blessings of the love of Netzach or, even more popularly, of Tiphereth, yet unlike the pentagram and hexagram rituals, it does not "light up" the astral realm as it creates sacred space. It is a quiet and meditative ritual. It is protective, but in a gentle way, as opposed to the more forceful banishing rituals of the pentagram and hexagram. Since it's done on the cross quarters, between the traditional quarters, it's not as "loud" astrally. Also, like the shaman's World Tree, it acknowledges the directions above and below, with the magician in the center. The Ritual of the Rosy Cross can be used for general protection (following the LBRP), for invisibility, to prepare for meditation, for general healing and blessing, and to seal your aura from outside influences.

When we look at the way the "rose" is drawn, as a crossed circle, we can see the glyph of Venus taken apart and the circle and cross placed one over the other. The connection to the Venus symbol, as well as the "disconnection" where the sphere of Tiphereth would be, show the unusual and powerful relationship between Netzach and Tiphereth, between Venus and the Sun. No wonder many magicians can't decide what this ritual really conjures, because in many ways it conjures the highest aspects of both sephiroth.

Rather than using a wand, blade, or even your finger as a tool in this ritual, a stick of incense traditionally is used. Any scent will do, though obviously rose or any Netzach or Tiphereth scent would work well.

Exercise 17

Ritual of the Rosy Cross

1. Perform the LBRP (exercise 5).

2. Light your incense stick.

3. Go to the southeast of the space and draw the circled cross with your incense stick, drawing the vertical line first and then the horizontal line, and finishing with a clockwise circle with the ends of the cross sticking out, similar to a Celtic cross rather than the planetary glyph for Earth (figure 45). Vibrate the divine name **Yeh-hah-shu-ah**. Finish drawing the circle on the syllable "shu" and then "stab" the center of the cross on the "ah" sound, filling the symbol with energy. As you do, you might feel an expansion of your aura or heart chakra, for this name has to do with the Pentagrammaton, a symbol of divine love and the saving principle embodied by the sacrificed gods (see chapter 5).

4. From the center of the cross, keep the incense stick level and trace one-quarter of a circle, moving clockwise to the southwest.

5. Repeat steps 3 and 4 three times more, drawing the rose cross in the southwest, northwest, and northeast, finally tracing a circle completed in the southeast. Do not repeat the circled cross in the southeast.

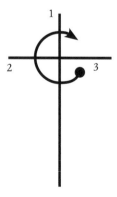

Figure 45: Circled Cross

6. Turn and face inward, toward the northwest. Raise your incense stick high and make a diagonal line from the southeast to the northwest. Stop in the center of the space and make the rose cross above you, vibrating the divine name (**Yeh-hah-shu-ah**).

7. From the center of this cross, continue onward to the northwest corner. Connect this line of smoke to the center of the rose cross in the northwest corner, without redrawing the rose cross. It is already present.

8. Turn and face inward, toward the southwest. Keep the incense stick at arm level, but pointed down. Move toward the southeast. Stop in the center of the space and make the rose cross below you, vibrating the divine name.

9. From the center of this cross, continue onward to the southeast corner, incense stick still pointed down. Connect this line of smoke to the center of the rose cross in the southeast corner. Vibrate the divine name here, but do not redraw the rose cross.

10. Keeping the incense stick level, retrace the one-quarter of the circle, moving clockwise to the southwest corner. When the incense stick is in the center of the previously drawn rose cross, vibrate the divine name. Do not redraw the rose cross.

11. Mirroring steps 6–10, turn and face inward, toward the northeast. Raise your incense stick high and make a diagonal line from the southwest to the northeast. Stop in the center of the space, at the previously drawn rose cross above you, and again vibrate the name. Continue onward to the northeast corner, connecting to the center of the rose cross in the northeast, without redrawing or vibrating the name. Turn inward again, facing the southwest, holding the incense level but pointing down. Move toward the southwest, stopping in the center to connect to the center of the rose cross below you, and vibrate the divine name. Complete the circuit to the southwest.

12. Keeping the incense level with the center of the rose crosses, move clockwise from southwest to northwest, northeast, and southeast, and return to the southwest.

13. Draw a large rose cross over the original smaller rose cross in the southwest, as big as you can make it. As you draw the bottom half of the circle, vibrate **Yeh-hah-shu-ah**. When you draw the top half, vibrate **Yeh-hoh-vah-shah**.

14. Go to the center of the space, facing east, and imagine the six rose crosses in golden light and the six rose circles in red, in the four cross quarters of SE, SW, NW, and NE, and above and below you. The lines connecting them are bright white, creating a sphere around you.

In the next chapter, as part of the hexagram rituals, you will learn the Analysis of the Key Word, which traditionally concludes the Ritual of the Rosy Cross, though the version of the ritual in exercise 17 is still very effective on its own. Though the Rose Cross can seem very complicated at first read, try doing a read through and walk through the steps, and you will see the pattern forming before you. With a little practice, it will become one of the easiest ceremonial rituals to perform. Unlike the LBRP, Middle Pillar, and Circulation of the Body of Light, the Rose Cross does not need to be done regularly. Use it when you feel called to do so.

FLUID CONDENSERS

Though many think the art of herbal magick is reserved for folk witches and medicine people, the plants of the green world, as well as the metals and minerals of other natural magick, play a strong role in the traditions of Western ceremonial magick. In fact, much of the lore that is passed on as witchcraft today was preserved through the writings of ceremonial magicians throughout history. Understanding the divine through nature is a key component of Western magick that many people overlook.

One particular form of natural magick prevalent in ceremonial magick and later absorbed into some of the more formal and ceremonial traditions of the Craft is the use of fluid condensers. The teachings have been used and adapted by many witches, particularly those associated with Alex Sanders and Sybil Leek. The teachings go back to the writings of P. B. Randolph and his work on sexual magick, and the writings of Franz Bardon.

Condensers are substances used to store etheric energy. They are used in magick to release energy with a particular kind of vibration. They usually are used to store the power of elemental energies, but also can be used for the planetary powers. Theoretically, Qabalistically inspired condensers, based on the sephiroth, could be formulated as well. They are made out of infusions of herbs and metals, preserved with alcohol. Though fluid condensers are usually liquid, some formulas call for solid or even gaseous substances.

The term *fluid condenser* refers not to the physical state of matter but to the idea that etheric energy is a subtle fluid flowing between the planes. The substance that contains, or condenses, this vital energy becomes the fluid condenser storing the energy. Technically, a wand, mirror, box, or other tool can be considered a fluid condenser, though now the term usually refers to herbal, metal, or mineral mixtures. They act as a battery, storing energy for later direction. The original teaching on this material is based on the concept that this flowing etheric fluid is associated with the two poles, described as electric and magnetic, but esoterically is identified with yang and yin or god and goddess. The fluid condenser is used in magick to anoint tools, paint charms, consecrate gems, make and paint statues, make magick mirrors, anoint the body, asperge the temple, cast spells, make poppets, and create magickal constructs. You also can add small amounts of a fluid condenser to incense or to food and drink, but use only the nontoxic ones and the ones to which you have no medical contraindications.

To a witch, a fluid condenser sounds like a potion, yet potions usually are made with a specific purpose, if not a specific goal, in mind. You create a love potion that can be used many times, yet do not tie it specifically to a particular kind of lover. A fluid condenser is associated with an elemental or planetary power, giving it a much wider range of use than most potions. Fluid condensers also are made a bit differently than most potions. They are said to be one of the most effective methods of storing, concentrating, and using magickal energy, so much so that many witches who are trained in the art use them only sparingly. Others use them for almost all magickal operations once they have been created. They can retain their power for many years, as long as the bottles storing them are corked tightly, kept out of the light, and shaken before every use. Though condensers work through the resonance and virtues of the herb used, the subtle forces are said to accumulate in the process of making them in a manner that is somewhat unlike that of traditional potions and herbal remedies.

A traditional ingredient in most fluid condensers is gold tincture. Franz Bardon was a great proponent of the belief that even tiny traces of gold can add great power to a fluid condenser. Gold is the perfect metal for the alchemist, as it's a symbol of the Sun, creative energy, and enlightenment. Using gold tincture is a way to add power to any condenser. The most traditional method of making gold tincture is to dissolve a gram of soluble gold chloride in twenty grams of distilled water. Store in a glass bottle.

An alternative method is take a piece of gold—nine carat or better, such as a gold ring or medal that has been properly cleansed physically and esoterically—and heat it in a flame, holding it safely with tongs. Drop the ring in a nonmetal bowl of water. Ideally, use filtered rainwater collected in a nonmetal container during a thunderstorm. Distilled or spring water also can be used. Protect yourself from any sputtering or scalding. Retrieve the gold with a nonmetal utensil, such as a heatproof glass ladle or cup. Repeat this process six times to saturate the water with gold atoms.

Scott Cunningham, in *Magical Herbalism*, suggests simply adding a small piece of gold to the mixture and then straining it out before use. I like to use a gold vibratory essence, made like a flower essence or gem elixir in sunlight, as described in chapter 13 of *The Temple of Shamanic Witchcraft*. Colloidal gold, though not as common as colloidal silver, is available as a health supplement. Many modern witches, feeling gold has solely a masculine energy, also use similar methods to make or obtain a silver tincture, and use silver tincture instead of, or in addition to, the traditional gold tincture.

There are two basic types of liquid fluid condensers and two methods of creating them. The formulas for fluid condensers can be simple or complex. Simple formulas contain one herbal ingredient, while complex ones have a mixture, ideally an odd number of herbs, though some would choose a number of herbs based on the corresponding sephira, if applicable. A Jupiter condenser could be made using four Jupiter herbs, for the fourth sphere of Chesed, rather than an odd number of herbs.

Fluid condensers can be created through an infusion or tincture process. Both are valuable, but the infusion process is quicker and has more steps. Both generally are begun when the Moon is waxing. For the tincture method, the New Moon is preferred, but if you are making planetary condensers, keep in mind planetary days and hours over Moon phase and sign. Some believe condensers should be made at dawn, while others prefer sunset or midnight. All of these are times of power. Choose the one that works best for you and the condenser's nature.

Infusion Process

Put one to two handfuls of the herb or herb mixture, usually dried, into a nonmetal pot. Pour cold water over the herbs to cover them completely. Let the mixture boil for about twenty minutes, with the lid on the pot. Cool it, again with the lid on, for at least thirteen minutes. Strain out the herbs. Place the pot back on the stove and heat it with the lid on, letting the mixture evaporate until it is at about half of where it was when you started. Let the mixture cool, and when ready, add to it an equal amount of clear alcohol, such as vodka or gin.

Tincture Process

Put one to two handfuls of the herb or herb mixture, usually dried, into a glass jar. Cover the herbs with alcohol, such as vodka, gin, or unadulterated grape brandy. Let the mixture steep for at least twenty-eight days in a warm, dark location without opening the jar. Then strain out the dry herbs.

Straining should be done through linen, not metal sieves, though I must admit I've used plastic strainers on occasion. At the end of either process, add 7 to 20 drops of your gold tincture. I usually use around 10. If you are using the fluid condenser for your own and only your own purposes, you can further increase its potency by adding a few drops of your blood, menstrual blood, and/or sperm/vaginal secretions. Shake vigorously, strain again, and then store in a dark glass bottle, away from direct light. Make sure you label and date it.

Though few works talk about "charging" the substance, basing its power on its natural vital electromagnetic correspondences, I think it's appropriate to call upon the spirit of the herb to aid you and be in alignment with your condenser. I also recommend thinking about the element, planet, or general spirit of the condenser when holding it and shaking it. Traditionally, chamomile is the first fluid condenser a magician makes, resonating with both fire and air, as well as the Sun and Mercury.

Elemental fluid condensers are great substances to aid you in working with a specific element. By now, you should be familiar with the purpose and energy of each element. Any spellcraft or visionary working involving a specific element can be enhanced by using the appropriate elemental condenser. Some formulas are based not on the traditional herbal usage but on other substances, such as juices or oils, as found in the Strega traditions taught by author Raven Grimassi. You can make your elemental condensers from these substances or from simple or complex herbal formulas, using the herbs listed for each element in the first four sephiroth lessons of this book.

Fire

Fire fluid condensers work best through combustion and are said to drive your will into reality. One method of using a fire condenser is to moisten paper or linen with your condenser as you focus on your intention. Fill the paper with your intention and then burn it, releasing the energy of your intention mingled with the condenser. A "hot" liquid such as a chili sauce or juice can be used as a fluid condenser. You can pass the fluid condenser through a candle or lamp flame a few times to truly align it with the element of fire as you concentrate on the element. Ideally, a fire fluid condenser should be made on a Tuesday or when the Moon is in a fire sign.

Air

Air fluid condensers work best through evaporation and are best for matters of communication, learning, and mental health. They also are used to aid respiratory health. A tried and true method of using an air condenser is to add a few drops of the condenser to water. Either heat the water on the stove, letting it evaporate into steam, or simply let the water in the bowl evaporate over time, particularly if working on a long-term intention. When adding the condenser, focus on your intention, infusing the charged water with your will. As the water evaporates, it releases your energy into the world to make your work a reality. When making an air fluid condenser, you can hang the bottle out on a tree for a short time or simply breathe life into it before you bottle it. A peppermint infusion is the most traditional base for an air condenser. Ideally, an air fluid condenser should be made on a Wednesday or when the Moon is in an air sign.

Water

Water fluid condensers are best for spiritual and emotional healing, as well as love, union, and psychic development. Mix a few drops of the condenser with water, preferably spring water or rainwater, not distilled water. Fill the water with your intention and then add it to a body of water, preferably running water, such as a river or stream, to manifest. Water condensers manifest through the mixing of waters. When making one, you can place the bottle in a natural body of water and later retrieve it. A great base for a water condenser is the juice of a water fruit or vegetable, such as a melon. Ideally, a water condenser should be made on a Monday or when the Moon is in a water sign.

Earth

Earth fluid condensers are best for manifestation and are said to influence, command, or compel others to do as you wish. They work through absorption in the ground and decomposition back to the basic elements of the earth. Take a small amount of condenser, either alone or mixed in rainwater. Load the fluid with your intention and pour it onto the ground where people will not be walking on it. If you are in an urban environment, you can pour it into a flower pot or into a hole cut into a large apple or potato that is then left out somewhere to rot or buried someplace. Along with the traditional earth herbs, mineral oil can be used for an earth fluid condenser. In either case, try to place the earth condenser in the ground after making it, to collect the earth energies, and then retrieve it later. The best time to make an earth fluid condenser is on a Saturday or when the Moon is in an earth sign.

Planetary fluid condensers embody the energies of one of the seven traditional planets. They are said to have a very strong and spiritual influence on the witch and can be used in both planetary and appropriately matching sephiric operations. Though any herb ruled by the planet can be used, alone or in combination, there are several herbs that traditionally are considered important to the planet, much as certain specific scents are ascribed to the sephiroth.

Planetary condensers should be made on the day and hour of the planet when possible (*OTOW*, Chapter 12). Magickal timing helps align the substances to the corresponding force, particularly for herbs that are ruled by two or more planets. Magickal timing stimulates the proper force to condense in the substance, for the time when something is "born" continues to influence its growth.

Planet	Time Period	Herbs
Sun	365 days	Rosemary, St. John's Wort, Eyebright, Cinnamon
Moon	28 days	Cucumber Skin, Willow Leaves or Bark, Mugwort
Mercury	10–11 months	Hazel, Valerian, Acacia, Mint
Venus	11 months	Vervain, Yarrow, Rose
Mars	22–24 months	Stinging Nettle, Untreated Tobacco, Pepper
Jupiter	12 years	Sage, Lemon Balm, Oak
Saturn	29.5 years	Horsetail, Poplar, Comfrey

For planetary condensers made through the tincture method, you might wait for a symbolic amount of time based on the planetary return. Using the length of some planetary returns, such as Saturn's twenty-nine years, usually proves to be impractical, so the number can correspond to days or months, depending on your patience, and still have a numerological resonance with the planet. I might do twenty-nine months for a powerful Saturn fluid condenser to keep for many years, or make a twenty-nine day condenser if I need it quickly. Those astrologically inclined might plan the exact moment of the planetary return, using an ephemeris or astrological software.

Universal fluid condensers, super powerful and all-purpose, can be made in several ways. An elemental universal fluid condenser contains equal amounts of each elemental condenser, with a few more drops of gold tincture, if applicable. A planetary universal condenser is made the same way, but with equal amounts of all seven planetary condensers. Here are the ingredients for a traditional universal condenser that can be used for any purpose, including elemental and planetary workings:

Angelica root

Sage leaf

Cucumber skin

Chamomile flowers

Violet leaves or flowers

Melon seeds

Tobacco leaves

Oak leaves or bark

Peppermint leaves

Solid fluid condensers can be made out of the herbs remaining from liquid fluid condensers. The herbal material is scattered on a paper towel to dry and then ground to a powder, traditionally by hand in a mortar and pestle, though modern mages might use an electric grinder. These powders can be added to potions and incense, scattered to the winds, dissolved in liquids, buried, or burned. They also can be added to paints, lacquers, or clay or used to fill hollow spaces in ritual tools, such as filling a hole drilled into a wand.

NETZACH PATHWORKINGS

Netzach pathworkings can be particularly intense. The pathway of the Moon card, which leads directly to Netzach from Malkuth, in its most basic form represents emotional magick, intuition, and separating illusions from truth. On its deeper initiatory level, the path of the Moon is the emotional trauma, in life or in vision, that awakens one to the higher reality. It can be quite difficult to describe this process in words. In a Netzach pathworking, we can revisit profound emotional memories that we carry with us. The emotional nature of personal traumas can prevent us from putting a certain amount of intellectual detachment and distance between us and the experience. With this pathworking, we can process the emotions and learn valuable lessons from the experience that will aid our overall spiritual evolution.

Many people enter magickal traditions believing that magick is only a form of psychology and auto-suggestion, and even when they have real experiences, the reality of magickal energy beyond the realm of the mind can be difficult to truly accept. Since Netzach really circumvents the realm of the mind, its experiences can be very intense. That's not to say that these experiences are detrimental or even unenjoyable. They most often are positive, and sometimes the emotion experienced is intense pleasure, love, or bliss. But they are intense emotional experiences for many explorers. One of my students, an experienced healer and shamanic practitioner who is well versed in all the teachings that precede level four, was almost overwhelmed by Netzach, experiencing a huge cathartic emotional release that led her to a greater understanding of the next step in her spiritual development. The pure emotions overwhelmed her because in this realm, she no longer had the ability to intellectualize and label specific emotions. She couldn't rest and reflect upon them, but simply had to experience them. The emotions had to "flow" or "burn" through her like a natural phenomenon, until they had run their course and the experience ended. Reflection took place after the ritual and pathworking.

The remaining paths out of Netzach can aid in our education of the sphere, giving us further context for the primal emotional sephira. We climb the Tree to Tiphereth through the thirteenth trump of the tarot, Death. The old personal self must die and be reborn to ascend to the heavens of Tiphereth. Ruled by the zodiac sign Scorpio, Death shows us that through intense emotional transformation we can rise, moving from the lower totem of Scorpio, the scorpion or snake, to the higher totem, the phoenix.

We climb from Netzach to Chesed, its higher octave, through the much gentler Wheel of Fortune card. While at first glance this card indicates a change in luck for the better, the true secret of the Wheel is to master at least two selves—the self that is personal, and on the wheel of life, experiencing ups and downs, and the self that is in the center, eternal, timeless, and bornless. By holding both images, you have both the personal energy of Netzach, below the veil, and the higher perspective of Chesed, above it.

EXERCISE 18

Netzach Pathworking

1. Perform the Lesser Banishing Ritual of the Pentagram (exercise 5) to clear your energy field and the space where you are doing this working. You also can do the Middle Pillar and the Circulation of the Body of Light (exercise 10), if you so choose, to open the middle path within you and energize you for the work. Performing the Ritual of the Rosy Cross is not required, but would be very appropriate to prepare yourself and the space for a Netzach pathworking.

2. While in this space, call upon the divine forces of Netzach. Burn your seven green candles and Venus incense. Try knocking on your altar seven times. Vibrate the divine name of Netzach, **Yod Heh Vah Heh Tzabaoth**, seven times. Call upon any of the Venusian deities of the sphere, or Archangel Haniel.

3. To count down into a meditative state, do exercise 1 through step 7 (page 76).

4. Let the familiar world around you fall away, as if the material reality you know is only a façade and beneath it lies the beautiful garden of the Goddess, a veritable paradise surrounding you. The land around you becomes a vast primordial garden, the garden of Malkuth, the familiar garden of the four paths.

5. Go to the heart of Malkuth, to the Temple of Malkuth. Decide which path you wish to take to Netzach. Will you travel via Yesod? If so, follow the path back to Yesod, as you did in exercise 12, and journey to the Temple of Yesod. Look for the gateway of the Star card to lead you to Netzach. Will you travel directly to Netzach, through the Moon card? If so, look in the Temple of Malkuth for the gateway of the Moon, and enter it.

6. While on your path, reflect on the symbolism of the path. Let the images of the associated tarot card and path come to you. Let your thoughts and feelings be guided by the power of the path. Learn what you can of the path, and of your process, to expand your consciousness to Netzach. Let go

of your analytical mind, and feel the primal creative powers of Netzach rise within you.

7. Feel the call of the green sphere from your path. The green light magnetically draws you in. You are bidden to enter the gates of Netzach. To enter, you might have to give a symbol of Netzach, such as the divine name (YHVH Tzabaoth), the glyph of Venus, or the name of a Venusian god. Enter the green light and feel the primal powers. Feel your blood, your life force, quicken. Feel your drives and desires. Walk the emerald-green sphere of Netzach and explore the primal passion of magick. Everything seems beyond time, yet full of life. You might encounter the beautiful creatures of Netzach, teachers in the lessons of creative fertility.

8. Make your way to the Temple of Netzach. You enter a seven-sided temple, a temple of the old world, beautiful and ornate. You smell the incense, see the flickering lights, feel the temperature, and hear the music. Your senses come alive. You see and feel the gateways out of Netzach, to the other spheres.

9. The figures of Netzach are residing in the temple. The beautiful goddess of this sphere awaits you. She might manifest as Aphrodite, Venus, Inanna, Freya, or any of the other goddesses of this realm. Haniel and the lynx are available as guides for Netzach journeys. Commune with the beings of Netzach, but don't be surprised if they are not big on words. Ask to learn the mysteries of Netzach, how to embody the virtue by working through the obligation and how to avoid the vices by not succumbing to the illusion. Ask for the Vision of Beauty Triumphant in a manner that is correct and for your highest good.

10. When done, thank all the beings who have communicated with you. They might offer you a gift, a token of their goodwill. If you accept, it is polite to reach within your being and offer them a gift of your goodwill.

11. Once you have said your farewells, leave the shrine and follow the path back. Return the way you came unless you feel guided to return via a different pathway and know the pathway back well. Now is not the time for fur-

ther exploring, but is the time to go back and integrate these experiences. Return to the garden of Malkuth. Focus on the waking world you know, and feel it return around the garden.

12. To return to normal waking consciousness and end your journey, perform steps 15–17 from exercise 1 (page 78). You can close the temple by repeating the LBRP.

İNITIATION OF NETZACH

Out of all the elemental grades in Qabalistic magick, I find assigning an element to Netzach the most difficult to understand and integrate. Though fire fits Netzach, the Venusian sphere, as most witches learn it, encompasses much more complexity than what most think of as strictly fire energy. Fire is the hardest element to describe, and most use terms such as soul, spirit, will, drive, energy, and desire as key words. Though Venusian principles are described as very primal, the archetype of drive is usually mated with her twin, Mars, while Venus is described as seductive and magnetic in her passion. The planet Venus draws to it what it desires, rather than going out and getting it, as implied in the fire imagery. It literally traps whatever energy passes through its atmosphere, holding on to it. Its magickal-magnetic qualities have more in common with lunar goddesses and the water element than with fire. Alan Moore, in his magickal comic book series *Promethea*, describes Venus as an ocean of emotion. That imagery works well for me and suits many of my own pathworkings. In astrology, Venus rules two signs, Taurus and Libra, an earth sign and an air sign, respectively. With these attributes—fire, water, earth, and air, all in one sphere—it's no wonder that Netzach has associations with the realm of nature, the fey, and the gods of the world. Aphrodite was born of blood and violence, yet came out of the foaming ocean. As she walked upon land, flowers bloomed. She then became the goddess of love and attraction, the force and desire of procreation.

The Philosopher grade ④=⑦ is the ranking of Netzach. The initiate undergoes moral training, to master the passions and drives, rather than be mastered by them. The devotion of the initiate to the magickal order also is tested. In this course, you might find that the testing of the fourth grade comes not as devotion to a specific order (though if you are a member of a coven, it might manifest on the physical plane as coven challenges), but as your devotion to the brotherhood and sisterhood of witch-craft. Whether we come from a broken or unbroken lineage is for scholars to debate, but spiritually, we are the inheritors of the ancient secret wisdom, the spiritual initiates of the mystery traditions, and when the time is right, we aspire to be members of that inner-plane order of teachers and healers, the Hidden Company or Withdrawn Order. Here, our passions, if not mastered, might derail us from the path of enlightenment. Here, our will must be mastered and applied to knowing our True Will.

Fire, like will, manifests on a variety of octaves and becomes our teacher in refin-ing our will. There is common fire—the candle flame or blazing bonfire—but it is terrestrial in nature. Yet there is always something supernal about it, as the first un-derstanding of fire comes from the flashes of heavenly lightning. The heavenly fire is akin to the celestial fire of the stars, the campfires of the gods and angels in old myths, and the hidden essence of our true natures. According to the Orphic mysteries, hu-manity's origins lie in the starry heavens, a teaching that Aleister Crowley reiterated in his Thelemic tradition. Terrestrial fire releases the hidden fire within all matter, the trapped energy, the spark of spirit residing in all things, awaiting release. Lastly, there is the secret fire of the initiate, the personal life force or kundalini, that must be refined. As it is refined, it forms our True Will. It is the fire of Prometheus, the occult fire that burns within all priestesses and priests in our order. It is that internal fire that is the true refining fire of the alchemist, and the fire we truly connect to in the fire festivals and fertility celebrations. Fire is our key to refinement.

Fire
Spiritual Lesson: Victory
Spiritual Tool: Spear of Victory, Spear Luin, Spear of Destiny
Fear and Challenge: Self-Sabotage
Virtue: Courage
Psychological Function: Intuition
Stage of Learning: Wisdom
State of Matter: Plasma

Environmental Sphere: Mangasphere
Scientific Force: Strong Force
Periodic Element: Nitrogen
Humor: Yellow Bile—Choleric
Body System: Nervous
Sacred River: Honey
Sacred Geometry: Tetrahedron
Celtic City: Gorias
Qabalistic World: Atziluth
Classical Age: Gold
Caste: Priest/ess
Sufi Breath: In Mouth/Out Nose
Mudra: Thumb and Ring Finger
Planets: Sun, Mars, Jupiter, Pluto
Fixed Sign and Animal: Leo—Lion
Egyptian Animal: Cat/Lion
Metal: Gold
Chakras: Solar Plexus, Crown
Time of Day: Noon
Season: Summer
Vowel Sound: I
Egyptian Syllable: Am
Hindi Syllable: Ram
Tibetan Syllable: Ra
Modern Syllable: Ra (Ka)
Obstruent Sounds: b, v, p, f
Time Signature: 9/8
Hebrew God Name: YHVH Tzabaoth or Adonai
Archangel: Michael
Angel: Aral
Ruler: Seraph
Elemental King and Queen: King Djinn and Queen Litha
Goetic Ruler: Göap
Enochian King: OIPTEAAPDOKE

Stones: Ruby, Citrine, Pyrite, Tiger's-Eye
Herbs: Chili, Heliotrope, Nettles, St. John's Wort, Sunflower

The fire tool of the True Will is traditionally the wand. Ceremonial magicians use several different types of wands to differentiate various energies being used, from a specific fire wand, to a lotus wand, to a rainbow zodiac wand. Witches have one all-purpose wand to serve all needs, though we might own several different physical wands, rods, and staves. Each one can be used for multiple reasons, from casting circles to charging objects.

In mythology, the staff or, even more commonly, the spear, is the symbol of this fire. In the Celtic myths, the fourth gift is the Spear of Lugh. Lugh is the Irish Celtic figure who led the Tuatha de Danann into battle. His tale begins with Lugh knocking on the door of Tara, the court of these gods. Through demonstrating his many skills, he quickly evolved from an outsider to a powerful divine figure. The festival of Lughnasadh was originally a celebration of the memory of his foster mother, Tailtiu. Lugh's story is a great tale of following your drive, your will, to manifest your highest divinity. His journey was not an easy one, yet he found success through pursuing what he felt called to do, with honor and courage. The translation of his name often is disputed, but he has been connected to solar, light, and lightning imagery, as well as "flowing vigor," which is perfect, as the fire element and his spear represent the power of drive. We need vigor to accomplish our True Will, and when we are connected to our True Will, we have access to an almost unlimited flow of energy.

The spear that aided Lugh in his victories was a very magickal tool indeed, needing not to be wielded by his own hand, or personal will. It acted like a living creature, struggling against its restraints until it was released, flashing fire, and tearing through the ranks of the enemy. The only way to quiet it was to steep its head in a potion of sedative poppy leaves. Other tales say the spear was so intensely hot, it had to be held down in the Cauldron of the Dagda, to prevent it from burning down everything around it. From the city of Finias, it was known as the Spear Luin, the flaming or flashing spear. It also is associated with the spear of Cuchulain, the Gae Bulg, or notched spear, made from the bone of a sea monster, as Cuchulain and Lugh were strongly associated with each other. Lugh had a second spear, known as the Spear of Assal, that would always hit its target and return to the thrower upon command.

In our modern mythologies identifying the four Celtic gifts with Christian mythos involving the grail, the spear was associated with the Spear of Longinus, the spear said to have pierced Christ's side. It was worked into the grail quest as the Holy Lance or Bleeding Lance. It later was associated with Nazi occultism and World War II mythology. Known as the Spear of Destiny, this spear was said to render its user undefeatable in battle. Seeking to be victorious, Hitler sought out and, some say, found and lost this ancient artifact, explaining his defeat.

The concept of destiny, or victory, associated with the fire element and spear is powerful. Most witches do not believe in destiny, for destiny implies there is no work to be done, no choice. Things simply happen because they are meant to happen. This doesn't fit our cosmology, or experience, for we know we must be active participants in the process. Destiny is really where opportunity and action meet, as a former business teacher of mine used to say. Destiny can pass us by if we are not vigilant.

When we find our True Will, and wield the stellar forces of light and power, anything in the purview of that True Will is possible. Anything. Though there will be struggles and work on the human level, an energy to accomplish a goal flows through the witch in a way that can't be understood before an aspect of the True Will is found. When we are following our True Will, we are in our center, peaceful, yet also working, striving, and moving forward. The paradox is that though we are putting forth effort, our work feels effortless on some level.

I think of this force more as victory than destiny, for victory implies more conscious action. When we hold the Spear of Victory in our hand, like Lugh's spear, it moves of its own volition, yet we must unleash and guide it, and take responsibility for it, or it will be power out of control. But when we hold the Spear of Victory appropriately in our hand, with our True Will in action, we can accomplish anything. For now, your "spear" might manifest as a smaller wand, scepter, or stick, and will grow into a spear or staff size with time and further training in the ways of the High Priest/ess.

Exercise 19

Elemental Fire Journey Seeking the Spear of Victory

1. This exercise is an expansion of the experiences in Exercise 13: Journeying to the Realm of Fire from *The Outer Temple of Witchcraft*. You can start by performing the LBRP before this journey to prepare yourself. Then perform exercise 1, steps 1–11, to go to your inner temple.

2. Orient yourself in the center of your inner temple. Look for the four doorways to the elemental planes. You might find that your guides bring you to the garden of Malkuth, with its four paths to the four elemental planes. In either case, orient yourself to the direction of elemental fire. Hold your intention to journey to the realm of fire and seek out the Spear of Victory. You know you might not receive it, but the journey will give you teachings to better master the element in your life so you can come back and claim it. Open the doorway of fire, perhaps using the invoking pentagram of fire as a magickal "key" (*OTOW*, Chapter 6). Enter the path or tunnel that leads to the elemental plane of fire.

3. When you are fully in the realm of fire, seek out the primal powers of the plane. Hold the intention to go to the heart of the realm, to seek out the elemental ruler, king, queen, archangel, or a deity of elemental fire. Perhaps a guide will take you there directly, or you will have to search, and the searching will be part of your lesson.

4. When you reach the heart of the elemental plane, state your request to receive the Spear of Victory. The keepers of the spear might ask you why you think you are worthy, and you might have to convince them you are ready to do so. You could be challenged to demonstrate your power to enact your will. Meet the challenges to the best of your ability. If you are ready to receive the spear, then the elemental teachers will give it to you, often embedding it in your heart, or in your dominant, or projective, hand. The spear might not even be a spear, but a wand, staff, or torch. Any of these tools will fulfill a similar function in this context. If you are not ready, they will instruct you in what you have to accomplish to be able to receive the spear in

the future. They may offer to tutor you in the ways of the fire element, giving you an assignment to complete before you return.

5. Travel back from the realm of elemental fire, back the way you came unless guided by the teachers to take another route. Go back to the inner temple. Close the gateway of elemental fire in a manner similar to the way you opened it. If you used an invoking pentagram, then use a banishing pentagram now.

6. To return to normal waking consciousness and end your journey, perform steps 15–17 from exercise 1 (page 78). Close with the LBRP if you opened with it.

This is the final journey that will help you gain greater mastery of the elements for deeper workings. If you receive the Spear of Victory, then you should reconsecrate your wand with this new energy. You can add something to it as well, such as a carving or mark. Some traditions will put on it the planetary glyphs for the first seven planets—Sun, Moon, Mercury, Venus, Mars, Jupiter, and Saturn. If your wand is wooden, you can oil the wand, both to preserve it and to add more power and increase its attunement to you, through the continual stroking of the tool with your body and energy field. Linseed oil is a particularly good choice, though use an appropriate oil that suits your own style of magick. Essential oils or, even better yet, fluid condensers, can be added to the oil. A small hole could be added to the wand and filled with a solid fluid condenser, then sealed with wax. Obviously, a fire fluid condenser would be best, though you also could use an all-purpose universal fluid condenser or one made from an herb that is one of your "power" herbs (*TOSW*, Chapter 13). If your wand is not wooden, you can still anoint it with fluid condensers, oils, or potions to increase its energy.

HOMEWORK

• Do Exercises 17–19 and record your experiences in your Book of Shadows.

• Learn and practice the Ritual of the Rosy Cross, the traditional version or your own personally reconstructed version.

• Continue to practice the LBRP, Middle Pillar, and Circulation of the Body of Light rituals, the traditional or personal versions. You can continue with the Four Adorations, but it's not a requirement.

TIPS

• Fill in the Netzach correspondences and colors on your own Tree of Life drawing. Contemplate them as you add them to the image. Start memorizing these correspondences.

• To gain greater mastery over the realm of Netzach and the element of fire, be aware of your passions, drives, and wants, and how they may serve or sabotage your life's purpose. This is not denial of passion by any means, but the healthiest expression of your desires.

• Study the Ritual of the Rosy Cross and deconstruct and reconstruct it to fit your worldview, if you so choose.

• Pick one other reality map from appendix I to contemplate. Understanding a variety of worldviews will help you when you construct your own reality map.

• Don't feel as though you need to master your Spear of Victory before going on to the next lessons. These are tools you can be using throughout the entire year-and-a-day course and beyond. Keep visiting the realm of fire, and integrate these lessons into your daily life.

• If you work with several different sets of tools, you might find your inner Spear of Victory extending out from your hands to empower a wand and then retracting back within you when the rite is concluded.

LESSON SIX
TIPHERETH

At the very heart of the Tree of Life is the sixth sphere, that of Tiphereth. Perfectly positioned as the connection point between the upper branches and the lower trunk in the middle of the Pillar of Mildness, between the Pillars or Severity and Mercy, Tiphereth is the lower point balancing the Ethical Triangle of mystical consciousness. The name of the sephira translates to "beauty" or "harmony," for that is its position and power. It is the harmonious center around which all things revolve.

Astrologically, the sixth point on the Tree is assigned to the Sun, as the solar body is both the heart of the Tree and the center of the solar system. The Sun provides us with interesting clues to the nature of the solar sephira. In astrology, the Sun indicates the personal self, the personal core of the individual, but spiritually oriented astrologers know that the zodiac Sun sign does not describe so much who you are personally but who you are learning to be, and there are many evolutions within each sign. The evolution of the personal, ego-based self, which is very solar in nature since it seeks to be at the center, leads to the transformation to the higher self, the magician's Holy Guardian Angel (HGA).

This Holy Guardian Angel acts as an intermediary between us and the highest divine self of Kether. Tiphereth itself is known as the Lesser Countenance, the lower octave of the Greater Countenance in Kether. In this Qabalistic scheme, the HGA and the individual personal ego associated with the Sun both correspond with Tiphereth, demonstrating to us that the ego and HGA are not that much different. Our introspective spiritual work transforms our ego consciousness, uniting it with the HGA. If we do not do the introspective work of the first four elements and sephiroth, then we can mistake the untransformed ego for the HGA, resulting in a journey of delusions and an overinflated sense of achievement. There is said to be a veil between the lower four spheres and Tiphereth, called the Veil of Paroketh. It is the veil of illusion, and in a sense, it is not really there. It is what separates fire from spirit, two elements that have much in common yet are different. Spirit is the entry point into the macrocosm, while fire is still part of the fourfold system of the microcosm. A magician, through training, knows both ritualistically and intuitively how to part the veil and have a clear, or at least clearer, vision of Tiphereth, while those who stumble into its power see with the veil of illusion over themselves and do not understand the beauty of this level of awareness. They are trapped in ego, while the true nature of Tiphereth is selfless, is sacrifice and harmony with the whole, the transcendence of the selfish side of the ego.

As a solar level of consciousness, Tiphereth could be said to be the first "ray" of en-"light"-enment in the process of magickal evolution. When we truly connect to Tiphereth and integrate its vision, we are utterly changed. When we make regular communion with this Holy Guardian Angel, we feel a sense of peace, balance, and harmony. There is a sense of detachment, yet an even deeper sense of love. It sounds contradictory, yet through this mystery we learn about the witch's Perfect Love, an unattached divine love, the rosy love that can be ever flowing through us if we are open to it. The true lesson is understanding that this step is one of many steps, not the final step, for there is always another level of the spiral of evolution for those of us incarnated. The universe continues to unfold in harmony, in ever more complex cycles of beauty, even when it feels like chaos or disaster to us from our human perspective.

Tiphereth

Meaning: Harmony

Level of Reality: Higher Astral

Parts of the Self: Imagination, Solar Plexus, Heart

Experience: Vision of Harmony, Understanding the Nature of Sacrifice

Obligation: Integrity

Illusion: Identification

Virtue: Dedication to the Great Work

Vice: False Pride

Name of God: YHVH Eloah va-Da'ath (Lord God of Knowledge)

King Scale Color: Rose Pink

Queen Scale Color: Yellow Gold

Prince Scale Color: Salmon Pink

Princess Scale Color: Golden Amber

Element: Spirit

Planet: Sun

Image: Sun Child

Archetypes: Sun Kings, Young Gods, Sacrificial Gods

Greek/Roman Deities: Apollo, Helios, Dionysus, Adonis, Bacchus

Egyptian Deities: Ra, Osiris, Horus

Middle Eastern Deities: Tammuz, Dumuzi

Celtic Deities: Lugh, Mabon, Lleu, Bel

Norse Deity: Balder

Hindu Deities: Krishna, Vishnu

Archangels: Michael (Archangel of Protection/Fire) and/or Raphael

Angelic Order: Malakim

Choir: Powers

Grade of Initiation: ⑤=⑥ Adept

Animals: Lion, Phoenix

Planetary Vowel Sound: I (ee)

Resonant Letter: y

Musical Mode: Ionian (Natural Major)

Musical Note: F

Tools: Lamen, Rose Cross, Cube

Incense: Frankincense
Tarot: Six of Wands, Swords, Cups, and Pentacles
      All Knights/Princes (young males)
      Temperance/Art—to Yesod
      Devil—to Hod
      Death—to Netzach
      Justice—to Geburah
      Hermit—to Chesed
      Lovers—to Binah
      Emperor—to Chokmah
      Priestess—to Kether
Metal: Gold
Stones: Topaz, Ruby, Yellow Diamond, Citrine, Pyrite
Plant: Sunflower

For this month's study, arrange your altar with the correspondences of Tiphereth. Use six yellow or gold candles in a hexagram formation. Use the colors yellow and gold and any solar symbols on the altar. Use frankincense as your incense in these workings. Wear gold jewelry. If you have made gold tincture, take a drop before working Tiphereth meditations and magick, or use a few drops in your chalice during solar rites. Yellow and gold stones, such as citrine and pyrite, are appropriate. Place the Tiphereth cards on the altar as a mandala, using the sixes of all four suits and the young male court cards, either princes or knights of all the suits, as well as the major arcana on the pathways leading out of Tiphereth, arranged at the edge of the altar. This time, you will have a more balanced altar mandala than you did with Hod and Netzach.

ᛖNTITIES OF ᛏIPHERETH

The solar gods are the obvious figures of Tiphereth. Solar figures come in many forms. The traditional image of this realm is the Sun Child. Look at the traditional image of the Sun card of the tarot. Though it connects Yesod and Hod on the Tree of Life, the imagery of the Sun card is the imagery of Tiphereth: a young, golden child, on the back of a white horse, open, jubilant, and free, riding eyes open into the next adventure. Sun mythologies are centered around the divine child, known as the Child of Light, or Child of Promise, for the child is the promise of the light renewed moving from the dark of the year to the light. Though most of us no longer pay close attention to the movement of the Sun in our daily lives, in ancient pagan cultures, the cycles of the Sun, the primary source of life, played a vital role in the cultural consciousness.

The outer Sun of the heavens is not the only manifestation of the child. For initiates, the Sun represents the mysteries of the inner child. The physical Sun corresponds to the spiritual solar forces within us. Descending into darkness is not just a metaphor, but an energetic reality. The Child of Promise must be found in the dark of the Underworld, and resurrected through our actions. Today, in our modern pop-culture psyche, we talk about the wounding of the inner child, and how to care for and play with our inner child. Though this sounds trite, it's an absolute necessity. To the magician, the inner child is not just a psychological construct or metaphor for innocence, but a real, living energy within each of us and reflected in the heavens. The movement of the Sun reflects upon the movement of the inner solar child, for they both are equal in the eyes of the magician. No wonder so many of us experience depression in the darkness of winter. The stories of the Child of Light can help us understand astrological and astronomical cycles, and the inner cycles they reflect. They are maps to find and nurture our inner light and relate to the God of the mysteries in a new way.

In the myths of the Sun Child, he is lost in the Underworld. We see this mythology played out in the sacred stories of Mabon and his mother, Modron, and of Pryderi and Rhiannon. Both children were taken unexpectedly to another realm, beyond the reach of the mother. The relationship of the Sun with the mother principle, be it the Earth as mother, or the universe, is very important. Both the Irish Lugh and the Welsh Lleu had an unusual relationship with their mother, and grew up in the care of another who guided, nurtured, and trained them. These figures grew up to be the warriors and potentially the king figures we also associate with the solar force. The idea of the golden regent, ruling from the solar heavens, is a popular form of the divinity. It's one of the reasons European royalty has been associated with lions.

Gods such as Apollo, Helios, and the Celtic Bel relate to light and our relationship with consciousness, as well as the seasons. Though Apollo and Helios are not considered ruling gods, next to Zeus and Chronos, rulers of the Olympians and Titans, respectively, they still play a prominent role in their mythologies and pantheon, being the light of the day. Not much is known of the figure Bel, yet one of the most prominent fire festivals, Beltaine, is named for him, indicating a place of prominence in his culture.

In the Egyptian cosmos, the Sun plays so vital a role that one of the many creation stories attributes the Sun lord Ra with the sole creation of the universe from an act of divine masturbation. To the Egyptians, the Sun was the primary generating force. The incarnation of the Sun's power on Earth continued through Ra's lineage, first through Osiris, the first pharaonic god figure. Osiris, and the gods who are similar to him, are the ones who bring the solar force down to the land, bridging the heavens to the Earth. He is a green and horned god, though most modern art does not depict him that way. He is the light within the vegetation of the Nile. He is the flowing of the waters to fertilize the land. He is growth, civilization, and enlightenment, here on Earth. Osiris was sacrificed through the act of his brother Set. Some interpret it as an act of vengeance and malice, while others think the original concept of Set was as the initiator, the teacher, or simply the forces of destruction in the cycle of life. Osiris then was resurrected through the magick and love of his sister-wife, Isis, and became lord of the dead, as he was lord of life. The solar energy descends into the Underworld, but it rises again through his son, Horus, another deity with solar and pharaonic attributes, though Horus also shares some martial attributes with the war godforms.

Though not quite the same story, we see similar themes in all the sacrificed god images, from the Norse Balder to Dionysus, Bacchus, Adonis, Tammuz, and Dumuzi. They all have strong goddess associations, with either a mother figure or a lover. Often this figure has Venusian qualities to her. These godforms are all transitions between the child figure and the divine king. Their resurrection brings them into full adulthood, yet with a dual perspective of life and death, one world and the next. They then become mediators between the gods and humanity, as the fertile land and plants are the main exchange between humans and later divinity, as humans both consume and make offerings and sacrifices to the divinities.

In the angelic realm, the archangel assigned to Tiphereth is another point of contention for Qabalists. Based on our previous work in Hod, I assign Michael as the archangel of the solar sphere. As Michael is the elemental ruler of fire, I find his presence quite strongly here. Out of all the angelic figures, it appears that Michael is one who is working with more people on a conscious level in magickal and New Age traditions. He seems to be guiding the people of the Earth in a very strong way, and this primary position, I believe, comes from this central sphere of solar light.

Other traditions of Qabalah put the archangel Raphael in Tiphereth, for the divine healing he brings. One of the main reasons the archangel of air is associated with Tiphereth is because this sphere is part of the middle pillar, the pillar traditionally assigned to the element of air. I would make the compromise that Raphael is a subruler, along with Michael, of Tiphereth, while Michael is a subruler, with Raphael, of Hod.

The traditional order of angels associated with Tiphereth is usually the Malakim, or Malachim, the kings or masters. They are the angels of balance and centralization, said to keep solar systems and galaxies balanced and harmoniously connected to one other. On a microscopic scale, they maintain the balance of subatomic particles in atoms and molecules. They also are known as Lords of the Pivot, as they hold the center. Many associate these angelic kings with the elemental kings. Though we think of the traditional elemental kings as elemental beings, their highest expression of these elements is said to be in Tiphereth, where the elemental world and the heavenly world intersect. The kings act as the "higher selves" of the elemental realms. The elemental archangels then act as even higher selves, guiding the kings.

In another version of angelic magick, the Powers, also known as the Dynamisms, Potentiates or Authorities, are associated with this sphere, maintaining the power and harmony of the universe. They are responsible for maintaining the balance between the heavens and the material world, guiding consciousness primarily through religious development and guiding lost souls who cannot find the afterlife.

The divine name of Tiphereth is YHVH Eloah va-Da'ath. Starting with the primal power of the Tetragrammaton, this name represents divinity, knowledge, and balance. This manifestation of divine power is the balance point, allowing us to access the divine core, the HGA, when it is vibrated.

THE VISION OF TIPHERETH

The spiritual experience of Tiphereth is twofold, much like the sphere's nature itself. We don't often think of the solar powers as twofold. Unlike the Moon and planets, the Sun doesn't have a dark side and a bright side. Tiphereth's twofold nature is not dual or polar, light and dark, but is due to the unique position it has in bridging the microcosm and personal spheres with the macrocosm and celestial spheres. It is the linking point between the circle and the cross of the heavens and Earth. That is why it can be associated both with the solar ego and personality and with the divine consciousness of the Holy Guardian Angel.

The experience of Tiphereth is known as the Vision of Harmony. That sounds all well and good, as this sphere is in the center of the Tree, the harmonious anchor around which all revolves. But the dual nature of the vision manifests as a secondary lesson, differentiated from, yet interlinked with, the first. This lesson is known as Understanding the Nature of Sacrifice, also known as the Crucifixion Mysteries. That doesn't sound like harmony, at least not at first. A lot of pagans studying Qabalah start to back off at this point, feeling the Christian symbolism is too inherent in the system to be overcome. One must keep in mind that the origins of the system, as we know it, are found in Hebrew Kabbalah, which has been greatly influenced by Middle Eastern magick and paganism. Our pagan world is filled with sacrificial gods.

Sacrifice does not necessarily mean crucifixion, nor does it mean altar sacrifice of plants, animals, or people, as potentially was done in the old pagan world. The true nature of sacrifice is the sacrifice of self, not in body, but in spirit, to spirit. Our sacrifice is of the personal self to the higher self, to embody our divine self more fully. We need not die bodily, or become a martyr to any cause, to enact this, but as we approach the higher spheres, their experiences are of an initiate, of a priestess or priest, who must become a minister, a servant, to the divine forces, and mediate them into the world. It is through this sacrifice, this offering of the self to spiritual service for the greater good, that we, too, become like the center of the Tree. We become the star, the solar fire of Aleister Crowley's Thelema.

To attain this understanding of sacrifice and actually accomplish it, you must maintain integrity in all that you do. That's not to say that you can't make mistakes.

This realm does not confer godlike omniscience, but it does require that you take responsibility for your mistakes, see yourself and others as objectively as possible, have compassion both for others and yourself, and integrate the lessons of the four elements to work with the integrity of spirit. To truly master Tiphereth, you come into harmony and union with the Holy Guardian Angel. The HGA is said to truly reside in Tiphereth. The virtue of this sphere is dedication to the Great Work, which is both fulfilling your True Will in this lifetime and the Great Work of all lifetimes, enlightenment and union with the source. Once you understand sacrifice and harmony, you continue to strive toward the Great Work. In Crowley's writings, the word Abrahadabra, a play on the word Abracadabra, is said to be the word, the name of the Great Work in this next age, and can be used as a magick word in rituals to strengthen your dedication to the Great Work.

The illusion of Tiphereth is identification. Sometimes seekers of the mysteries identify strongly with this sphere, and its powers, yet haven't done the work to integrate it fully, and they think they are already "there," with no further work to do. Other times, these practitioners identify so strongly with a divine force or patron deity that they take on many of the attributes of the patron god, but forget they are still human and still have to do their own personal spiritual development work. They forget about their own spiritual identity in favor of aligning with a deity. And who wouldn't want that, at least at first? The deities are grand, powerful, and mysterious, things we often aspire to be. But in their sacrifice to the divine, these seekers lose sight of their own Holy Guardian Angel, their own higher self, and lose sight of many other facets of the divine, focusing only on one being. This type of identification can lead to mystical delusion, martyrdom, and dogmatic theology, believing only one view of the divine is correct. The harmony conceived of is an illusion, for the harmony of Tiphereth must be dynamic, not static, adjusting to the changes and flow of creation.

The illusion goes hand in hand with the vice of Tiphereth, false pride. It is not the pride of an accomplishment well earned, but the false pride of something assumed without the work having been done to support it. The nature of sacrifice is both strong and loving, strong in conviction yet compassionate toward others. The Sun both heals and grows, and burns away what doesn't serve. If you see only one side of its power, you are missing the vision. You are not truly in balance, in dynamic harmony with the unfolding universe.

Tiphereth Magick

All solar magick is the province of Tiphereth, from seasonal celebrations that are really about harnessing solar energy to turn the Wheel of the Year, to traditional success, health, and inspiration magick. Like the sphere itself, solar magick is dual in nature. In one sense, it is transcendent, self-sacrificing, and performed for the good of all. It is "white" magick in the sense that it is ritual to find enlightenment, commune with the higher self, and become more conscious and aware. Basically, it is magick to become a better human being, living as a divine being in the world of form.

On the second side, solar magick is magick for material success, as the Sun has so much material power. It is for physical health and vigor. It is for financial success, as its metal, gold, is also one of the most highly valued metals on the market. Solar magick is for general career success, to shine like gold, or be the "golden child" in any situation, where you can do no wrong and everything you touch is successful. It is the magick of poetic inspiration, to fuel the imagination of artists, musicians, and writers by their muse, as the Greek Muses had a strong connection to the worshippers of Apollo. But this second side occurs only when you become more in tune with the nature of the higher reality and your higher self. As you attune to your higher self and follow your bliss, your divine calling, you naturally are more successful, healthy, and inspired. So all solar magick leads back to this highest form of magick, becoming a better person. It is part of the nature of the Vision of Harmony and Understanding the Nature of Sacrifice.

Gold and all other solar gems and plants correspond to the work of Tiphereth. Gold is the symbol of the Sun, of Tiphereth, of the Philosopher's Stone, as it is a pure and untarnishing metal, both solid and malleable. It possesses qualities of both male and female, the central point of balance in the spiritual evolution of metals. Alchemists once believed that all metals in the earth eventually would evolve into gold, just as all humans eventually would move toward enlightenment. Frankincense is the traditional incense and oil, though bay and acacia also are used. Grape vines have a strong connection to this sphere through the Dionysian imagery. The traditional stones associated with the sixth sphere are topaz and yellow diamond, though for some reason ruby is sometimes listed. I find ruby to be more of a Geburah stone myself. Citrine, pyrite, yellow calcite, and anything golden yellow works well to direct this energy.

The totems associated with Tiphereth also have strong alchemical imagery. The lion and the phoenix are the primary animals. The lion of Leo, the zodiac sign ruled by the Sun, is a natural for a Tiphereth correspondence with its fiery disposition. The phoenix is the highest expression of Scorpio, a water sign, but sometimes is described as fiery in its intensity. Another totem associated with Tiphereth is the pelican, as the pelican also is associated with alchemical retorts used to refine and perfect the substances of the laboratory as the alchemist refines and perfects him- or herself in spirit.

All the sixes of the tarot suits are associated with Tiphereth, and as you look at each, you will find points of balance and harmony in the elemental journey. The young male figures are associated with Tiphereth, be they knights in the traditional tarot setup, or princes. They are the embodiment of the young solar king, the Tiphereth energy, in each of the elemental journeys. They are the potential Child of Promise in earth, air, fire, and water.

The geometry implied in the sixth sphere is the hexagram. The six-pointed star is seen as the symbol of Jewish faith, as the Star of David, but the symbol has a much broader meaning. As part of the mandala of the heart chakra, it is the union of Goddess and God, Shakti and Shiva, in the center of the body. It is the union of fire and water in the alchemical triangles, giving birth to the symbols of air and earth, all implied in the hexagram shape.

In the modern resurgence of sacred geometry, a hexagram-based figure known as the Flower of Life is said to be the basic sacred structure underlying all form (figure 46). It consists of nineteen interlocked circles, surrounded by a larger set of two circles. Brought to popular consciousness through the work of the controversial New Age figure Drunvalo Melchizedek and his Flower of Life workshops and books, the five Platonic solids, the underlying sacred geometry shapes of creation, can be mapped upon the image of the Flower of Life, through the related image known as Metatron's Cube

Figure 46: Flower of Life

(figure 47). The cube is not literally a cube, but a mandala based on the Flower of Life in which all the centers of the circles are connected through straight lines. Many figures of sacred geometry, including the very Tree of Life, can be mapped upon the Flower of Life (figure 48). Study of and meditation upon the flower can yield great insights into the nature of life. The physical source of life, water, has a hexagonal molecular structure, seen in the formation of snowflakes. While the pentagram is the common shape of organic life, the hexagram, as the structure of function and order, is associated most strongly with inorganic creation. Water, quartz crystals, vitamin C, uranium hexafluoride, sugar, pencil graphite, and aspirin all have hexagonal formations.

In ceremonial magick, the hexagram is the star of the macrocosm, as the pentagram is the star of the microcosm. One symbolizes the heavens, while the other symbolizes the terrestrial world. If we place the Sun in the center, as it is on the Tree of Life, and move the position of Saturn to the top point, we have all the planets of the cosmos arranged on the star (figure 49). This symbol is used in magick for the hexa-

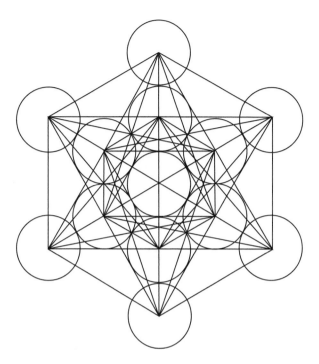

Figure 47: Metatron's Cube

gram rituals, to banish or invoke planetary forces, just as the pentagram rituals can banish and invoke elemental forces.

The Lesser Banishing Ritual of the Hexagram, or LBRH, sometimes known simply as the Banishing Ritual of the Hexagram (BRH), is one of the fundamental rituals of ceremonial magick, done regularly like the LBRP. It is said to banish all "positive" influences. Students hear that and wonder why on Earth they would want to banish positive forces. Remember that, in magick, "positive" doesn't necessarily equal "good." It is simply an energy, like yang to yin. More accurately, one can say that the LBRH banishes all celestial forces, while the LBRP banishes all terrestrial forces. Together, they leave a working space completely neutral.

Some forces, both terrestrial and celestial, are not inherently bad, but can be in conflict with the working you have planned. I teach a lot of workshops in public places. Often the room has been used recently by others for ritual, healing, and meditation, and

Figure 48: Flower of Life with the Tree of Life

their "vibes" linger. These vibes aren't bad or evil, but they're not in harmony with what I want to do in the room next. If I'm doing a dark goddess Underworld working, and the last class was "Finding Love with Your Angels," then the angelic vibe is not necessarily conducive to my Underworld work. Performing an LBRP and LBRH clears that space completely. When I'm done with the working, doing both rituals again creates a neutral zone, so whoever comes in next won't have to clean up my energy. Performing only a traditional LBRP or smudging might not make the space completely neutral, for the planetary, zodiac, and angelic forces may not necessary be ruled by the pentagram.

On a deeper and more spiritual note, regular use of the LBRH ritual aligns you with the cosmic forces, the planets and stars of the zodiac. It changes your aura and consciousness. The elements are oriented differently in the circle of the hexagram, aligned with the cardinal zodiac signs rather than the familiar positions known to witches. The elemental order follows the cycle of the zodiac, with fire, earth, air, and water, like Aries, Taurus, Gemini, and Cancer. The LBRH is like a prayer to be united with your HGA and have a view that is both on the Earth yet from the heavens.

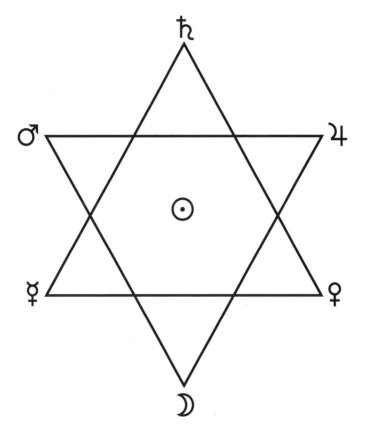

Figure 49: Hexagram with Planetary Attributes

One of the most difficult parts of the LBRH, particularly for pagans, is the Analysis of the Key Word. The key word is the word, or formula, for the evolving age. When a magician recites this, he or she is aligned with the evolution of the age, the spirit of the age, just as when a magician performs the Qabalistic Cross, he or she is aligned with the Tree of Life. The Analysis is a part of the Golden Dawn's ⑤=⑥ initiation ritual. In the Golden Dawn system of magick, adopted by most, the key word is *INRI*, which is familiar to many people as the inscription above Jesus on the cross. Many pagan occultists turn away from this ritual for this reason, but there are deeper meanings to the four letters, associated with the Hebrew occult correspondences.

Letter	Hebrew	Element	Astrology	LVX	Godforms
I	Yod	Water	Virgo	L	Isis
N	Nun	Fire	Scorpio	V	Apophis/Typhon
R	Resh	Air	Sun	X	Osiris
I	Yod	Earth	Virgo	—	Isis

Though some of these correspondences might seem unusual at first, they show that, in ceremonial magick, INRI refers to more than just Jesus's crucifixion, though it does have a lot to do with the sacrificed-god, Tiphereth principle. The key word is a formula for the basic generative, destructive, and sustaining forces of the universe. They are embodied by three Egyptian gods that are familiar to most pagans—Isis, the great mother, Typhon/Apophis, the destructive principle often equated with Set, and Osiris, the resurrected pharaoh god, husband to Isis and brother to both Set and Isis. The notarikon (acronym) of their names, *IAO*, is also the name of the Gnostic supreme god, and is equated with a wide spectrum of trinity forces, from astrology's cardinal, fixed, and mutable energies to the modern pagan's image of the triple goddess. Seen as a Sun figure, Osiris brings the spiritual solar light of Tiphereth to the world. The Latin word for light, *LVX*, pronounced "lux," is used as part of this invocation of light in the current age. There are four signs known as the *LVX signs*. These signs, found in chapter 4, are performed during the LBRH ritual. *L* is for the Sign of the Mourning of Isis, and *V* is for the Sign of Apophis and Typhon. The Sign of Osiris Slain is an intermediary step with no LVX letter, and *X* is for the Sign of Osiris Risen.

The last unfamiliar part of the ritual is the formulation of the hexagrams. Four different symbols, each consisting of two equilateral triangles, are drawn. One "hexagram" in each of the four directions is drawn, each of which corresponds to an element. The divine word used to empower them is *ARARITA*, a seven-letter word for the seven planets and a notarikon for "Achad Rosh Achdotho Rosh Ichudo Temurahzo Achad," a phrase in Hebrew that means "One is his beginning, one is his individuality, his permutation is one." Though I'm sure the use of the male pronoun will upset some of us witches, the concept is of the Divine Mind, the Great Spirit, beyond form or gender.

EXERCISE 20

Lesser Banishing Ritual of the Hexagram (LBRH)

1. Perform the LBRP (exercise 5). Traditionally, the LBRH is done with the ritual wand, held in the right hand. As in the LBRP, you can use either a tool or your hand.

2. Perform the **Analysis of the Key Word**. Face east and say:

   INRI
   Yod, Nun, Resh, Yod.
   Virgo, Isis, Mighty Mother,
   Scorpio, Apophis, Destroyer,
   Sol, Osiris, Slain and Risen.
   Isis, Apophis, Osiris.
   IAO

3. Make the Sign of Osiris Slain (page 111). Say: **The Sign of Osiris Slain.**

4. Make the Sign of the Mourning of Isis (page 109). Say: **The Sign of the Mourning of Isis.**

5. Make the Sign of Apophis and Typhon (page 110). Say: **The Sign of Apophis and Typhon.**

6. Make the Sign of Osiris Risen (page 112). Say: **The Sign of Osiris Risen.**

7. Make the Sign of Osiris Slain. Breathe deeply. When ready, move on to the next step.

8. Make the Sign of the Mourning of Isis. Say: **L.**

9. Make the Sign of Apophis and Typhon. Say: **V.**

10. Make the Sign of Osiris Risen. Say: **X.**

11. Holding the Sign of Osiris Risen, say: **L . . . V . . . X . . . LUX.**

12. Spread your arms open as you say: **The Light . . .**

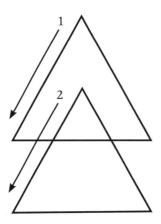

Figure 50: Banishing Hexagram of Fire

13. Make the Sign of Osiris Risen and say: **. . . of the Cross.**
    Feel the space fill with the creative light of the divine.

14. **Formulation of the Banishing Hexagrams.** Face east and draw a banishing
    hexagram of fire in bright golden flame (figure 50). The hexagrams should
    be roughly equivalent in size to the pentagrams in the LBRP. You might
    even perceive the blue-flame pentagrams behind the golden hexagram.

    Technically, you will assume the Sign of the Enterer to charge the hexagram
    with energy, chanting **ARARITA**, followed by the Sign of Silence. Many ma-
    gicians dispense with the use of these signs in this complicated ritual, simply
    vibrating the divine word.

15. Point to the center of the hexagram with your tool, and draw one-quarter
    of the circle with a line of light, bringing you to the south, just as you did
    in the LBRP.

16. Face south and draw a banishing hexagram of earth in bright golden flame
    (figure 51). Empower it as you did before (step 14) with the divine word
    ARARITA.

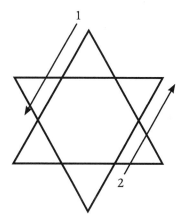

Figure 51: Banishing Hexagram of Earth

17. Point to the center of the hexagram with your tool, and draw one-quarter of the circle with a line of light, bringing you to the west.

18. Face west and draw a banishing hexagram of air in bright golden flame (figure 52). Empower it as you did before with the divine word **ARARITA**.

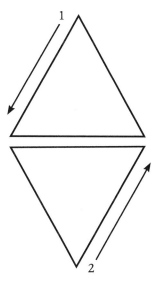

Figure 52: Banishing Hexagram of Air

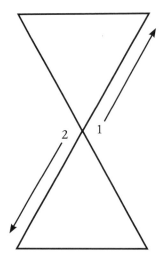

Figure 53: Banishing Hexagram of Water

19. Point to the center of the hexagram with your tool, and draw one-quarter of the circle with a line of light, bringing you to the north.

20. Face north and draw a banishing hexagram of water in bright golden flame (figure 53). Empower it as you did before with the divine word **ARARITA**.

21. Point to the center of the hexagram with your tool, and draw one-quarter of the circle with a line of light, bringing you back to the east, completing the circle.

22. Repeat the Analysis of the Key Word, steps 2–13. Many magicians also repeat the LBRP to close the space.

There are many variations of this ritual, simpler and more complex. For example, many magicians draw the Hebrew letters Yod, Nun, Resh, Yod with the wand, from right to left in blue flame, and then vibrate them, and/or the Hebrew letters for ARARITA. Others omit or add to the many repetitions of the four main signs in the Analysis. Some omit the line "the Light of the Cross" and replace it with "Let the Divine Light Descend." Others repeat step 2, adding "Let the Divine Light Descend" between steps 13 and 14. Some magicians omit the circle of light connecting the hexagrams, relying on the ring created by the LBRP. There are even variations on how to draw the hexagrams themselves.

One of the most profound magickal practices that I relate to the mysteries of Tiphereth cannot really be taught. It's not a technique to learn or a bit of lore to memorize. It's tapping into the ever flowing spring of inspiration, of divine light, that flows from this sphere and letting it inspire your magick and ritual. Apollo and the solar gods are linked to the arts and inspiration. There comes a time in your training when you have learned the foundation and you have to stop playing so strictly by the rules.

A musician learns scales and practices patterns and then learns to read a piece of music as it sits on the stand. Then the piece is memorized. But at some point, the piece becomes internalized—it becomes part of the musician. Then, once the piece is part of the musician's consciousness, certain liberties are taken. The expression of the same piece of music by various artists will all be different, as each internalizes and then expresses it differently. Professional musicians learn to improvise, to jam, to take their range of experience and, in the moment, create something new. They can work well with others who have that same level of experience, and together, through inspiration and group synergy, a magickal form of music is created, whether any of the musicians identify as a magician or not.

All artists go through a similar process. Graphic artists learn perspective, design, and how to mix color. They learn their mediums of paints and pencils. But once they have a foundation of skills, internalized, they let inspiration move them to create spontaneously yet still retain their technique. Dancers, like musicians, learn their moves and techniques and train to align the body and mind, but an inspired dancer becomes one with the music and infuses life into the series of moves through a partnership between body, mind, and music. Poets or writers learn their craft of words, voice, rhythm, and meter, but also allow inspiration to dictate to them. But the flow of words comes through their own psyche and is shaped by the skills they have developed. One only has to look at modern channeled material to see that the best of it is written by those who are writers to start with. The translations from the supernal realm to the page leave a lot to be desired when coming through someone with poor grammar and spelling and a lack of basic communication skills. This doesn't invalidate the message, but it does make it less palatable.

As witches and magicians, we too are artists. Witchcraft is a science, art, and religion. All are interconnected. Yet so many people, seeking to "get it right," lose sight of the artistry. This is not to say that anything you want to do is right and is witchcraft. A lot of people confuse freedom and spontaneity for "anything goes," and then feel they don't have to learn technique, style, or discipline. They think they can't do it "wrong" no matter what, so why learn anything in a specific or orderly way?

Well, it's true, you can't really do things "wrong," but you can do them well, executing them both beautifully and effectively. True, anybody can dance, but to dance well as an artist, you must learn rhythm, movement, and technique and train your body. Anybody can write, yet there's a world of difference between a shopping list and a well-crafted story. Anybody can draw, though despite some modern art, we tend to value the art that combines a statement with technique over a scribble. Anyone can hum or sing, yet it takes some form of training to play an instrument, and a basic understanding of the language of music to play with others.

It's the same with magick. Anybody can hold a ritual, yet not everybody can do effective magick. Fewer still are those who do magick that leads them to evolve and transform. That is the art, science, and religion of our Craft. We learn the fundamentals, the techniques and style, yet have a freedom to create and improvise in a particular format. We know our "scales." We know the "key" the ritual is in, and when we get good enough, we find ourselves putting down the ritual notes and books and not necessarily using a memorized speech, but flowing with the moment, with the words and inspirations that come to us, doing things that we might not have learned in that particular way, but the combination works at that moment. We become inspired—in spirit. The gates open, the power and knowledge flows through us, and we are capable of anything.

When we reach this point, we realize that all magick becomes both art and prayer, and see how art is a form of magick. Our life becomes more and more infused with magick, in every moment. It was already there—we just awaken to it because we are more inspired. Our life becomes both art and prayer in every moment.

There is no exercise I can give you to complete, for we each come to this point of magickal inspiration differently. What I can do is urge you to master the fundamentals and then let go of your fear and let inspiration come into the moment. For some, you always have been doing this. That's great. Continue. For others, it's hard. I know that, as a musician, I had a hard time improvising. I didn't want to go off the paper, off the sheet music, for fear of doing it wrong, when the "right" way was before me, in black and white. It was a struggle. And in music it still is. I no longer really identify as a musician. But as a magician, as a witch and will worker, I have found my love and inspiration. Some of my best rituals, even for large public groups, were based on a vague outline and intention of the ritual, and then I went for it, in the moment. This can work well alone, but if you have a small group of like-minded individuals, who can pick up on your energetic cues and you can pick up on theirs, you can have quite a divinely inspired group ritual. If this is your path, you have to find the same type of flow, of divine inspiration, in your magick. It is like raising the storytelling magick, the guided imagery used in Yesod, to the next level, the next octave of inspiration. For your next esbat or sabbat or any circle you are doing, put down the notes. Hold the intention of the ritual. Remember your training. Ask for inspiration and the partnership of the hidden world to guide you, and let it flow.

ŤIPHERETH PATHWORKINGS

Tiphereth has more paths connected to it than any other sphere on the Tree of Life. Being in the center, it is connected to three paths below it and five paths above it. The heart of the Tree links all the realms to create harmony. Journeys on the paths above the veil have a different quality than those on the paths below the veil. Though Tiphereth presents many challenges, the challenges are of a less personal nature than those of the first four spheres.

The central path leading directly to Kether is ruled by the Priestess card. At this higher level, the Priestess force is the guardian of the gate, the opener of the way, standing between the Pillars of Severity and Mercy, guarding the paradise of pomegranates behind her. She is the lunar guardian into the depths of spirit guarding the

Abyss. The masculine path corresponding to the Emperor card leads to Chokmah. Here we learn about cosmic strength through the male mysteries. Its reflection, the path of the Lovers card, leads to the feminine mysteries of Binah. The Lovers path is the true alchemical wedding, the merging of opposites. A lesser manifestation of such merging occurred on the path of Temperance / Art, but the Lovers path brings the union to completion. The path of the Hermit leads to Chesed. This is the period alone that any king or spiritual ruler must go through, to gain self-knowledge in preparation for true service. The path of the Hermit is reflected in the path of Justice, linking Tiphereth to Geburah. We must learn the wise application of power, for a balanced or just cause, before we can claim the power of Geburah.

EXERCISE 21

Tiphereth Pathworking

1. Perform the Lesser Banishing Ritual of the Pentagram (exercise 5) and the Lesser Banishing Ritual of the Hexagram (exercise 20). Do any other ritual you feel is appropriate.

2. While in this space, call upon the divine forces of Tiphereth. Burn your six gold candles and frankincense or bay leaves. Knock on your altar six times. Vibrate the divine name of Tiphereth, **Yod Heh Vah Heh Eloah va-Da'ath**, six times. Call upon any of the solar deities of the sphere, or Archangel Michael. Call upon your Holy Guardian Angel.

3. To count down into a meditative state, do exercise 1 through step 7 (page 76).

4. Let the familiar world around you fall away, as if the material reality you know is only a façade and beneath it lies the beautiful garden of the Goddess, a veritable paradise surrounding you. The land around you becomes a vast primordial garden, the garden of Malkuth, the familiar garden of the four paths.

5. Go to the heart of Malkuth, to the Temple of Malkuth. Decide which path you wish to take to Tiphereth. The easiest way is up the middle pillar, through the World/Universe to Yesod and through Temperance/Art to Tiphereth. Or you can follow the lightning strike—World/Universe to Yesod, Sun to Hod, Tower to Netzach, and Death to Tiphereth. There are many other possibilities. Choose your route and follow the gates from the Temple of Malkuth.

6. While on your path, reflect on the symbolism of the path. Let the images of the associated tarot card and path come to you. Let your thoughts and feelings be guided by the power of the path. Learn what you can of the path, and of your process, to expand your consciousness to Tiphereth. Feel the call of your higher, golden self welcoming you onward.

7. Feel the call of the golden-yellow sphere from your path. You are bidden to enter the gates of Tiphereth, the realm of beauty, but you might have to give a symbol of Tiphereth, such as the divine name (YHVH Eloah va-Da'ath), the solar glyph, or the name of a solar being. Once you enter, the light warms and welcomes you, filling you up as you feel yourself radiating golden light and love. Feel the harmonious and beautiful energy of this sphere. Explore the golden realm. You might encounter the beings of Tiphereth as you make your way to the golden temple.

8. Make your way to the Temple of Tiphereth. You enter a six-sided temple, golden and ornate beyond comprehension. You feel the power of the spiritual Sun illuminate all things and are aware of the eight gateways leading out of the temple. You have come to the temple by one path; seven more remain to be explored in the future.

9. The entities of Tiphereth are residing in the temple. The solar god is manifest, perhaps as a child, king, or sacrificial god. The lion and phoenix are present, along with the archangel Michael or Raphael. Commune with the beings of Tiphereth. Ask to know the Vision of Harmony and Understand the Nature of Sacrifice in a manner that is correct and for your highest good. Ask

to learn the virtue and obligation of the sphere and ways to avoid the vice and illusion. Most importantly, feel the golden love of devotion emanating from every being here, from the very walls of the temple itself.

10. When done, thank all the beings who have communicated with you. They might offer you a gift, a token of their goodwill. If you accept, it is polite to reach within your being and offer them a gift of your goodwill.

11. Once you have said your farewells, leave the shrine and follow the path back. Return the way you came unless you feel guided to return via a different pathway and know the pathway back well. Go back to the garden of Malkuth. Focus on the waking world you know, and feel it return around the garden.

12. To return to normal waking consciousness and end your journey, perform steps 15–17 from exercise 1 (page 78). You can close the temple by repeating the LBRP.

İNITIATION OF ȚIPHERETH

In the traditional orders of ceremonial magicians, passing from the grade of Netzach to the grade of Tiphereth, the Adept or Adeptus Minor, ⑤=⑥, is to pass from the First Order to the Second Order, going deeper into the mysteries. The initiate must learn the Portal grade, having the ability not just in technique but in all ways to rend and close the veil between worlds, the veil between the lower Tree and Tiphereth. The signs found in the Hexagram ritual are the ones of this rank, that of the IAO formula—Mourning of Isis, Apophis and Typhon, Osiris Slain, and Osiris Risen. In this working, the initiate is sacrificed through the Vision of Sacrifice, knowing that the life of the initiate is not totally his or her own but is dedicated to the service of all life, of the Great Spirit and creative intelligence.

One at this level of initiation already must have performed the first stage of the Great Work, the Knowledge and Conversation of the Holy Guardian Angel. Briefly experienced as the Vision of Malkuth, this level of knowledge and conversation now must be a daily reality. The initiate must be in regular, if not constant, communion with this higher soul self, and be acting more and more from this higher perspective. You do not lose the personal perspective at all, but you must be able to look, act, and feel beyond it. From a personal energetic perspective, you really must be operating out of the heart space, balanced and harmonious, rather than the lower three chakras. True mastery of the Tiphereth sphere comes with integration of the Holy Guardian Angel identity with the personal identity, to truly live from the perspective of the higher self every day.

Spirit

Spiritual Lessons: Humility, Illumination
Spiritual Tool: Crown
Fears and Challenges: Fear of Ego Loss, Fear of Guilt/Moral Lapse
Virtue: Humility
Psychological Function: None
Stage of Learning: Direct Revelation
State of Matter: Dark Matter
Environmental Sphere: Biosphere
Scientific Force: Life Force
Periodic Element: Sodium
Humor: None
Body System: Endocrine
Sacred River: Starlight
Sacred Geometry: Dodecahedron
Celtic City: Tara
Qabalistic World: Entire Tree of Life
Classical Age: Platinum
Caste: Master
Sufi Breath: In Nose/Out Nose
Mudra: Thumb and First Two Fingers
Planets: Sun, Jupiter, Uranus
Fixed Sign and Animal: None
Egyptian Animal: Phoenix
Metal: Electrum

Chakra: Crown
Time of Day: All Day
Season: Entire Year
Vowel Sound: U
Egyptian Syllable: Sa
Hindi Syllable: Ham
Tibetan Syllable: Kha
Modern Syllable: Ka (Ra)
Obstruent Sounds: None
Time Signature: None
Hebrew God Name: Eihehe
Archangel: Metatron
Angel: None
Ruler: None
Elemental King and Queen: None
Goetic Ruler: None
Enochian King: None
Stones: Quartz, Diamond, Herkimer Diamond, Phenacite
Herbs: Mistletoe, Oak, Vervain

In our comparison of the grades of the elements to the Celtic gifts, there is no fifth gift in the legends. Tiphereth is compared to both the Philosopher's Stone (or Stone of Destiny) and the Holy Grail. Both legends are connected to emeralds and, in the modern age, the tektite moldavite. A great stone was said to fall from the Lightbringer's brow and descend into Earth, into the cycle of form and time. It is both the source of the "fall" in Christian mythologies and the key to redemption. Pagans know that redemption is within us all, for we never truly fell anywhere. We've always been in paradise. We just haven't always remembered it, or acted like it. But the emerald of the heart, carved into the sacred cup, is really an allegory for the heart space, which connects us to the timeless heavens. Only through awakening the heart chakra can we connect to the heavenly crown.

In Gareth Knight's book *The Secret Tradition in Arthurian Legend*, the Qabalistic influences are clearly spelled out. Malkuth is the forest or later wasteland, where the

Grail knights wander. Yesod is the lake, with the Lady of the Lake as guardian of the astral forces and inner-plane guides. Hod is the realm of the knights, questing forward, swords in hand. Netzach is Camelot, ultimately ruled by the queen, for the king rules only through his relationship with the Goddess and the land, as represented by the queen. The sacrificed king necessary to enter the realm of Tiphereth is Arthur himself, and Tiphereth is the Holy Grail itself, capable of restoring all to true health and vigor, if it is rightly found. This is a slightly different spin on our take of the four gifts and their elemental associations, but again, it leaves us with no fifth tool to work with.

In meditation, I have found the Crown of Humility. It is the Crown of Service and Sacrifice, for contrary to popular opinion, true kings and queens cannot do as they like, but do as they must, to maintain their "right" relationship with the land and the spirits, for the greater good of the people. In days of old, kings and queens were priest-kings and priestess-queens. They were not just political leaders, or even religious leaders, but conduits to mediate the forces of the land and Otherworld for their people. One simply has to look at the Egyptian pharaonic line or the Celtic kings to see this theme. Heavy is the head that wears the crown, literally and metaphysically.

In this day and age, the Age of Aquarius, we are all called upon to mediate our own spiritual forces and not have others do it for us. We are each called to be our own queen or king in the world. To do that, we must master the first four elements.

Though the lessons of this book span to the first sphere of Kether, the student is not expected to attain that level of initiation. Spiritual enlightenment can take many lifetimes, and much spiritual growth occurs between lifetimes. For those of us in a body, the Tree of Life is a map to understand higher consciousness, and nothing more. I don't claim to have reached these high levels of metaphysical evolution, and neither do most Qabalistic writers. But we do understand the maps, and sometimes understanding what's ahead helps you tackle whatever is before you.

Rather than perform a ritual or meditation to find the Crown of Humility or undergo a Tiphereth initiation of any kind, you are charged to continue to master the first four elements and see clearly past the veil as this yearlong training continues. The work and lessons of the rest of this book, culminating in the lessons of Kether, will prepare you to more fully invoke the HGA, while rituals to work with the Crown, in service to both your spiritual growth and the planet, will be part of the training in the fifth book of this series, The Living Temple of Witchcraft. Through this fifth book, you will develop the skills and awareness to live from the perspective of the higher self.

No book, and even no teacher, can hope to bring you beyond Tiphereth consciousness. For the purposes of the Temple of Witchcraft series, your only goals in this course are an intellectual understanding of the entire Tree of Life, the creation of your own reality map, and a greater mastery of the four elemental grades and their tools. You can and should develop a relationship with your HGA as a result of this work. You can explore the concepts of the higher spheres to understand them to the best of your ability at your present level of spiritual initiation, but don't mistake greater knowledge for spiritual mastery of the higher spheres.

Homework

- Do Exercises 20–21 and record your experiences in your Book of Shadows.

- Learn and practice the Lesser Banishing Ritual of the Hexagram (exercise 20), the traditional version or your own personally reconstructed version.

- Continue to practice the LBRP, Middle Pillar, and Circulation of the Body of Light rituals, the traditional or personal versions. You can continue with the Four Adorations and the Ritual of the Rosy Cross, but this is not a requirement.

Tips

- Fill in the Tiphereth correspondences and colors on your own Tree of Life drawing. Contemplate them as you add them to the image. Start memorizing these correspondences.

- Review and reflect on all you have learned in this lesson.

- Continue to work with the four elements. If you have not yet mastered the Stone of Sovereignty, the Cup of Compassion, the Sword of Truth, and the

Spear of Victory, work toward that mastery. If you have, make sure you are continuing to use their energies effectively, both in ritual and daily life.

• Continue working with the lower sephiroth. They are not just one-time destinations, but psychic destinations and temples with which you should become intimately familiar.

• Study appendix VI to deconstruct and reconstruct the Lesser Banishing Ritual of the Hexagram to fit your worldview, if you so choose. If you are reconstructing it, make sure your symbolism is consistent with the pentagram rituals and other rites.

• Pick one other reality map from appendix I to contemplate. Understanding a variety of worldviews will help you when you construct your own reality map.

• The Analysis of the Key Word can be done as a ritual by itself, either preceded and followed by the Qabalistic Cross or LBRP.

• To bring the macrocosm into their work and ritual attire, some witches and magicians tie the cords of their belt in the reef knot, left over right and right over left, forming a hexagram shape.

• Like the Lesser Banishing Ritual of the Pentagram, there are many variations of the hexagram ritual. You can adapt it to be the Lesser Invoking Ritual of the Hexagram (using the invoking hexagrams in figure 54), to align yourself with the stellar forces for a working. The Greater Invoking Ritual of the Hexagram can be used to both banish and invoke specific planetary or zodiac powers. This will be covered in chapter 12.

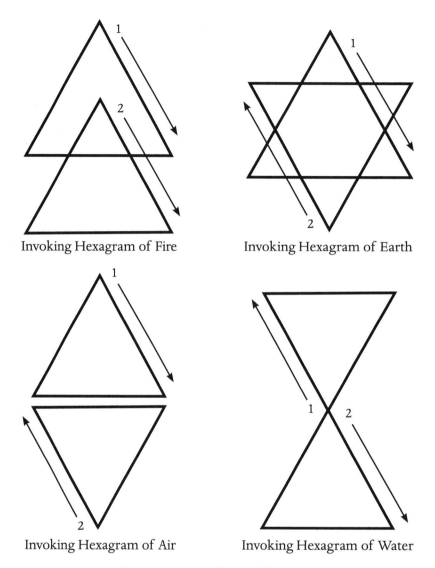

Invoking Hexagram of Fire

Invoking Hexagram of Earth

Invoking Hexagram of Air

Invoking Hexagram of Water

Figure 54: Invoking Elemental Hexagrams

Lesson Seven
Geburah

The crimson sphere of Geburah is the first of the higher powers above Tiphereth on the Tree of Life. The powers of Geburah and its twin, Chesed, are the forces that can be wielded safely only by an initiate who has made communion with the higher self in Tiphereth. The left corner of the Ethical Triangle, Geburah, is power. Geburah is, quite literally, force. Its name means "strength" or "might," and it is the strength of will and power. It is the energy needed to manifest will. Though power to manifest will can be accessed by all manner of people, the most effective use of power is power applied to True Will, showing us why Tiphereth comes first on the climb of the magician. Geburah is the higher octave of Hod, and where Hod is individual thought and the personal ideas the magician can choose to manifest, Geburah is the raw power, the higher will or higher thought, the divine component in the formula, supplying the energy.

Astrologically, Geburah corresponds to the red planet Mars, which is the indicator of will in a natal chart. Mars is the drive forward, named after the war god. It is the impetus and our ability to act. The sign that Mars occupies in our birth chart shows the style in which we act. When you look at the environment of Mars as a planet with magickal symbolism in mind, its extreme power becomes more apparent. What little water, or emotion, that is present on it is frozen, suspended. Though the planet has an Earth-like size and shape, and much pseudoscientific speculation abounds regarding former life and even civilizations on Mars, it is not currently supportive of life or nurturing in any way. The environment is tough, martial, and unforgiving. Sandstorms continue to scar the surface, scourging it of the past and making it fresh.

The power of Geburah, though it can be used to accomplish things, is described as catabolic. It is destructive in nature, like the metabolic process breaking down energy sources to then release the energy. The martial might of Geburah can break down forces, seemingly destroying them, only to use that energy for a higher purpose. The power of Geburah is the power to destroy what no longer serves your highest will. Sometimes that destruction isn't easy or pleasant, but it is a necessary part of the process. The power of Geburah is impersonal and does whatever must be done to create change and make space. Unlike with the lower sephiroth, there is no sentimentality in the way Geburah functions. In our world, we can see the power of Geburah manifest in disasters and accidents, such as fires and floods, as well as the long and continuous shaping of the land by weather and wind. Although sometimes traumatic, these occurrences bring change and new creation. Another name for Geburah is severity, as it sits in the center of the Pillar of Severity. Geburah is said to be devoid of mercy, the quality of Chesed with which it must be balanced.

Geburah

Meaning: Strength, Might, Power
Levels of Reality: Force and Motion
Parts of the Self: Will, Volition, Right Shoulder
Experience: Vision of Power
Obligation: Courage
Illusion: Invincibility
Virtue: Courageous Behavior
Vice: Wanton Destruction or Cruelty
Name of God: Elohim Gibor (Gods of Strength, Gods of Power)

King Scale Color: Orange
Queen Scale Color: Red
Prince Scale Color: Bright Scarlet
Princess Scale Color: Red flecked with Black
Element: Fire
Planet: Mars
Image: Warrior in Chariot
Archetypes: Warrior Deities, Forge Deities
Greek/Roman Deities: Ares, Mars, Athena, Minerva, the Furies
Egyptian Deities: Horus, Sekhmet, Maat
Middle Eastern Deities: Ninurta, Nergal
Celtic Deities: Bran, Morrighan, Macha
Norse Deities: Tyr, Thor
Hindu Deities: Kali, Durga
Archangel: Kamael (Archangel of Strength)
Angelic Order: Seraphim (Fiery Serpents)
Choir: Virtues
Grade of Initiation: ⑥=⑤ Advanced Adept
Animal: Basilisk
Planetary Vowel Sound: O (oh)
Resonant Letters: ng
Musical Mode: Lydian
Musical Note: F#
Tools: Scourge, Spear, Chain, Sword, Pentagon
Incense: Tobacco, Dragon's Blood
Tarot: Five of Wands, Swords, Cups, and Pentacles
       Hanged Man—To Hod
       Justice—to Tiphereth
       Strength/Lust—to Chesed
       Chariot—to Binah
Metal: Iron
Stones: Ruby, Bloodstone, Carnelian
Plant: Cactus

For this month's lesson, Geburah's themes are done in fives, and are associated with martial correspondences, the fives of the four tarot suits, red candles, iron and steel, red fiery stones, and stimulating, powerful incense. The traditional scent is tobacco, but many witches dislike meditating with this. If you do use tobacco, choose a natural, untreated tobacco. Asafoetida is a substitute. Used to banish spirits and demons, it actually smells a lot worse than regular tobacco, and many believe it will neutralize the charge of all your ritual tools. The best substitute for tobacco is dragon's blood, as it is just as powerful and stimulating magickally but has a less offensive smell. I suggest making an altar using your peyton as the center, surrounded by your five red candles and other tools, along with the major arcana cards representing the pathways in and out of Geburah. It's interesting that, through the pentacle, there is a resonance between Geburah and Malkuth.

ENTITIES OF GEBURAH

The glyph of Mars, the ruling planet of this sphere, is also the male symbol used in our modern culture, just as Venus's glyph is the female symbol. The glyph has been characterized as the shield and spear or arrow of a warrior. The powers of Mars have been equated with the warrior, as the planet was named after the Roman war god, with his corresponding association with the Greek war god Ares. The traditional image of Mars is the warrior in his Chariot, riding out to battle.

All warrior figures and deities can be assigned to Geburah. Tyr, of the Norse, is the Mars cognate, but it is important to remember that Tyr is not only a warrior, but a god of justice and sacrifice. He sacrificed his hand to bind the Fenris wolf and protect all the nine worlds. Justice is a strong component of the entities of Geburah, as the implication is that the conflict, the war, is just and necessary, not foolhardy and ill-conceived. Bran is the Welsh warrior king who led the forces to battle Ireland to avenge the honor of his sister, the goddess Branwen. Horus of the Egyptian pantheon, though seen as a solar figure and child king, is also a war god and mighty avenger who battled his uncle for the throne of Egypt.

Almost any of the gods with warrior aspects can be assigned to Geburah. Many of these gods have other attributes as well, so Geburah can include a wide range of traits other than just martial force. I find it interesting that so many warrior gods have agricultural or fertility aspects associated with them. At one time, Ares was tied to agriculture and healing, revealing another link from Geburah to Malkuth.

The forge and furnace gods also can be associated with Geburah. It is the fire of destruction to then create new forms and shapes. Metals must be melted in the forge before being reshaped. Hephaestus in the Greek mythos and Vulcan in the Roman are the best-known forge gods. Other gods with similar associations include Ptah, Nusku, Tubal Cain, Volund, Weiland, Govannon, Goibniu, Goban, Luchtaine, and Creidne.

Despite all this male-god imagery, much of the lore surrounding Geburah is distinctly feminine. Some people are shocked by this, but Geburah appears on the left, or negative, side of the Tree of Life. Some believe that the pillars spiral like DNA or the caduceus; the active principle alternates from Chokmah to Geburah to the fiery Netzach, while the receptive principle alternates from Binah to Chesed and down to mercurial Hod. Nevertheless, Geburah is on the dark pillar and could be described as the feminine side of the active principle. Besides all the war-god imagery, we have the warrior goddess and destructive feminine principles. We have the warrior queen, sovereign over life and death.

Athena of the Greeks and Minerva of the Romans both are said to embody the higher aspect of the warrior—the strategist. They have a relationship to their brothers Ares and Mars, yet take a "higher" road that is symbolized perfectly by Geburah, being a higher sephira. We could see the male gods as the lower expression of will, with the goddesses as the higher expression. In European traditions, many of the goddesses are warrior goddesses. The Celtic traditions are filled with dark warrior queens associated with the battlefield. The Morrighan, a triple goddess of the battlefield and the Underworld, consists of the three goddesses Anu, Badb, and Macha or Badb, Macha, and Nemain, all of whom have dark warrior aspects.

In terms of primal Geburah goddess figures, a perfect fit would be the lion-headed Egyptian goddess Sekhmet. In a display of the destructive power of the Sun, she conducted an enraged slaughter of humanity that had to be quelled by the gods. But her priestesses and priests were also great healers, able to remove illness and disease with the power of the Sun's destructive light, brought down in carefully measured ways.

Kali from the Hindu traditions is another Geburah figure. Though Kali is truly a goddess of nature, and is both creative and destructive, many in the West choose to focus on her more fearsome and destructive aspects. She is fiery, black-skinned, many-armed, and demon-like, instilling fear and panic. She wears a necklace of skulls and a skirt of severed arms. She represents destruction, but one cannot create if one cannot destroy.

Looking through the lens of Geburah, we cannot help but see that the province of the warrior, the avenger, the destroyer and creator, can be found in both the gods and the goddesses. The divine name of Geburah sums it up quite nicely: *Elohim Gibor*, the gods and goddesses of strength, might, and power.

The archangel assigned to Geburah is traditionally Kamael, the archangel of strength, courage, justice, and severity. His name has been translated as "He who seeks God," "He who sees God," or "Burner of God." Each name relates to his ability to see the divine within another, as an archangel of testing. Kamael is linked to the great tester Samael, a controversial figure in angelic mythology, related to death and sometimes to the angel of the "fall." The angel of the Geburah station tests our convictions and motivations, purifying them. He also is responsible for making sure the power of the Tree of Life is modified as it descends into the spheres below Geburah.

The traditional angelic order of Geburah is the Seraphim, the fiery serpents or burning ones, said to carry out the divine's destructive and purifying will, removing imperfection from the divine order. In another system, the Seraphim are related to the highest spheres, and separated from humanity, simply singing the praises of the divine. In this system, the angels of the martial sphere are known as Virtues. They infuse creation with blessing, with virtue, particularly those who have demonstrated valor or are in need of valor.

Vision of Geburah

Geburah's divine experience is the Vision of Power, which is the key to understanding and unlocking your power to manifest your divine will, and not necessarily your personal will, in the world. The obligation of this vision is courage, for if you are not courageous, if you cannot follow the road, follow the call of divinity even when things look rough and the outcome is uncertain, then you cannot have access to this divine power. The virtue of Geburah is much like the obligation. Those who attain the Vision of Power find that courageous behavior comes naturally, for they are in touch with the primal forces of power and can wield them. The illusion of Geburah is that one is invincible. Some have not yet attained this vision but think they have, and believe themselves to be invincible in the face of all challenges. Others do attain this vision, but then fall, confusing divine will with personal will. Sometimes it is in accord with divine will and power to not get what you want. Sometimes your defeat serves you and serves creation. Those who attain a certain measure of power, but abuse it through wanton and unnecessary destruction and cruelty, thinking they are beyond such moral constraints, have great difficulty reaching the true Vision of Power.

Geburah Magick

Geburah magick is that of creation and destruction. More appropriately, it is the correct use of power—magickal power, psychic power, and worldly power—in the context of a spiritual life.

Once you ascend past Tiphereth, there is no single elemental correspondence for each sephira, as there is for the lower spheres. These higher spheres are simply too powerful to be limited by one element. Though we may glance at the astrological correspondences and make some assumptions, the upper spheres are too complex to pin down neatly. Geburah is the sphere of Mars, and obviously of fire because of that association. It forms a nice balance with Netzach, diagonally across Tiphereth, as they are both related to fire. But as the sphere of judgment and catabolic processes, Geburah is much more than that. Mars rules both Aries and, in traditional astrology, Scorpio, associating the planet with both fire and water. Geburah is the fire of destruction, but also the cleansing flood of the ancient legends. It is storms, earthquakes, volcanoes, and other natural disasters on the planet and their symbolic correspondences in our lives.

The totem of Geburah is the mythical basilisk, one of the most dangerous totemic figures on the Tree. Nobody knows for sure what the basilisk looks like, as it's impossible to see it and survive, but it's believed to be a serpent or dragon-like creature, with a gaze that would kill. Some legends say the basilisk was created from Medusa's blood, as she is a Gorgon whose gaze turns the viewer to stone. We must be vigilant with our Geburah power, lest it destroy us rather than our target.

All the tools of Geburah are martial. Iron is the sacred metal, and one of the tools most useful to humanity. Without iron, many of our technologies and innovations would not have been possible. Yet the Iron Age in our mythologies experienced a decline in spiritual awareness from what has been termed the Golden and Silver Ages of great innocence and harmony with the planet. Iron oxide is a key component of Mars the planet and Geburic magick. The red quality of the "star" of Mars is due to the oxidation of iron. Did the ancients know that the iron on our planet corresponded so well to the iron of Mars? Probably not, but it's an interesting question. In magick, iron is used for protection, to block harm like a lightning rod, grounding it. It is also a substitute for blood, as it mimics the redness of our blood and is considered to be a form of blood from the Earth. Older traditional spells calling for blood as an ingredient can be performed using iron/rust, salt, and water as a substitute. Martian energy is stimulating, and any herb, oil, scent, or stone that is stimulating is a good match. The scent of tobacco is a stimulant, and thorny plants such as roses, thistles, and stinging nettles also are associated with Mars. High-energy stones, like ruby, or stones working with the blood, like bloodstone and hematite, are aligned with Geburah.

To witches, the tool associated most strongly with Geburah is the scourge. It is the tool of discipline. Although not popular in most modern traditions of witchcraft that are not from a British Traditional line, scourging the self is both a part of initiation rites, to ritually teach the threefold law, and a method of raising power and altering consciousness. Interestingly enough, the markings of the traditional scourge are those of the three degrees of traditional witchcraft, all involving the pentagram (figure 55).

Figure 55: Degree Markings on the Scourge (First, Second, and Third Degrees)

The pentagram, pentacle, and pentagon all are aligned with Geburah, being the fifth sphere. The initiation symbols of the scourge can be outlined quite easily on the Tree of Life (figure 56).

Figure 56: Tree of Life with the Degree Markings

It is interesting how stars are associated with the military in general, and the pentagon shape is the one chosen for the American military headquarters, giving it further Geburah connotations. Known by many names, such as the endless knot, goblin's foot, or witch's cross, the pentagram was said to be the symbol on the knight Percival's shield, and is aligned with the old Celtic war goddesses, giving it another Geburah association. In the medieval tales of Sir Gawain, it also is on his shield, but is given Christian symbolism of the five wounds of Christ as well as the virtues of the knight: frankness, fellowship, purity, courtesy, and compassion. The image of the five-pointed star is not simply a symbol of earth and the combination of the five elements, but a symbol of mastery over the elements and the material world. When one attains the power of Geburah, one has a certain level of power to achieve goals and accomplish divine will in the world at large. This is one of the many reasons why the various versions of the star are used as initiation symbols and carved on the scourge.

The pentagram also is aligned with mastery over the physical world because of the very magickal mathematical proportions encoded in its very structure. Within the proportions of the pentagram are the geometries to reproduce itself perfectly (figure 57). This magickal star is a prime example of the Principle of Correspondence, showing that patterns repeat themselves on many scales and levels.

The most remarkable thing about the pentacle is that encoded within its proportion is the phi ratio, also known as the Golden Section. The Golden Section is a remarkable ratio and pattern, observed and revered by the ancients. Plato saw it as the mathematical key to the universe, the underlying pattern of everything, while the Egyptians saw it as the process of creation. And it is. The Golden Section is an asymmetrical division of unity that results in the diverse creation of life yet shows the fundamental and underlying unity among all things. It describes a progression of forms, shapes, or numbers expanding or contracting so that the new measurement is to the original as the original is to the whole. In geometry, one could say that B is to A as A is to $A + B$ (figure 58). The pattern is best seen in the pentagram, but also can be seen in the human body and the Western musical scale. It also roughly describes the proportions of the solar system, at least of the inner planets, as the ratio begins to break down the further out you go. The phi ratio shows us the wisdom of "as above, so below."

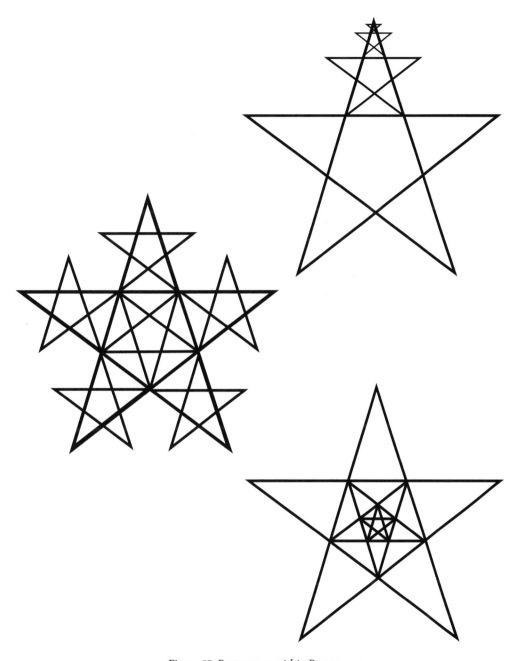

Figure 57: Pentagrams within Pentagrams

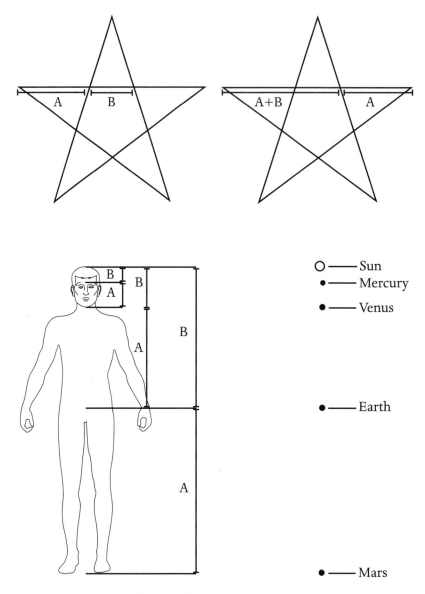

Figure 58: Pentagram Proportions

We can see the proportion in a sequence known as the Fibonacci sequence: 1, 1, 2, 3, 5, 8, 13, 21, 34, 55, 89, 144...Each new number is generated by adding the previous two. This sequence is how the infinite spiral is brought into form in the material world (figure 59). The ratio is infinite, but often is expressed numerically as 1.618. Each number is in the phi ratio to the previous number, moving infinitely closer to perfection yet never reaching that mathematical perfection in the physical world, which is why we call it an irrational number.

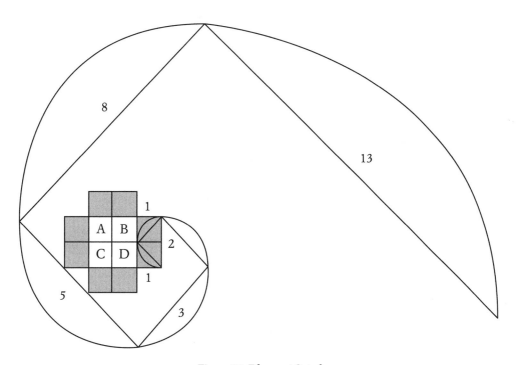

Figure 59: Fibonacci Spiral

These sequences appear in nature. The Fibonacci can be found in the branching patterns of grasses, flowers, bushes, and trees. It is in the spiraling patterns of a pine cone, as well as the patterns in horns and shells of animals. The pattern is found in the ancestry of bees. You see it in the proportions of the human body. The length of your elbow to the tip of your fingers is in the phi ratio to the length of your entire arm. The length of your body from your waist to the top of your head is in the phi ratio to the entire length of your body, head to toe. The pattern continues to all the divisions of the body, down to the joints in your fingers. Much of the art of the ancient world, and then the Renaissance, used the proportions of sacred geometry, including the phi ratio, while most modern art does not. Though both bring their blessings, there is something vastly different between art that uses sacred geometry and art that does not.

The pentagram, with this proportion encoded within it, is the key to linking the perfected supernal world of the upper triad with the manifestation of life in the material world. This is one of the reasons why it is the shape that grants mastery over the physical world and encompasses all the elements. As a symbol of incarnation, a human with two arms, two legs, and a head, it brings the perfected divine spark into the material existence. The flowers that repeat its pattern of five petals are the most spiritual, yet they are either very healing or very toxic, bringing this life force in and out. Fruits with five-petaled flowers, such as the apple, usually have the pentagram in their seed pattern and have long been revered for their connection to witchcraft. The pentagram, containing the geometry to replicate itself, is the power of regeneration in the living world, and the regenerative life force of nature, sacred in the ancient world both to the goddess Venus and to Pan, the All. The pentagram holds the key to the mysteries of life, death, infinity, and power.

As the aspiring ceremonial magician starts with the Lesser Ritual of the Pentagram, the logical expansion is to the Greater Ritual of the Pentagram. Many witches forgo learning the Greater Ritual of the Pentagram, feeling that the traditional magick circle of witchcraft is more than adequate for their work. I must agree that, when the two are compared, I favor the magick circle found in witchcraft, and detailed in the second book of this series, *The Outer Temple of Witchcraft*. Before the advent of the Golden Dawn, ritual magicians all had personal and unique ways of creating their circles, in chalk or other markings on the floor, inscribing rings within rings with sacred names of the divine and angelic symbols. The traditional nine-foot "circle of the art" aligned the force of the Moon, as Yesod is the ninth sphere. The diameters of subsequent inner rings also can have Qabalistic symbolism attached.

With the Greater Ritual of the Pentagram, we start to unravel the deeper mysteries behind the pentagram. Witches often look at the associations of the elements with the points on the pentagram and wonder if they are arbitrary or not. If not, what is the logic behind them? If you draw the pentagram clockwise, starting from the top, you move from spirit to fire, air, water, and earth, and back to spirit again, arranging the elements from least dense to most dense, starting from and returning to spirit. It also goes in the order of the alchemical circle, with fire and air connected with one line and earth and water connected with one line. Those two lines are not used in the traditional drawing of invoking and banishing the four elements by pentagram. They are used in the active and passive spirit pentagrams (figure 60). Drawn as either invoking or banishing pentagrams, the active pentagrams of spirit are drawn first in the quarters of the active elements—fire and air—followed by the appropriate traditional elemental pentagram. The passive pentagrams of spirit are drawn first in the quarters of the passive elements—water and earth—and likewise followed by the appropriate traditional elemental pentagram. The invoking spirit pentagrams are known as *equilibrating*, while the banishing pentagrams are known as *closing* pentagrams. By starting with the spirit pentagrams, the four elemental gateways are fully empowered, making it truly the greater ritual in power and purpose when compared to the Lesser Ritual of the Pentagram.

When working with the Greater Ritual of the Pentagram, one must decide how to formulate it, as either invoking or banishing. Usually the traditional preliminary banishing of the LBRP and LBRH are done to clear the space, and then the sacred space is created through the Greater Invoking Ritual of the Pentagram. Next, the work is done, and then the space is released through the Greater Banishing Ritual of the Pentagram, followed by a repetition of the LBRP and LBRH.

The practical witch might look at all these steps and wonder why on Earth anyone would go through this when you could just cast a witch's magick circle. The complexity and precision of the steps really are meant to short-circuit your doubts, fears, and

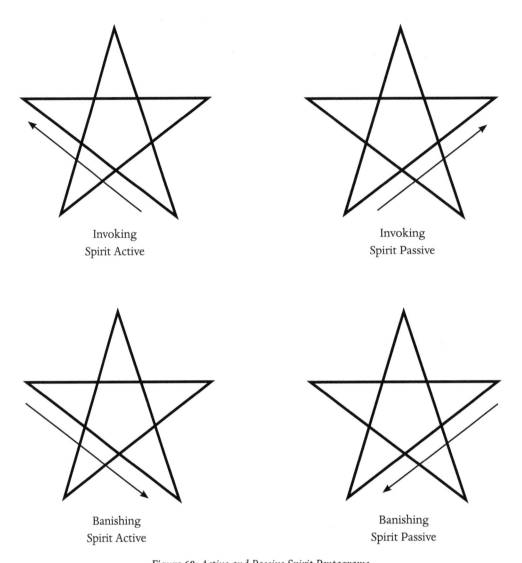

Invoking
Spirit Active

Invoking
Spirit Passive

Banishing
Spirit Active

Banishing
Spirit Passive

Figure 60: Active and Passive Spirit Pentagrams

much of your conscious mind, allowing you to fully engage your magickal self once you are in the space to do the working you have chosen, be it spell casting, energy work, divination, or meditation. Much like a martial discipline, a vigorous yoga, Eastern martial art, or extended circle dancing, these complex movements become second nature to the trained practitioner. These movements teach the practitioner how to make new connections between his or her personal energy, thoughts, physical body, and vocalizations, to make some truly spectacular magick.

EXERCISE 22

Greater Invoking Ritual of the Pentagram (GIRP)

1. Perform the LBRP (exercise 5). Ideally, also perform the LBRH (exercise 20), though some magicians would consider that step optional.

2. Repeat the Qabalistic Cross (exercise 2).

3. Facing east, draw an equilibrated active invoking pentagram of spirit in white light. Vibrate the divine name: **Eh-heh-yeh**.

4. Make the Active Sign of the Portal, the Sign of Rending the Veil (page 107).

5. Draw an invoking pentagram of air in yellow light. Make the Sign of the Enterer (page 102), empowering the air pentagram while vibrating the divine name: **Yud-Heh-Vahv-Heh**.

6. Make the Sign of the Practicus Grade, ②=⑨, for air (page 104). Point your finger/blade in the center of the pentagram, and trace one-quarter of the circle in the air with a line of light, bringing you to the south.

7. Facing south, draw an equilibrated active invoking pentagram of spirit in white light. Vibrate the divine name: **Eh-heh-yeh**.

8. Make the Active Sign of the Portal, the Sign of Rending the Veil.

9. Draw an invoking pentagram of fire in red light. Make the Sign of the Enterer, empowering the fire pentagram while vibrating the divine name: **Elohim**.

10. Make the Sign of the Philosophus Grade, ④=⑦, for fire (page 106). Point your finger/blade in the center of the pentagram, and trace one-quarter of the circle in the air with a line of light, bringing you to the west.

11. Facing west, draw an equilibrated passive invoking pentagram of spirit in white light. Vibrate the divine name: **Ah-glah**.

12. Make the Passive Sign of the Portal, the Sign of Closing the Veil (page 108).

13. Draw an invoking pentagram of water in blue light. Make the Sign of the Enterer, empowering the water pentagram while vibrating the divine name: **El**.

14. Make the Sign of the Theoricus Grade, ③=⑧, for water (page 105). Point your finger/blade in the center of the pentagram, and trace one-quarter of the circle in the air with a line of light, bringing you to the north.

15. Facing north, draw an equilibrated passive invoking pentagram of spirit in white light. Vibrate the divine name: **Ah-glah**.

16. Give the Passive Sign of the Portal, the Sign of Closing the Veil.

17. Draw an invoking pentagram of earth in green or black light. Make the Sign of the Enterer, empowering the earth pentagram while vibrating the divine name: **Ah-doh-nye**.

18. Make the Sign of the Zelator Grade, ①=⑩, for earth (page 103). Point your finger/blade in the center of the pentagram, and trace one-quarter of the circle in the air with a line of light, bringing you to the east.

19. Repeat the Qabalistic Cross. When the working is done, it should be followed by the Greater Banishing Ritual of the Pentagram, following the same steps yet using banishing pentagrams. Many also close the temple with the LBRP and LBRH.

As with the previous rituals, there are many variations of the Greater Ritual of the Pentagram. Often the portal signs are omitted entirely, or only the active signs are used in the invoking rituals and the passive signs are used in the banishing rituals, which I prefer. Remember that in our elemental ranking system in *The Temple of High Witchcraft*, the Theoricus and Practicus signs have been switched in name, yet the elemental symbolism is consistent with each of the four quarters. The most complicated version of this ritual, involving Enochian words of power, is known as the Supreme Invoking Ritual of the Pentagram, or SIRP.

The Greater Ritual of the Pentagram can be adapted from invoking to banishing by drawing all banishing pentagrams, for both the spirit and the four elements, in place of invoking pentagrams. Unlike the end of a traditional witch's circle, the Greater Banishing Ritual of the Pentagram moves deosil (clockwise) to close the space.

If desired, the Greater Ritual of the Pentagram can be focused on one specific element. You can focus on only one quarter and fill the space with elemental energy from that quarter, or you can draw the same spirit pentagram and same elemental pentagram in each of the four quarters, as in the traditional LIRP or LBRP.

Some practitioners have special words they use to both open and close a powerful ritual, particularly the Greater and Supreme Rituals of the Pentagram and Hexagram. To open the space, they use **Hekas, Hekas, Este Bebeloi**, meaning "Be ye far, all ye profane." At the end, they use a declaration that the temple is duly closed: "I now release any Spirit that may have been imprisoned by this ritual. Go now, with blessings. May there always be peace between us, and may you always come when you are called. I now declare this ritual duly closed."

BARBAROUS WORDS OF POWER

If Geburah is said to be the higher octave of Hod on the Pillar of Severity, and Hod magick includes alphabets and language, then I place the use of powerful words and phrases, that do not necessarily conform to an intelligible language or script, in the primal realm of Geburah magick. Known as the *barbarous names (or words) of power*, they are words and phrases that have no specific meaning to the magician, yet their power is twofold.

One theory holds that the function of their magick is in the sound of the words, not in the meaning. For example, many of us start to do the LBRP without a full understanding of the Hebrew, yet we find something powerful in the sounds and tones and the ritual is supremely effective. This theory would hold that magick words, the sounds themselves, are keyed in to the powers of the universe and help make the magick. One shouldn't try to decode them, even if it's possible, for in that decoding they might lose their magick.

The second theory is that even though the sounds may be unfamiliar, if they are said with authority in the context of the ritual, they have a profound psychological and magickal effect on the magician. The power of the ritual comes from the magician's own connection to the universe, enhanced by the flavor of the ritual, rather than any power inherent in the sounds themselves. The words should be uttered "thunderously" to command and direct power. We can find this technique effective in that same LBRP, even if in retrospect we find that we were unsure of the pronunciations, or find that our pronunciations differ from those suggested in the manual.

In truth, I think it's a little of both, and although the barbarous names are not as popular in magick today, I've found them very effective. I've done several exorcism rituals in my healing practice for those with attached spirit entities, and in some of the most effective of these rituals, I used foreign languages and untranslatable words of power. I started with the popular phrase "Hekas, Hekas, Este Bebeloi." Not only did this connect me to a sense of magickal history, but the unfamiliarity of the words helped my client release. Combining this phrase with words of power and the Hebrew version of the ceremonial rituals induced a profound psycho-magickal state in both myself and the client in which this difficult magick could be done effectively and completely.

The term *barbarous name* comes from the Greek *barbaroi* and is the root for our word *barbarian*, which simply meant "one who didn't speak Greek." A barbarous name referred to any word in a ritual, possibly a god name, that didn't make sense in Greek. The term *voces magicae*, meaning "words of power," also can be used. The *Ephesia Grammata*, literally "Ephesian letters" in Greek, were the best-known and most commonly used words of power in the classical Greek world. They were used widely to confer power and victory, and eventually became equated with the concept of barbarous names to mean any unintelligible name. The Ephesia Grammata are *askion, kataskion, lix, tertrax, damnameneus,* and *aision (aisia).*

The idea of barbarous words of power was later adopted by other cultures to mean any magickal word that didn't make sense in the well-known tongue. Such names of power were derived from Egyptian, Hebrew, Persian, and later Greek, though many words cannot be traced to any root language and just appear to be gibberish. A major source for such names is the *Graeco-Egyptian Magical Papyri,* mixing pagan, Jewish, and Christian forms of magick and terms of power. Such words have been used in a variety of cultures and forms of magick, from curse tablets to love spells. The tradition was powerful up through the Middle Ages, yet other than in the modern revival of Enochian, Goetia workings, and a ritual known as the Bornless Rite, very few modern magicians use the classical barbarous names of power. Examples of these names include *ablanathanalba, akrammachamarei, anaboria, baldachia, asanexhexeton,* and *sesengenbarpharanges.*

Certain other barbarous words have been passed down. In *The Key of Solomon,* to consecrate water, or to prepare what some call the Bath of Solomon, the following names are used:

Mertalia, Musalia, Dophalia, Onemalia, Zitanseia, Goldaphaira, Dedulsaira, Ghevialaira, Gheminaira, Gegropheria, Cedahi, Gilthar, Godieb, Ezoil, Musil, Grassil, Tamen, Pueri, Godu, Huznoth, Astachoth, Astachoth, Adonai, AGLA, On, El, Tetragrammaton, Shema, Aresion, Anaphaxeton, Segilaton, Primeumaton.

To consecrate the salt, to add to the water, other barbarous names are used:

Imanel, Arnamon, Imato, Memeon, Rectacon, Muoboii, Paltellon, Decaion, Yamenton, Yaron, Tatonon, Vaphoron, Gardon, Existon, Zagveron, Momerton, Zarmesiton, Tileion, Tixmion.

Many modern witches of British Traditional lineages are taught to use abridged versions of these words of power: "Mertalia, Musalia, Dophalia, Onemalia, Zitanseia" for the water and "Yamenton, Yaron, Tatonon, Zarmesiton, Tileion, Tixmion" for the salt.

Witches also have adopted a form of barbarous words known as the *Bagahi Rune*. Like the Witch's Rune (*OTOW*, Chapter 11), it refers to a chant, not the Teutonic symbol system. The origin of the Bagahi Rune is disputed, but many believe it began with the Basques, a people known for their connections to witchcraft, secret languages, and magick. Some speculate that it is a listing of god names in Basque, though we don't know that with any certainty. The first written account of the Bagahi Rune appeared in a thirteenth-century manuscript attributed to the French troubadour Rutebeuf. Now it is used in Gardnerian and Alexandrian rites, particularly initiation ceremonies, and at Samhain. It also can be used to add power to any working of magick. Here is a phonetic suggestion to help you recite the Bagahi Rune, from *The Goodly Spellbook: Olde Spells for Modern Problems* by Dixie Deerman (Lady Passion) and Steven Rasmussen (*Diuvei):

Bagahi laca bachahe — Bah-GAH-hee LAH-ka BAH-khah-hey
Lamac cahi achabahe — Lah-MAHK kah-HEE ah-KHAH-bah-hey
Karrrelyos! — Kah-RREL-yohs!

Lamac lamec bachalyos — La-MAHK lah-MEKH bah-KHAH-lee-ohs
Cabahagi sabalyos — Kah-BAH-hah-gee sah-BAH-lee-ohs
Baryols! — Bah-RREE-oh-lahs!

Lagozatha cabyolas — Lah-goh-zah-THAH kah-BEE-oh-lahs
Samahac et famyolas — Sah-MAH-HAHK EHT fah-MEE-oh-lahs
Harrahya! — Hah-RRAH-hee-yah!

Modern magicians can make use of power words in similar ways. Here are some options.

Classic Barbarous Words

Through researching classic texts and grimoires, and the writings of those magicians who use them, you can find barbarous words that have been used in the past.

Foreign Languages

You don't have to use any words that you are completely unfamiliar with, but you can ritualistically use the words of a foreign tongue that you are not as familiar with. I have found great use in translating rituals into Latin and Greek. This provides a mechanism for me to add power to my rituals, or at least sections of rituals, even though I'm not an expert in either of these languages, and even if my translations wouldn't sound proper to a native speaker of the language.

Sigilization Method

You can make words of power with very specific intentions in the same manner in which you would create a sigil. Rather than using the remaining, unrepeated letters of a phrase to create a geometric design, you would use them in a chant (see *OTOW*, Chapter 13, and *TOSW*, Chapter 13).

Notarikon

In the tradition of notarikon, you can use the first letters of a statement to create a magick word. Our previous example, "I ASK THE GODS TO BE FINANCIALLY PROSPEROUS. SO MOTE IT BE," would then become IATGTBFPSMIB, which I might divide as IATG TB FPS MIB.

Otherworld Languages

You can travel to the other realms and receive words of power from spirits, angels, and deities, and use them as instructed (see *TOSW*, Chapter 13). You can find your own divine names and power words for each of the sephiroth.

The use of any of these names of power is personal. Some magicians use them for evocation of spirits and creating sacred space. Others use them to raise energy for a spell. The recitation of a series of magickal words also can be the catalyst to cast the spell. If you so choose, experiment with the technique of using foreign words and sounds, researching both the psychological effect this has on you and others, but also determining if the sound itself has an effect on reality. Working names and words into melody and chant, particularly using the tones associated with the sephiroth, can be quite powerful.

GEBURAH PATHWORKINGS

Based on the previous lessons, only two paths from Geburah remain, the path of Strength/Lust and the path of the Chariot. Each path is a process focused on the appropriate use of power. The path of Strength/Lust links Geburah to Chesed. Strength must be learned to properly apply both the power and mercy of these two spheres. The classic image of the woman holding open the jaws of the lion shows us that we must be fearless in balancing these mighty powers. Compassion without power is weakness. Power without compassion is dangerous and can run wild. We must learn to integrate the two, yet not fear the appropriate use of both power and compassion.

Geburah is linked to its highest form, Binah, through the mysteries of the Chariot card. The Chariot is the power of movement, of travel, and ultimately of the sacred quest. After a period of introspection and drawing boundaries, the withdrawal into the armor of the knight, the Grail Knight, the seeker must cross the Abyss and find the highest form of the divine feminine, the form found in Binah. This is the ultimate sacrifice for the understanding that comes with Binah.

EXERCISE 23

Geburah Pathworking

1. Perform the Lesser Banishing Ritual of the Pentagram (exercise 5) and the Lesser Banishing Ritual of the Hexagram (exercise 20). Do any other ritual you feel is appropriate.

2. While in this space, call upon the divine forces of Geburah. Burn your five red candles and dragon's blood incense. Knock on your altar five times. Vibrate the divine name of Geburah, **Elohim Gibor**, five times. Call upon any of the martial deities of the sphere, or Archangel Kamael.

3. To count down into a meditative state, do exercise 1 through step 7 (page 76).

4. Let the familiar world around you fall away, as if the material reality you know is only a façade and beneath it lies the beautiful garden of the Goddess, a veritable paradise surrounding you. The land around you becomes a vast primordial garden, the garden of Malkuth, the familiar garden of the four paths.

5. Go to the heart of Malkuth, to the Temple of Malkuth. Decide which path you wish to take to Geburah. Plot out the path in your mind, through the appropriate sephiroth and pathways. Perhaps try choosing pathways that you haven't yet explored.

6. While on your path, reflect on the symbolism of each of the paths of wisdom. If you have walked a particular pathway before, let the wisdom reach a deeper level within you. Let the images of the associated tarot card and path come to you. Let your thoughts and feelings be guided by the power of the path. Learn what you can of the path, and of your process, to expand your consciousness to Geburah.

7. Feel the call of the red sphere from your path. You are bidden to enter the gates of Geburah, the realm of fire and smoke, the forge of power. You might have to give a symbol of Geburah as the key to enter the realm, such as the divine name (Elohim Gibor), the Mars glyph, or the name of a warrior deity. Once you enter the realm, you feel the heat and power of the sphere. Feel your power rise. Feel your strength. Notice how you feel about these qualities, as your body and psyche are stimulated by the energy. Explore the realm of Geburah, and welcome any beings that may come across your path, but be wary, as they might challenge your power, your strength, and your right to be there. And beware the basilisks.

8. Make your way to the Temple of Geburah. You enter a five-sided temple, made of ruby and iron, stark and powerful. You feel the essence of Geburah, of might and power emanating from the walls. Notice the gateways to the other paths in the temple, the gate from the direction in which you came and the other three gates.

9. The entities of Geburah are residing in the temple. The warrior gods and goddesses are present. Forge deities and destructive goddesses are potentially manifest, depending on your relationship to Geburah. Archangel Kamael also is available. Commune with the beings of the sphere. Ask to know the Vision of Power in a manner that is correct and for your highest good. Ask to learn the virtue and obligation of the sphere and ways to avoid the vice and illusion.

10. When done, thank all the beings who have communicated with you. They might offer you a gift, a token of their goodwill. If you accept, it is polite to reach within your being and offer them a gift of your goodwill.

11. Once you have said your farewells, leave the shrine and follow the path back. Return the way you came unless you feel guided to return via a different pathway and know the pathway back well. Return to the garden of Malkuth. Focus on the waking world you know, and feel it return around the garden.

12. To return to normal waking consciousness and end your journey, perform steps 15–17 from exercise 1 (page 78). You can close the temple by repeating the LBRP.

GEBURAH INITIATION

In traditional ceremonial orders, the Geburah initiation is known as the ⑥=⑤ ranking, that of an Adeptus Major or Advanced Adept. The training and obligation of this level of initiation is to master all forms of practical magick. This is why the five-pointed star, a symbol of magick and all the elements, is such a good emblem of this level.

A true witch or magician has a thirst for all things magickal. We seek to know all systems of magick, to understand and expand our own worldview, even if we find that those traditions are not for us. We want to know, to learn, to understand the flow of magick in all things, in all people and cultures. There is a drive to explore and experience. That is the higher drive of Geburah, to have mastery over these skills, for we never know when we'll be called upon to use them. Part of this fourth-level training is to prepare modern witches to understand and potentially use Qabalah in their personal magickal systems. Once they have achieved a certain level of mastery, it's up to the individual witches to decide what aspects to synthesize into their worldview and what to leave behind, but only after attaining a thorough understanding of the tradition.

HOMEWORK

- Do Exercises 22–23 and record your experiences in your Book of Shadows.

- Learn and practice the Greater Invoking Ritual of the Pentagram (exercise 22), the traditional version or your own personally reconstructed version.

- Explore working with words of power.

- Continue to practice the LBRP, LBRH, Middle Pillar, and Circulation of the Body of Light rituals, the traditional or personal versions. You can continue with the Four Adorations and the Ritual of the Rosy Cross, but this is not a requirement.

TIPS

- Fill in the Geburah correspondences and colors on your own Tree of Life drawing. Contemplate them as you add them to the image. Start memorizing these correspondences.

- Review and reflect on all you have learned in this lesson.

- Continue to work with the four elements.

- Continue working with the lower sephiroth.

- Study the Greater Invoking Ritual of the Pentagram to deconstruct and reconstruct it to fit your worldview, if you so choose. If you are reconstructing it, make sure your symbolism is consistent with the pentagram rituals and other rites.

• Pick one other reality map from appendix I to contemplate. Understanding a variety of worldviews will help you when you construct your own reality map.

LESSON EIGHT
CHESED

Chesed is the balance to Geburah. While Geburah is all fire and power, direct and confronting, Chesed is mercy and divine love, tempering the martial fire of Geburah. While Geburah is catabolic, breaking things down, Chesed is anabolic, forming structure and building things up. It encourages growth and expansion.

Chesed is the realm of the loving principle in a divine and detached state, being a higher octave of the passionate love of Netzach. Chesed's name means "mercy," for it is the merciful and benign aspect of the Tree of Life, situated at the center of the Pillar of Mercy. It is an elevated form of Netzach, but a more comprehendible form of Chokmah. At its ultimate level, it is the divine parental love, embodied by the astrological figure of Jupiter, father of the gods. Jupiter is known as the Greater Benefic, the planet of good fortune, in medieval astrology. Modern astrologers might say it's the planet of the higher self, the higher octave to the personal self of the Sun. Jupiter is the planet the Sun mythically aspires to be, like the Sun god Apollo aspiring to his father's throne. While the Sun is physically bigger than Jupiter, Jupiter's magnetosphere is the largest "object" in our solar system. As "king" of the gods and planets, Jupiter has a presence that is larger but more subtle than that of the Sun. Jupiter even transmits signal noise that usually sounds like static to scientists, but when it is listened to carefully, there is a pattern, as if Jupiter is trying to send a message or code, guiding others. Jupiter's signal is much like how our own meditations can be—mostly static punctuated with some patterned message that needs to be decoded.

On a personal level, Jupiter seems to portend good luck and fortune coming our way, but in reality it brings about a greater alignment with the higher self. When we are more aligned with this true self, the way opens up to us, creating what appears to be good luck to anybody unaware of the higher reality. Jupiter's nature is to expand whatever it touches. We initially see this as a good thing, for if we are focusing on blessings, Jupiter and Chesed expand what we focus on. Sometimes this expansion becomes too much for reality, and this force must be balanced with an equally strong yet opposing energy, as embodied by Geburah.

Chesed is said to have a special relationship with the astral plane, and the world of form in general. As the first sphere beyond the Abyss, beneath the three supernals, it is the first power to give abstraction form. It represents the highest, most lofty, royal and benign manifestations of reality. It contains all archetypes and potentials, at their most perfected state, to be made manifest in the lower realms. What we experience in the lower spheres, particularly in Yesod, is clouded by our emotions. Fear and anger, in particular, cloud our vision. We have to reach through to Chesed to see the highest expression of whatever force we are seeking.

Chesed

Meaning: Mercy
Level of Reality: Time, Space, Manifestation
Parts of the Self: Memory, Left Shoulder
Experience: Vision of Love
Obligation: Humility
Illusion: Self-Righteousness
Virtue: Obedience
Vices: Bigotry, Tyranny, Hypocrisy, Gluttony
Name of God: El (God)

King Scale Color: Deep Violet
Queen Scale Color: Blue
Prince Scale Color: Deep Purple
Princess Scale Color: Deep Azure flecked with Gold
Element: Water
Planet: Jupiter
Image: Ruler on a Throne
Archetypes: Sky Father, Wise King
Greek/Roman Deities: Zeus, Jupiter, Poseidon
Egyptian Deity: Amon-Ra
Middle Eastern Deity: Marduk
Celtic Deities: Dagda, Taranis
Norse Deities: Thor, Bragi
Hindu Deities: Indra, Brahma
Archangel: Tzadkiel (Angel of Mercy)
Angelic Order: Chashmalim (Brilliant Ones)
Choir: Dominions
Grade of Initiation: ⑦=④ Perfect Adept
Animal: Unicorn
Planetary Vowel Sound: Y (ü)
Resonant Letter: n
Musical Mode: Mixolydian
Musical Note: G
Tools: Wand, Crook, Scepter, Pyramid, Equal-Armed Cross
Incense: Cedar
Tarot: Four of Wands, Swords, Cups, and Pentacles
       Fortune—to Netzach
       Hermit—to Tiphereth
       Strength/Lust—to Geburah
       Hierophant—to Chokmah
Metal: Tin
Stone: Amethyst
Plants: Olive, Rush, Lemon Balm

For this month's lesson, arrange your altar with the correspondences of Chesed and Jupiter. Blues are the colors of Chesed, and the number is four. Cedar is the traditional incense, and blue and purple stones are suitable. Anything royal and rich would be appropriate for the embodiment of Chesed, as it is the king beneath the Abyss. Arrange the fours of the tarot on your altar, as well as the major arcana leading to the pathways in and out of the sphere. Fortune reaches down to Netzach, while the Hierophant goes above to Chokmah. Strength/Lust reaches across to Geburah, while the Hermit leads to Tiphereth.

Entities of Chesed

The realm of Chesed is the realm of royalty, marked by the self-mastery and sovereignty that comes from attaining the powers of the previous sephiroth yet not ascending across the Abyss. The classic image of Chesed is the Ruler or King upon a Throne. Chesed is the loving father, the benevolent and proud dad, wanting to provide for and protect his children. All the best father qualities we sentimentalize in greeting cards are part of Chesed. As the sky shelters the planet below, protecting it from too much heat and light, the sky of Chesed protects creation from the Abyss and the supernals, sheltering us under its clouds and gently encouraging our growth. The planet Jupiter protects the Earth by attracting space debris in its gravity that could otherwise endanger our planet.

The planetary archetype of Chesed is Jupiter, the ruler of the Roman gods. His Greek cognate is the ruler of the Olympians, Zeus. While the more Titanic forces of the previous generation of gods can be seen in the powers of the Supernal Triad, Zeus and his siblings represent the gods closer to humanity and the material world. He is a storm king and sky father. His weapon of choice is the lightning bolt, said to be forged by Hephaestus, a Geburah figure, showing the intimate link again between Geburah and Chesed. In many stories, Zeus is a figure of life, of wisdom, healing, and blessings. He is seen as a wise and magnificent ruler. Other times, he is seen as jealous, oversexed, rash, quick to anger, unforgiving, and unaware of the feelings of others.

Other pagan sky fathers and lightning gods are related to Chesed. Thor of the Norse gods is a Jupiterian figure. Though his father, Odin, is considered to be the all-father and wise ruler, Thor is the god of the people of Midgard, our Earth, or Malkuth in Norse cosmology. His tool wields the lightning of the storm. Though goodhearted, he is not considered as wise and cunning as his father.

The early Celtic figure of Taranis is seen as a lightning, storm, and sky king, though we know little of the early Celtic figures. The Dagda is equated with Jupiterian figures. The Dagda has much more lore from the Irish myths, as a primal giant and leader of the gods, yet he is not necessarily associated with the sky or storms. He is a great teacher and an archdruid, jovial and powerful. His cauldron is the cauldron of plenty, while his harp's music turns the seasons. He is linked to the goddess of war and death, the Morrighan, to gain insight to defeat the Fomorians and carries a staff of life and death, killing and resurrecting a foe with alternate blows. He embodies the principles of Jupiter, of expansiveness and true royalty.

Coming from the Hindu cosmology, Indra is the god king associated with Chesed. He is the lord of storms and thunders, leader of the devas, and a great warrior defending humanity from the forces of evil. His weapons are the Vajra, the lightning, as well as a net, bow, and hook. He brings water to the Earth and can resurrect slain warriors, much like the Dagda. He is the ruler of the lesser gods beneath him in power and prestige, yet the more primal powers of Binah, Chokmah, and Kether are still above him.

To the Egyptians, the primal father figure usually is associated with the Sun, not Jupiter. When looking at our Qabalistic correspondences from an Egyptian perspective, the gods of Tiphereth, Chesed, and Kether overlap and share characteristics. With multiple creation stories, many see Ra, the Sun god, as the primal creator and closest to the godhead, and embodied by his successors in the lower planes.

One Egyptian figure I associate with the rulership of Chesed and Jupiter is Amon-Ra, a later addition to Egyptian mythology fusing aspects of Amun and Ra. Amon-Ra is the invisible breeze and is seen as a god of wind and air, and eventually became fused with the Sun god Ra and the ruler of Thebes. Later he was made the supreme god of Egypt. Depicted with a ram's head and man's body, Amon-Ra holds the rulership qualities of the enlightened king upon the throne.

El is the divine name of Chesed, meaning "God," and some believe there is a connection to the names Baal and Bel. Cosmologically, many in traditional orthodox religions are actually focusing their attention not on the godhead, on the YHVH creative force of the universe, but on the aspect of God in Chesed. We can find parallels between the sky fathers of pagan cosmologies and the biblical father god of the Old Testament, linking them both with Chesed, while the less capricious god of the New Testament is linked with the godhead of Kether. Figures such as Jupiter have a beneficent side, as exemplified by the sphere's lessons, and a tyrannical side, the vices and corruption of the sphere. As Chesed is the highest sphere of the Tree before the Abyss, many make the mistake of thinking this is the highest sphere, and that stems from a fear of going beyond, or arrogance. The early Gnostics and Gnostic Christians had a concept that the figure of the Old Testament was not the true God, what the Qabalist would call YHVH, but the Demiurge, the god of the material world, and equated this Demiurge with the concept of the Devil. The Demiurge has been linked to figures such as Lucifer, Prometheus, and Melek Taus.

When the Demiurge or his followers believe him to be the supreme god, he manifests as the jealous, tyrannical, and fearful god of wrath, fire, and brimstone. The Demiurge is in fear, because he doesn't want you to figure it out. He is in ego, and the religions built up around him are in ego. Many would argue that this is the type of Christianity that focuses on the Old Testament stories.

When the figure clearly is not the ultimate creator, he becomes a liberator, a giver of celestial light to the material world. He is like Prometheus, the light bringer, or the Gnostic Lucifer, the light bringer, not the Devil. He becomes the secret shadow god that acts as an ally to help the mystic cross the Abyss and attain higher experience. Orthodox religions hide this aspect and demonize it, so those involved in the religion will not seek out the liberator, for if you have the guidance of the liberator, you do not need the Church. In essence, they are two sides of the same coin, both several rungs short of the ultimate godhead and source.

Tzadkiel, or Zadkiel, the archangel of mercy, is the angelic minister to this sphere, as the archangel of Jupiter. He is associated with magick and transmutation, as well as the hidden orders of masters that aspire to this plane. He is the leader of the order of the Chashmalim, the "brilliant ones" or "shining ones." Some see the Chashmalim as aspects of gods or demigods, as the gods were called the ancient and shining ones, and these angels are a higher octave of the Elohim of the sphere of Netzach below. Another system relates the choir of the Dominions to this sphere. They are the divine organizers, the architects of the universe, bringing form and function, neatly fitting in with Chesed's theme of form, as the fourth sephira.

As a realm of perfected forms, Chesed is called the Hall of Masters, or the Hall of the Ancient Ones. The template of the divine ascended human, the inner-plane master, comes from this place. Many ascended masters, moving on from the station of guiding Malkuth, help guide the inner orders from the consciousness of Chesed. Chesed as a principle encourages and nurtures structure and order. This manifests as promoting learning, philosophy, art, science, and magick. The masters of magick can guide and teach the initiates through this sphere.

Vision of Chesed

The spiritual experience of Chesed is simply known as the Vision of Love. This is the experience of Love, not the conditional love seen in many relationships, but a true experience of unconditional divine love that is best symbolized as the relationship between parent and child, though in this case it is the love between the divine parent and child. It is the witch's Perfect Love of the magick circle. When we cast our circle in Perfect Love and Perfect Trust, we are invoking the highest power, expansive and uplifting, and contractive and protecting. One might say that in the Ethical Triangle, these forces, Perfect Love and Perfect Trust, are Chesed and Geburah, mediated by the solar sphere of Tiphereth.

The obligation of Chesed is humility. Like a regent, a divine sovereign, we must aspire to humility, for it is only in the spirit of humility that we can serve the divine purpose with divine love. The illusion of this sphere, self-righteousness, is a turn that many take when they believe they have touched upon the divine mercy of Chesed. Many do experience Chesed's mercy, but rather than integrate it and embody it, they then feel they have a license to drive everybody toward their path, as it obviously worked for them, and if it worked, it must be the way. In an effort to be "right" and have everybody see they are "right," they lose sight of the mercy and love, and cannot manifest mercy and love. When this lack of love is exposed, no potential follower will feel this is the path to divinity. We see this in many of the "merciful" forms of Christianity, that are so only in name, but turn out to be some of the most bigoted, tyrannical, hypocritical, and greedy organizations. They embody all the vices of Chesed, yet believe, in their hypocrisy, that they are fulfilling divine will, and fulfilling the obligation to the divine—obedience. The virtue of Chesed is to be true to your own higher self, not to force others to the will of what you perceive your divinity to be demanding. It is easy to experience bigotry once you attain this level, for you feel as if you are looking "down" upon the rest of the cosmos. Without the balance of humility, we lose the mastery of self that got us to Chesed.

To truly embody the merciful principle of Chesed is to realize this mercy is all-inclusive and does not distinguish anyone, at their spiritual core, as better than anybody else. That is the mystery of Chesed. In the end, we all are deserving of receiving, and then giving, Perfect Love. Without this love and mercy, we are not serving the true spirit of Chesed, but the shadow of Chesed, the Demiurge, the lord of the world, not of spirit.

Chesed Magick

Chesed is a powerful force to work with in any magick. For spiritual goals, it is the highest force beneath the Abyss, and generally is characterized as wise, gentle, and loving. For material goals, it is the root of all form beneath the Abyss, and holds the idea patterns and archetypes of creation. It is a complex, generating force.

Elementally, Chesed has multiple correspondences. Like Geburah, it cannot be neatly pinned down. Chesed is ruled by Jupiter, which rules Sagittarius, a fire sign. Jupiter is considered a spiritual Sun, as it is a gas giant that has never ignited into a star. But in more traditional astrology, Jupiter also rules Pisces, a water sign. Both have very strong spiritual associations, being the first and last of the four transpersonal zodiac signs. At their heights, Jupiter is expanded consciousness, while Pisces is unconditional love, the mercy of Chesed. Like its twin, Geburah, Chesed has fire and water associations. Mythically, the sky king of Jupiter also would give it air associations. Though the least tangible of the sephiroth beneath the Abyss, Chesed rules form by being the root of manifestation, also giving it an earth quality.

Chesed's divine rulership is symbolized by the totemic figure of the unicorn. Though many would assume that the unicorn belongs to the realm of the fluffy-bunny explorer of fantasy games rather than serious Qabalah, the unicorn has a rich mythical history. Traditionally associated with innocence and purity, unicorns are something incorruptible in the material world, beyond simple and basic animal instincts yet more evolved and advanced than humans. They make contact only with those similarly pure and in alignment with spirit. The unicorn has been a symbol of royalty, as part of the crests and banners of kings, as well as a symbol of the Christ principle, the resurrection god. A famous tapestry named "Unicorn in Captivity" shows the innocence of spirit, embodied by the unicorn, in the bondage of the material world. From a Qabalistic perspective, the natural realm of the unicorn is Chesed, not Malkuth. As the unicorn is the mythical animal of kings, all rich and royal correspondences match with Chesed and Jupiter.

Traditionally, the wood of cedar is burned as an incense, or its oil as a scent. Strangely, tin is the metal of Jupiter. One would think Jupiter's metal would be the gold of the Sun or even something richer, like platinum, but tin is traditional, for it is a metal to transform. Alchemists believed metals transformed from lead into tin first, moving through the metallic "spectrum" to get to gold. Rich and royal blues and purple are the colors of Chesed. Amethyst is its traditional stone, bearing out the Jupiterian association with Pisces, as amethyst is the traditional birthstone of Pisces.

Chesed's ability to move the abstract form and energies of the upper triangle into more concrete concepts is both part of its anabolic building function and its inherent geometry. As the fourth sphere, it is directly tied in to the four directions and, as we've seen, the four elements. Four is the power of manifestation, as we need all four elements to make something a tangible reality. It is the stability of the four legs of a table or the four walls of a building. One could say that the devas, when defined as the architects of nature, the pattern holders, reside here. They are the spirits that guide the elemental and nature spirits to build our physical reality and maintain the flow of energies between the worlds and that reality. Ceremonies involving the four directions and four powers help align us with these powers of creation. We need only look at the witch's magick circle, the variety of rituals in ceremonial magick, and the native medicine wheel ceremonies to see the universality of the four powers.

The sacred geometries based on the tetrad, tetrahedron, square, and cube are fundamental building blocks of nature, both organic and inorganic creations, from the subatomic structures of atoms to viruses, crystals, and living cells. Though the three points of Binah form the first shape, it takes a minimum of four points in space to define volume and form the first object. This is why four is associated with solid manifestation in the material realm. The sacred geometric figure known as the Decomposed Square, a square continuously divided into four, creates a woven pattern, the Net of Indra or the Web of the Goddess (figure 61). This pattern shows up both as the underlying form of sacred ancient art and in microscopic atomic patterns.

Almost all the rituals of ceremonial magick have the four-directional symbolism inherent in them, yet there is no ritual specifically aligned with the four-pointed star, or specifically the square. Yet the cube, the six-sided hexahedron, is born out of tetrad geometry, as each face of the polyhedron is four-sided, mixing the four and six geometric forms. For this lesson, I have chosen the Greater Ritual of the Hexagram. The

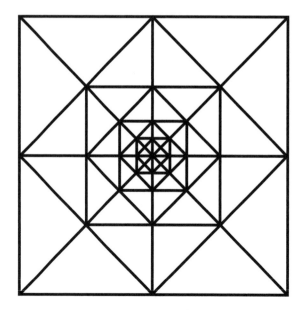

Figure 61: Decomposed Square

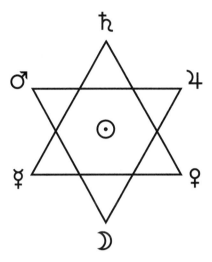

Figure 62: Planets on the Hexagram

two triangles of the hexagram are the alignment of the Upper and Lower Worlds, the macrocosm and microcosm. In Tiphereth, you learned the elementally aligned version of the hexagram ritual (exercise 20). In the Greater Ritual, you will learn the invocation or banishing of planetary forces. As Chesed is our link, or bridge, to the upper triangle, the Greater Ritual of the Hexagram, using all seven planets, is an alignment across the Abyss to the upper triangle, for the last planet, Saturn, is assigned to Binah, the first sephira of the Supernal Triangle (figure 62).

The Greater Ritual of the Hexagram is used to invoke or banish specific planetary forces. Just as the pentagrams can be used to invoke or banish specific elements, so can the hexagrams be used to invoke or banish planetary energies. In the form given here, the ritual is written as the Greater Invoking Ritual of the Hexagram.

Unlike the Greater Ritual of the Pentagram (exercise 22), which works with all four elements, the Greater Ritual of the Hexagram involves invoking or banishing a specific planetary power, not all seven. Some versions of the ritual use the basic Star of David–style of hexagram (two interlocked triangles) for each direction, while other, more complicated forms of the ritual use the variant east, south, west, and north forms of the

Invoking   Banishing

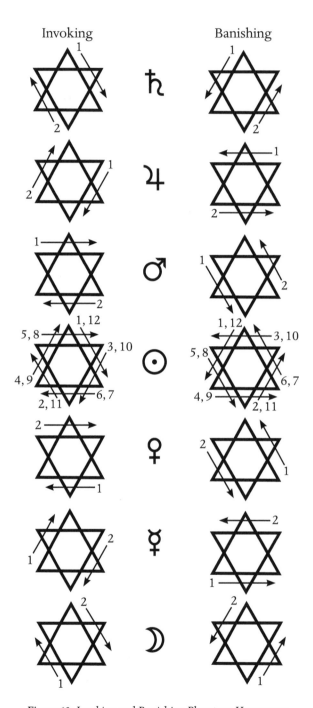

Figure 63: Invoking and Banishing Planetary Hexagrams

hexagram, with the same movements to invoke or banish but with the triangles arranged differently. For our work here, I prefer to use the traditional interlocked hexagram.

To invoke, start at the point of the hexagram with which the planet is aligned, and trace a clockwise triangle (figure 63). For the second triangle, start at the opposing point of the hexagram, and draw a clockwise triangle. Draw the planetary glyph in the center of the hexagram. To banish, start at the planet's point on the hexagram and draw a counterclockwise triangle. For the second triangle, start at the opposing point of the hexagram and draw a counterclockwise triangle. Draw the planetary glyph in the center of the hexagram.

For the Sun, all the previous hexagrams must be drawn, either invoking or banishing, depending on the ritual. To draw an invoking hexagram of the Sun, you must draw an invoking hexagram of Saturn, Jupiter, Mars, Venus, Mercury, and the Moon, all without planetary glyphs, but end by drawing the glyph of the Sun in the center. To draw a banishing hexagram of the Sun, you must draw a banishing hexagram of Saturn, Jupiter, Mars, Venus, Mercury, and the Moon, all without planetary glyphs, but end by drawing the Sun's glyph in the center.

Technically, in the LBRH, all of these banishing hexagrams are of Saturn, for each of the four directions. An LIRH would use the invoking hexagrams of Saturn. Much as the earth pentagram is used as an all-purpose form in the earlier pentagram rituals, the Saturn hexagram is used as an all-purpose form in the earlier hexagram ritual.

EXERCISE 24

Greater Invoking Ritual of the Hexagram (GIRH)

1. Perform the LBRP and LBRH (exercises 5 and 20). As in the LBRH, in the GIRH you can use your wand, held in your right hand, or you can just use your hand. (A rainbow-banded lotus wand, with twelve colors, can be used for this rite. For each planetary ritual, you can hold the lotus wand by the zodiac color associated with the sign that is ruled by the planet. I prefer to just use my traditional wand.)

2. Performing the Analysis of the Key Word is optional (refer back to exercise 20). It is repeated here in certain versions of this ritual, but as it was just performed in the LBRH in step 1, I do not find it necessary to do so again here, as the LVX signs will be performed at each quarter. You can omit the Analysis of the Key Word in favor of the Qabalistic Cross, or omit step 2 all together and move right on to the hexagram ritual itself.

3. Facing east, draw the invoking hexagram of the planet you wish to work with, in bright light. You can imagine the hexagram and planetary glyph in the colors associated with the planet. You might perceive the previous banishing blue pentagram and golden hexagrams behind it. Make the Sign of the Enterer to charge the hexagram with the appropriate-colored planetary energy, vibrating **ARARITA**. Draw the glyph of the planet you are invoking in the appropriate planetary color, and vibrate the divine god name associated with its sephira. (Optional: Follow with the LVX signs: Sign of the Mourning of Isis—Sign of Apophis and Typhon—Sign of Osiris Slain—Sign of Osiris Risen.)

4. Point to the center of the hexagram with your tool, and draw one-quarter of the circle with a line of light, bringing you to the south, just as you did in the LBRP and LBRH.

5. Facing south, draw the invoking hexagram of the planet you wish to work with, in bright light of the planet's color on the Queen Scale. Make the Sign of the Enterer to charge the hexagram with the appropriate-colored planetary energy, vibrating **ARARITA**. Draw the glyph of the planet you are invoking in the appropriate planetary color, and vibrate the divine god name associated with its sephira. (Optional: Follow with the LVX signs.)

6. Point to the center of the hexagram with your tool, and draw one-quarter of the circle with a line of light, bringing you to the west.

7. Facing west, draw the invoking hexagram of the planet you wish to work with, in bright light of the planet's color on the Queen Scale. Make the Sign of the Enterer to charge the hexagram with the appropriate-colored

planetary energy, vibrating **ARARITA**. Draw the glyph of the planet you are invoking in the appropriate planetary color, and vibrate the divine god name associated with its sephira. (Optional: Follow with the LVX signs.)

8. Point to the center of the hexagram with your tool, and draw one-quarter of the circle with a line of light, bringing you to the north.

9. Facing north, draw the invoking hexagram of the planet you wish to work with, in bright light of the planet's color on the Queen Scale. Make the Sign of the Enterer to charge the hexagram with the appropriate-colored planetary energy, vibrating **ARARITA**. Draw the glyph of the planet you are invoking in the appropriate planetary color, and vibrate the divine god name associated with its sephira. (Optional: Follow with the LVX signs.)

10. Point to the center of the hexagram with your tool, and draw one-quarter of the circle with a line of light, bringing you to the east.

11. Optional: Draw the invoking hexagram of the planet you wish to work with, in bright light of the planet's color on the Queen Scale, above the altar and/or in the center of the ritual circle. Make the Sign of the Enterer to charge the hexagram with the appropriate-colored planetary energy, vibrating **ARARITA**. Follow with the LVX signs.

12. Optional: Circumambulate around the ritual circle the Qabalistically corresponding number of times associated with the planet. (Saturn rituals would have three movements around the circle, Venus would have seven, etc.)

13. Do your planetary working, such as ritual magick, meditation, pathworking, or consecration.

14. Optional: Reverse circumambulate around the ritual circle the same number of times as in step 12. (If, in a Saturn ritual, you went clockwise around the altar three times, then go counterclockwise around the altar, starting and ending in the east.) This is one of the few times in traditional ceremonial magick that a widdershins movement is used. Notice that even in banishing rituals we are "creating" a clear space, and moving deosil.

15. Perform the Greater Banishing Ritual of the Hexagram for the planet you have chosen, repeating steps 3–11, but with banishing hexagrams of the appropriate planet rather than invoking hexagrams.

16. Repeat the LBRP and LBRH.

The hexagram rituals can be adapted and further expanded. One adaptation is to use them as invoking and banishing rituals for zodiac signs or the sephirothic powers. Another is to combine the planetary powers in the Supreme Ritual of the Hexagram, used to invoke or banish all seven planetary forces in one ritual. This ritual is much like the Greater Ritual of the Hexagram, yet instead of orienting to the four directions, the orientation mimics the Golden Dawn's septagram-style Vault of the Adepti. It can be adapted by simply drawing all seven hexagrams in the center, above the altar, after the LBRP and LBRH, rather than following the intricate pattern of the Vault.

MAGICKAL CONSTRUCTS

Since Chesed is the root of creation beneath the Abyss, a form of magick that aligns well with this creative force is the creation of magickal constructs. Constructs go by a variety of names, such as artificial elementals, artificial familiars, spirit golems, tulpas, and servitor spirits. At first glance, it's a controversial technique, particularly among witches, but when you delve deeper, it's not much different from what we already are doing in our magickal workings. I think it's a problem of packaging. Call anything "artificial" and witches want nothing to do with it. Likewise, call something a "servant" and witches shy away. The technique is more popular among Chaos magicians.

In essence, a construct is a semipermanent spell with open-ended instructions. If you have created a ward (a protection shield around your home or vehicle), you already have created a type of construct. In the more advanced stages, it is a semipermanent thoughtform programmed with your instructions. It's semipermanent because if you don't do any upkeep on it, "feeding" it energy, it will dissipate. It's not a living being generating life force on its own, but a packet of energy with specific instructions. With most spells, once the spell completes its task, it runs out of energy, because it used its energy to manifest your goal, and it dissipates. A construct has a semblance of life and can last for an indefinite or predetermined period of time. It's a spell with a longer shelf life than that of your typical candle or petition spell.

For example, if you run a shop, you could create a construct that protects your store, preventing people from shoplifting. It might broadcast a fear of getting caught to those who intend to shoplift, or it might help expose their theft before they reach the door. Your spell would not target a specific time, day, or person, but would be open-ended, for the life of the store. If you work with the public, particularly in the social services, you might create a construct to devour harmful unbalanced energy and transmute it to balanced healing energy. You can create a construct to help find lost objects, maintain a computer network, or inspire you at work. You are limited only by your imagination and the physical requirements of the task. Unfortunately, I've yet to find a magician who created a construct that physically vacuums or washes windows.

Some of my friends who are witches wonder why you would go to the trouble of creating a construct when you could partner with a spirit who would do the same thing with you. It's a good question, and a matter of personal magickal style. You can summon/conjure/partner with a spiritual being to protect your home, transmute energy, find lost objects, or anything else, but some feel it would be binding a spirit to a specific location and task, even if the spirit agrees of its own will. Some magicians would argue that most spiritual beings do not have free will in the same manner that humans do, and they do not have the same freedoms that we do. Creating a construct allows a spell to be in place without binding a specific spirit. It was common practice in medieval magick to summon and bind a spirit to do your bidding, but today, most witches tend to avoid forced servitude of another being. There is nothing wrong with summoning and working with a spirit and taking all the necessary precautions, but I personally want to work only with spirits who want to work with me, and who come in love, trust, and harmony.

Many witches wonder if they are creating life, only to enslave it. Sometimes constructs take on a persona and spark, and practitioners question their right to force the spirit to do their bidding. To the practical magician, that's like saying you are enslaving your toaster or computer. Its natural function is to fulfill a task. Many people personify their cars, homes, and electronic equipment by giving them a name or talking to them, yet don't worry about freeing them.

An even more controversial theory is that most spirits, and possibly even the gods, are simply built-up thoughtforms that have gained enough energy to be self-sustaining. I know that in some instances I intuitively feel drawn to work with a spiritual ally, and other times I choose to create a construct, an artificial servitor spirit that is specifically oriented to my will.

Here are the basic steps of construct creation:

1. Decide on the intention of the construct. What is its goal? What are the operating instructions? Be as specific as you can without limiting the servitor spirit's ability to fulfill its function. Think of it as writing instructions for an employee.

2. What powers most strongly correspond to the intended use of the construct? Does the construct resonate with a particular element? Some constructs are made entirely of one elemental force, which is why they often are referred to as artificial elementals. Does the construct resonate with a particular planet? What energetic qualities does it need to fulfill its purpose? Look at your tables of correspondences for the planets and elements in this book, *The Outer Temple of Witchcraft*, your BOS, and any other resources at your disposal.

3. Create an identity for the construct spirit. Name the spirit and/or create a symbol for it, to be used for this spirit and only this spirit. You can create a barbarous name for it by taking the basic intention and reducing it by crossing out the repeated letters (*OTOW*, Chapter 13). You also can create a geometric sigil for the spirit, aligning it further with the spiritual powers of the universe. Take the letters of the name and convert them to numbers. Then choose a *magick square*, a numeric grid that is aligned with your intention. Each of the seven planets has a magick square, also known as a *kamea* (figure 64). Each one is based on a specific pattern, in which each of the rows, horizontal or vertical, adds up to the same number. The numbers associated with each of the planets are Sun = 111, Moon = 369, Mercury = 260, Venus = 175, Mars = 65, Jupiter = 34, and Saturn = 15. When you make sigils on these grids, the shape of the sigil is naturally aligned with the power of the

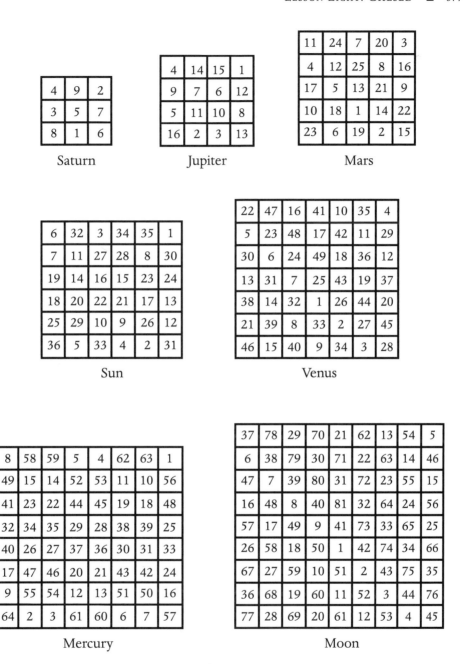

Figure 64: Planetary Squares

planet. Choose the planetary square that is appropriate for your working. Or, if your intention is not as specific, you can keep it in letters and make a sigil using the witch's wheel (*OTOW*, Chapter 13). Letters can be converted to numbers using this chart:

1	2	3	4	5	6	7	8	9
A	B	C	D	E	F	G	H	I
J	K	L	M	N	O	P	Q	R
S	T	U	V	W	X	Y	Z	

Sigils are not absolutely necessary, but they certainly help with this type of magick. Planetary squares also can be used to make more traditional amulets and talismans. They need not be linked with servitor constructs.

4. With a name and potentially a sigil for the spirit construct, you can create a binding vessel for it. Anything that can hold energy can be used as the home base and resting place of the spirit. You can bind the spirit to a location or vehicle, but I have found it best to bind it to an object that you can later move. Statues, crystals, and charms are the best vessels. Some vessels can become "containers" when the spirit is not in use, while others serve simply as anchors so the spirit doesn't wander.

   For artificial elementals, you can make a talisman and anoint it or fill it with a fluid condenser of the appropriate element. Statues can have holes drilled into them, or objects such as the traditional piggy bank, hollow in the center, can become vessels. Decorated bottles also work. Perhaps this is the idea behind the genie and the magick lamp. To make a more intricate servitor, you can use four condensers, one for each of the elements, plus a drop of your own blood to give it life and to make it in harmony with your will. For planet-aligned servitors, working with the appropriate planetary condenser is effective.

   A tradition in ceremonial magick is to simply make a *geometric charm*, an amulet/talisman that is aligned with the planet you have chosen. Such geometric charms can be one-sided, two-sided, or sometimes even four-sided, with the charm folded in, covering two sides and leaving a front and a back. The charm can be designed with the sigil of its name and planetary symbols, as well as a few drops of liquid fluid condenser or pinches of dry magickal condenser placed in the center before the two sides of the charm are glued and sealed shut. Circular and square shapes always are appropriate for this work, but to further align with your planet, you can make something in the geometric shape corresponding to your planet's sephiric number.

5. Get all the materials you need for your servitor spirit and vessel. Charms can be made before or during the ritual, depending on your personal style. Create your sacred space. You can cast a magick circle or, if working with a specific element or planet, work with the appropriate invoking pentagram or hexagram ritual. For example, if you were working with a Mercury-oriented construct, you would do the Greater Invoking Ritual of the Hexagram of Mercury.

6. Using your will, visualization, spoken word, and/or chanting, gather your energy and program it with what you want the construct to do. Be clear and precise in your instructions. As with many spells, I repeat the words of the instructions three times. In this process, make sure you name the spirit and hold its symbol/vessel to bind the instructions, energy, and intention all together.

7. Bind the construct to the vessel by holding it up, if possible, and visualize the energy linking to the vessel.

8. Complete your ritual, releasing the sacred space and returning to normal. Place the vessel in the most appropriate place for its function and purpose.

9. Decide how you are going to "feed" the construct to maintain its energy, and do so regularly. Feeding does not necessarily involve physical material, but energy, though physical offerings, such as food, drink, and coins, contain energy when blessed by you, and act as an appropriate medium to transfer energy. Recognizing the work of the construct and sending it energy can feed it the necessary energy. Recognizing it each day for its service builds up both its energy and the resolve of its function. The more the construct is used, and used successfully, the stronger it can become.

If a construct has fulfilled its purpose, it should be "dismantled." If you have a protection construct around your home and are moving, the polite and responsible thing to do would be to remove the construct, either taking it with you or dismantling it, so its energy does not linger or change with the new owners, who don't know about its presence or how to work with it. Ritually deconstruct it in sacred space, thanking it for its service. Explain what you are doing, and destroy the vessel and sigil. I imagine grounding the energy into the Earth and Underworld.

Some practitioners feel the servitor has a consciousness of its own (particularly if it has been developed over a long period of time) and should have a choice in the matter. If the spirit does not want to be grounded, give it another option. Speak to your guides and gods about the situation. Perhaps the spirit can be freed from its vessel and sent to another realm. If you simply let it go, make sure you instruct it on how to responsibly find a food source to sustain it, rather than becoming like a hungry vampire ghost or mischievous spirit. Many of our reinforced yet unconscious thoughtforms become mischievous and rogue spirits. Those that have been created ritually are even more powerful. A practitioner must take responsibility for his or her creations.

If you don't remove a construct and don't care for it, you run the risk of it becoming a problem. Most constructs will wither and dissipate without an energy source, but some will disconnect from their "anchor" and seek out energy from other sources, attaching to someone or something. Often called *rogue elementals*, they are the true source of many hauntings and the bad vibes people get at certain locations. They are not evil, but they do become parasitical in nature and are unhealthy.

Another method of sigil construction that does not involve planetary squares is outlined by Ian Corrigan in his book *Celtic Sorcery*. He uses Fionn's Window (*TOSW*, Chapter 5). Each of the ogham is linked to a letter in our alphabet (figure 65). A word or letter sequence can be traced on the window, following the curved lines, to create a much more rounded form of sigil, perhaps more in harmony with the Celtic witch than the Hermetic magician, but the technique itself is the same as the magician's.

Here is an example of how to create a servitor spirit:

My goal for the construct is to create an entity that will protect me when I'm in large crowds of people, doing spiritual work and having to remain open when teaching, healing, and leading ceremonies. Sometimes I'm so focused on the work that I'm

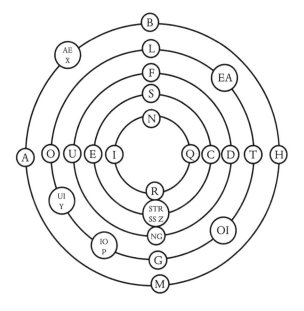

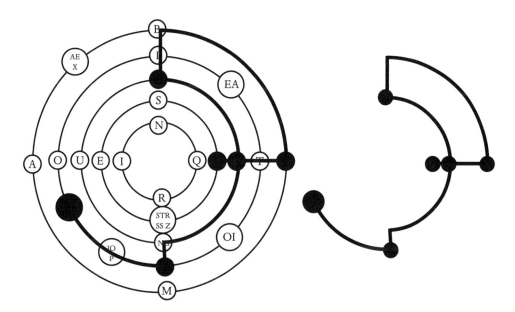

Figure 65: Fionn's Window and Sigil

not focused on my own defenses, so I want something that will focus on protecting me from random energy and intense attention so I can continue with the work and not be distracted. As a public speaker, anybody can show up at events, and you never know what the energy of the group will be like. I can't let a few people spoil the experience for everybody there, myself included, or endanger participants in the working. So I want a construct that will intercept any harmful or unbalanced energy sent my way, and transmute it into healthy, balanced energy.

Magickally, my intention to protect and transform corresponds with fire. In terms of planets, I naturally would choose Pluto for transformation, but Pluto is not one of the planets with a magick square grid. Mars for fire would be appropriate, yet the imagery of the Sun, as golden protective light, also appeals to me. In the end, I'm going to stick with Mars, for Geburah has the pentagon shape, and I associate that with protection more than the hexagon structure.

To name this new spirit I wish to create, I make a statement of intent:
SPIRIT INTERCEPT AND TRANSMUTE ALL HARMFUL ENERGY

- I reduce this intention to nonrepeating letters: C D H F G Y.

- Then I convert these letters to numbers: 3 4 8 6 7 7.

- Next, I plot out the intention on the Square of Mars, omitting the repeated seven letters, starting with the traditional circle and ending with the perpendicular line (figures 66 and 67).

My binding vessel will be a traditional paper charm. I'm making it pentagon style, double folded, so I can put something inside it. I'm going to color it red, the traditional color of Mars, and its opposite color, also known as its flashing color, green. On one side I have my sigil of the spirit, to be the outside front of the amulet, and on the back I have a pentacle (figure 68). In the center I have the glyph of Mars and the glyphs of its zodiac signs—Aries, for aggression to intercept, and Scorpio, to transmute and transform. I dip a small piece of cotton into a Mars fluid condenser (stinging nettle) and add a drop of black pepper essential oil. I let the cotton dry to avoid blemishing the design of the amulet, and then place the cotton in the amulet and glue it shut. If you want to wear the amulet, you can put a bit of string, yarn, or cord through it before you glue it shut, to make a necklace.

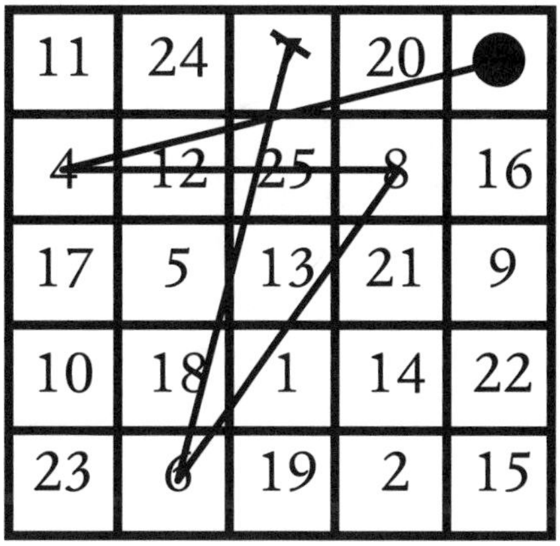

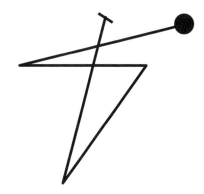

11	24	⁊	20	●
4	12	25	8	16
17	5	13	21	9
10	18	1	14	22
23	6	19	2	15

Figure 66: Sigil on Mars Square

Figure 67: Sigil

Though I'd like to say I performed the Greater Invoking Ritual of the Hexagram of Mars, in truth I simply cast a traditional witch's circle, drew the invoking hexagram of Mars in the center of it, and asked for the spirit of Mars to fill the circle with protective energy. I imagined the hexagram of Mars in red as I burned dragon's blood incense and a little tobacco. I passed the amulet through the smoke of the incense, and visualized the smoke and red light becoming a ball of light, the size of a baseball, with a big mouth, something like the video game *Pac-Man*. I also imagined some gold and green light in the amulet, and programmed it with my intention. I visualized it orbiting my aura like an electron around a nucleus, and as energy came to me that was dark and

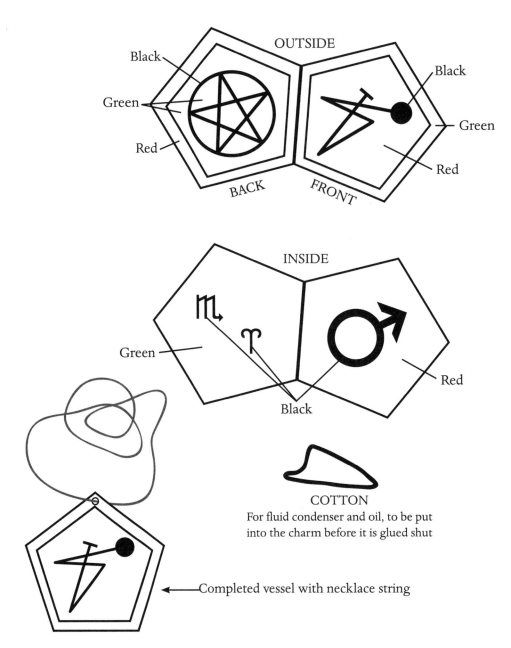

OUTSIDE

Black

Green

Red

BACK

FRONT

Black

Green

Red

INSIDE

Green

Black

Red

COTTON
For fluid condenser and oil, to be put
into the charm before it is glued shut

Completed vessel with necklace string

Figure 68: Construct Vessel

discordant, it gobbled up the energy and put it through its internal fire. When the spirit construct "exhaled," out came a golden white light, adding to the general peace and healing vibe of the environment around me. I released the space and carried the talisman with me only in situations in which I needed it. When it was not in use, it was in a little red box I keep in my altar drawer.

Each time I worked with the talisman, I instructed the spirit construct in its task. The spell itself naturally fed the construct, but after every event, I would leave it on my altar and light a red candle, placing the talisman under the candle holder and anointing the candle with something Martian, like the fluid condenser or pepper oil. I would visualize the energy of the flame feeding the construct, making it stronger.

CHESED PATHWORKINGS

Only one path of Chesed remains to be explored—the path upward, across the Abyss to Chokmah. This path is ruled by the priest king, the Hierophant. While the lowest expression of this card is read as institutional authority or dogma to be overcome, the higher form is the great teacher and initiator. The Hierophant passes blessing and knowledge on to the student, so the Abyss can be crossed and the initiate can reach the father-god force found in Chokmah. The student then becomes the initiator, able to help others cross the Abyss.

EXERCISE 25

Chesed Pathworking

1. Perform the Lesser Banishing Ritual of the Pentagram (exercise 5) and the Lesser Banishing Ritual of the Hexagram (exercise 20). Do any other ritual you feel is appropriate.

2. While in this space, call upon the divine forces of Chesed. Burn your four blue candles and cedar incense. Knock on your altar four times. Vibrate the divine name of Chesed, **El**, four times. Call upon any of the Jupiter deities of the sphere, or Archangel Tzadkiel.

3. To count down into a meditative state, do exercise 1 through step 7 (page 76).

4. Let the familiar world around you fall away, as if the material reality you know is only a façade and beneath it lies the beautiful garden of the Goddess, a veritable paradise surrounding you. The land around you becomes a vast primordial garden, the garden of Malkuth, the familiar garden of the four paths.

5. Go to the heart of Malkuth, to the Temple of Malkuth. Decide which path you wish to take to Chesed. Plot out the path in your mind, through the appropriate sephiroth and pathways. Perhaps try choosing pathways that you haven't yet explored.

6. While on your path, reflect on the symbolism of each of the paths of wisdom. If you have walked a particular pathway before, let the wisdom reach a deeper level within you. Let the images of the associated tarot card and path come to you. Let your thoughts and feelings be guided by the power of the path. Learn what you can of the path, and of your process, to expand your consciousness to Chesed.

7. Feel the call of the blue sphere from your path. You are bidden to enter the gates of Chesed, the realm of gentle mercy. You might have to give a symbol of Chesed as the key to enter the realm, such as the divine name (El), the Jupiter glyph, or the name of a sky father deity. Once you enter the realm, you feel as if you are passing through mist or clouds. Feel the compassion and mercy of this realm of blue light. Everything appears soft and fuzzy and gently out of focus, as the atmosphere actually blurs your vision over a distance. Feel your heart open. Explore the realm of Chesed, and welcome any beings of the sphere that come across your path.

8. Make your way to the Temple of Chesed. You enter a four-sided temple, made of tin, amethyst, aquamarine, and blue sapphire. You feel the essence of Chesed here in the heart of the realm. Notice the gateways to the other paths in the temple, the gate from the direction in which you came and the other three gates.

9. The entities of Chesed are residing in the temple. The sky fathers and good kings are present. Archangel Tzadkiel also is available, as well as the unicorns, if you haven't seen them already. Commune with the beings of the sphere. Ask to know the Vision of Love in a manner that is correct and for your highest good. Ask to learn the virtue and obligation of the sphere and ways to avoid the vices and illusion.

10. When done, thank all the beings who have communicated with you. They might offer you a gift, a token of their goodwill. If you accept, it is polite to reach within your being and offer them a gift of your goodwill.

11. Once you have said your farewells, leave the shrine and follow the path back. Return the way you came unless you feel guided to return via a different pathway and know the pathway back well. Return to the garden of Malkuth. Focus on the waking world you know, and feel it return around the garden.

12. To return to normal waking consciousness and end your journey, perform steps 15–17 from exercise 1 (page 78). You can close the temple by repeating the LBRP.

CHESED INITIATION

With the initiation of Chesed, we enter the mythical realm, yet we know such mythical perfection is part of Chesed and part of our path of magickal enlightenment. The ⑦=④ initiation is that of the Adeptus Exemptus, or Perfect Adept. One is said to attain perfection in all matters at this stage of development, yet one embodies this perfection while in the physical vehicle, as Chesed is before the Abyss. One might say the seventh initiation is one for who is as close to an ascended master as one can be and not ascend, and be physically incarnate. At this stage, all magick, high and low, has been mastered and perfected, and the initiate is the result of that mastery, conferring mastery of the material world, as well as the emotional, mental, and spiritual forces that move through the material world. The next step of initiation takes us across the Abyss into an entirely different realm of being, just as the jump from Netzach to Tiphereth brings the initiate to an entirely new level of understanding.

HOMEWORK

- Do Exercises 24–25 and record your experiences in your Book of Shadows.

- Learn and practice the Greater Ritual of the Hexagram, the traditional version or your own personally reconstructed version.

- Explore working with constructs if you so choose and feel ready to do so.

- Continue to practice the LBRP, LBRH, Middle Pillar, and Circulation of the Body of Light rituals, the traditional or personal versions.

TIPS

- Fill in the Chesed correspondences and colors on your own Tree of Life drawing. Contemplate them as you add them to the image. Start memorizing these correspondences.

- Review and reflect on all you have learned in this lesson.

- Continue working with the four elements.

- Continue working with the lower sephiroth.

- Study appendix VI to deconstruct and reconstruct the Greater Ritual of the Hexagram to your liking and worldview, if you so choose. If you are reconstructing it, make sure that your symbolism is consistent with the pentagram rituals and other rites.

- Pick one other reality map from appendix I to contemplate.

Lesson Nine
Da'ath

The Abyss lies between the Ethical Triangle of Geburah, Chesed, and Tiphereth and the Supernal Triangle of Binah, Chokmah, and Kether. A vast chasm of understanding separates what mortals can comprehend and what is beyond true comprehension. In biblical mythology, the Abyss represents the divide created by the "Fall," whether it be the fall of the archangel Lucifer into the depths after the war in heaven, the fall of Adam and Eve leaving the Garden of Eden, or the Gnostic fall of light into the world of matter. In its most enlightened telling, the Fall is not the fall of angels or men, but the fall of God, as the prime creator, into form to experience life, and in that process the separation that God experiences from himself/herself. We are that portion of God in manifestation. In the Abyss lies the mysterious sphere that is not a sphere—the world of Da'ath, which separates the manifested form of the universe, represented by the lower seven sephiroth, from the supernal ideal of creation, embodied by the upper three.

Called the mysterious eleventh sephira, Da'ath is not really a sephira, as it is not on, or connected to, the Tree of Life. There is a great deal of confusion and controversy over this point. The *Sepher Yetzirah* clearly states that the Kabbalah consists of ten sephiroth, not nine and not eleven, as we see its pattern modeled in our ten fingers and ten toes. Yet the mysterious eleventh sphere has popped up in our mythology. Whether you love or hate the idea of another sephira, it has become a part of our magickal cosmology and deserves at least some understanding and consideration.

Technically, Da'ath is not numbered, and is sometimes depicted as a dotted circle with a *D* in the center of it. This sphere floats mysteriously on the middle pillar between Kether and Tiphereth. It fits well into our power centers for the Middle Pillar ritual as the point of the traditional throat or neck chakra. For many witches, the model of the Tree of Life, with its decadal symbolism, is not satisfying. In modern paganism we learn of the sacredness of the numbers nine, twelve, and thirteen. My own quest into a more New Age version of the Tree, with twelve or thirteen points, is what sparked my serious study of reality maps and the Qabalah.

Da'ath means "knowledge," and magickally it represents all knowledge, but not necessarily the understanding or wisdom to use it properly. The knowledge of the invisible sephira is the knowledge beyond reason, the knowledge that becomes apparent by its absence, not by its direct revelation. Da'ath is claimed to be the closest thing humanity can understand of the Supernal Triad while incarnate. It is knowledge, but not the power to work appropriately with that knowledge. Some magicians recognize that as they climb the Tree, while others mistake Da'ath for Kether, mistake knowledge for the Godhead. As wonderful as knowledge is, it is not a substitute for divinity. Such magicians are said to get lost in the Abyss, obsessed with magickal knowledge but lacking the understanding to apply it properly to their spiritual journey.

Da'ath is the union of the Great Mother and Great Father. It can be conceived as an alternate point to a triangle involving Binah and Chokmah, pointing down into manifestation. It is a transition point from the supernal world to the more manifest world, and back again. One could think of it in terms of the transition point between matter and energy. The more supernal concepts must be translated into something more "concrete" when crossing the Abyss to enter Chesed, while more formed energies must be stripped to their most supernal components and patterns when rising through the Abyss to Binah. On the way down the Tree, Da'ath can be seen as the birth canal of the Binah goddess, sending the new soul out into the world. When returning, it can be seen as the cosmic grave, as the goddess, bringing us from womb to tomb, strips us of our individualization in our quest to become one with the Godhead.

The knowledge of Da'ath is important, for it is with that knowledge that one can bridge the Abyss, if the knowledge is applied correctly rather than mistaken for divinity and sought out simply for knowledge's sake. One must use the knowledge of Da'ath without losing sight of the light of Kether. The climber on the Tree must not mistake the eclipsed light of Da'ath for the supreme Godhead. As the sphere of the throat, Da'ath can be linked to the mind, or the mental body. The mind is a trap at times, where we get lost thinking about things but never doing anything. We can get caught in a form of mental masturbation, mistaking knowledge for the experience. We can mistake our thoughts of the divine for the divine itself. The throat center is also where knowledge is expressed, and the windpipe is like a "hole" within us.

It is said that Da'ath is the invisible sephira. Unlike the other sephiroth, Da'ath does not act as an emanation, but instead functions like an invisible gateway, a doorway. It is a gateway across the Abyss and into what many see as another dimension, the realm of the *Qlippoth*, the shells of divinity, or the reverse of the Tree of Life. It is through the gateway of the Qlippoth that a mage can use knowledge to truly get lost and never make it across the Abyss. Because of this function, occultists debate whether Da'ath is a sephira or a pathway.

The implied numerology of Da'ath gives us some interesting concepts. If we accept its placement as the eleventh sphere, then we can look to numerology to know that eleven is considered a master number, signifying spirituality, with an emphasis on one, or the creative force, and the ego being held in balance with the spirit. Eleven plays an interesting role in Thelemic magick, as some rituals are opened with a series of eleven taps, in the rhythm of 1–3–3–3–1 and closed with eleven taps in the 3–5–3 sequence.

One, ten, and eleven all have an emphasis on the digit one, and each of these spheres on the middle pillar has a strong relationship with other spheres. Da'ath often is seen as a shadow and reflection of the light of Kether. Others see a strong relationship between Da'ath and Malkuth, with the mythology of the Fall. The Tree of Life, though symmetrical around the vertical axis, is asymmetrical around the horizontal axis. Malkuth makes it slightly off-center. Some Qabalists believe that Malkuth once occupied the position of Da'ath, creating a perfectly symmetrical Tree, and the realm of the Kingdom was in harmony with the supernals. Malkuth formed a strange link with the upper and lower spheres. The transitions between the spheres did not incorporate an Abyss. During the Fall, Malkuth dropped through the worlds into its current position as the lowest and densest of the spheres. One could think of Da'ath not so much as a sphere, but as the hole through which Malkuth fell. In its original position, Malkuth/Da'ath as the daughter principle held a "higher" station on the Tree of Life than the son principle of Tiphereth.

Such mythologies are hard for pagan magicians to understand or accept, for our cosmology doesn't have a Fall. We don't believe the angels fought the divine and were cast down. We believe that we never left paradise. We have no original sin. In more feminine-reverent and Earth-reverent forms of Gnostic philosophy, the Fall is seen as the descent of spirit into the world of matter, and it is believed that the angels of matter and the world voluntarily entered the cyclical rhythms of creation. Their descent is what set the physical worlds into motion. Before that, everything was nontangible. Some tales tell us that the faeries are simply angels that descended into flesh, and that the Lucifer figures are the light bringers guiding the world and watching the gates between the heavens and the more material planes. With this thought in mind, detached from Judeo-Christian morality, the Fall doesn't seem so far-fetched. It embodies well the paradox we have of divinity as both immanent and transcendent.

Author Alan Moore, in his *Promethea* comic book series, makes an interesting point, stating that Da'ath is not the eleventh sphere at all, but is pi (π) with the top bar missing. Da'ath's real number is the irrational number, the ratio of a circle's circumference to its diameter. Pi is infinite, but is expressed as 3.14159..., a number moving infinitely between three (Binah) and four (Chesed). Such an irrational number creatively expresses the infinite and irrational nature of the Abyss and its sephira, Da'ath. Pi is a great symbol for the bottomlessness of the Abyss, where the mysteries appear to go on forever. It takes knowledge to find this number, but that knowledge does not equate with wisdom.

Astrologically, Da'ath has been associated with a number of heavenly forces. The star system of Sirius is the most prominent. Sirius has been venerated as a point of wisdom in many ancient cultures, particularly Egypt. The pyramids possibly were used as initiation chambers, according to some mystics, and were aligned with the light of Sirius. Perhaps the ancient priests and priestesses found a way to bridge the Abyss. In Theosophical teaching, Sirius is said to act like the higher self of our Sun, with our group of ascended masters being an outpost for the original "lodge" of masters from Sirius. It is interesting that Chesed often is associated with the ascended masters, and the next step is the higher "lodge" of masters on Sirius.

The outer planets also have an association with Da'ath. The one that most often is aligned with Da'ath is Uranus, a planet of unorthodox communication that is associated with the throat, spine, and nervous system. Others put Pluto, the gateway to life and death, the Lord of the Underworld and hidden riches, at the gate of the Qlippoth. The psychedelic aspect of Neptune also can be part of Da'ath's imagery. Lastly, some equate the asteroids, the "missing" planet between Mars and Jupiter, as the zone of Da'ath. As Da'ath is the shattered and collapsed sephira, this zone is for the shattered planet, as many esotericists believe a planet once occupied the orbit of the asteroids and was destroyed early in the creation of the solar system. Others think of the asteroid belt as a planet that never formed. The four main asteroids of the belt all are assigned to goddesses—Ceres, Juno, Pallas, and Vesta. Lastly, the mysterious planetoid Chiron, between the inner and outer planets, between Saturn and Uranus, is sometimes given rulership over Da'ath. Chiron is known as the "wounded healer," and as Da'ath represents a "wound" in the universe, this rulership, too, would be appropriate. The wide variety of correspondences to Da'ath adds to the mystique.

The correspondences of Da'ath are tricky, as ultimately Da'ath's symbolism is the absence of all symbolism. The following correspondences have been culled from authors both in print and online who tackle the difficult subject of Da'ath.

Da'ath

Meaning: Knowledge
Level of Reality: Abyss
Parts of the Self: Shadow Self, Throat
Experience: Vision Across the Abyss
Obligation: Detachment
Illusion: Attachment

Virtues: Self-Knowledge, Mastery of Demons

Vices: Self-Delusion, Ignorance of Self, False Enlightenment

Name of God: (YHVH Elohim)

King Scale Color: Lavender

Queen Scale Color: Pale Silver Gray

Prince Scale Color: Pure Violet

Princess Scale Color: Gray flecked with Gold

Element: Air

Planets: Uranus, Pluto, Neptune, Sirius, Chiron, Asteroids, Black Holes

Image: Two-Faced God

Archetypes: Dual Deities, Threshold Deities

Greek/Roman Deities: Janus, Hecate, Persephone

Egyptian Deities: Set/Horus, Osiris/Horus, Dark Isis, Ma'at

Middle Eastern Deity: Tiamat

Celtic Deities: Oak King/Holly King, Green/Red Knight

Norse Deities: Loki, Hel

Hindu Deity: Shiva

Archangels: Uriel, Mesukiel, Zagzagel

Angelic Order: Serpents

Choir: None

Grade of Initiation: Crossing the Abyss

Animals: Raven, Cthulhu Creatures

Planetary Vowel Sound: None

Resonant Letters: None

Musical Mode: None

Musical Note: None

Tools: Chain, Prism, Black Hole

Incense: Wormwood

Tarot: All Cards

Metal: None

Stones: Obsidian, Opal, Moldavite, "Artificial" or Treated Stones

Plants: Psychedelics

You can build a Da'ath altar using any of these correspondences. There really is no "right" way to build any of these altars, but this is true particularly with Da'ath, as it has no traditional, universally respected correspondences.

ENTITIES OF DA'ATH

The archetypal image of Da'ath is the two-faced god, with one face looking forward and one looking back. Here we have the synthesis of polarity, as past and future, above and below, mother and father, and life and death. The image is found in Roman mythology, in the figure of Janus. He is the god of gateways, doors, and both beginnings and endings. At one time, Janus's image was of one face smooth and young and the other bearded. Later images had both faces bearded. His symbol, beyond gateways, is the key, the opener of the gates, which he has in common with many other threshold deities, such as Hecate.

I also think of the two-faced god in the general Wiccan mythos as The God, the Lord of Life and Death (*OTOW*, Chapter 5). He is the god of light and green in the growing season and the god of death and the Underworld in the waning. One side is the golden green man and grain god, and the other is the horned one. Like the Da'ath figure, he is a synthesis and a guardian of the gateways between the worlds. As Da'ath is a portal, the God is an ideal figure to focus upon in his entirety, for beneath the Abyss, he manifests separately as the Holly King and Oak King, Green Knight and Red Knight.

Janus and the two sides of the witch's God in the sphere of Da'ath can be seen as initiators, having more in common with Hecate and the feminine mysteries than just keys. Any figure that is seen as a divine initiator, an opener of the spiritual gate, can be considered a Da'ath figure. Depending on the planetary associations, figures such as the Uranian divine rebels, the Prometheus and Lucifer figures, fit here, or the Plutonian death gods and goddesses, such as Hades, Persephone, Hecate, and Osiris. Gareth Knight suggests working with Isis and the mysteries of the goddess as a way to invoke Da'ath's positive attributes, as it leads to Binah, the Great Mother. Isis certainly can be seen as an initiator. The path of the Priestess card, from Tiphereth to Kether, runs right through Da'ath's position on the Tree, and figures like Isis certainly resonate with the Priestess card. Likewise, the figure of Set can be seen as Osiris's teacher through conflict. His mythology, with his seventy-two accomplices, has a relevant connection to Goetic magick.

The god name of Da'ath is YHVH Elohim. It is the creative power of the Tetragrammaton linked to the plural form of the divine, meaning "Lord of Gods" or "Lord God." It is truly the divine name of Binah, for Da'ath is said to not have a true god name.

As a gateway to another, possibly corrupt dimension, Da'ath rarely is associated with the angelic realm. Demonic associations are more likely. When angels are used, Uriel, the archangel of Uranus, is a possibility. Another option is the archangel of the Abyss, Mesukiel, whose name possibly means the "Veiler of God." Author D. J. Conway, in *Magick of the Gods & Goddesses*, associates Zagzagel, as an archangel of wisdom, with Da'ath. The angelic "order" known as the Serpents is associated with Da'ath. These Serpents are like the Seraphim, but unlike the Seraphim, they lack the flame of spirit, residing in the dark Abyss. The fallen angels of many traditions, which are akin to the demons and devils of mythology, all find a home in Da'ath as the gateway to the demonic realm.

The demonic associations come from Da'ath's link as the doorway to the Qlippoth. The Qlippoth are the reverse of the sephiroth. The Qlippothic Tree of Life, sometimes known as the Tree of Evil or Tree of Death, the reverse of our familiar Tree of Life, is sometimes depicted as behind the traditional Tree or a mirror image beneath that Tree (figures 69 and 70). Though the Qlippoth could be seen as the shaman's Underworld, their meaning is quite different. While the sephiroth are divine emanations, the Qlippoth are "shells." They are not evil, as popularly believed, but empty. When you look at the Qlippothic correspondent of any sephira, if you remove the divine attribute of that sephira, emptying it out, then you have the Qlippothic force. The Qlippoth embody the vices, not the virtues. Chesed without mercy and compassion is simply bigotry and arrogant power. Geburah without divine power is simply wanton force and destruction. Tiphereth without selfless offering is needless suffering or egotistical martyrdom. These are the empty shells of the Qlippothic Tree.

The mythology of the Qlippoth can be seen in the Abyss. One teaching on the Abyss looks at it as a cosmic dumping ground. At one time, the Creator, the force behind Kether, made previous universes that were imperfect. These broken universes were swept into the Abyss, until our current universe was created. The remnants of the broken universes still exist, and we experience them when we enter the Qlippothic spheres. They are seen as a broken shadow of our universe. When we don't embody the virtues of the sephiroth, we enter the reverse Tree of Life.

Some magicians see no purpose in trafficking with the reverse Tree, while others seek it out, in an effort to know all, and to conquer all fear and all aspects of the

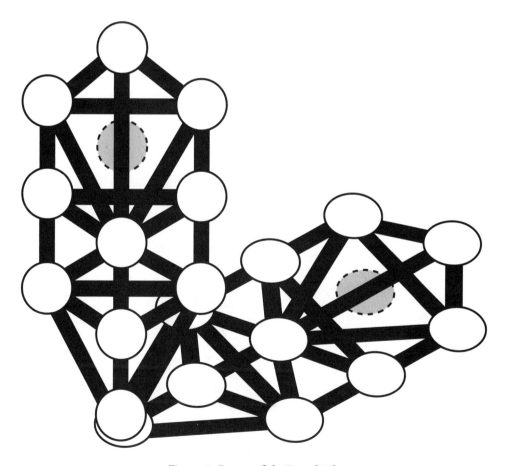

Figure 69: Reverse of the Tree of Life

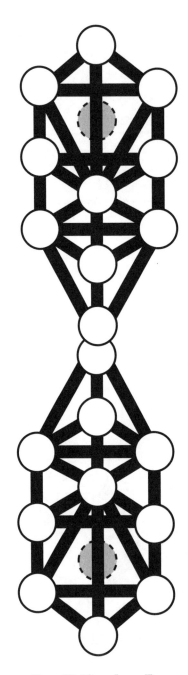

Figure 70: Mirror Image Tree

Qabalistic Sphere	Qlippothic Order	English Equivalent
Kether	Thaumiel	Twins of God
Chokmah	Ogiel	The Hinderers
Binah	Satariel	The Concealers
Chesed	Gasheklah	The Smiters
Geburah	Golachab	The Arsonists
Tiphereth	Tageriron	The Hagglers
Netzach	Oreb Zaraq	The Raven of Dispersion
Hod	Samael	Poison of God
Yesod	Gamaliel	The Obscene Ones
Malkuth	Lilith	Queen of the Night

Chart 4: Qlippothic Correspondences

shadow. The mythology of the Qlippoth assigns alternate names and titles to each of the ten sephiroth. While the sephiroth have angelic orders and archangels, the Qlippoth have demonic orders and archdemons (chart 4). Understanding the shadow, the shell of a sephira, can aid in understanding the "full" manifestation of the sephira's power.

In modern magick, the paths of the reverse Tree are known as the "Tunnels of Set," while the bright paths are the "Tunnels of Horus," showing the Set and Horus cosmology embodied in the concept of the dual Tree. Modern magick also has associated the mythos of H. P. Lovecraft, in the Cthulhu series, with the sphere of Da'ath, feeling that Lovecraft unconsciously connected to this gateway of power and mystery. The Cthulhu mythos was continued onward in a magickal context by comic author Grant Morrison in *The Invisibles* series, describing the Reverse Tree of Life as Universe B, a sick and twisted yet integral component of our own reality.

Da'ath is the only sphere to exist both on the day side and the night side of the Tree of Life, yet it belongs to neither. The archdemon of Da'ath is Choronzon. Popularized by Aleister Crowley, Choronzon stands at the gateway, and is the keeper of false knowledge and the deceiver of the initiate. But he is a necessary part of the Tree of Life, as the magician must conquer, integrate, or make peace with this force before ascending higher. Choronzon is the force continually ripping apart the universe and the mage potentially crossing the Abyss. It is in the dissolution of the self that one finds Binah, union with the Cosmic Mother. Choronzon seems like a modern interpretation of the "root monster" in the World Tree of the shaman, like Nidhogg in the roots of Yggdrasil. One of Crowley's most controversial workings involved the invocation of this demon. I'm reminded of the shamanic dismemberment initiations when I think of Crowley's Choronzon working. One can think of Choronzon as the cosmic Dweller on the Threshold, the collective shadow guardian preventing us from going up further. Though Choronzon is seen as an evil figure by some, in many ways he (and all Da'ath figures) is the higher octave of the child of light in Tiphereth, as the child of the union of Binah, understanding, and Chokmah, wisdom.

The Qlippoth seem so frightening and powerful to the new student, yet they are not. By their very definition, the Qlippoth are empty. They are shells devoid of divinity. It is simply that we live in a culture that puts more power to the fear. Because we are not in touch with many of these divine forces as embodied by the sephiroth, we think their opposing forces are more powerful because they are equally unknown, yet seem fiercer in our imagery. If we are truly in touch with the divine powers, then we will know just how powerful the energies of the Tree of Life really are.

The qualities of Da'ath are the primal and primordial powers. Da'ath is the unknown creature of the dark. It is the serpent power, and its parallel in the body can be found in the serpent power of the Kundalini as it rises upward to reach the stem of the brain. While Da'ath is the throat, it also is the primal reptilian brain at the back of the skull, guarding the doorway with no key, the gateway to the higher dimensions. The earthly aspects of the higher position of Malkuth give Da'ath associations with all sorts of primal yet earthy creatures—the Leviathan, the Beast, the Midgard Serpent, the coiling Kundalini. This serpent power is the primal power of the deep unconscious. It is the power of the void. These creatures bring power, but often instill fear in us. So much of what we don't understand or like is labeled demonic. And if that is the label we use, then that is the label we must come to terms with as we work with this sphere.

Vision of Da'ath

There is very little formalized agreement on Da'ath's visions and experience. One might say the spiritual vision of this sphere is simply to get across the Abyss. Such a feat can be described as the realization of attachment and nonattachment, as crossing the Abyss forces us to relinquish much of our personal self and personal attachment characterized by the lower sephiroth. It's like a higher octave of the process that occurs when we pierce the veil between the lower four sephiroth and Tiphereth. Instead of simply piercing the veil, we are called to cross the Abyss. We must go beyond the illusion, beyond the seduction of knowledge, to attain the vision across the Abyss. As the zero point between the lower and upper parts of the Tree, the experience of moving from one realm to another can be seen as the shattering of self, the disintegration of the ego self. In this process of detachment, the magician truly no longer practices the magick that he or she has been mastering in the lower spheres, but transforms, to become the magick fully. This is the true mystery of magick. One could see the vision of crossing the Abyss as the vision of disintegration or the vision of transformation.

As Da'ath is the sphere of the Qlippoth, one might not find any virtues to this realm, yet the highest virtue is mastery of the demonic forces in our lives. Since the demons of the universe most often manifest in personal ways, the vision of attachment and nonattachment creates the virtue of detachment. One is in the world, yet detached from the outcome, the fruit of the labor, as one manifests the principles of Malkuth restored to the supernal world, rather than focusing strictly on the material results. One sees the truth about the self. This is the ultimate knowledge embodied by Da'ath's name. Not the knowledge of things, but of self, and that knowledge comes only from a detached, objective look at oneself. Another virtue of mastering Da'ath is embodied in the two-faced Janus image—mastery of being in between, which is simply another way of looking at detachment. One has a knowledge of, intention for, and confidence in the future, but with detachment, knowing the future will work out as it must, and we are part of that process. The initiate has an awareness of the past, culling the knowledge from past successes and failures, yet an ability to remain in the moment, the time and place between. Magicians, witches, and shamans are known to be threshold beings, walkers between the worlds, not fully belonging to any one place or time.

The vice is manifested in one who is trapped in Da'ath. If one is seduced by the illusion, one cannot make the leap across the Abyss. Attachment, the inability to move forward, is the illusion. One is inert because one is chained down by personal attachment, by the lure of hidden knowledge, by worry and fantasy about the past or future, or by the ego self. The inertia of attachment can be considered a higher octave of the Malkuth vice, inertia or laziness.

To fulfill the obligation of Da'ath, needed to truly cross the Abyss, one must be starkly honest with oneself, seeking not the knowledge of the world or the esoteric realms but knowledge of the self. Esoteric knowledge serves only if one uses the macrocosm to find enlightenment. The oracles of Delphi, those who sat in an "in-between" place, urge all to "know thyself," for this is crucial in looking into the darkness of the Abyss. Self-knowledge is the key to the gateway, leading across to Binah. Da'ath is much like a mirror, in which one must look truly at the self. We might not see things as they really are. Through a trick of light and perspective, we may convince ourselves that we are something we really are not. The philosopher Nietzsche's famous quote on the Abyss is, "When you stare into the abyss, the abyss stares back into you." Like the reflected self, each image takes stock of the other.

The illusion of Da'ath is truly self-delusion. One has climbed so high only to be blocked by the self. Ignorance of the self is the true illusion, fully manifested when one is attached to the self-image, rather than taking identity from the divine self. With self-delusion, one can mistake this attachment for attainment of the realm beyond the Abyss. One has attained a sense of false enlightenment. One can continually fall in the Abyss, yet create a self-deluded fantasy of enlightenment and the Godhead, all taking place in the mental realm, not the realm of spirit.

As the ascended masters often are associated with both Chesed and Binah, the corresponding "black brothers" are linked with Da'ath. Though the definition of such black brothers has been misinterpreted in our popular fiction as black magicians who seek to destroy the world, the true definition is those magicians who are satisfied with the illusion of Da'ath, with the smaller ideas of divinity, who wear the False Crown of Da'ath as it is known, rather than seeking the True Crown of Kether. The realization of having to release the ego self is too much for such magicians, brothers and sisters alike, to bear, and instead, they succumb to the illusions and vices, thinking they have attainted enlightenment, merging with the Godhead. In truth, they have abandoned their HGA for the material knowledge of Da'ath and invoked the corresponding shadow of their HGA, the so-called Evil Genius.

Da'ath Magick

In many ways, the traditional magickal structures and correspondences don't work when invoking the powers of Da'ath. Its primary symbol is no symbol, emptiness and absence, as it is the transformation point between vastly different levels of consciousness. Typical images that can be used for Da'ath are the empty cell or empty room and the void or black hole. Each suggests the absence of light or, even more, the absorption of light into the Abyss, and both can be useful images to meditate on in a pathworking.

Rituals tools are somewhat harder to use with the absence of symbolism. A common association is the chain, symbolizing the chain of attachment that must be broken to cross the Abyss. Another tool I happened upon through Internet posts and discussion is the prism. The lens that refracts white light into the spectrum suits Da'ath quite well, as we must look at each aspect of the self in our introspective process. Otherworldly colors and dark iridescents are associated with Da'ath. Uriel's colors are sometimes described as the oil slick or peacock, iridescent but dark. The image of Melek Taus, the peacock god, also is quite helpful in Da'ath. The spectrum of light for Da'ath is ultraviolet, and though I've never used them, black light and trippy images from black-light poster art would be helpful for such rituals. Imagery of Promethean fire, the fennel stalks burning with the knowledge of heaven, is also a tool, though it can be difficult to keep fennel stalks burning during a ritual. A good substitute tool for a similar concept is the apple, as the apple of knowledge and the apple of immortality from the tale of Eden.

The edge of the sword, not the sword itself, is a tool of Da'ath. One is said to walk the sword or razor's edge across the Abyss, without error, keeping a steady gaze on the light of Kether. The sword edge also demonstrates the part of the mind that is needed to truly cross the Abyss, the part that separates, divides, and detaches.

All dark creatures are associated with Da'ath, from the primordial serpents and creatures that go bump in the night to more traditional dark images, such as the raven or crow, with their dark iridescent wings, bringing the night color into full daylight.

In terms of spell correspondences, herbs that open the gates, that induce trance, would be appropriate, from the full-trance-inducing psychotropic plants to safer alternatives. The use of the Artemisia family, particularly wormwood, in an incense would be very helpful for conjuring Da'ath powers.

Shining iridescent yet dark stones are the gems of Da'ath. Obsidian, in general, and rainbow obsidian, in particular, are wonderful choices. Obsidian is the mineral of the classic witch's mirror, used to stare into the otherworlds, and to stare into the self. Opal, as a stone of Uranus, and in particular black opal, is a powerful gem for Da'ath. I also would include labradorite/spectrolite, an iridescent form of feldspar, in the sphere of Da'ath.

The most appropriate form of magick for Da'ath is the magick of the *Goetia*. Goetia is a word that has both referred to witchcraft in general and meant "howling," possibly a reference to the practitioners of rural and "illicit" religions when compared to the state-sanctioned temple priests and priestesses. Such rural rituals were probably more primal, wild, and loud.

Originally, Goetia was the art of the *goes*, a ritual mourner at funerary rites. A goes was one who lamented for the dead. Later, the term was associated with necromancy, meaning one who could summon the spirits of the dead. Eventually, goes became a term for sorcery and witchcraft, but with negative connotations. Despite the modern pagan opinion that all witchcraft was embraced by the ancient world, even in the very pagan times of ancient Greece, some forms of magick were looked down upon harshly. Classical magicians and philosophers deeply wanted to disassociate themselves from Goetic practitioners. Goetic magick refers to spirit summoning, a practice that spread throughout Europe in the Middle Ages, primarily among underground practitioners in the Church, and parts of it eventually made their way into folk magick traditions. The Goetia played an important role in the Golden Dawn revival, as Mathers was one to translate the text of the Goetia, and then Crowley published a version with his own modifications.

Today, the Goetia most often refers to a system of magick found in the first book of a famous grimoire known as *The Lesser Key of Solomon*, or *The Lemegeton*. Attributed to the biblical magician king Solomon yet most likely having no direct link to ancient Hebrew magick, it details a system for summoning, binding, and controlling seventy-two spirits, often considered demons, each with a realm of power. Now the "howling" of the Goetia is said to refer to the noise these demons make, as Solomon was said to have imprisoned them in a brass vessel, but later they escaped to plague the world.

You might be wondering what a section on "demon" summoning is doing in a book on modern witchcraft. We so often are trying to fight the stereotype of witches being a cult of devil worshippers and demon summoners, so why would we embrace this? If you look to other world traditions, without the moralistic tones of Christianity, you will see traditions rich with demons. Beyond more politically correct forms of the shamanic revival, one will find anthropological tales of shamans battling demons as the spirits of illness. Tibetan traditions, influenced by both the native Bön religion and Buddhism from the Hindu-dominant India, are filled with fierce imagery. The first-generation creatures of many a pagan-based creation story are quite demonic. Most nature-based traditions of the ancient world recognized destructive forces, both in nature and within the individual, yet did not get trapped in a moralistic dualism of true divinity against an ultimate evil. The divine was beyond both, and encompassed both.

Until fairly recently, such demon-summoning magick was part of a magician's training. I've spoken to British Traditional witches active at the dawn of the Witchcraft Renaissance in the 1950s and 60s who had Goetic training as part and parcel of witchcraft training. When you look at classic accounts of witchcraft, including the famous biblical story of the Witch of Endor, it is obvious that witches trafficked with the spirits of the dead, with the ancestors, for divination and guidance. Necromancy, when defined as such, was a component of our Craft. The older book *Mastering Witchcraft*, by Paul Huson, included a section on Goetic spirit summoning, but as more books on witchcraft became mainstream and acceptable to society, with the concept that witches are just like practitioners of any other religion, aspects of magick that seem less acceptable were omitted from the books and never learned by most new practitioners.

When viewed with a modern eye and away from medieval superstition, the Goetia appears to be both a very practical and spiritual form of magick, somewhat akin to a magickal form of psychoanalysis, yet invoking real and powerful forces. Each of the seventy-two spirits rules over aspects of our lives that we see as demonic, as out of control and ruling us, just as angels rule over the creative aspects of life and the universe. Whereas angels are very impersonal in the fulfillment of their function, simply enacting divine will, these "demons" are very personal and intimate, ruled by personal will. These demons are like the spirits, the rulers, of the shadow self. Each one rules one aspect of the shadow. This is not to say that all these demons are simply internalized forces. As above, so below—they are reflections of the self, but are also the spirits of the universal shadow.

Though usually thought of as demons, the classic texts refer to them generally as spirits, yet in the context of a medieval Christian infernal hierarchy. One has to look at the source material and filter out what is universal and what is a biased product of the times. Many look to the names of the Goetia and see corrupted names of pagan gods and goddesses, as Christian magicians saw any pagan spirit as a potential demon. When looking to the Egyptian mythologies, Set had seventy-two accomplices in his betrayal of Osiris. Perhaps he is the leader, or chief aspect, of these seventy-two spirits.

When a magician feels an aspect of life has gotten out of control, through obsession or seemingly uncontrollable emotion, he or she summons the spirit that rules that particular area of life. The magician uses rituals, seals, and binding to bring the spirit, and the force it rules, under the direction of the magician's divine will, the Holy Guardian Angel, rather than the personal will. Medieval magicians working in a Christian framework would recite the Hebrew names of God and the angels and assume the authority of God in the ritual, with the right to summon, bind, and command these spirits. A modern magician or shamanic practitioner might befriend, negotiate, or compromise rather than compel, but in the end, as long as the spirit is now under the direction of the divine will, the same end result is achieved. The spirit then is given a task compatible with its nature, that the magician is fully conscious of, and the result is constructive in the life of the magician, not destructive. The magician has given all the built-up frustrated power of the demon a healthy outlet, and thereby has created a healthy outlet for the magician's own energy to manifest his or her desires, rather than rage out of control or unconsciously self-sabotage. Naming your demons, identifying them, both literally and metaphorically, is a huge part of the introspective process.

You must identify your faults, your blind spots, your vices, and you can do that only when you are truly reflective and honest about yourself. That is why the mirror is such a common tool for this magick. You can only deal with the things that you are consciously aware of.

Though most look at these spirits as beings who promise wealth and power, when you read their full description, many are teaching spirits who emphasize the virtues of stones, plants, the arts, and the sciences. There is quite a bit more to them than temporal power. Some see the images of wealth and power as metaphors for spiritual wealth and power, and when the magician truly understands the rituals, then these symbols become clear, though I must admit that my own Goetic rituals have led to some pretty spectacular real-world, not just purely psychological, results.

Goetic magick introduces some concepts and working tools that many witches are not familiar with. The circle is familiar enough, yet this ritual circle serves a somewhat different purpose than most. Rather than be a container for the forces you wish to work with, it separates you and the forces you are summoning. Technically, the Goetic spirits are evoked, not invoked. The circle becomes a semisolid boundary, usually drawn or marked on the floor in chalk, paint, dust, or salt with the traditional nine-foot diameter, and inscribed with divine names. The magician must never cross the circle during the operation. Modern witches often are sloppy with the boundary of the circle, but in Goetia, it's treated like a solid line that must not be crossed. If one needs to reach outside the circle, a long sword is used to move objects in and out of the triangle, add more incense to the triangle's burner, or threaten the spirit, as iron disrupts the matrix of a spirit, grounding it. This is why spirits, demons, and faeries are said to fear cold iron or steel. The metal of Mars has that grounding effect.

In ceremonial magick, invocation usually refers to spirits that are brought into the circle, with you, while evoked spirits are put into another space, usually known as the Triangle of Manifestation, or the Triangle of the Art. In witchcraft, invocation is taking a spirit or godform within your body, while evocation is just a call for the spirit to appear and participate. In Goetic invocation, you put the spirit in a triangle, as you are trying to separate yourself from the spirit, so you can see it and deal with it objectively. In alchemy, the various stages of a chemical process usually include a separation phase, where a substance is divided based upon its conflicting properties, then purified and recombined. Goetic magick is a bit of spiritual alchemy, as the same process occurs. This is similar to acts of sorcery found in Tibetan Bön traditions, in which a practitioner constructs an elaborate circle mandala in sand with which to "trap" a summoned demon spirit and bind it into service. Instead of using a triangle, the Tibetan magician is simply on the outside of the circle, separate from the spirit. Then when the pact is made, the spirit is released, to act as a guide and teacher.

The three points of the triangle stand for the first three powers, the three mother letters of the elements air, fire, and water. The Hermetic "fire" triangle points upright and is sacred to Michael, the archangel of protection. By his power, the spirit remains bound in the triangle. The triangle is also a symbol of Binah, a power over Da'ath and the Abyss, with the ability to bind. Within the triangle is often a dark reflective mirror, as the gateway to the astral realm, for the spirit to manifest an image and commune with you, and/or a traditional incense burner, a thurible or brazier, to burn thick smoke through which the spirit also may manifest. The smoky incense Dittany of Crete is used as the scent of Malkuth. I've had good luck using patchouli leaves as another smoky and earthy incense. Oregano, a relative of Dittany, also can be used as a poor man's substitute. I also like to use resinous incense, like myrrh or dragon's blood, in Goetic workings. Some magicians keep asafoetida and a second brazier in the circle with them, as asafoetida is a noxious herb guaranteed to banish all spirits. Sulfur on burning coals also can be used to banish a spirit that has gotten out of your control. A candle can be put either in the triangle, reflecting in the mirror, or, better yet, in the circle, behind the magician, yet still reflected in the surface of the mirror.

Magicians disagree as to where the triangle should be placed in relationship to the circle. Traditions that face east place it in the east. Others use south, the classic direction of Archangel Michael. I start and face the north, so I place my triangle in the north (figure 71). Many magicians do not use the triangle, but instead place a magick mirror or dark bowl of water directly in front of them to scry and use their own dark reflection as the method for communing with the demon. Though this is an effective tactic, I suggest working with reflections in the triangle, not in the circle with you.

The spirit is controlled by the use of its seal. The seal is a sigil, a geometric talisman keyed to the very nature of the spirit based upon its geometry. The Goetia has a different seal for each of the seventy-two spirits. The seals are similar in shape to Eastern meditation yantras or Voodou vevers, used to call the lwa spirits. The seal must be constructed prior to the ritual, from metal, leather, wood, or parchment. As a modern magician, I tend to use wooden disks from a craft store, with permanent magic markers. The medieval magician would threaten the spirit, passing the seal over a fire in a sealed metal box and reciting the "Curse of Chains," seemingly "burning" the spirit and threatening to destroy the seal and never mention the spirit's name again. Modern magicians might enter into what would appear to be more like a modern psychotherapy session,

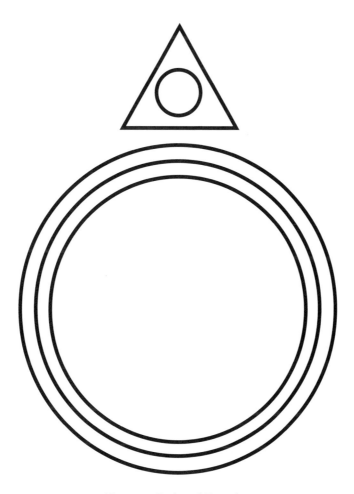

Figure 71: Circle and Triangle

trying to understand why the spirit is out of control, its motivations, and how it can be brought back into divine balance, much like dealing with the shadow self. The only difference is that this system works with specific aspects of shadow forces, not their entirety. Many read about this type of magick and believe that "binding" a spirit is wrong, feeling that we are harming a spirit and binding it against its own free will. These spirits, unlike humans, are not operating under the same parameters of free will. It is their nature to rebel if we are not in full alignment with divinity. They can be wonderful teachers because they bring us lessons, yet they are not our friends. We bind wounds and broken bones in order to heal. We bind demons for the same reason. This situation aids both the magician and the demon in the long run.

The last tools of the Goetic ritual are the ring, pentacle, and hexagram. The ring is held to the face, to protect the magician from any harmful energy, described as the "flaming breath" of the spirit. The pentacle is worn at the heart in silver, gold, or the metal appropriate to the spirit's rank. Often the seal of the spirit summoned is on the reverse side, which can be done on parchment. The Ordo Templi Astartes has an interesting technique of using temporary greasepaint on a metal lamen, so the sigil can be changed with the working. The pentacle helps control the spirit and protect the magician. In the spirit world, symbols are things, not just symbols of things. The upward-pointing pentagram symbolizes the power of spirit over the lower powers. The spirit responds to this energy. The hexagram, traditionally in calf skin, is hidden in the "skirt" of the magician, revealed to the spirit to make it take human form and obey the magician.

In my opinion, all the implements of Goetic magick can be adapted to suit the modern practitioner. As witches, we adapted the principles of medieval Christian magick to suit our own theology, so it only makes sense that some of the tools and symbolism will change. I use my level-one initiation pentacle for my lamen and keep a separate seal for the spirit, which I simply hold up during the invocation. I use my second-degree pentacle ring for the magick ring. I omit the use of the hexagram, or draw one in the air as needed. For my circle boundary, I use a ring of carefully placed stones, reserved solely for the purpose of Goetic circles. I mark the boundary of the triangle with stones as well. I do not draw them in chalk, nor do I inscribe them with holy names. If you choose to inscribe them with holy names, use the names and symbols of the gods that are appropriate to your magickal beliefs. Witches might draw pagan god names in Theban. Thelemites might use the names of Thelemic gods in Greek. You should study the original instructions and diagrams in *The Lesser Key of Solomon* before you begin adapting this material to your own needs. In fact, the next section is entirely for your intellection education, your Da'ath knowledge, but should not be applied until the completion of this course, and all the exercises contained within it, culminating with the successful completion of chapter 17 and a stronger connection to your own HGA. Like Da'ath, this lesson is almost like a test, to not be seduced by forbidden knowledge at the expense of your spiritual growth. I repeat, *Goetic magick SHOULD NOT be attempted before you complete the entire course outlined in this book.*

My friend and student Diane, well versed in shadow work and personally facing her demons, both magickally and through other channels such as successfully using twelve-step programs, urges fellow students to become comfortable with the material in *The Temple of Shamanic Witchcraft*, and the shadow work, and to have a connection to personal divinity before tackling this Goetic material. If *The Temple of Shamanic Witchcraft* was a ritualized form of conjuring the shadow, then Goetia is much like dissecting the shadow, and working with the universal forces that rule each part of the shadow.

Once you have consulted the Goetia text and determined the appropriate spirit to evoke and bind, and have set up the altar, circle, triangle, and all the appropriate tools, the basic Goetic ritual consists of the following:

Cleansing of the Space and Magician

It is essential to make sure you are centered and purified before such a working. I suggest performing a brief meditation or prayer before the ritual.

Dressing of the Magician

Anything that heightens the experience or separates you from more usual rituals should be used. If you don't often wear ritual clothing, wear it. If you have a usual robe, have a separate robe for Goetic workings. I almost never do rituals skyclad, so for Goetic workings I work skyclad, heightening the emotional intensity of the ritual, for it's not part of my usual pattern.

Appropriate Banishing Rituals

The LBRP and LBRH are certainly appropriate for this working.

Creation of Sacred Space

Though the invoking pentagram rituals could be used, as a witch, I use the traditional witch's magick circle with one difference. I cast it on the floor, through the stones I've laid out. Before I cast the circle, I "cast" the triangle, drawing the triangle with my wand three times in a clockwise fashion, and evoke Michael to guard the circle. Before I do this, I light the triangle's incense.

Preliminary Invocation

Perform an invocation to the divine and, most importantly, to the higher self. Modern Goetics use Crowley's Bornless Ritual. This will be discussed in detail in the last lesson, which is why this ritual should not be attempted until the course has been completed.

Conjuration

The conjuration is what summons the spirit to the triangle. When holding the spirit's seal, call it by name to appear in the triangle. Call upon the divine names of appropriate deities, angels, and archangels to appear.

Welcoming the Spirit

One you feel the spirit has arrived, welcome it. Scry into the mirror or smoke to contact the spirit. I see the spirit in my psychic vision, while others see shapes and images form in the smoke and mirror. The experience, despite many writings to the contrary, takes place in the magickal planes, and is not a physical manifestation, though it can be so intense as to almost seem physical to the magician. Name the spirit again and mention its rank and areas of rulership. By listing its correspondences, you are strengthening your connection to it. Charge the spirit to give you "true and faithful answers and faithful service" and to remain until given license to depart.

Binding and Commandments

Commune with the spirit, questioning it for the information it holds, either personal information or general information attributed to its nature. Command it to do as you desire, as long as your request is consistent with the spirit's nature. I promise to honor and recognize the spirit if it fulfills my commands, as I have asked and as I have intended, because as demons, they often will fulfill what you ask to the letter of the request, but not what you wanted. Keeping a magickal journal of what you ask is important in case you have to go back and "reprogram" the spirit. If certain colors are naturally associated with the entity, I burn candles of those colors, with the seal beneath the candle. I also make an offering of alcohol, either as a libation upon the seal, or set on fire in a flameproof bowl, with the seal next to it. This is a form of positive reinforcement, rather than the negative act of "burning" the seal.

Exorcism

The exorcism, also known as the License to Depart, is done when the working has been completed. If the spirit does not depart, a stronger exorcism is used. A full-on banishing rite, with banishing pentagram and banishing hexagram, can be used over the triangle. I often close the License to Depart with a banishing pentagram, drawn with the sword or athame, to seal the space, even when the spirit leaves quietly, just to make sure it's gone.

Devocation

Say farewell to your Bornless Self/HGA, and perform the release in the Bornless Ritual to return to a normal consciousness.

Closing the Sacred Space

I release the circle first and then release the triangle. Before releasing the circle, I often do a muscle test (*ITOW*, Chapter 13) to confirm the entity has fully departed from the triangle and the gateway to its world is closed.

Appropriate Banishings

The repetition of the LBRP and LBRH is appropriate. I also burn a lot of purifying incense after the working. Then I deconstruct the ring and triangle of stones.

Goetic magick, though not directly tied into the mythology of the Qlippoth, is one of the most powerful ways to work with the realm of demons, to master the self and not fear the unknown. When you start this work, I suggest you follow Paul Huson's teachings in *Mastering Witchcraft*, and begin such spirit summoning with the third spirit of the Goetia, Vassago (figure 72). He is "of a Good Nature, and his office is to declare things Past and to Come, and to discover all things Hid or Lost." As a good-natured spirit, Vassago is the easiest to work with when beginning, giving you an idea of how to work Goetic summoning before tackling harder entities. The Goetic techniques of spirit summoning can be adapted for a variety of spirits, demonic and nondemonic in origin. Another book that explains the art of spirit summoning in layperson's terms and in a manner friendly for the witch or pagan is *Summoning Spirits: The Art of Magical Evocation* by Konstantinos.

DA'ATH PATHWORKING

Unlike the other sephiroth, Da'ath has no specific paths leading into or out of it. The gateway nature of Da'ath makes it more akin to a pathway than a sephira anyway. Da'ath represents the part of our consciousness that is off the map, quite literally. The process of experiencing Da'ath often is perceived as alien. We are in the void, detached from the Tree, between the more traditional levels of consciousness and supernal consciousness. On the path of the Priestess and the image of Gimel, the camel, the void manifests as the desert, the spiritual wasteland that one must cross to reach the "waters" of enlightenment. The camel carries enough water to get to the oasis at the top. In the process, the initiate who rides this ship of the desert is transformed from individual seeker, to become part of the mystery.

Da'ath is said to have a hidden path, the unnamed and unnumbered part of the lightning strike. The path of the lightning strike is one across the Abyss from Chesed to Binah. The dark and stormy skies at the edge of Chesed lead to the primordial waters of Binah by way of the Abyss. One must personally experience the mystery of this path, of the crossing. *Promethea* author Alan Moore details the "broken" paths named after tarot archetypes that he calls the Beggar, from Da'ath to Chesed, detailing the form the divine often takes to manifest in the world and test humanity, and the Fountain, from Da'ath to Binah, as the primordial waters of Binah cross the void. They rep-

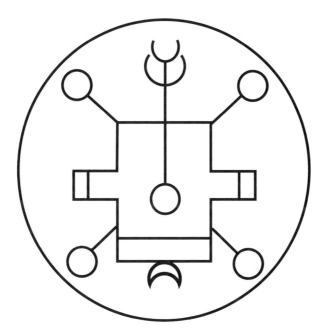

Figure 72: Vassago Seal

resent two concepts that have been lost during the Fall to human consciousness, yet their fractured skeletal paths remain. Though an invention of Moore, they provide us with some interesting insights and ideas when experiencing our own Abyss.

Since Da'ath (and the Abyss) is not an actual sphere, but a transition point, it is difficult to do a pathworking to Da'ath without continuing onward to one of the three supernal sephiroth. As we continue to work with the Tree of Life in the next three lessons, use the knowledge of lesson 13 to aid you in transitioning from the Ethical Triangle to the Supernal Triangle.

DA'ATH INITIATION

Though Da'ath has no traditional rank, in many ways it represents one of the most profound initiatory experiences on the Tree of Life—the transition between the ethical and supernal levels of consciousness.

One could argue that such a transition cannot occur when one is still incarnate in a body, and any experience a magician has of Da'ath and the supernal spheres is simply an experience of the "fractal" Tree, an experience of the supernal aspects of one of the lower spheres. As each sephira has its own inner Tree that must be climbed (chapter 5), you might cross the Abyss and move through the Da'ath of a lower sphere. That way, we have many Abysses to cross before our journey is over. The most an enlightened sage in the world can hope for until the transition beyond this body and world is to cross the Abyss within the realm of Chesed and attain the supernal sephira of Chesed, but not cross the "true" Abyss of the full Tree of Life. In this way, we can safely learn about Da'ath, or any sephira, at the level of our own current initiation. A magician can never truly know if he or she is experiencing the true sephira in the larger Tree of Life or an aspect of that sephira in another sephira. A magician might experience Kether but truly be experiencing the Kether aspect of Malkuth, Yesod, Hod, or any of the other more accessible levels of consciousness.

One who can cross the true Abyss is one who has reached such a level of enlightenment that the material plane is not his or her point of origin any longer, becoming closer to an ascended master. Perhaps some ascended beings, capable of all forms of magick, have been here incarnated in a body in the past, and some are here now, but generally one working on this level of initiation is focused on other realms of existence, and no longer attached to the world of form and function. Once we move beyond Tiphereth, we lose much of our sense of personal attachment, and when we cross the Abyss, our sense of divinity is no longer personal, but transpersonal.

HOMEWORK

- As stated in this lesson, DO NOT practice Goetic magick until you have made a solid and strong connection with your own HGA, deities, and divine powers through completion of all the exercises in this book. Complete the course work in this book, culminating in chapter 17, and then go back to apply knowledge of the Goetia if you feel it should be a part of your spiritual practice. It is not necessary to explore the Goetia to continue on to the last book in the Temple series, *The Living Temple of Witchcraft*. This chapter is as much for your intellectual understanding as your actual practice.

- Continue to practice the LBRP, LBRH, Middle Pillar, and Circulation of the Body of Light rituals, the traditional or personal versions.

TIPS

- Fill in the Da'ath correspondences and colors on your own Tree of Life drawing. Contemplate them as you add them to the image. Start memorizing these correspondences.

- Review and reflect on all you have learned in this lesson. Reflect particularly on the lesson of seeking out forbidden knowledge rather than seeking divinity.

- Begin contemplating designs for your own reality map. What correspondences, images, and geometries are important to your own worldview?

Lesson Ten
Binah

The third sphere of the Tree of Life is the one that most Qabalistic witches relate to the best. Binah is the sphere of the Great Mother, the cosmic goddess. Here is where true life begins, and where life ends. The Great Mother is both the source of life, and the reunion with the cosmos.

Binah means "understanding," for this sphere is the truest understanding of all that has come before. It moves beyond the intellectual knowledge of Da'ath, for knowledge without understanding is useless. Binah is the understanding of the universe, of the cosmos, of the powers of creation, for creation first takes hold in Binah. Binah is the understanding of how to use all that we have learned before this. What does it all mean? Why are we on the path? How do we best serve? Binah is the understanding of the great mysteries of life. Understanding differs from knowledge and wisdom, for knowledge is what we seek; we must initiate the process and go out to find it. Knowledge is seen as something beyond us. Wisdom is something that issues forth from us, sometimes bidden and other times unbidden. It's an alchemical result of the knowledge applied. Understanding simply happens, in that deep dark place within us, like the womb of the Great Mother. Understanding suddenly occurs, as if things suddenly come into focus.

The primal Godhead of Kether projects the seed of life in Chokmah, but it is Binah that provides the fertile cosmic "ground" to receive the seed. In Binah, the idea grows into form. Binah is the womb, the cosmic ocean, the vast darkness where spiritual procreation takes place to manifest the universe. The interaction between Binah as Goddess and Chokmah as God creates, sustains, and ultimately destroys the universe. The planet Saturn is the correspondent to Binah in the solar system. It is the only one of the seven traditional planets to be placed across the Abyss. Saturn holds a special place among the seven planets, as the oldest, wisest, and furthest out, setting barriers to and limits on the others. It is the planet of endings, boundaries, and gates. Saturn is the planet of death, but also of manifestation, which suits the function of Binah quite well. In the past, when life expectancy was much shorter, Saturn's thirty-year cycle signaled the end of life, but now the Saturn return signals the start of "cosmic adulthood." Working with Saturnine energy requires a certain degree of maturity, for it is so powerful.

Though Saturn and his Greek counterpart, Chronos, are masculine in classical mythology, Qabalists see Saturn as a feminine force, the top of the Pillar of Severity. As the polarities shift beneath the veil, the goddess force of Netzach, of love and nature, represents the lower octave of this force, just as Hod has a correspondence with Chokmah. Some also see Saturn as a higher octave of the Moon. While in astrology the placement of the Moon represents the emotions and karma you are manifesting in this life, Saturn represents the past, and the karma from previous actions manifesting in the world. For this reason, Saturn is said to be the taskmaster, the teacher of discipline, and its lessons sometimes are seen as punishment. In this case, Saturn has much in common with Geburah, as its higher note on the Pillar of Severity. Yet at the same time, Binah and Saturn teach the lessons beyond life, death, and attachment to the material world.

Binah

Meaning: Understanding
Level of Reality: Highest Form of Manifest Creation, Divine Mother Love, Eros

Parts of the Self: Divine Soul, Intuitive Self, Right Side of the Head

Experience: Vision of Sorrow, Vision of Compassion

Obligation: None

Illusion: Death

Virtue: Silence

Vice: None

Name of God: YHVH Elohim, Tetragrammaton Gods

King Scale Color: Crimson

Queen Scale Color: Black

Prince Scale Color: Dark Brown

Princess Scale Color: Gray flecked with Pink

Elements: Water, Earth

Planet: Saturn

Image: Mature Queen

Archetypes: Dark Mother, Underworld Goddess, Universal Star Goddess, Sea Mother, Fertile Mother

Greek/Roman Deities: Hecate, Persephone, Demeter, Hera, Rhea

Egyptian Deities: Isis, Nepthys, Maat, Nuit

Middle Eastern Deities: Inanna, Erishkigal, Tiamat

Celtic Deities: Danu, Morrighan

Norse Deities: Hel, Frigga

Hindu Deity: Shakti

Archangel: Tzafkiel (Angel of Protection against Strife and Evil)

Angelic Order: Aralim, Thrones

Choir: Thrones

Grade of Initiation: ⑧=③ Master

Animal: Woman

Planetary Vowel Sound: O (oo)

Resonant Letter: m

Musical Mode: Dorian

Musical Note: A

Tools: Cup, Wine, Outer Robe of Concealment, the Veil, Yoni, Vesica Pisces, the Cup or Chalice

Incense: Myrrh

Tarot: All Queens
>> Chariot—to Geburah
>> Lovers—to Tiphereth
>> Empress—to Chokmah
>> Magician—to Kether

Metal: Lead

Stones: Pearl, Star Sapphire, Jet, Onyx

Plant: Cypress

For this month's journey in Binah, decorate your altar in black and in threes. The threes of all the tarot suits, as well as all the queens of the deck, are designated for Binah. The Chariot, Lovers, Empress, and Magician are the gateway cards in and out of the realm. Myrrh is the classic scent, and while the lead tools can be difficult to obtain for ritual use, anything dark and dull will correspond to Saturn. Dark black stones, as well as the star sapphire and pearl, resonate with Binah.

ENTITIES OF BINAH

Binah is the Great Mother, the matron queen. She sometimes is described as the sterile mother, for when we return to her again, she is the receiver, the principle of ending, not the giver of life, though she also is the cosmic void from which creation flows. Binah is the feminine aspect of all of creation. She is the Greater Goddess, with a capital *G*, of the neopagan movement, and we see her reflection in all of the other goddesses and gods. The divine name of Binah is also the name used for Da'ath in the Middle Pillar exercise—*YHVH Elohim*, Lord of Gods. She rules over the rest of the gods of the Tree, yet rules from a distance, simply creating and receiving them, and all things.

Binah has a special relationship with goddesses of Malkuth, as the Mature Queen has a special relationship with her daughter, the Young Queen enthroned. Malkuth is the world of matter, but Binah is the root of all matter, the root of all form and formation. Without the power of Binah, none of the other spheres would take shape and lead to the formation of matter. Mother Gaia, as our planet, is like the reflection of the Supernal Mother in the microcosm. That is why the Earth is such a link and connecting force to the transcendent forces of the cosmos. They sing the same "note," the same "songs," in a different octave.

Binah consecrates and makes holy all things, for it brings all things into formation. Binah, as the third sphere, has three names and aspects, known as the Sanctifying Intelligence of the Tree. The first is Marah, the great sea, but she is not the sea of the world, but the sea of the cosmos. The second is Aimah, the fertile mother, the life-giving force that rises from the sea. The single-celled organisms of our ocean that developed into multicellular life, crawling out of Earth's primordial sea, are a reflection of what occurred on a cosmic level, as creation crawled out of Binah, across Da'ath, and onto the "land" of the four directions, Chesed. Lastly, Binah manifests as Ama, the dark mother.

Influenced by Thelemic mythos, Alan Moore's comic-book teaching of Binah looks at the three aspects of this sphere as Marie, Revelation, and Babylon. Marie is the virginal Queen of Heaven, the uncorrupt and endless sea of compassion. Revelation is she who reveals herself to us. She is wanton and shows her mysteries, inviting those who seek them. The Goddess is revealed all around us, in the life force, in the unions all around—human, animal, and plant, and in the stars and sky. You simply need to be paying attention to experience Revelation. She reveals the vision of Binah. And she is Babylon. Babylon is a Thelemic reinterpretation of the Whore of Babylon. She is the goddess of the Lust card of the Thoth deck, with her roots in the original image of Strength. She rides the great beast. She is the lust for the divine, for revelation, but also the destruction of all things. With a neopagan background, it is easy to see in this triple sphere the triple goddess, as the Goddess manifests as maiden, mother, and crone, or the creating, sustaining, and destroying principles of the universe.

All the primordial goddesses of creation fall in the sphere of Binah, as each culture tried to express this goddess in myth and art. Binah is the Dark Mother and the Underworld Queen. In this form, she is Hecate and Persephone. She is Erishkigal. She is the Morrighan and Hel. She is Dark Isis. She is Nepthys. She is the Earth Mother as the material cosmos, not just our planet, but all land and matter everywhere. She is the mother of the gods, Danu, and the greater form of Gaia. She is the Queen of Heaven and Earth, Inanna. She is the universal Star Goddess quoted in *The Charge of the Goddess*. She is Nuit.

The archangel associated with Binah and Saturn is Tzafkiel, or Tzaphkiel, the angel who protects against strife and evil. This being often is confused with Tzadkiel, the archangel of Jupiter, but Tzafkiel is the one to invoke when you feel overwhelmed by the forces of Saturn in your life and the karmic darkness becomes too much to bear. Tzafkiel mediates these forces, so you actually have the opportunity to learn from them and not be destroyed by them. Tzafkiel is an angel of endings and, with Saturn, is sometimes seen as an archangel of death, but he can be called upon to initiate change by ending situations, relationships, and patterns in life, much like the image of the Death card in the tarot. His being is said to be so cosmically vast that one cannot see him in his entirety in spirit vision, but only a limb or an eye at a time.

The angelic order of Binah in both angelic systems of magick covered in this text actually matches. The Aralim (the Mighty Ones) or Thrones of the angelic world reside here. Interestingly enough, the throne of the queen is a symbol of Binah and the daughter sphere of Malkuth. These are the angels of understanding, ministers to the Great Mother in the process of creation issuing forth from the womb of creation. Despite the receptivity of Binah, they are known as angels of action and often divine justice. They also are known as the Many-Eyed Ones, and often are linked to the Living Creatures of Ezekiel's vision as he ascended to the Throne of God. The path linking Geburah and Binah is the Chariot, a metaphor for the merkaba whirlwind that brought Ezekiel upward to the throne.

Vision of Binah

Binah's spiritual experience is the first above the Abyss, and relates to a deep and profound mystical event that is quite difficult to experience, let alone explain. Known as the Vision of Sorrow, it is the realization of the state of the world, the state of creation. We live in a paradox of wholeness and separation. We are born only to live and die again. We are in a cycle of creation, and the process of transition always brings sorrow on some level. The Divine Mother here has many natures, and the understanding and reconciliation of her vast nature is what can create the Vision of Sorrow, but also the complementary Vision of Compassion.

The Dark Goddess—triple in nature as the sea, the fertile mother, and the sterile mother—has many other names. She is the sacred priestess of ancient times, known as the temple prostitute, a role that has been downcast and degraded in our world. As all women are goddesses, the way those of us in the world (both male and female) treat women is the way we treat the Goddess, our true and cosmic mother. The Great Mother is the wanton harlot, the sacred whore or scarlet woman, for in truth, she shuns and refuses no one. Though none can fully embrace her, she embraces all of us, for she must receive us at the hour of our death. Eventually she will receive the world, the cosmos, as the cycle of life ends to begin anew in a different form. Think of how we treat the Great Mother as reflected in how we treat our blood mothers, our sisters, daughters, and all women. Think of how we treat the woman who explores the power of sexuality. Think of how we treat the planet Earth. Though our cultural attitudes are slowly changing, women have not held a place of value, esteem, and holiness for a very long time. Think of how our myths have changed to reflect our beliefs, as the ancient myths became more patriarchal and less goddess reverent. This mistreatment is the source of sorrow. The Mother walks our world all around us, yet we have ignored her. Now we see her in all things at Binah. We remember how we have acted, individually and collectively, and we feel the sorrow.

Those who seek out the Great Mother, seek out the taboo. They seek out magick and spirit through the feminine, through the body and through sex. They seek her intentionally and unintentionally, through the Underworld, through karma, through their pains and addictions and vices. These people are seen as dark and corrupt, and eventually are rejected by much of society, yet they are purified and cleansed, more so than anyone who walks the straight and narrow, never giving in to temptation or sorrow. When they enter the womb of the Goddess, when they taste the nectar of her royal blood, they know that it is truly ambrosia that flows from her gates, as she has been implanted with the seed of wisdom, the seed of Chokmah, and they may taste of true wisdom. The Aztecs have a goddess named Tlazolteotl who is known as the eater of shit or eater of filth. She takes the impure and devours their sin, the karmic lead, as we might call it, and transforms it into pure, incorruptible gold. Those who have been touched by her can never be touched, corrupted, or made unclean again, regardless of what happens to their bodies in the world. Tlazolteotl is a goddess of Binah.

When we understand this sorrow, when we understand the state of creation and realize our involvement in it, we can move into compassion for ourselves and for those who follow, for we have been there. We move beyond the mercy of Chesed, which is fatherly and protective yet can be bigoted and judgmental of those who do not overcome their problems in a manner we find acceptable. There is no judgment in Binah. There is no protection or desire to save. There is simply the holiness of the Goddess, witnessing, accepting, and loving.

When we move through the sorrow, we see her again, as the sacred mother, the divine and virginal queen of heaven. She has not changed in the slightest, for the whore is the virgin and the virgin is the whore. She is both Isis Veiled and Isis Unveiled. A true virgin is one who is in control of her sexuality, not one who abstains from it. Yet we see the queen of heaven with a royalty, a grace. She is the understanding of the cosmos, through the sorrow and compassion. She is endless compassion, like the ocean. She is the Shekinah, the goddess of wisdom and understanding, the great bride and queen of the world. She is the Gnostic wisdom goddess Sophia. She is the royalty that she has always been, but now we understand it, and understand it for all women, for the planet, for the cosmos, for she is the Star Goddess whose feet hold the hosts of heaven. She is all that we have ever known. The understanding that comes with sorrow is like an old wine that is left open, degraded by time and the world, made bitter, yet it opens the gates to higher power. The understanding that comes from compassion after sorrow is like a second flow of wine blood, straight from the Mother, untainted by the lower worlds, pure and full of wisdom. This is the true *sang real*, the royal blood.

There is no obligation beyond the Abyss. There is nothing you have to do once you have reached the Mother. She accepts all unconditionally, giving her the image of both whore and divine mother, depending on how you go to her, yet she is both and neither. There is no vice. All vices have been stripped away, forgiven, and culled for their understanding and later wisdom.

The virtue of the sphere is silence, for nothing more can be said here. What is, is. You are here. You are loved. You are given the drink of understanding. These things are felt and experienced, not spoken of. A non-initiate can talk about the mysteries until he or she is blue in the face, but two who have experienced them can silently nod in understanding, as no words are needed.

The ultimate illusion of this sphere is death, for death is an illusion once you move beyond the sorrow. Things are born, live, and die only to be born again. There is no end, but only change. Those who fear death have an attachment to the individual self, while those who cross the Abyss no longer have that personal attachment. They see the paradox of individuality and union. They then can become the devoted adepts of understanding, enflamed in their love, drunk upon the honey blood wine of the Great Mother, and seek no more than to be of benevolent service to her and thereby to all of creation.

BINAH MAGICK

Binah magick is all goddess magick—creation, life, and death. Binah's color is black, and its incense is all dark and earthy things, reminding us of the root of the material world and creation. Myrrh is the traditional scent, though older texts also include the animal scent civet. Most modern witches no longer use the animal products civet, musk, or ambergris, due to both ethical and practical considerations, though some natural and synthetic substitutes have been used. Likewise, the metal lead, the earthly manifestation of the virtues of Saturn, is not always easily accessible to modern witches, but it is the best metallic correspondence. Dark stones such as jet, onyx, and obsidian can be used, as well as brighter luminescent stones, particularly star sapphire and pearl. The hexagonal shine of the star sapphire alludes to the geometry of Binah by doubling it. Through such stones, we can see the triad.

It takes a minimum of three points to form a shape. The first shape formed is the triangle, the symbol of Binah. The downward-facing triangle is the alchemical symbol of water, the element of the ocean mother, as well as a symbol for the yoni, the feminine organs that epitomize this sphere. The three legs of a stool or tripod are the minimum number needed to stand upright. In sacred geometry, three represents the first step in creation, as nothing can take form without a minimum of three points. The triad becomes the fundamental shape that gives birth to many others. The principle of three in creation is essential, be it the three faces of the goddess of the Fates, or the scientist's electron, proton, and neutron. Three shows up in our visible spectrum, the red, green, and blue violet that make things visible to us, or the pigment spectrum of red, blue, and yellow. Both of these triads, when mixed, create the rest of the rainbow, all of visible creation. The ability of the three to balance the two, and generate something new, is the power of this sphere. When a binding element is introduced into something that is polarized, a new whole is created, rather that just two complementary points. Negative and positive points come together through a field and make a magnet. Reactant and reagent chemicals come together with a catalyst and make a new chemical process. The proton and electron come together with a neutron to make an atom. The third part grants the powers of creation.

The working of all feminine magick is the province of Binah. It is here that the magician, regardless of gender, becomes one with the feminine mysteries, that which must be experienced, not intellectualized. Binah's correspondences show us the intimate feminine connection of this sphere. All the queens of the tarot are aligned with Binah, and the animal of Binah is woman. People often are insulted to hear that, but above the Abyss, the actual and mythical animals are not the manifestations of the sphere's power. Above the Abyss, the human body, the human vehicle, is the "animal," for we all have an animal nature and animal structure in our bodies. Woman is the expression of our physicality that relates to Binah, as man is the expression of Chokmah. Here we explore that physical archetypal nature of woman.

Binah's ritual tools are the expression of woman. The first tool is the outer robe of concealment, as in the tarot's Magician, with the outer garment of red protecting the inner robe of white. The veil, symbolizing the covering of the holiest of holies, and the unveiling, the mystery and experience, play a similar role. The veil is power and purity rolled into one. We begin to plumb the mysteries of how something like sex can be both sacred and profane at the same time. Something can be primal and animalistic but also holy and divine. Something can be wanton and lustful yet saintly. It's the paradox of spirit that we find in these feminine mysteries. These mysteries have been suppressed because they are so powerful and so easy to misunderstand. Many of the orthodox religions fear feminine mysteries, and fear the role of the Goddess, of all women, in the initiation process, so we have suppressed our sexuality and have been encouraged to be as unconscious as possible when actually engaging in it. If we were truly present and conscious in all acts of sexuality, then the gates would open and we'd climb the Tree and pick the fruit for ourselves. That is the true secret of the Garden of Eden. The serpent power, the kundalini, is what informed us, our inner Eve, to pick the apple, the witch's fruit, and have a Gnostic experience, a direct knowledge of the divine. With such simple instructions to experience divinity, we'd have little need for organized religion and its institutions.

Beyond the robe and veil, all yoni figures, art, and tools that emulate the divine feminine, the vagina, the vulva, are symbols of Binah energy. Yoni is the Sanskrit term for the feminine reproductive organs, and in that tradition, the word contains a host of sacred associations with the Goddess and with feminine powers, including rites of passage, death, and agricultural fertility. Yoni statues, or goddess images with enlarged yonis, were used in rituals. This imagery bears a striking similarity to the Sheela-na-gig figure found in the United Kingdom. Like the qualities of Binah, the Sheela-na-gig is not a young and fertile figure, but often is associated with crones, comical images, or fairly monstrous-looking women rather than voluptuous and beautiful young maidens (figure 73). I know many witches who work with Sheela-na-gig as a primal goddess, and her yoni is a gateway to the Otherworld.

In sacred geometry, the *Vesica Pisces* is the yoni figure (figure 74). Though made of two circles, seemingly relating it to the second sphere of Chokmah, it is the union of the two that creates the third, new shape that is the gateway to all of creation, like the Goddess and God coming together. Both are needed for creation, but ultimately it is this yoni shape that generates the universe. When you look at the lines and relationships extrapolated from the Vesica Pisces, many of the other figures of sacred geometry are "born."

Called the Eye of God and the Gate of Creation, the term Vesica Pisces actually refers to a fish bladder, as the symbol has been associated with fish and, in particular, Christianity. Jesus is known both for performing the miracle of the fishes and loaves and for being the "fisher of souls." Yet the fish is born out of the primal ocean of the Mother. This is why many pagan mythologies start with the birth of the universe

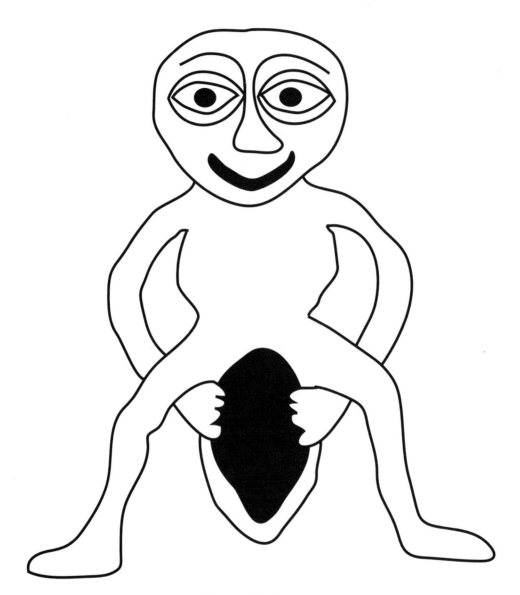

Figure 73: Sheela-na-gig

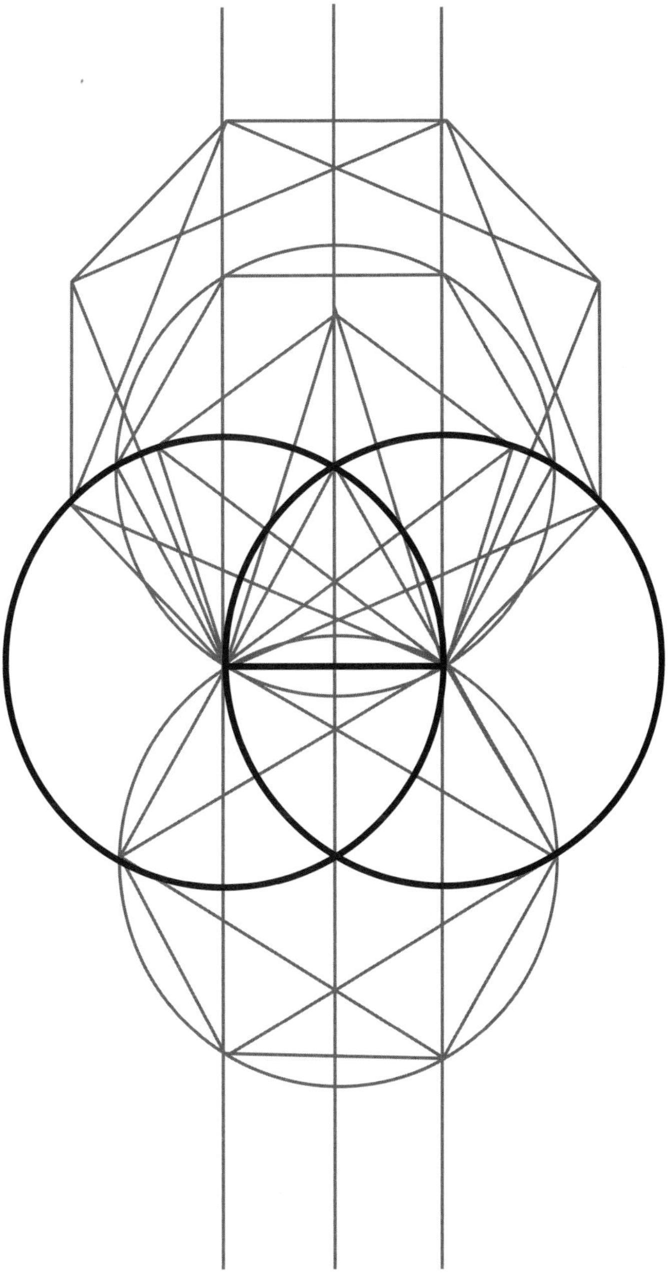

Figure 74: Vesica Pisces and Sacred Geometry

through the Goddess, the void, the Great Mother. It is the first act of creation we can really understand, appearing to be a self-generating, bisexual mother goddess.

The yoni and Vesica Pisces both are receptive feminine symbols, which, to the magician, are best embodied by the cauldron or cup. The chalice represents the Holy Grail, the San Greal but also as the sang real, the sacred royal blood, for the blood is a sacred mystery. The true royalty comes in recognizing our own sovereignty, our own divinity and right to rule ourselves as spiritual beings. The power of Binah is both of vessel and of blood, for the two are linked. When we start to learn about the powers of the chalice, as we did together through the lessons of Yesod, we look to water as love, as compassion and healing. It is all the best, the brightest, and the most gentle of the feminine mysteries. In Binah, water is the cup of blood, the cup of ancestry, of the Underworld and life through death. It is the lineages of the priestesses and the sexual relationships of body and spirit mating, such as the legendary unions with the fey, angels, gods, and demons found in our mythology. Through such matings we have an intermingling of the supernal and the material, the mythical and the mundane. It is all the things we know to be true, yet we cannot express them in our sciences and languages. We must experience them, for they are a mystery. It is because of that mystery, that secret union of flesh, spirit, and all the elements coming together in perfect proportion, in this space and time, that we are here—as individuals, as a race, as a planet. It is the divine mystery we seek to know as we climb the Tree. No amount of talking about it is a substitute for the experience.

Wine is a powerful ritual tool for Binah, for the true royal wine, the royal blood, is hers to share, flowing from her yoni, and stilled into purified and corrupt currents that ultimately give the same gift. Bitter or soured wines often are used as an offering to the dark goddesses, such as Hecate, while untainted wines are used in many traditional Wiccan rituals. Honey wines, or meads, are very appropriate, as the bee, a creature of solar light and the Upper World, distills the light and Venusian flower power into honey, feeding both body and soul. That is further transformed into a fluid to open the gates of perception. Bees have a strong esoteric connection with the Goddess, as the Queen Bee, and with sexual reproduction. Honey is used as a description of sexual fluids. The chalice filled with wine or honey wine is the ritual vagina of the Goddess in the Great Rite.

The art of winemaking and the use of honey in magick and medicine are the province of both the witch and the alchemist. Distillation of fluids to open the gates and transform the soul is part of the alchemist's work. The practical application of alchemy is one of the best forms of magick to help one understand the powers of creation. Its physical nature balances the cerebral focus of Hermetic magick and helps ground the magician. Alchemy and herbalism are strongly connected to witchcraft and the Goddess-oriented traditions. Binah is an excellent sphere to learn to work with nature in a hands-on creative process. A basic knowledge of alchemy was expected from those in the lower ranks of the Golden Dawn.

Alchemy is the art, science, and spiritual tradition of finding enlightenment through the study of the natural world. An alchemist seeks to understand the self through studying the natural world. By learning how the divine manifests in nature, there comes a greater understanding of how the divine manifests in humanity. The Principle of Correspondence—as above, so below—is the guiding theme. The use of metals, gems, and plants is part of the alchemist's repertoire, as each is said to contain an interior star, a light, that corresponds to the stars in the heavens. To study things on Earth is to study the patterns of the heavens.

An alchemist seeks the refinement of the self through the refinement of natural materials. By studying the breakdown of natural materials, and then their purification and recombination, the alchemist learns how to break down, purify, and recombine the self. The guiding principle of this later form of alchemy is embodied in the maxim *solve et coagula*, meaning "dissolve and coagulate" or "dissolve the body and coagulate the spirit." Dew is probably one of the holiest of fluids used in alchemy, because by its very nature, it demonstrates the properties of something that has gone through the circulation process of solve et coagula. Water evaporates through the action of the Sun, of light, rising to the heavens. But dew cools through the action of the night, of dark, and descends back to the Earth, yet doesn't really touch the ground, existing in some heavenly liminal state, purified. Dew is a physical manifestation of life force, a condensation of spirit, collected and used in alchemical workings.

Alchemical processes are really rituals of sympathetic magick. When an alchemist puts material through a dissolution and coagulation pattern, the results are not based on controlled scientific conditions; rather, more in the spirit of our modern quantum physicists, alchemists believe the alchemist directly affects the result of the experiment. An alchemist who has refined his or her body and spirit to a certain extent will have better results, seemingly defying our normal laws of physics, than the alchemist who is not spiritually refined. The chemical experiments are like tests. As you refine yourself, you refine the materials, and vice versa. Repeated experimentation brings the understanding of the true nature of the materials, of creation and ultimately the self. This is epitomized as the transmutation of lead into gold. Known as the Philosopher's Stone, this ultimate transmutation of matter was said to transmute the elements, prolong life, and cure any illness. The Philosopher's Stone is really the alchemist's own body, united fully with the spirit, and enlightened, capable of healing all illness and transforming matter, much like the concept we have of divine and ascended beings bending the laws of physics to reveal their connection to the divine by performing miracles.

Like high and low magick, alchemy can be divided into outer alchemy and inner alchemy. One is focused on the refinement of substances and the use of medicines, while the second is focused on inner change. Like high and low magick, knowledge of both is needed to be a truly successful practicing alchemist. The alchemist's pictorial texts and mandalas form some of the most sophisticated modern reality maps we have.

Alchemy follows many of the same fundamental concepts of all occult traditions. Its theories of the cosmos eventually evolved into a triune understanding of creation, using the symbols of sulfur, mercury, and salt. Like the four elements, which were also a critical part of the alchemist's cosmology, these three chemicals stood for greater principles rather than the substances they represent.

Sulfur is the energetic and volatile principle. It has strong associations with fire, the Sun, yang, and the cardinal triplicity. Mercury is the fluid and interactive principle. It corresponds with water, the Moon, yin, and the mutable triplicity. Salt is the stable and grounded principle, the material component. It is associated with earth, planet Earth, and the fixed triplicity.

Modern witches and magicians can apply the intellectual knowledge of Hermeticism in the making of planetary herbal tinctures. Known as plant alchemy, it is the lesser working of the alchemist, for the greater working is with metals. The lesser working is known as the Way of the Vegetable Stone, rather than the Philosopher's Stone. Many alchemists consider this working a prerequisite to the fabled Philosopher's Stone. Though plant tinctures cannot turn lead into gold, they do produce marvelous results. Such medicines work very similarly to both magickal herbal preparations and medicinal herbal preparations, but the purification and coagulation process intensifies the properties, so only drops are needed for profound physical and spiritual healings. The Way of the Vegetable Stone is to separate the sulfur, mercury, and salt of a plant, purifying them and recombining them. The process of making planetary tinctures transforms the alchemist, aiding his or her own enlightenment and healing process and ability to help heal others.

EXERCISE 26

Planetary Tinctures

Materials needed:

  2 glass canning jars with lids

  Plastic wrap

  Funnel

  Cheesecloth

  Metal spoon

  Heatproof glass baking dish with lid

  Mortar and pestle

  Airtight jar

  High-quality alcohol

Decide what kind of planetary tincture you desire to make. What planet will serve you best in the current stage of your enlightenment process? Traditionally, alchemists will choose lemon balm, an herb ruled by Jupiter, as the first herb, though lemon balm also has lunar associations. Others might start with a tincture of a Saturnine herb, and move through all seven stages of the alchemist's planetary view—Saturn, Jupiter, Mars, Venus, Mercury, Moon, and Sun. Once you have selected a planet, choose an appropriate herb ruled by that planet. Use a nontoxic plant, as planetary tinctures are typically consumed in ritual. Traditionally, the dose of tincture is a few drops. Tinctures also can be used to anoint ritual objects and charms.

1. Begin making your planetary tincture on the first day ruled by that planet, after the New Moon. If you are using the Jupiter/lemon balm tincture, start on the first Thursday after the New Moon. Ideally, start in the hour of the planet on the day of the planet (*OTOW*, Chapter 12). Try to time major operations in the process using the appropriate planetary day or planetary hour whenever possible, to keep the energy as focused as possible. Traditional alchemists purified themselves and prayed before doing any work on their experiments.

2. If possible, begin the process by harvesting the herb and drying it naturally. If you cannot harvest the herb yourself, you can purchase it. Grind the dried herb into a fine powder with a mortar and pestle. As you do, meditate on the powers of the planet and herb. Spending time with the herb physically attunes your energy field to it. Your attitude will directly determine the effect the experiment has. I've been very focused while making tinctures and had marvelous results, and I've made them while distracted, not giving them my full attention, and they did not turn out as powerful. Once you have ground the herb, add the herbal powder to a canning jar until it is one-third full.

3. Add a high-quality, high-proof alcohol or, better yet, an ethanol or grain alcohol until the jar is full. The Everclear brand, at 151 or 190 proof, is ideal. Lower-proof alcohol can be consecrated by freezing it for a few hours, to separate the water, which freezes, from the alcohol. Pour the alcohol out of the container after putting it in the freezer for a few hours, to remove some water. Next, put a piece of plastic wrap over the jar to prevent any contact with a metal lid, and then place the lid over the plastic, sealing it. Put the jar in a warm place, such as a boiler room. I've kept mine in a cabinet under my altar. Traditionally, it takes a minimum of two or three weeks, and ideally six weeks, to draw out the plant properties into the liquid. This is the incubation process. The length of time is up to you, but six weeks is a good medium.

Others time it as they would with a planetary fluid condenser (see page 280). I suggest shaking the jar daily and thinking about the planetary properties of the tincture. The tincture must be treated with respect, as it is the birth of the "higher self" of the plant in material form. It is considered the alchemist's child. If the tincture is solar-oriented, you can put the jar out in the sunlight. Warm days are ideal to help the tincturing process. If the tincture is lunar-oriented, you can put the jar under the moonlight. Lunar tinctures should be brought inside before sunrise. The alcohol and water component is the mercury separating the volatile sulfur, or essential oils, of the plant from the dross matter, or salt, of the plant.

4. Pour out the mixture through cheesecloth and a funnel into a second jar. Now the liquid is in the second jar, with the herb strained out. Seal the jar with plastic wrap and the lid. Label "Tincture of (Herb Name/Planet)." The tincture alone, being the sulfur and mercury components of the plant, heals the spiritual and soul levels of the individual.

5. Take the herb out of the cheesecloth filter, and place it in a non-aluminum baking pan. Glass baking dishes work well too. Take the pan outside on a non-windy day, and set it on a fireproof surface. Drop a match on the alcohol-soaked herb, setting it on fire. Let the herb burn to ash. Stir it with a metal spoon, to make sure it all burns. Be careful, and use oven mitts if necessary. Do not lose the ash. If the herb does not burn, particularly if you used a lower-grade alcohol, splash it with a higher-grade alcohol or ethanol to ignite it more easily.

6. Bake the ash at 500° F or more for over an hour. Calcinate the herb, making the ash turn gray or white. This is the salt of the herb. This process can create smoke, so be prepared to temporarily disconnect or cover your fire alarms and reconnect them when the experiment is done. Let the ash cool after it has turned color, and when cool, grind it up using a mortar and pestle. Place the dry ash in a separate jar and label as "Salt of (Herb Name/Planet)." You can take a few grains of the salt in a glass of distilled water for

healing, particularly for physical healing, as it contains the alchemical salt principle of the herb. Look up the physical healing properties of the herb in a reputable medicinal herbal book. The salt of the herb should aid in healing that body part or system. You also can add appropriately corresponding planetary salts to planetary fluid condensers, to make them more powerful. Ideally, the condensers should contain the same herb from which the salt is made, but this is not absolutely necessary, as long as the planetary attribute is the same.

7. If you want to make a planetary tincture, add the salt of the herb to the tincture of the herb, creating a true planetary tincture, what is also known as a *spagyric tincture*. This heals the body, soul, and spirit simultaneously, unlocking the secret powers of the herb, its true divine nature. Label it appropriately and put a date on it. Take no more than ten drops in a glass of water or wine daily. You can take it to attune to a specific planet or herb for a ritual, or have a regimen of taking the tincture daily, starting on the day of the planet, to attune yourself to the spiritual forces of the planet for a long period of time. Alchemists might go through a regimen of the seven planets, from densest Saturn up to the gold of the Sun, to refine their vibration, making seven tinctures and completely consuming them all, only a few drops at a time.

Binah Pathworkings

As Binah is the first sphere above the Abyss, working with it directly in vision is very intense. Though many would say that we are incapable of reaching Binah directly, we can touch the Binah aspect of any sphere to which we can ascend.

Only two paths from Binah remain to be discussed, the path of the Empress across to Chokmah and the path of the Magician up to Kether. The bridge between Binah and Chokmah is the mystery of the Empress. Viewed as the Venusian Mother Nature, the Empress embodies the formation of nature as a force of creation. The path of the Empress is the fertility path, connecting the seed of Chokmah to the womb of Binah.

The path from Binah to Kether is ruled by the Magician, the divine androgyne who is the keeper of cosmic knowledge and the ability to manifest will in the world.

EXERCISE 27

Binah Pathworking

1. Perform the Lesser Banishing Ritual of the Pentagram (exercise 5) and the Lesser Banishing Ritual of the Hexagram (exercise 20). Do any other ritual you feel is appropriate.

2. While in this space, call upon the divine forces of Binah. Burn your three black candles and myrrh incense. Knock on your altar three times. Vibrate the divine name of Binah, **YHVH Elohim**, three times. Call upon any of the Saturn goddesses or Archangel Tzafkiel.

3. To count down into a meditative state, do exercise 1 through step 7 (page 76).

4. Let the familiar world around you fall away, as if the material reality you know is only a façade and beneath it lies the beautiful garden of the Goddess, a veritable paradise surrounding you. The land around you becomes a vast primordial garden, the garden of Malkuth, the familiar garden of the four paths.

5. Go to the heart of Malkuth, to the Temple of Malkuth. Decide to follow the paths up to and from Tiphereth to the realm of Binah. Walk the path of the World/Universe up to Yesod. Experience the consciousness of Yesod for a time. Walk the path of Temperance/Art to Tiphereth. Bask in the golden light of your HGA. Then, from the temple of Tiphereth, use your will to ascend the path of the Lovers.

6. The path of the Lovers is the path of the Gemini Twins and of Zayin, the sword point of the intellect, cleaving away all that does not serve. Move through the Lovers card, and feel yourself coalesce and polarize, dividing into your inner king and inner queen as your higher self witnesses all from

a third point of view. Feel yourself separate. Look at all that is feminine within you. Take in the beauty of the Goddess within. Look at all that is masculine within you. Take in all the power of the God within. Through the power of love, divine love, feel these two selves coming together. Through a psychic alchemical process, feel your awareness merge, king and queen becoming one, and overshadowed by the higher self. Feel yourself become the rebis, balanced in view and energy. Move toward the blackness of Binah.

7. Feel the call of the black sphere, the dark waters lapping at your feet as you tread the cosmic ocean. You might be tested to enter the realm of the sacred mother, though as silence is its virtue, you might not be required to say anything as part of the test. Enter the dark womb realm that is holy, like a temple or church. Binah is like all the sacred ground of every religion coming together in one place. It is the cathedral, the labyrinth, and the stone circle, come together. It is the cave of the shaman's initiation and the classical temple all in one. Everything here is holy. This is the realm of the Sacred Mother, both virgin and whore.

8. Make your way to the sacred Temple of Binah, three-sided and filled with triangular geometry. Some of the triangles manifest with hard, straight lines, and others are soft and rounded. This is the temple of lead, of pearl, sapphire, and jet. This is the temple of the Mother. Feel the essence of her holiness, the beginning and ending of all that was, is, and ever shall be. Notice the gateways in and out of the temple, for the Chariot, the Empress, and the Magician, as well as the entrance you came through for the Lovers. Experience the paradox and simple beauty of one force, embodying fertility, sterility, and endless compassion. Experience the paradox of wanton sexuality, virginity, and destruction. When the paradox is resolved, you will have understanding.

9. The entities of Binah are residing in the temple, all surrounding the Great Mother. The illuminated adepts, the benevolent masters who find under-

standing through the love of the Goddess, are here, making it across the void. They are inflamed by their prayer and love. The holy inner-plane priestesses are present, mediating the forces of the Mother and her three faces. From the angelic realms, Tzafkiel and the Thrones are available. All of these beings attend the Great Goddess in her aspects of the fertile mother, the dark sterile mother, and the lady of the cosmic sea. Commune with the Mother and her children. This may be silent communion, in feelings rather than words. Through this silent communion, ask to find understanding and learn compassion through the Vision of Sorrow. Ask to learn the virtue of this sphere and how to avoid the illusion.

10. When done, thank all the beings who have communicated with you. They might offer you a gift, a token of their goodwill. If you accept, it is polite to reach within your being and offer them a gift of your goodwill. Be sure that what you give reflects the energy and intention you plan to put into the sphere's lessons.

11. Once you have said your farewells, leave the shrine and follow the path back. Return the way you came unless you feel guided to return via a different pathway and know the pathway back well. Return to the garden of Malkuth. Focus on the waking world you know, and feel it return around the garden.

12. To return to normal waking consciousness and end your journey, perform steps 15–17 from exercise 1 (page 78). You can close the temple by repeating the LBRP.

Initiation of Binah

The initiation of Binah is that of the True Master, the master of the temple, which is the cosmic temple, where one is moving toward a point beyond the shape and form of the human world into something we on the lower paths cannot truly comprehend. The ⑧=③ ranking is conferred cosmically on one who is the master of Samadhi. This

Sanskrit term has been borrowed by and incorporated into Western magickal traditions. Though it is difficult to describe, Samadhi is said to indicate a state of nondualistic consciousness in which you become one with whatever you are experiencing, yet you still remain conscious. The broader meaning is to gain a sense of wholeness and integration, not only with the individual self but with the universe. Samadhi literally means to "make firm." A master of Samadhi is in a continual and effortless state of perfection with the universe. This is ultimately the master of the ascension traditions, who can move effortlessly throughout the Tree of Life, being in harmony and union with Binah and all spheres below it. The master then is responsible for "tending" or guiding the disciples on the path. Here we have the Secret Chiefs, guiding the lodge traditions, or the Theosophical masters, guiding the world. Magicians, witches, and shamans all ultimately aspire to be of service to the divine as the inner-plane priestesses and priests.

Homework

- Do Exercises 26–27 and record your experiences in your Book of Shadows.

- Continue to practice the LBRP, LBRH, Middle Pillar, and Circulation of the Body of Light rituals, the traditional or personal versions.

Tips

- Fill in the Binah correspondences and colors on your own Tree of Life drawing. Contemplate them as you add them to the image. Start memorizing these correspondences.

- Review and reflect on all you have learned in this lesson.

- Integrate the tools of the four elements into your magickal and daily life.

- Continue to work on designs for your own reality map. What correspondences, images, and geometries are important to your own worldview?

LESSON ELEVEN
CHOKMAH

As Binah is the supernal Mother, the Goddess, the divine feminine, God as a woman, Chokmah is her partner, the supernal Father, the God, the divine masculine, God as a man. Together, they are the primal powers, the first yin and yang, the pagan's true Lord and Lady. Many make the mistake of thinking they are lesser powers, being labeled sephiroth two and three, but they are, along with Kether, the Divine Creator. The Divine Creator simply has three faces—female, male, and one beyond shape and form.

Many look to the supreme father and expect to see the face we explored in Chesed—the sky father, the paternal figure of benevolence. We find that image most popularly pursued in the Yahweh or Jehovah image of biblical lore. Yet magicians, witches, and other mystics know that the God is more than this one face of the Father. The God is the universal father, of all life. Chokmah is the life force, the divine power of all of creation. Witches see the father god in many "octaves" in our mythos, yet he always expresses life force, and all his forms emanate from the Qabalist's Chokmah.

Chokmah is the solar light in the sky, from newborn child to redeeming king. It is the green man, the light flowing within the vegetation, giving it life. The solar light and its interaction with the Goddess of the Earth through the green world is the basis of all cellular life, plant and animal, upon the Earth. Life feeds life. Plants feed off the soil and light. Animals feeds off the plants, and then other animals feed off of animals. Chokmah is the life force sacrificed to feed others, projected to the Underworld, the land of the dead, to be reborn as light once again. In each case, it is the life force, the secret seed of creation.

Chokmah is the life force spurting out into the cosmos. It is the seed of the divine that then will fertilize Binah. Chokmah is the outpouring of vital energy and power, all things male in their utmost ideal, that then must be given shape and form by femininity, by Binah, to make anything useful.

Chokmah is wisdom. Wisdom is the application of all the other virtues and visions. Wisdom must come forth. Wisdom that is not expressed, in word, in writing, in vision, is simply understanding and knowledge that has not been put into action. Wisdom must gush forth. Sometimes it is asked for, and sometimes it wells and rises, and must be released.

Such wisdom is equated with the power of the "Word," the divine Logos, or manifestation of the divine in terms of vibration. The Logos is the word of God that sets forth creation. The concept of the Logos was originally Greek, and relating to the concept of guiding universal logic, for it is the pattern of creation, the guiding force and principle, that brings form, order, creation into being. The Logos has been mingled with many esoteric concepts and most often is associated with Christianity, but ultimately it is much more than any one religion can contain. It is like a spoken blueprint. It is the Om, or Aum, of the Hindus, the sound of creation. In this regard, with spoken sound, Chokmah has the higher-octave associations of Hod, the sphere of Mercury, just as Binah has a special relationship with Netzach.

Traditionally, no planet is assigned to Chokmah, as the ancients used only seven magickal planets. The stars, specifically the zodiac, correspond with Chokmah. As the light first issues forth from the void of creation, Chokmah is the foundation of stars, the light illuminating the sky. Chokmah is the first light, turned on in the universe, which is also a metaphor for self-awareness, the "I" or "I Am" of the universe. It is the projection of the god force into the cosmos. With the discovery of the outer planets, occultists most often have equated Neptune with Chokmah, as the sea father's planet corresponds nicely with the image of fluids flowing to infuse life in the womb of the Great Mother. The sea contains a bit of every naturally occurring periodic element. It is a pattern for creation, as life first began in the sea. Uranus, as the first father principle in Greek cosmology, is also an appropriate correspondence.

Chokmah

Meaning: Wisdom

Level of Reality: Seed of Creation, Logos, Flow, Expansion

Parts of the Self: Life Force, Creative Self, Right Side of Head

Experience: Vision of the Source

Obligation: None

Illusion: Independence

Virtue: Devotion

Vice: None

Names of God: YHVH, Tetragrammaton Gods

King Scale Color: Pure Soft Blue

Queen Scale Color: Gray

Prince Scale Color: Iridescent Pearl Gray

Princess Scale Color: White flecked with Red, Blue, and Yellow

Element: Fire

Planets: Zodiac; some now say Neptune or perhaps Uranus

Image: Bearded Man

Archetypes: Universal Father, Ancient One, Cosmic Seed, Utterer

Greek/Roman Deities: Uranus, Chronos, Pan, Zeus, Jupiter, Poseidon, Neptune, Janus

Egyptian Deities: Thoth, Osiris, Ra

Middle Eastern Deity: Anu

Celtic Deities: Dagda, Cernunnos

Norse Deities: Ymir, Odin

Hindu Deity: Shiva

Archangels: Raziel (Angel of Hidden Knowledge), Jophiel

Angelic Order: Auphanim (Wheels)

Choir: Cherubim
Grade of Initiation: ⑨=② Magus
Animal: Man
Planetary Vowel Sound: None
Resonant Letters: None
Musical Mode: None
Musical Note: A#
Tools: Phallus, Wand, Standing Stone, Inner Robe, Tower
Incense: Musk, Amaranth
Tarot: All Kings/Knights
   Hierophant—to Chesed
   Emperor—to Tiphereth
   Empress—to Binah
   Fool—to Kether
Metal: Platinum
Stones: Star Ruby, Turquoise, Jade, Tourmaline
Plant: Amaranth

Build your Chokmah altar in the color gray and in pairs, working with twos of everything, to signify the dual qualities of this sphere. Corresponding tools are difficult to find as we climb the Tree, particularly with no clear planetary attribute. Chokmah is the highest male vibration, so it can share correspondences with Jupiter/Chesed and the Sun/Tiphereth.

ENTITIES OF CHOKMAH

Chokmah is the masculine side of God. Traditional images are of the old patriarch, the wise king, as the elder or higher octave of Chesed, but Chokmah is much more than that. Chokmah is the first father, first principle, that gives rise to all things. As the universal father, we can look to many images of God. Some would see Chokmah as the ancient one. As this sphere is the first conscious separation from Kether, mythologies would represent Chokmah as the first separated being, the first god that takes a role in the creation of the entire cosmos. In Greek mythology, the sky father Uranus can be seen as the first god, separating from Gaia. Others look to Chronos, or Saturn, as the ancient one and primal father, as Uranus did little in the way of actual fathering, but as the cosmic principle, perhaps Uranus is the most correct manifestation. Chokmah is not the doting and protective father, but simply the seed and pattern. In terms of planetary attributes, Poseidon, as the Greek godform attributed to Neptune, would be appropriate, though the pre-Olympian deities work better in terms of Qabalistic qualities.

In Sumerian mythos, Anu is the great sky father and great father to all the gods. Anu is the cosmic sky father, not the terrestrial sky father. He created the stars as great soldiers to destroy the wicked. He is the ruler of the heavens and is equated with the heavens themselves. Anu the Sumerian god should not be confused with Anu, another name for the Celtic goddess Danu or an aspect of the Morrighan.

In Norse myth, though Odin takes part in the creation cycle with his brothers, the first two beings are the frost giant Ymir and the great cow Audumla. These two were the first father and Earth Mother figures of Norse mythology, though Ymir also was androgynous and created a race of frost giants alone. Audumla licked Ymir's ice and, through her action, created the first god, Buri, who later fathered the gods.

In Egyptian mythology, at least three figures can be associated with Chokmah, as the Egyptians had many creation stories. Ra often is depicted as the great progenitor of the universe, through an act of masturbation. The masturbation imagery fits well with the seed and spurting symbolism of Chokmah. If Isis is equated with Binah, then her brother and mate, Osiris, is an obvious Chokmah choice. Many see Isis and Osiris as the primal figures, and the flooding of the Nile is seen as Osiris's life-giving seed, impregnating the land to bring the harvest. In essence, the Nile is the microcosmic manifestation of the life-giving flood for which Osiris is responsible, bringing awareness to others, as symbolized in his development of culture in ancient, primitive Egypt. Lastly, Thoth is attributed to Chokmah, as the wisest figure of the Egyptians, beyond the daily concerns of the gods, keeper of secret wisdom. Some myths have him hatching the universe from an egg, as he manifests as the Ibis bird.

Though he's also seen as a Jupiter figure, the Dagda plays the role of the cosmic father in some Celtic neopagan traditions. Danu is seen as the Great Mother, or Binah principle, with the Dagda as her complement and the entity known as the Dryghten as the Great Spirit or androgynous Kether principle.

For the modern pagan, the best god to embody Chokmah is Pan. Modern ceremonialists and witches look to Pan as the "All," as his name is translated, though we can't be sure that ancient pagans viewed the god of Arcadia, the Land Before the Moon, in this way. Pan is the life force of not only nature in the land of our planet, but all of nature in the universe. Pan manifests in many octaves, from the lustful god of fear and inspiration to the uncrowned king of the nature spirits, faeries, and elemental forces. His highest manifestation is the cosmically lustful principle, desiring creation. The phallic imagery, both literally and through the horn symbolism and cosmic connotations as the "All," is woven together in his mythology. Pan's desire for sexual release is the principle of Chokmah put into microcosmic terms.

Pan is the Lord of the Witches, complementing the many faces of the Lady in Binah. He is the life force of everything and everyone, from the tiniest quark to the light of the brightest stars. The Celtic correspondent of Pan—Cernunnos or Herne, to modern pagans—also is associated with Chokmah. Though, like the Dagda, he has some very fatherly attributes, Cernunnos is a lord of life and death, creation and destruction. Some witchcraft traditions, looking at the complementary powers of the Lady and Lord, of the Qabalists' Binah and Chokmah, say we are born through the gates of the Goddess, through her womb, and we return in death through the horns of the Hunter, through the gates of God.

Lastly, Chokmah is the Utterer. The Utterer is the one, the being, who utters the divine Logos, to manifest creation. The god name of Chokmah is *YHVH*, often looked at as Yahweh or Jehovah in the penultimate sphere, reserving the true power of the Tetragrammaton for the entire Tree and four worlds. This is the Lord. In biblical mythology, the Logos, the utterance of the Word of God, is the power of creation. "God" speaks, whether you think of the God of Genesis as YHVH, Yahweh, or the Elohim, and through that use of words, creation occurs. Chokmah is the Utterer of creation, and Binah then takes the utterance and uses it as the seed to grow creation.

Traditionally, the archangel of Chokmah is considered to be Raziel, Ratziel, or Ratzkiel. Raziel is known as the archangel who guides the creative force and is the keeper of mysterious lore. His name is said to be the "Secret of God," and he is the author of the mysterious tome called *Sefer Raziel*, given to Adam and Eve after their expulsion from the Garden. Copies of it were passed to Enoch and Noah.

Other systems place Jophiel, the "Beauty of God," as the archangel of Chokmah. Jophiel is the companion to Archangel Metatron and, like Raziel, is associated with the expulsion of the first couple from Eden, as in some versions of the tale, Jophiel was one of the angels to actually do the expulsion.

The Qabalistic order of angels beneath Raziel is the Auphanim, or the Wheels. They are the whirling forces of creation, wheels within wheels, with many eyes. They are difficult for humans to comprehend. They are a cosmic order of beings, guiding the creative forces of Chokmah. When looked at symbolically, the wheel is the human device that moves things. We have this image symbolically in the wheel of life and the Wheel of the Year. We observe it in the Wheel of the Zodiac. When we use it as a tool, it moves things along, making creation and development easier. In the secondary angelic system, the second choir is the Cherubim, the angels of wisdom, contemplating the divine essence and form. They are the angels of light and the guides to the stars. Though we now think of cherubs as childlike angels, traditionally they are described as fearsome four-winged beings, guarding sacred places with flaming swords.

VISION OF CHOKMAH

In the sphere of Chokmah, the spiritual experience is the Vision of the Source. One is not yet united with Kether, but from Chokmah, the Vision of the Source is at its clearest. Sometimes known as the Vision of the Gods, or Vision of God, it is the closest one comes to understanding the ultimate reality without being one with that reality. One truly sees God.

As with Binah, there is no vice or obligation for Chokmah, for the supernals are above such things. The illusion of Chokmah, independence, was the virtue of Yesod. Here, we know that independence is an illusion, for all things are connected. All nature is dependent upon itself. Chokmah is nothing without Binah, and vice versa. Without the other, there is no creation, so there is no true and absolute independence. This is a necessary lesson before attaining oneness with Kether. The virtue of Chokmah is devotion, as one will be devoted to the divine life force expressed in the Tree and devoted to union with that life force when integrating the lessons of Kether.

CHOKMAH MAGICK

The correspondences of Chokmah are even more diffuse than those of Binah, as there is no absolute planetary correspondence for this sephira. Traditional incense, herbs, colors, and scents are not readily available, though some use Neptunian associations. The traditional scent is musk, for the virile sexual aspect of the scent, as well as its being filled with life force, as an animal product. Because musk is not as politically correct or eco-friendly, many witches opt to not use it, but instead use combinations of certain herbs to produce a musklike smell. Amaranth and olive are traditionally associated with Chokmah. Fennel, hops, lotus, wood aloe, and ylang-ylang have Neptunian influences and can be used in incense and potions for Chokmah.

No metal is attributed to Chokmah, though platinum, pewter, or electrum are potential correspondences. The stone of the star ruby, as well as turquoise, jade, and all forms of tourmaline (for tourmaline grows in a straight-line formation), fit the geometry of Chokmah.

All the maleness of Chokmah shows us its primary tool. As the yoni is to Binah, the phallus is to Chokmah. Ceremonially, Chokmah's tool is the wand, the directing tool of creative energy and life force. Another variation of the theme is the thyrsus, the Greek wand or staff used by the followers of Dionysus, a fennel stick topped with a pine cone. All phallus-oriented gods, from Dionysus to Kokopelli, could be found in this sphere. Though Dionysus is a younger god in the Greek pantheon, his most primal cosmic Neptunian associations, as the life force entering the dark, entering the world, could give him rulership here. In the world, the phallus is associated ritually with the erect standing stone, and the Tower. The standing stone is associated with both healing and fertility mysteries. By sleeping next to certain standing stones in the United Kingdom and Europe, infertile women or couples were said to increase their fertility and conceive easily afterward. The Tower, as the wizard's sanctum, the magickal place of refuge and study, is part of the male magician's imagery. The magician's inner robe, the white robe beneath the red in the tarot, is assigned to Chokmah as well, for it is the seed within the flesh, rather than the manifestation of the seed.

The geometry of Chokmah is the line. In terms of numerology, one is a point and three is a triangle, so two is the line, two points connected. Here we have the phallic imagery of a straight line. It is also the geometry of the Logos. First we have one divine being, indivisible and indistinct. That being is everything, yet is not necessarily aware that it is everything. When that being utters the word of creation, an aspect of the Creator is speaking while another aspect is listening. In effect, the act of utterance divides the Divine Creator into two—speaker and listener. To be able to say "I" or "I am" on any level is to differentiate the speaker from whoever is listening. There we have the manifestation, the point of self-awareness in the creation process that separates Kether from Chokmah.

The process of dividing into two parts, or uniting two parts, is the magick of Chokmah. Kether is like the Great Spirit, the creative force known as the Logos, the Word. But for the Word of creation to be relevant, something must hear it. Kether emanates to Chokmah, so there is both the speaker and the listener, ushering creation onward. Chokmah follows suit, being a male, projective energy. It wants to reach out to Binah, to create the universe as God and Goddess, or reach back to Kether, to be reunited with the source. Both paths imply a form of spiritual ecstasy or bliss when uniting with another.

One of the most important ways to discover this mystery is through the use of actual sexual energies through sexual action. As with the Great Mysteries, no amount of talking, fantasizing, or intellectualizing about sex is a substitute for actually experiencing it. Sexual energy is hard-wired into us. Sex is one of the eight gates of witchcraft to raise power, and ultimately, all of those gates, when used with deep intention, open the ways to the mysteries. Each is a path up the mountain of spirituality. The desire to direct our sexual energy, what is really our creative impulse, is the power of Chokmah.

Historically, sexual magick has been a powerful part of both Western and Eastern traditions of magick and spirituality. When referring to the Eastern traditions, the word *tantra* is used. Tantra does not exclusively concern sexuality, since it refers to a wide number of ritualistic practices and customs. Western investigators of the Eastern mysteries often focus on the sacred-sexuality aspects of tantra. A practitioner may visualize having sex with a particular deity, or, when having sex with another, visualize himself/herself and/or a partner as a deity, as a method of uniting strongly with the divine.

Western sex magick customs can be just as spiritually focused, though much of the modern literature tends to use sex—solo, coupled, or group—as a method of generating energy for outward manifestation through the use of spells and charms rather than personal enlightenment. Masturbation is the typical method of charging personal sigils in the traditions of Chaos magick. The mix of Western and Eastern teachings in modern sex magick, balancing spirituality and practicality, is bringing a healthier view of sexual power. The greater availability of texts makes this process easier, but the roots of such mixing date far back. Many believe the Knights Templar and other esotericists brought back sexual magick lore along with many other treasures from their journeys in the East.

In the ancient pagan world, we have the custom of the *Hieros Gamos*. The Hieros Gamos, or hierogamy, directly translates from the Greek to "holy wedding" or "holy coupling," and refers to the sexual union and sometimes marriage of a deity and a human. As a ritual, this was done in ancient days as an act of fertility magick, where the ruler would mate with a priestess to ensure the fertility of the land. Members of the community also would also have sex at this time, further adding to the fertility of the land through sympathetic magick, but also ensuring that their children would be born in the winter, after the growing season, so there would be more time to care for the children and fewer distractions for those working the land.

Examples of the Hieros Gamos can be found in Sumerian history when the king of a city-state would unite with a high priestess of Inanna. Celtic witches also observed the traditions of the sacred land, with the king being wed to the land through the queen as a remnant of this tradition. We see this mystery played out, rather confusingly for most, in the myths of King Arthur and Camelot.

The concepts remain in our traditions of Beltane. Most witches look to the Great Rite (in act or in token) and the fertility rites of Beltane as our experience of the Hieros Gamos. The Great Rite is a blend of both Western and Eastern ideas, which, at their core, lead to the same place. The Great Rite, done in ritual and initiations, can be profoundly moving. Though it can be the "fuel" for a spell, bringing lunar or solar energies into the circle through the rituals of drawing down, it is much more than that. The Great Rite is a profound experience of the union of the Goddess and God to create, as they are united in the circle, between us and in us. We hold that divine power of union, each and every one of us. It is through that union that we do our truest magick, in alignment with the highest will. That is the key to the witch's theurgy.

We find similar ideas, but just as veiled, in the Hermetic traditions of alchemy and Qabalah. Many of the instructive drawings of alchemy, which leave the uninitiated perplexed, depict this process. Through a series of operations, the divine King and Queen, what the psychologist might see as the animus and anima, are brought out, crowned and sovereign. They are brought together in a hermaphroditic figure of king and queen mixed, the rebis, looking more like an otherworldly wizard. The rebis is the mixture of the feminine lunar quicksilver principle with the masculine golden sulfur principle. It is the conjunction of the soul and the spirit. This is the figure of enlightened humanity, balanced in all things, incorruptible, like gold, the alchemical metal of enlightenment. Within the hermaphrodite, all paradoxes are resolved.

Like the Great Rite, the birth of the rebis shows that while this act can occur on the physical plane, as sexual union between king and queen, male and female, it also must occur on the inner planes, with the magician. In fact, that is where it must occur. Physical sex infrequently results in enlightenment. Yet sexual union, the act on the physical plane, can lead us to inner union if we are aware when engaging in it. It is the overall relationship you have with another that informs you about your inner relationship, your inner king and queen. One of my favorite alchemists is Nicholas Flamel. He found the secrets to the Philosopher's Stone, to riches of matter and spirit, not by sequestering himself away like a monk, toiling away alone, but along with his wife, who was an alchemist herself. Everybody forgets about Perenelle Flamel, but she was a critical partner, in all ways, to Nicholas's successes. Their relationship was as much the root of their enlightenment as were their alchemical experiments.

The use of sex magick in the Craft and ceremonial magick is a powerful way to work your magick. Sex magick is not restricted to just fertility magick, nor is it restricted to heterosexual pairs. Sexual energy can be used in homosexual and polyamorous situations, as well as solo experiences. In fact, many sexual rites don't actually involve physical sex. The Great Rite, done in token, is not just symbolic. Energy is moved, be it in a solitary Great Rite with the blade and chalice, or with a priestess and priest wielding the blade and chalice.

Here are some ideas for incorporating sexual magick into your workings. As with all other rituals, they are most effective when done in a ceremonial setting. Candles, incense, oils, purifications, and incantations all add to the atmosphere to turn an ordinary sexual experience into a sexual ritual.

Divine Celebration

Sexual touch is a powerful and moving way to celebrate the life force within you and can be an appropriate addition to any ritual. By viscerally feeling the life force in your blood and body, you are in touch with it in a manner that is far more primal and powerful than simple visualization and intention. Such union can be a culmination of dance, play, or ritual drama as a part of the rite. Through this, we remember the words of the Goddess in the Charge: "All acts of love and pleasure are my rituals."

Worship Through Sexual Union

We can worship the divine, physically, through a sexual partner. On one level, our modern pagan theology says "thou art god" and "thou art goddess" from the teaching of the Church of All Worlds. When we stare into the eyes of anyone, we are staring into the eyes of the divine. Through ritual sex, we honor the divine by giving pleasure to another. Through the act of giving love and pleasure to the divine being that is our partner, we connect to the divine source. In more formal rites, one or more of the participants can do a traditional invocation of a godform, in effect becoming a manifestation of a goddess or god. The union is then a form of the traditional ritualized Hieros Gamos, in which the deity is physically in union, through a priest/ess, with the worshipper. The energy of the act can be put forward for a multitude of magickal intentions or simply as an act of worshipping and honoring the divine.

Energy Working

Through sexual acts, energy can be moved through an individual's body, or between and through partners, awakening the chakra energy centers and meridian pathways. Through sex, energy is always exchanged. Magicians can focus and direct the exchange to where they want it to go. For most, the exchange occurs only through the lower chakras. For some, the exchange also goes through the heart center. In tantric magick, energy can be used to rise through the chakras, cycling from one partner to the other, to awaken the crown chakra in a manner that can be much more intense and profound than when simply visualized alone in a meditation. The additional component of physical sexual energy, beyond the visualized intent, makes it a powerful way to awaken. Also, an experienced partner can guide a less-experienced one to a deeper awakening than could be achieved alone without sexual energy, though the less-experienced partner ideally should have a foundation of knowledge to know what he or she is getting in to with the ritual. The energy raised also can be used in direct magickal working and the empowerment of tools.

Magickal Empowerment

Sexual energy, raised alone or with others, can be used to manifest magick. A traditional method of solo sex magick, drawn from the work of Austin Spare and forming a foundation of Chaos magick, is to make a sigil (*OTOW*, Chapter 13) and to stare at that sigil while masturbating. Most important is to be completely focused on the sigil upon orgasm and then release the spell by throwing out the sigil paper, burning it or tearing it up. All your energy generated by the sexual act is now focused on the intention of the sigil. You need not focus on the intention itself, just the sigil that represents it. This method can be adapted with partners, and sigils can be used with body paint so you can focus on the sigil while pleasuring your partner. Sex is not the only method of charging sigils, but it is by far the most enjoyable one. Some methods use the sexual body fluids produced by these rituals, supercharged with intention, in both spellcraft and alchemical elixirs for enlightenment and awareness. They are used to anoint charms and ritual tools. One should always be very cautious about consuming the sexual fluids of another and follow safer sex guidelines.

Inner Planes Hieros Gamos

One doesn't need a physical partner to experience sexual magick with another. Much of our shamanic lore relates to the concept of spirit marriages. A shaman will mate with a spirit guide, to be a spouse. Faery seers often enter into a marriage arrangement with a fey king or queen, who acts as an indwelling presence. Voodou practitioners sometimes experience rituals of marriage to a particular lwa spirit that confers them certain rights and obligations. Witches can experience shamanic journeys and visions, particularly at the seasonal holidays of Beltane and Samhain, mating with the Goddess and God. Their relationship with their deities and patrons, and other guides, can take on a sexual note, as they experience a Hieros Gamos between the worlds, on the inner planes. For those unprepared for such contact, it can be startling and difficult to talk about, lacking cultural context. In reality, it is a natural part of the enlightenment process for many priestesses and priests who embrace sexuality as a part of spirituality.

Taboo Power

Let's face it, in our culture, mixing sex and spirituality is taboo. People see them as completely distinct. Actual intercourse raises a lot of energy just because of the taboo factor alone. Things that excite us, titillate us, or make us afraid on some level have power. A modern witchcraft wisdom is "Where there is fear, there is power." As we become desensitized to sex in general, other taboo areas in the use of sexuality in ritual can produce a similar rise in energy. They continue to be effective, if not overdone or used too often outside of a ritualized context. Role play, fetishes, BDSM practices, gender role reversal, and fantasy fulfillment release a lot of suppressed energy in the psyche and body that can be put forth for magickal purposes, and the added side benefit is that the practice is very healing, removing the energy that is blocked, and helps us integrate our shadow self better in the areas of sexuality.

Polarity Rites

Working magick in a polarized union of priestess and priest is the manner in which many ceremonial magick groups and British Traditional branches of witchcraft always work, using a combination of techniques. One generates the power and the other guides and directs it. In many traditions of magick, the polarities are seen to reverse beneath the veil, and the priestess wields the active blade while the priest holds the receptive cup in ritual, revealing further mysteries of the gods. The two are not locked into one role or form. The energy of the polarity working is used to fill the circle, bless objects, cast spells, and move energy within the consciousness of the priest and priestess as well as those in attendance. The polarity working can be enhanced by directly invoking the Goddess into the priestess and the God into the priest, either the generalized Great Goddess and God or specific and compatible godforms. The officiants then mediate the energies of the deities, often through channeling and prophecy, for the rest of the group. One can look to the novels of Dion Fortune, in particular *The Sea Priestess* and *Moon Magic*, for valuable information on how the sexual energies of dynamic individuals can be harnessed for grand magickal operations without actual physical consummation. In fact, for some forms of sex magick, consummation actually grounds the connection and ends the dynamic tension of the magickal working.

Because sexual energy is so powerful, in any context, a witch must be very cautious when using it. Make sure that your intentions and motivations are clear before entering into sexual rites. The power of the experience can lead to a lot of difficulties and reveal hang-ups. Many feel that in sex magick with another, they are in a "performance" and have to produce a good act. Magick has much ritual drama, and that can be a part of sex magick, but not to the point that it is debilitating for the participants. There is pressure to perform sexually, to keep a state of arousal while simultaneously holding on to other magickal factors and details. The intensity of workings can make them all the more powerful, but when they go awry, they can feel even more personally defeating and affect self-image and self-esteem. Use sex magick with care, but don't be afraid to explore your sexuality as a part of your spirituality. Such exploration will help you better understand the energies of Chokmah, and the relationship between Chokmah and Binah.

The power of uniting ritually is done by witches through the Great Rite, the mysteries of the chalice and the blade. In ceremonial magick, the ritual can be done with the chalice and the wand, uniting Binah and Chokmah. Modern Qabalists also have the rite known as the Mystic Repast. Similar to the Wiccan Cakes and Ale, or Christian Eucharist, it is a ritual of recognizing and consuming the sacred in the material world, to unite with it and make it one within you. The Ceremonial Repast also is an invitation to align and commune with the beings of the elemental realms.

EXERCISE 28

Mystic Repast

The traditional Mystic Repast uses the Golden Dawn elemental associations. Upon the altar, place a rose in the east, a red candle in the south, a cup of wine in the west, and a platter of bread and salt in the north. This version has been adapted from the ritual presented in *The Essential Golden Dawn* by Chic and Sandra Tabatha Cicero.

1. Perform the Qabalistic Cross (exercise 2).

2. Still facing east, raise both hands in the air and say:

   I invite all you beings of elemental air, archangels, angels, kings, rulers, and elementals, to partake with me of the mystic repast of the four elements.

3. Pick up the rose and say:

   I invite you to inhale with me the perfume of this rose, as a symbol of air.

   Smell the rose.

4. Pick up the candle and say:

   To feel with me the warmth of this sacred lamp, as a symbol of fire.

   Hold your hand over the flame.

5. Pick up the platter and say:

   To eat with me this bread and salt, as types of earth.

   Dip a piece of bread into the salt and eat it.

6. Pick up the cup and say:

   And finally, to drink with me this wine, the consecrated emblem of elemental water.

   With the cup, trace a cross in the air—up, down, left, right. Drink the wine, and place the empty cup back upon the altar.

7. Then say:

   It is finished.

CHOKMAH PATHWORKINGS

There remains only one path to explore on the Tree of Life—the last path, which in many ways is the first path, that of the Fool. It leads from Chokmah to Kether. In the study of the tarot, it is said to be the "first" card, preceding the Magician. In the tarot, the trumps represent the stages of the magickal journey and evolution. And it's true, for they descend from the top of the Tree into manifestation. The path to enlightenment and back up to the source is the reverse of the trumps. Instead of starting with the "birth" of the cosmic Fool, we rise through the lower cards—the Moon, Judgment/Aeon, and the World/Universe. The path of the Fool is ruled by Uranus, the divine rebel or cosmic light bringer, kicking off the possibility of manifestation by choosing to descend from Kether.

EXERCISE 29

Chokmah Pathworking

1. Perform the Lesser Banishing Ritual of the Pentagram (exercise 5) and the Lesser Banishing Ritual of the Hexagram (exercise 20). Do any other ritual you feel is appropriate.

2. While in this space, call upon the divine forces of Chokmah. Burn your two gray candles. Musk incense is a difficult scent to use, though there are some herbal formulas that attempt to replicate the smell and quality of musk that are appropriate. Burning fennel seeds on charcoal or wearing ylang-ylang oil also can attune you to Chokmah, even though they both smell very different from musk. Knock on your altar two times. Vibrate the divine name of Chokmah, **YHVH**, twice. Call upon any of the ancient ones or Archangel Raziel.

3. To count down into a meditative state, do exercise 1 through step 7 (page 76).

4. Let the familiar world around you fall away, as if the material reality you know is only a façade and beneath it lies the beautiful garden of the Goddess, a veritable paradise surrounding you. The land around you becomes

a vast primordial garden, the garden of Malkuth, the familiar garden of the four paths.

5. Go to the heart of Malkuth, to the Temple of Malkuth. Decide to follow the path up to and from Tiphereth to the realm of Chokmah. Walk the path of the World/Universe up to Yesod. Experience the consciousness of Yesod for a time. Walk the path of Temperance/Art to Tiphereth. Bask in the golden light of your HGA. Then, from the Temple of Tiphereth, use your will to ascend the path of the Emperor.

6. The path of the Emperor is one of cosmic strength. One who travels this path must find the Divine King within. We must find our ability to rule ourselves and our lives, and through that we discover that we are generating force, the Chokmah force, in our own lives. We must find that inner king, the force that connects our HGA to the generative principle of Chokmah.

7. Feel the call of the gray sphere, the origin of light, or the stars in our creation. You might be tested to enter the realm of the divine father, though if you have made it this far, there might be no need for any intellectual testing. Enter the starry gray light of the realm of Chokmah. Enter the realm of the primal life force. The stars are within a vast garden, like the highest pattern that eventually becomes the garden of Malkuth in the material realm.

8. Make your way to the sacred Temple of Chokmah. Unlike the other temples, this is not a temple or room, but a hallway, a line, moving from one point to another. This is the Temple of the Father, the movement from one place to the next, constant movement and change. You see the gateways for the Hierophant, Empress, and Fool, as well as the path of the Emperor, through which you arrived.

9. The entities of Chokmah are residing in the temple and surrounding areas, yet the place is very peaceful. You feel the presence of the Great Father all around you. You are breathing in this life force. Ask to know the Vision of the Source in a manner that is correct and for your highest good.

10. When done, thank all the beings who have communicated with you. They might offer you a gift, a token of their goodwill. If you accept, it is polite to reach within your being and offer them a gift of your goodwill. Be sure that what you give reflects the energy and intention you plan to put into the sphere's lessons.

11. Once you have said your farewells, leave the shrine and follow the path back. Return the way you came unless you feel guided to return via a different pathway and know the pathway back well. Return to the garden of Malkuth. Focus on the waking world you know, and feel it return around the garden.

12. To return to normal waking consciousness and end your journey, perform steps 15–17 from exercise 1 (page 78). You can close the temple by repeating the LBRP.

CHOKMAH INITIATION

The Chokmah initiation is the penultimate step toward true enlightenment in the Qabalistic model. It is the ninth initiation, known as the ⑨=②. Here one becomes a true Mage, a Magus, the master of all forms of high magick, or the ability to relate to the divine higher self. Chokmah is the highest level of consciousness at which we still have some level of individualization, for Kether is the complete merger with the divine. In Chokmah, the mage unites with the Logos and is able to declare the "Law" of the Aeon. In other words, the mage become one with the Logos of this creation. Not only does the mage declare it, but the declaration is in his or her entire being; the mage vibrates or resonates with the Law. Here the initiate becomes completely attuned to the power of the Aeon in which he or she resides, and discovers how best to bring the fulfillment of that Aeon's forces.

The mage's mundane or worldly declaration of the Law is made through his or her teachings. In *The Book of the Law*, Aleister Crowley declared the "Law" of the Aeon of Horus, outlining the formative principles of the next age of the world. Crowley was the prophet of the Aeon, the true Mage, and was able to see and shape the coming of the Aeon and its manifestation. Ultimately, we all are called to not simply follow the Law as it is presented to us, but to become one with the Law of the Aeon, and our material expression of it might differ substantially from Crowley's. We must seek to be our own magickal genius, like Crowley himself, rather than simply following a prophet blindly.

Homework

- Do Exercises 28–29 and record your experiences in your Book of Shadows.

- Continue to practice the LBRP, LBRH, Middle Pillar, and Circulation of the Body of Light rituals, the traditional or personal versions.

Tips

- Fill in the Chokmah correspondences and colors on your own Tree of Life drawing. Contemplate them as you add them to the image. Start memorizing these correspondences.

- Review and reflect on all you have learned in this lesson.

- Integrate the tools of the four elements into your magickal and daily life.

- Seriously think about your own reality map. When you reflect, what ideas come to mind, based on both your understanding of the universe and your experiences? Begin taking notes for constructing a map.

LESSON TWELVE
KETHER

We are now at the top of the Tree of Life, at Kether, the crown. From our vantage point here on Malkuth, it does appear to be the highest branch, reaching into the Three Veils of Negative Existence. But once we reach Kether, or the aspect of Kether that we can reach at this point, we realize that it is not necessarily a branch, but the root. This Tree is rooted in the heavens, issuing forth into the world of manifestation, and Malkuth is its fruit. Malkuth contains Kether's essence. All that was, all that is, all that ever shall be is found in Kether, and its potential is in Malkuth, as Malkuth will be the Kether of another Tree. From the seeds of Malkuth will grow another Tree.

Kether is the "highest" point, the purest manifestation of the divine in our concept of creation, issuing forth from the Three Veils. We realize that the terms *high* and *low* no longer apply, but Kether is the most indistinct of the sephiroth, for it encompasses all potentials. There are few distinct characteristics and symbols. It sits on the top of the middle pillar, but issues forth the Pillars of Mercy and Severity. It is the source of the entire Tree, the emanation that is at the root of creation, from which all other sephiroth are formed.

Kether is said to be beyond all astrological associations. If Chokmah is the fixed and formed stars, then Kether is the forming stars, the wellspring of light that has not yet taken fixed shape. It is the Great Central Sun of the universe that everything else revolves around. Modern astrological Qabalists have associated the outer planets with it, particularly Uranus. I favor Pluto for Kether, for it is the planet embodying the highest will. Kether is the sphere of divine will, and if you are going to assign any corresponding planet to this sphere, I think Pluto suits it well. Pluto is commonly seen as the planet of death, named for the Underworld lord Pluto, the lord of riches.

In Kether, Pluto shows us how the individual self really dies and is reborn not only as the higher self but as the merged higher self, uniting personal will and the HGA's will with the total divine will of Kether. You receive all the riches of creation, literal and figurative. It is said that a true initiate owns nothing, yet has use of everything. These are the riches of Kether, for in the end, everything is a manifestation of the divine, and you can't truly own the divine. It's like the indigenous people of America not comprehending how the Europeans could say they "owned" the land, for the land was the skin of the Mother, who belongs to herself. We are here by her good graces.

Yet those who are aligned with divine will have everything they need. Every resource is at their disposal, as long as they don't become attached and desire ownership of it. Kether, as the "Crown," can have associations with Pluto as well, for as the lord of the dead, Pluto wears the crown of the Underworld. As Pluto (or Hades, in ancient myth) shares creation with his brothers Zeus/Jupiter, who rules both the heavens and all gods, and Poseidon/Neptune, who rules the seas, he ultimately has eventual rulership over the brothers. Everything that lives must die. In the cosmology of the Greeks, even a god can die. From our view, they eventually return to Kether, reunited with the divine source, but that puts the true "crown" in the hands of the lord of the dead.

Kether

Meaning: Crown

Level of Reality: Highest Manifestation of Consciousness That Can Be Contemplated by Humanity, Great Spirit, Creator, Beyond All Shape and Polarity, Unity

Parts of the Self: Indivisible Self, Highest Self, Bornless One, Crown

Experience: Reunion with the Source

Obligation: None

Illusion: Attainment

Virtue: Completion of the Great Work

Vice: None

Name of God: Eheieh (I Am)

King Scale Color: Pure Brilliance

Queen Scale Color: Brilliant White

Prince Scale Color: Brilliant White

Princess Scale Color: White flecked with Gold

Elements: Air, Spirit

Planets: Traditionally No Planet but the Primum Mobile; some now say Pluto

Image: Bearded Man in Profile

Archetypes: Great Spirit, Gods of Creation, Life and Death

Greek/Roman Deities: Zeus, Jupiter, Chaos, Eros, Hades, Pluto

Egyptian Deities: Ptah, Ra, Khephra, Osiris

Middle Eastern Deity: Tiamat

Celtic Deities: Dryghten, Danu, Don, Modron, Pywll, Annwn

Norse Deities: Buri, Bor

Hindu Deities: Parabraham, Brahman

Archangel: Metatron (Angel of Spiritual Evolution)

Angelic Order: Chaioth ha-Qadesh (Holy Living Creatures)

Choir: Seraphim

Grade of Initiation: ⑩=①Ipsissimus

Animals: Hawk, Swan, Eagle

Musical Note: B

Tools: Lotus, Skull, Single Candle, Crown

Incense: Ambergris, Bay Leaves

Tarot: All Aces

       Priestess—to Tiphereth

       Magician—to Binah

       Fool—to Chokmah

Metals: White Gold, Manganese, Chromium, Carbon Steel

Stone: Diamond

Plant: Almond

White is the strongest correspondence of Kether, so use white imagery for your altar for this lesson. A sparse altar actually is appropriate for Kether. Having a single white candle would embody the energy of this sphere quite well. The aces of the four tarot suits represent Kether's power in each of the four elemental worlds, while the three cards leading out from this sphere—the Magician, Priestess, and Fool—all can be displayed.

Entities of Kether

The well-accepted image of Kether is the "bearded man in profile," alluding to our most common Qabalistic and biblical images of God, as a patriarchal father god. A modern pagan/magician interpretation is that this god is in profile, for he is really a hermaphrodite, a rebis, half male and half female, both God and Goddess, and you would see this if he turned the other cheek. Kether embodies both aspects of the two other supernals, Binah and Chokmah, Mother and Father, so it seems only fitting that Kether would not be solely male.

I see the force of Kether as beyond male and female. Early on in my witchcraft experiences, I learned the Great Goddess as Danu, while the Great God was the Dagda, her mate. Though the most common stories depict Danu not as an actual mythical character but simply as the mother of the gods, and the Dagda's most famous mating was with the Morrighan at Samhain, this partnership as primal female and male made sense to me. We had a third spirit, the Dryghten, an indivisible "lord" who is neither male nor female. The three d sounds together worked well in ritual, and I loved the concept of two deities and an overarching androgynous spirit. When my own practice and public teachings became more multicultural, I simply began saying "Goddess, God, and Great Spirit," using three g sounds together, and it worked quite well for everybody involved. I think of Kether as the Great Spirit of Dryghten. I think of it as the Divine Mind. I think of it as the Tao of Asian mysticism, manifesting Goddess and God as yin and yang. I think of it as the collective consciousness of creation, manifesting a cosmic anima and animus. Kether is the Great Architect of the Masons, who designs and engineers the rest of the Tree of Life. These are all ways to describe the light that is Kether.

The divine name of Kether is simply *Eheieh*, where all the lords and titles are dispensed with in favor of the simple "I am" or "I am that I am." My teachers tried to explain this name as not only "I am" but "I was that I was, I am that I am, I shall be that I shall be." It is the divine "being" in all tenses, really beyond shape and form but encompassing everything.

For specific archetypes, our primal creative gods and goddesses, androgynous in nature, can be seen here in Kether. Tiamat, dragoness goddess of the primordial waters, can be seen as both a Binah and a Kether figure. The Irish Celtic Danu, and her cognates in Don and Modron, share similar attributes with both Binah and Kether as the source of creation. Chaos, the primordial voice from which Gaia and Uranus sprang in the Greek creation myth, can fill the place in the triad as Kether. In early versions of the Greek creation tale, Eros was a primal god, not just a god of sexual love and attraction, but the binding force responsible for the embrace between Gaia and Uranus, to bring life into this world. Eros in this primal form can be seen as the power of Kether.

Some of the more familiar and gender-specific gods have androgynous manifestations. There is an image of Zeus as many breasted, in his creator aspect. There is a bearded Aphrodite. Many of the creator gods, such as Ra, Ptah, and Thoth, created the universe alone. Using the Plutonian imagery, the lords of the Underworld—Hades, Pluto, Osiris, Pywll, Annwn—can be associated with Kether. Less common in ceremonial magick, but equally valid as Plutonian archetypes, are the queens of the dead—Persephone, Proserpina, Erishkigal, and Hel—though they share much in common with Binah, as do the lords with Chokmah.

The archangel associated with Kether is Metatron. The most unusual of all the archangels, he is considered the prince of archangels. Some descriptions have his own crown in Kether and the rest of his body stretching out through to Malkuth, as he acts as an intermediary on all planes. Other descriptions say he manifests as a small child, or a monstrous giant, with thirty-six wings and countless eyes. Out of all the angels, with the possible exception of Michael, Metatron is said to be closest to "God" as the creator.

The angelic order under the rule of Metatron is known as the Chaioth ha-Qadesh, or Holy Living Creatures. They are the highest of all the angelic orders, save the ruling archangels of the Qabalah, who exist on an entirely higher plane. The Holy Creatures are said to bear the "throne" of God in the heavens. In our secondary system of angelic lore, the highest choir of angels is known as the Seraphim. Not to be confused with the fiery serpents of more traditional Qabalistic lore, these angels are said to be at the throne of the Creator, burning with the bright and blinding light of creation and singing the song of the celestial spheres, chanting, "Holy, Holy, Holy is the Lord of Hosts, the whole Earth is full of His Glory." These Seraphim are described as having six wings, with two covering their face, two covering their feet, and two for flying. Their vision is said to be so intense that even other divine beings fear to gaze upon them.

VISION OF KETHER

The vision of Kether is beyond description. It is not a vision, but the experience of Reunion with the Source, the divine source of creation. The magician becomes one with the magick of creation, and unites with the source of all that was, is, and ever shall be. We may have glimpses of this experience, as we touch the aspect of Kether in the lower spheres, but the vision of the true Kether is a merging with the source of all that is. Many would choose to never leave this place, while others still return, going through the cycle of creation and rebirth to climb the Tree of Life yet again.

At Kether's level of consciousness, there is no obligation. There is no vice. There is no illusion. You are beyond all of it. The only virtue is the successful completion of the Great Work, and if you truly make it to Kether, you have fulfilled your divine will in all the lower sephiroth and truly have attained the Great Work, becoming one with the Philosopher's Stone, the diamond of divinity, the primal fount from which all things flow.

KETHER MAGICK

There are not a lot of magickal correspondences for Kether, as the primal Godhead. This sphere's principle is union, so in effect, all things are part of Kether. Ritually, we have created some associations with forces that seem to be more helpful in connecting with Kether.

All the aces of the tarot are the "roots" of the four elements, Kether manifest in each of the four worlds. The four tools we have worked so hard to obtain for the four elemental degrees are the highest forms of the elements and are the links to Kether. Our reconsecrated ritual tools lead us back to Kether.

Another great alignment with Kether is the diamond, often used as a symbol for divinity itself, in plurality with its many facets, and in unity as a single object (*OTOW*, Chapter 5). Diamonds are one of the hardest substances on Earth, yet are formed from coal, mimicking the alchemical enlightenment process of transforming something dark into something clear and dazzling. None of the seven classic metals are used for Kether, though Pluto often has an alignment with chromium, carbon steel, and manganese. I also like the image of white gold, a more refined and purified form of gold, for Kether, as the yellow gold is associated with the lower octave of enlightenment, Tiphereth. In terms of herbs, few items are associated with Kether. Ambergris, an animal product coming from whales, is the traditional scent, though many use bay leaves instead, again having a strong corollary to Tiphereth, as bay is sacred to Apollo. I also think mistletoe is an appropriate herb, though it's toxic and shouldn't be used in incense or potions to be consumed. Mistletoe has Kether, Chokmah, and Chesed associations, but it was the most sacred herb of the Druids. Vanilla is a scent associated with Pluto that can be used ritually for Kether.

In terms of totems, all the highest-flying birds are associated with Kether, like the eagle, hawk, and falcon. Strangely, the swan, as a bird of divinity and great beauty as well as transformation, is a totem of Kether. One could see angels, as a race of "animal" in creation, like man and woman are the "animals" of Chokmah and Binah, being appropriate for Kether, for they are the closest beings that are not gods yet are aligned with the divine.

The geometry of Kether is quite simple—the single point or monad. It is the core of all things and the beginning of the creation process. The term *monad* will be familiar to students of John Dee's work. Through a treatise called the *Monas Hieroglyphica*, or *The Hieroglyphic Monad*, he created an esoteric symbol and teaching based on the monad, which was divinely inspired and which he believed would revolutionize astronomy, mathematics, alchemy, mechanics, music, optics, and magick. Though we think of the monad as a single point, this version is an amalgam of several different esoteric astrological glyphs (figure 75).

If any magick can be considered appropriate for the lessons of Kether, I think Enochian magick fits the bill. Though introduced in the early stages of the Golden Dawn training, it is not covered in detail until the Adeptus Minor rank. Enochian magick is another creation of John Dee, and his scrying partner, Edward Kelley. Though the history of Enochian magick and its founders would make an excellent modern-day thriller, few people outside of the more learned realms of the esoteric arts know of the existence of Enochian magick. Enochian is a complete language and alphabet as well as a magickal system. It is said to be the pure language spoken before the Fall—some speculate in the day of Atlantis. The system uses grids of letters to spell the names of various Enochian angels that can be summoned, along with a variety of ritual tools specialized for the Enochian workings. The language is used in the Supreme Ritual of the Pentagram and its variation, the Opening by Watchtower ritual. Unfortunately, a complete introduction to Enochian magick goes far beyond the lessons of this text.

Figure 75: Hieroglyphic Monad

For those desiring to explore Enochian and the SRP, this book provides a strong foundation for going deeper into your high magick studies.

KETHER PATHWORKINGS

Now that we have explored all of the twenty-two paths of the Tree, it is time for you to touch the aspect of Kether that you are ready to experience. Exploring Kether, if you are successful in making contact with an aspect of it, doesn't confer instant enlightenment. Seeking guidance on the Great Work, and experience in working with the entities of the Source, does not equate to attainment of the Great Work and a merging with the divine in totality. Through visionary pathworking, you can cross the Abyss, commune with the supernals and in Kether, and have a partial merging with the divine light that is the Crown. If your entire being were to merge, then you would cease to be here on the physical plane. We do not truly touch Kether in its highest and most exalted state, but that aspect of Kether in whatever lower sephira we are anchored in. If you are working through the realm of Tiphereth, you can reach the Kether aspect of Tiphereth, and that experience will help you master Tiphereth and move on to the next sephira. You will have a taste of Kether, like hearing a lower note on a piano gives you an idea of what the higher note is. You can almost imagine it. You will know it if you hear it, but for now, the lower note is in your normal range of hearing and you can safely work with it.

EXERCISE 30

Kether Pathworking

1. Perform the Lesser Banishing Ritual of the Pentagram (exercise 5) and the Lesser Banishing Ritual of the Hexagram (exercise 20). Do any other ritual you feel is appropriate.

2. While in this space, call upon the divine forces of Kether. Burn your single white candle. Burn bay leaves upon charcoal to release a vibration corresponding to Kether.

Knock on your altar one time or ten times, to show that Kether is in Malkuth and Malkuth is in Kether. Vibrate the divine name of Kether, **Eheieh**. Call upon the Great Spirit and Archangel Metatron.

3. To count down into a meditative state, do exercise 1 through step 7 (page 76).

4. Let the familiar world around you fall away, as if the material reality you know is only a façade and beneath it lies the beautiful garden of the Goddess, a veritable paradise surrounding you. The land around you becomes a vast primordial garden, the garden of Malkuth, the familiar garden of the four paths.

5. Go to the heart of Malkuth, to the Temple of Malkuth. Decide what path you will be taking to Kether. I suggest either following the route of the Magician, sequentially up the Tree as we have learned, for a longer pathworking extending a basic "rising on the planes" experience into a detailed visionary journey, or taking the most direct route, up through the middle pillar, passing through Yesod and Tiphereth, and following the route of the Priestess across the Abyss to Kether.

6. Feel the call of the brilliant white sphere beyond the gray shadow of starlight in Chokmah and the dark cosmic night of Binah. Go to the source of both and feel the call of Kether. As with the other spheres, you might be tested before gaining entrance to the Great Central Sun of our universe, or you could be beyond such tests. Enter the pure white light of Kether.

7. There is nothing to distinguish you from Kether. You feel yourself in the white light, and you are the white light. The light is brilliant and dazzling, white yet multicolored like light reflected off a diamond or opal, shining with the potential of all colors and forms. You feel the whole Tree with you in Kether, and you realize you always have been here. A part of you has never left.

8. There is no temple. There is no structure. There are only the patterns of swirling light suggesting images and mesmerizing you. You feel the presence of Metatron, of the Great Spirit, of everything and everyone that ever

has been, is, or will be here in Kether. Commune with Kether and the intelligences of Kether. Feel the loving connection, the power of both Eros and Chaos, surrounding you, for nothing is what you expected it would be. Ask to know the vision of the Reunion with the Source in a manner that is correct and for your highest good here and now.

9. When done, thank the Source and all beings who have communicated with you. Those in Kether do not offer you a gift or token, for the experience is the gift itself, and you always have been there, so when you are ready, your conscious awareness can return anytime. You have completed all the steps to get there.

10. Say your farewells, knowing that you are not really leaving, and go back the way you came unless you feel guided to return via a different pathway. Return to the garden of Malkuth. Know that Malkuth is in Kether and Kether is in Malkuth. One is simply the root, the other the seed, but both contain the entire Tree. Focus on the waking world you know, and feel it return around the garden.

11. To return to normal waking consciousness and end your journey, perform steps 15–17 from exercise 1 (page 78). You can close the temple by repeating the LBRP.

KETHER INITIATION

In our Qabalistic scheme, Kether is the tenth initiation, marking completion. It is the ⑩=☐ ranking of Ipsissimus, usually translated to be the "very very self" or true self beyond all image and illusion of manifested creation. The Ipsissimus is beyond all understanding of those below this level, and is said to be incomprehensible to us. Here we have the images of the mad monks and crazy mystics, reaching enlightenment but completely beyond earthly concerns or traditional society. They are heading toward this final level of enlightenment. The Ipsissimus is the master of all forms of consciousness, because this initiate is merged with the Source. This is beyond even ascension from the physical body. This is ascension from individualization and identity, to know that your very very self is the same as the Creator. You integrate the mystery of being God/dess on all levels, and you enter into manifestation to create something new, to know yourself better, to experience separation and form.

HOMEWORK

- Do Exercise 30 and record your experiences in your Book of Shadows.

- Continue to practice the LBRP, LBRH, Middle Pillar, and Circulation of the Body of Light rituals, the traditional or personal versions.

TIPS

- Fill in the Kether correspondences and colors on your own Tree of Life drawing. Contemplate them as you add them to the image. Start memorizing these correspondences.

- Review and reflect on all you have learned in this lesson.

- Prepare to make your own reality map, the full process of which will be outlined in the next and final lesson.

Lesson Thirteen
Initiation of High Witchcraft

Unlike the first two levels of this tradition, *The Inner Temple of Witchcraft* and *The Outer Temple of Witchcraft*, this level of training does not include a self-test. There is no pass/fail minimum body of knowledge that must be ascertained before completing this level, though there very easily could be. Between Hebrew names and letters, sephiroth definitions and angelic orders, there certainly is enough information to know. While this information is important, it isn't that important. Information always can be looked up. If you don't have certain esoteric lore at your fingertips, but know how to find it when you need it, and more importantly know when and why you would need it, how to use it, and what it means, then you have all the skills you need for high magick.

You are learning new ways to think, view the universe, and process information. You are learning new ways to relate to the divine and the universe. That is the challenge of *The Temple of High Witchcraft*. Like *The Temple of Shamanic Witchcraft*, with its challenge in the shadow realm, a personal initiation of the dark and lower self, this course challenges you with the intellectualism and creativity of the higher self, forcing you to find and embody it, through both action and ritual.

The initiation of *The Temple of High Witchcraft* is twofold. One part of the initiation is intellectual and academic, and the other is ceremonial. Both are extremely magickal and can be life changing. The final challenge of the fourth level is making a deeper connection to the divine, a true and direct knowledge of the divine, Gnosticism in the truest sense of the word. This comes in part through the challenge of creating your own reality map, your own magickal model and mandala, personalized to your own view of reality, your own experiences and the symbols you find moving. The second initiation experience is a ritual invocation of the higher self.

CREATING YOUR OWN REALITY MAP

Through the twelve previous lessons, you have gained a comprehensive overview of the traditions of modern high magick and the most popular reality map, the Tree of Life. You understand how the Tree works both in a practical and a spiritually profound way. You understand how it organizes and forms information systems, to help you relate to the many aspects of the divine and the many aspects of yourself.

But, if you are anything like me, as a witch, the Tree of Life might not be your favorite symbol system. I know it has taken me many years to value the profound wisdom of the Qabalah. I forced myself to learn about it because, like many witches, I got tired of reading the same books over and over again, with the same quarter calls, circle castings, and Wheel of the Year, without anybody going further. I knew intellectually the impact that Qabalah and the ceremonial magicians played in the witchcraft revival, but I wasn't particularly moved by it. Witches I admired seemed to spend at least a little time becoming familiar with high magick, and as I was running out of new challenges, I decided to take on the Qabalah challenge. Now I know that the "basic" wisdom of Wicca is not mastered easily and the most simple of rituals can have profound benefits for the rest of our lives, and open us deeper and deeper to the mysteries, but we often need to change our perspective to see the wisdom we already have. The time I spent exploring the Tree of Life, and looking for pagan associations with the Tree, changed my magickal perspective. It started with Ellen Cannon Reed's *The Goddess and the Tree*, which later became *The Witches Qabalah*. This book is an excellent place for pagans to start their exploration of the Tree of Life.

If you feel the same way about the Tree of Life, and even if you don't, it is an extremely worthwhile experience to create your own reality map. Use the examples in appendix I as inspiration. If you have been studying them along with your monthly lessons, as suggested in the homework, then you have a grasp of how varied magickal models can be. Use your ideas, experiences, thoughts, and inspirations to form your own reality map.

EXERCISE 31

Create Your Reality Map

There really is no specific set of instructions to create your own reality map. You can use any mediums you desire, though most maps are two-dimensional and able to be reproduced on paper. Most are able to be inscribed in some way on the back of a ritual disk or wax disk to act as a peyton, but I've had students create multilayered reality maps using colors and tracing paper. Some have produced multimedia presentations on the computer or three-dimensional sculptures and dioramas. Others have converted their reality map into music. Some have created logarithms and mathematical formulas that were, quite frankly, a bit over my head yet seemed to work for them.

All of this can seem quite overwhelming, because you are solely responsible for your creation. By asking yourself the following questions, you will begin to narrow your focus for your reality map.

1. What aspects of the reality map are most important to you? A good reality map will have aspects of all of the following, but some will be more dominant than others.

    • Powers of the universe

    • Multiple levels of reality

    • Organization of life

    • Humanity's place in the cosmos

    • Path of transformation

    • Magickal correspondences

2. What symbol systems are important to you?

- Elemental

- Planetary

- Zodiac

- Shamanic worlds

- Holidays/seasons

- Numerology

- Magickal alphabets

3. What images are important to you? Finding a good image can be the anchor for your map.

- Geometric designs—circles, stars, shapes

- Animal imagery

- Plant imagery

- Abstract imagery

4. What magickal correspondences, if any, should be incorporated into the design?

- Colors

- Deities/angels/spirits

- Sounds

- Herbs

- Stones

- Metals

- Animals

- Astrology (planets and signs)

- Divination—tarot, runes, I Ching, ogham

Keeping the following tips in mind can be helpful as well:

- No one reality map can have it all, so choose to incorporate the things that are important to you. Notice that even the Tree of Life doesn't really have the cycle of the seasons or a solar or lunar calendar.

- Not all the systems you choose will be compatible with one another. No reality map will be perfect, because you are attempting to capture perfection in a static image. It can't be done. Just as you think you have it figured out, one aspect of the map won't fit the rest. You have to use your judgment to discern which elements to keep and which to remove. This is not the only reality map you are allowed to make. You can make another later on to express a different view you have of reality. Look at the example of the Golden Dawn. In an effort to keep the fire-air-water-earth order of the elements from the Tetragrammaton, the Golden Dawn instituted a strange association of Hod with water and Yesod with air. Preserving that pattern was more important than working with the more obvious symbolism of Mercury and Yesod.

- Though you will be very attached to your first reality map, part of the experience is to learn that your map is just a map, just like everybody else's. There is no one way to see the truth; all reality maps are just representations. It can be quite helpful to repeat this exercise after a number of years, to see how you look at reality differently after different experiences.

- Look through your old journal entries of rituals, spells, and journeys. What are the repeated themes, images, and symbols? These are the parts of your experience that are most important to you, whether you realized it or not at the time.

- Reality maps are intellectual, creative, and divine. If you are having trouble finding your vision for this project, do a meditation, either to the inner temple or to a specific sephira on the Tree of Life, and ask for inspiration and advice. Do some dream magick (*TOSW*, Chapter 10). Do a shamanic journey. Use the techniques that you want to incorporate into the Tree and ask for divine guidance.

• You might want to wait until you complete the Bornless Ritual (exercise 32), as it might provide you with a valuable experience or inspiration, a direct revelation of your divine paradigm.

When I teach this book as a course, I make each student present his or her reality map to the rest of the group. Sometimes this is just as much of a challenge as making the map. The ability to communicate your vision to others is a critical part of the air element training. If you have a magickal study group, mentor, or magickally oriented friends, prepare a short lecture describing your reality map and take any questions. Learn to communicate your thoughts and ideas. Even if you don't feel it goes well, the very act of communication is a huge accomplishment. If possible, put the image of your reality map in your Book of Shadows.

The Bornless Ritual

The second initiatory experience to complete this stage of learning is a ceremonial magick ritual known as the Bornless Ritual. The *Bornless One* is a name for the eternal self, what we might call the higher self or monad combined. It is the essence of the divine self, who is never born, who never dies. It is our eternal identity, guiding our incarnation. The Bornless Self really is another name for the Holy Guardian Angel.

The Bornless One is invoked in ritual, most commonly in rituals that involve summoning and controlling spirits, particularly Solomonic-style Goetic rituals, for only by divine authority can we perform such rituals and bindings. Though it can be used as a preliminary operation for other workings of ceremonial magick, it is also a ritual unto itself, a simplified and truncated version of the Abramelin Operation, to commune with your Holy Guardian Angel. The Abramelin Operation, from *The Sacred Magick of Abramelin the Mage*, is a magickal program popularized by the Golden Dawn. It involves a six-month period, equinox to equinox, of spiritual preparation, calling the initiate to "enflame thyself in prayer" to finally make communion with the Holy Guardian Angel. Aleister Crowley adapted much of the material, shortening the length of time and making it a preliminary invocation to be used before Goetic workings, so that by the divine power of your godself, your HGA, you could command the spirits of the Goetic text. Many versions of the operation exist, incorporating barbarous words of power or formal Enochian calls. Most are drawn from material in Aleister Crowley's *Liber Samekh*. One of the most accessible modern versions of the Abramelin Operation can be found in Jason Augustus Newcomb's *21ˢᵗ Century Mage*, in which he adapts the archaic language and instructions to effectively suit a modern practitioner, and explains the reasons behind the archaic instructions.

Some would criticize the Bornless Ritual as being a misunderstanding of a phrase referring to a "headless" deity, as the ritual originally came from the *Graeco-Egyptian Magical Papyri* and was a ceremony for exorcisms. The magician takes on the role and identity of this headless deity, through invocation, and banishes a malevolent spirit. This is nothing like the Abramelin Operation.

The ritual entered British esoteric circles in 1853 through Charles Wycliffe Goodwin and later was reworked and added to the training material of the Golden Dawn. Crowley then used it as the preliminary ritual of his printed version of *The Goetia* and revised it again for *Liber Samekh*, which has become one of its most popular and powerful forms. Though it originally may have referred to a headless god or Beginningless Deity, it has been used successfully to commune with the personal daimon, or Holy Guardian Angel.

I partook of a Bornless Ritual with Enochian calls rather than the classic barbarous names, and I must admit that, while the setting was very magickal and moving, I did not feel much during the invocation. The leaders of the group gave us time to meditate after the invocation, and there I felt its power. I received a long list of specific instructions on how to commune further with my Bornless Self and continue my initiatory process. I am still in the midst of completing these instructions, for they span several years, but I did immediately notice amazing changes in my life.

The traditional Bornless Ritual uses a set of barbarous words of power, from the Hellenistic Hermetic formulae from ancient Alexandria. These barbarous words are said to be at least 2,000 years old, and such a history seems to confer a sense of power. Yet, I think anything alien to our conscious mind helps us break through the personal self and reach the expanded consciousness of our higher self.

The Holy Guardian Angel comes in many forms. Known not only as the Bornless Self, it also takes shape throughout traditions as the Augoeides, Silent Watcher, Great

Master, Genius, and Logos. The concept of the higher self has developed in our mystic traditions as humanity has developed. Knowledge of this self is the knowledge of both the deep self and the universe, for they are one and the same. Working with the HGA is a lifelong process.

In *The Equinox*, Crowley wrote that the HGA is "the first and the last of all Spiritual Experiences. For though He is attributed to Malkuth, and the Door of the Path of His overshadowing, He is also in Kether" and "all things are in Ourself, and all Spiritual Experience is a more or less complete Revelation of Him." Thelemite Rodney Orpheus, in his book *Abrahadabra*, describes the HGA with a mathematical formula: "HGA = Infinity – me." Everything that you are personally, subtracted from the cosmos, gives you your Holy Guardian Angel. Together, you are everything.

Many think such concepts are strictly ceremonial and have no place in any form of witchcraft, yet Alex Sanders, founder of the Alexandrian line of British Witchcraft, claimed this in the "Book of Hermes" from his *Alex Sanders Lectures*: "Behold me, mortal, for I am thy God, the true image of thyself, and the very essence of life, yet within me lieth a magnitude greater than you can ever behold without. For I am both macrocosm and microcosm; only your petty vanity could decree otherwise. Worship me, and I shall give you the stars. Reject me, and I shall give thee the depths of the Abyss, for I lie within your own being."

When I think of both the HGA and the immanent divinity that is a part of pagan theology, I am reminded of the beautiful line in the Gnostic Mass of the O.T.O.: "There is no part of me that is not of the gods." For we all are divine, and divine on all levels. That is the essential teaching of paganism, witchcraft, magick, and even the Qabalah, despite all its complexities. Every part of you is God.

You will notice that working directly with the HGA, or Bornless Self, is an important facet of Qabalistic magick. The first vision, that of Malkuth, is Knowledge and Conversation of the Holy Guardian Angel. In *The Temple of Shamanic Witchcraft*, you learned how to commune with the higher self (*TOSW*, Exercise 17). Knowledge and Conversation is not the same as having a strong relationship with the Holy Guardian Angel. In Tiphereth, one is said to truly achieve the vision of Tiphereth by developing a strong relationship with the HGA, either as a guide or by merging with it on some level. Technically, the Bornless Ritual would be even more appropriate as Tiphereth magick, as a regular ritual to more fully embody the HGA. Yet for the purpose of this training, I prefer to give you an understanding of the entire Tree of Life before performing the Bornless Ritual. Though Kether is beyond personalized forms of divinity, our best understanding of divinity while in human form is through the HGA. The final enlightenment on the Tree, with Kether, comes through the true union with the highest self and the forces beyond. As Crowley said, it is the first and last of our spiritual experiences.

MAGICKAL NAMES, MODELS, AND PERSONAL SIGILS

As a part of this very personal and initiatory ritual, to make sure you are able to commune with and, in effect, become your highest self when needed, releasing you from the need to look for your authority solely from another, you can take another initiatory name. Like the witch names of the previous lessons, the name can embody who you feel you are—not only the qualities you aspire to have, but the qualities you feel at this point you truly are embodying as a part of your divine will. High magick traditions are filled with the practice of using magickal mottos to sum up your work. Crowley had many magickal names and mottos, such as *Mega Therion*, or the "Great Beast." One of the most inspiring was *Frater Perdurabo*, which means "I will endure." Crowley certainly did endure through his works. His personal sigil is shown in figure 76. Violet Firth, better known to us today as Dion Fortune, took her name from her family motto, *Deo, non fortuna*, or "God, not fate." You can take a similar name and/or motto, keep the magickal name you are using, or ask your HGA what magickal name you should go by after performing the Bornless Ritual. Another tradition is making a magickal sigil that reflects you as a magician and your Great Work and will.

As in the three previous initiation ceremonies for the levels of fire, earth, and water, a cord can be used as your tool to signify the working of this level. Take a piece of yellow cord (the traditional ceremonial color of the air element) the same length as your braided cords of red, green, and blue. Untie the braid and creatively weave all

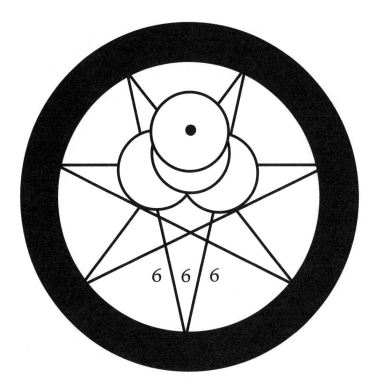

Figure 76: Aleister Crowley's Personal Sigil

four lengths of cord together into one belt for your ritual attire. Bless and consecrate the cord as a ritual tool during the Bornless Ritual.

Exercise 32

Bornless Ritual

This really should only be done once you have worked through the lower four elements and obtained the elemental gifts from the guardians.

1. Perform the LBRP (exercise 5) and the LBRH (exercise 20).

2. You can create sacred space through the GIRP (exercise 22) or a traditional magick circle of your own style. Many feel this is not necessary, for the

Bornless Ritual requires you to face all four directions and commune with the elemental powers, thus automatically creating sacred space.

3. Light any candles and incense you desire and feel are appropriate. Frankincense is a good choice. I also like a variation of what I call "Tree of Life Incense," mixing one part of each of the ten spheres, plus Da'ath, using some substitutions from the traditional correspondences.

Tree of Life Incense
1 part patchouli leaves (Malkuth)
1 part storax (Hod)
1 part frankincense (Tiphereth)
1 part dragon's blood (Geburah)
1 part cedar wood (Chesed)
1 part myrrh (Binah)
1 part fennel (Chokmah)
1 part bay leaves (Kether)
1 pinch wormwood (Da'ath)
9 drops jasmine oil (Yesod)
7 drops rose or rosewood oil (Netzach)

4. If you desire to anoint yourself with Abramelin Oil (chapter 7) or any other high-vibrational substance you feel will help you commune with the higher self, the Bornless One, then do so.

5. Bathe yourself in the divine light from above, as if you are starting the Middle Pillar (exercise 9), but do not go through chanting the divine names of power. Simply fill and surround yourself with the light as you focus on the concept of your Bornless One.

6. **Oath of Invocation.** Speak this in the center of your circle:

I invoke you, Bornless One,
Beingness that has no beginning and no end.
You who create the Earth and the heavens.

You who create the night and the day.

You who create the darkness and the light.

You are myself made perfect that no one has ever seen.

You are matter, destroying to create, you are force, destroying to create.

You have distinguished the just from the unjust, the female from the male.

You produce the seed and the fruit, making all to love and to hate one another.

You create the moist and the dry and that which nourishes all life.

I am your prophet to whom you have given your mysteries.

Hear me, for I am yours.

You are myself made perfect.

7. Face east, and feel yourself connected to the powers of the east. You can hold your blade, if you desire. Feel the yellow elemental energy of air. Feel the guardian of the element of air, either in animal, human, angelic, or deity form. Feel yourself becoming one with the guardian. Feel its powers within you. Feel yourself and your consciousness expand to the reaches of the universe as you recite the sacred words:

   AR...THI-A-O...RHE-I-BET...A-THE-LE-BER-SET...A...BE-LA-THA...AB-E-U...EB-E-U...PHI...THE-TA-SO-E...IB...THI-A-O

   Say to yourself and the spirits of the east:

   Hear my word, and make all spirits subject to my command, so that every spirit, whether of the heavens or of the air, of the Earth or beneath the Earth, on land or in the waters, and every force, feeling, and form in the cosmos is mine to command.

8. Face south, and feel yourself connected to the powers of the south. You can hold your wand, if you desire. Feel the red elemental energy of fire. Feel the guardian of the element of fire, either in animal, human, angelic, or deity form. Feel yourself becoming one with the guardian. Feel its powers within you. Feel yourself and your consciousness expand to the reaches of the universe as you recite the sacred words:

AR-O-GO-GO-RU-BRA-O . . . SO-TO-U . . . MU-DO-RI-O . . . PHA-LAR-TA-O . . . O-O-O . . . A-PE

Say to yourself and the spirits of the south:

Hear my word, and make all spirits subject to my command, so that every spirit, whether of the heavens or of the air, of the Earth or beneath the Earth, on land or in the waters, and every force, feeling, and form in the cosmos is mine to command.

9. Face west, and feel yourself connected to the powers of the west. You can hold your cup, if you desire. Feel the blue elemental energy of water. Feel the guardian of the element of water, either in animal, human, angelic, or deity form. Feel yourself becoming one with the guardian. Feel its powers within you. Feel yourself and your consciousness expand to the reaches of the universe as you recite the sacred words:

RU-A-BRA-I-A-O . . . MRI-O-DOM . . . BA-BA-LON-BAL-BIN-A-BAFT . . . A-SAL-ON-A-I . . . A-PHE-NI-A-O . . . I . . . PHO-TETH . . . A-BRA-SAX . . . A-E-O-O-U . . . I-SCHU-RE

Say to yourself and the spirits of the west:

Hear my word, and make all spirits subject to my command, so that every spirit, whether of the heavens or of the air, of the Earth or beneath the Earth, on land or in the waters, and every force, feeling, and form in the cosmos is mine to command.

10. Face north, and feel yourself connected to the powers of the north. You can hold your peyton/stone, if you desire. Feel the green, brown, or black elemental energy of earth. Feel the guardian of the element of earth, either in animal, human, angelic, or deity form. Feel yourself becoming one with the guardian. Feel its powers within you. Feel yourself and your consciousness expand to the reaches of the universe as you recite the sacred words:

MA . . . BAR-RI-O . . . I-O-EL . . . KO-THA . . . A-THO-RE-BA-LO . . . A-BRA-OT

Say to yourself and the spirits of the north:

Hear my word, and make all spirits subject to my command, so that every spirit, whether of the heavens or of the air, of the Earth or beneath the Earth, on land or in the waters, and every force, feeling, and form in the cosmos is mine to command.

11. Stand back in the center. Feel the power of the center, of spirit, of your Holy Guardian Angel. Feel the light descend from the heavens, rise from the Earth, and surround you. Feel yourself dissolving in the light. Feel yourself expanding in all directions, the four around you, above, and below. Feel your consciousness dissolve in the light, as you become your Bornless Self. Feel yourself expand as you say the words:

A-OT...A-BA-OT...BA-SA-U-M...I-SAK...SA-VA-O...I-A-O

Say in the center:

This is the ruler of the universe, whom the winds fear... This is who made voice and all things were created. Ruler, master, helper...

I-E-O-U...PUR...I-O-U...PUR...I-AOTH...I-A-E-O...I-O-O-U...A-BRA-SAX...SA-BRI-AM...O-O...U-U...E-U...O-O...U-U...A-DO-NA-I...E-DE...E-DE...AN-GE-LO-STON-THE-ON...AN-LA-LA...LA-I...GA-I-A...A-E-PE...DI-A-THAR-NA...THO-RON

I am the Bornless One.
Having sight in the feet: strong and the immortal fire. I am the truth.
I am the one in lightning and in thunder.
My sweat is the rain that showers the Earth with life.
My mouth is ever flaming.
I am the maker and the begetter of the light!
I am the grace of the world.
The heart girt with a serpent is my name.

I-A-O...SA-BA-O

12. Feel yourself totally and completely become the Bornless One. Do your working of magick or commune with the Bornless Self. You might simply know things and perceive things differently through this union, or have a very different internal dialogue between your middle self and your higher self. If this is your first invocation of the higher self, you can ask your higher self its name, or dedicate your relationship with it through the consecrating of your magickal name and/or sigil. The HGA might give you a different name or sigil than you had planned on using. Follow the higher guidance you are receiving in this space and at this time. Bless your newly crafted cord at this time.

13. Thank and "release" the Bornless Self. Technically, we know that we are the Bornless Self and this is unnecessary, but doing something to ground yourself back to your "ordinary" persona is helpful at this time. If you created a sacred space, close the space as you opened it. If you performed a magick circle, release it. If you performed the GIRP, then use the GBRP.

14. Close with the LBRP and the LBRH if you have not done so already.

The version presented here is very similar to the modernized version of Jason Augustus Newcomb, in his *New Hermetics* book. If you would like Crowley's line-by-line commentary on the Bornless Ritual, as well as his interpretations of the barbarous names, I again suggest *The Magick of Aleister Crowley* by Lon Milo DuQuette, who goes to the trouble of arranging two of Crowley's essays by the appropriate sections of the ritual, while also offering his own version of an Invocation of the Holy Guardian Angel. A more pagan-themed ritual can be found in appendix VII.

Ultimately, regardless of the tradition or technique, we all are seeking to make contact with our own higher self and, through it, the divine forces manifested as Secret Chiefs, inner-plane masters, angels, and deities. Once we have that divine connection, and realize that we are part of the great chain of divinity, not separate from it, we no longer need the authority of others. We gather in community as equals, but we need not accept anyone else's truth as the absolute truth.

Ceremonial magick is an amazing system for those who apply themselves to its practice and find the spirituality in its construction. It is a great asset for the modern witch to know the traditions of ceremonial magick, to work with them and grow from them. It's much like letting the seeds of your neighbor's garden blow into your garden, or letting the bees cross-pollinate the two, creating a new hybrid, different from both parents but still in your garden. It is still where your spirit grows.

History, unfortunately, has shown us just as many practitioners whose own derailment from the path can serve as a lesson. Looking at the history of the Golden Dawn and its associated groups, we see the machinations of egomaniacs and escapists and, in some shining moments, true adepts of the Great Work. Magick historians, with their favored personalities, simply disagree as to who was the egotist and who was the adept, leaving us all room for interpretation, just as reality is open to interpretation. The finding of your own higher self is what must guide you. With that, it matters not how history judges you, if it judges you at all. You will have worked your True Will in the world, and no magician, no witch, can ask for more.

Many say there are "mistakes" in a variety of modern texts that detail the rituals of high magick, from the old grimoires to modern printings of the Golden Dawn and related material. They argue that the public tarot cards and revealed documents contain purposeful flaws to throw off the uninitiated and uneducated, and that anyone trained in such magick can see and correct such obvious flaws in the formula. This is a means of protecting the secrecy of such rituals, for some believe that if they are revealed, they will lose their power. I disagree. Although such measures may or may not have been taken by the authors, purposely or not, all that it has succeeded in doing is creating variations of the traditions, which, when fueled with the proper will, still work. There is no one path up the mountain, even for the magician.

THE EVOLVING SPIRAL

With a rededication to the elemental training and exploring the elements through the paradigm of the Tree of Life, witches begin to see the elemental spiral we are walking in the Temple of Witchcraft. This is our path up the mountain, one that crosses many others. It might take longer, but it is full and rich and the witch who walks it will be well traveled. When you look at the alchemical orientation of the magick circle—north/earth, east/fire, south/air, and west/water—we are walking the widdershins path to the center, to the heart of the Underworld and the Goddess. But we also are aligning with the stars and solar consciousness, as the heavens appear to go counterclockwise in the night sky. We began with fire in the east in *The Inner Temple*, then moved to earth in the north for *The Outer Temple*. Water in the west was the third level of training in *Shamanic Witchcraft*, and now air in the south for *High Witchcraft*. The next step is to the center, in the forthcoming *The Living Temple of Witchcraft*. Our movement in some ways parallels the rise through the lower five spheres, though the elemental scheme doesn't always fit. For the first level and Malkuth we learned discernment, the science of magick, the theory, and how things work. For Yesod as the second level, we learned Moon circles and the virtues of stone, herbs, and oils. The third level relating to Netzach was almost overwhelming in the intense emotions, while the fourth level relating to Hod matched perfectly with our training in Hermetic Qabalah. The fifth step, as always, is spirit, in Tiphereth, where we put the Bornless Self to work manifesting our True Will in the world. Here we learn service, sacrifice, and living in union with the higher self.

Thus we conclude our teachings in high witchcraft and high magick. You have all the skills to move on to the next level. You understand that which has influenced modern witchcraft, even if you choose not to embrace it. You will never again feel disconnected or uninformed about these traditions. You have faced the final point of our witches' pyramid: "To Dare." You must be daring to put this knowledge to use. You must be daring to find your own divine authority and break from the pack, reworking and rewriting things to suit your own divine self. You truly must be daring to create your own map of reality, and use it as a guide.

Many people feel their way is the only way. They feel their tradition is the "true path," or the special transmission from the Secret Chiefs for the new aeon, or the lineage of an ancient family heritage. Some groups have kept alive the "wells" of ancient symbolism and memory, both through folk practices and lodges such as those of the Masons, which have played such a pivotal role in the initiation systems of both ceremonial magick and Wicca. The modern revival traditions and their splinter groups have given us the gifts of reconstruction. If they can do it, then so can we. They have taught us how to take the old and synthesize the new, even though giving us that freedom might not have been their intention. Don't stop where they have stopped. Take it to the next level, what will be the new magickal concepts of the next generation. If you don't dare to go beyond what you were taught and try to do things differently, you certainly won't be on the next wave. Yet at the same time, you have to make sure your feet are firmly on the ground, or you will have no support or foundation. Do you know where your traditions come from and how they work? If so, then build upon them.

On a personal level, you can look at all these splinter groups, both lodge and coven traditions, and all the political infighting and wonder how we ever will get along and move together into the next age. I admit that it can look quite depressing. But from an elevated perspective, the fractured groups are like pieces of glass or stone. Each holds a place within a powerful mosaic, a beautiful pattern with individual pieces. Each piece has its own size, shape, and color, yet together they become a greater whole. This mosaic pattern is the next age we are entering, the Aquarian Age, which holds many paradigms and traditions side by side, where they each can be "right" if they contain the timeless and eternal wisdom of the mysteries.

In the Aquarian Age, there is room for all traditions, cultures, and individual perspectives. The work in *The Temple of High Witchcraft* is designed to aid witches in the transition. Though not always easy, or fun, or what we expected, the mental training is necessary, as Aquarius is an air sign—not just any air sign, but the sign of individuality and innovative genius. Here we must learn to tap our own genius, which we now know is not just a word for intelligence, but is our higher self, our Holy Guardian Angel and Bornless Self. That is where inspiration comes to us. With this training, we learn how to transition from our point of view so we can see the beauty in the many. We learn to be creative and modern and yet not lose our mysteries and magick to innovation. Ultimately, we learn how to bring our collective piece to the mosaic of world wisdom traditions and take our place as leaders in the coming age of balance and harmony, devoted equally to the Mother, the Father, and the Child.

Appendix I: Examples of Reality Maps

When you are preparing to make your own reality map, it is useful to see other models and paradigms to give you a greater understanding of what a reality map is and how it functions. Some examples are very specific to an individual's worldview, while others are specific to a tradition. The most useful to learn are those that apply universal shapes and symbols.

To assist you in the lessons in this book, I have prepared this appendix outlining several reality maps. Obviously, none are as detailed as the Tree of Life. Few have such a history and level of detail, and if they did, it obviously would be too much to cover in this text. If you are intrigued by a reality map that is drawn from other texts, I suggest you seek out the source information and study it firsthand. I also suggest meditating on the symbol and working directly with it on the inner planes.

Some students who have taken the classes on which this book is based have complained that knowing too many reality maps confused them, giving them too many choices. They felt that everything already had been created, so how could they develop a unique map? They didn't want to be too influenced by any of the models they had learned. Unfortunately, that is the risk you run. Like a self-taught musician who "discovers" a chord progression because the notes sound pleasing together, only to later study music formally and discover that the particular chord progression first was used centuries before, we experience the same joy of exploration and then a letdown to learn our map wasn't completely original. The same could be said about the scientist who is not educated in the body of knowledge that comes before him or her. The scientist might come to the same conclusion by a unique path, but it is the same conclusion. By actively learning what generations before us have developed, we can build new trails and paths in the development of our art. Without education, we spend most of our time "rediscovering" what the ancestors already have given us. Think of these models as gifts from those who have walked the path before us.

Here are some other reality maps you already have been exposed to in the Temple of Witchcraft training.

World Tree

First outlined in chapter 12 of *The Inner Temple of Witchcraft* and then in greater detail in *The Temple of Shamanic Witchcraft*, the shaman's view of reality comprises three basic worlds. The Upper World of higher spirits and deities, the Middle World of humanity and nature, and the Lower World of chthonic deities, ancestors, and power allies all exist in a balance. The spirit wheel (*TOSW*, Figure 4) gives us a graphic representation of the worlds and our potential allies. Various world mythologies further subdivide these three planes, as the Norse have nine worlds (*TOSW*, Figure 13) and some Celtic traditions have twelve, as described in Fionn's window (*TOSW*, Figures 10 and 11).

Planes of Reality

Detailed in chapter 12 of *The Inner Temple of Witchcraft*, the seven planes of reality—physical, etheric, astral, emotional, mental, psychic, and divine—neatly divide the spectrum of reality into various levels of consciousness. An enterprising student easily could find correspondences among the seven planes and many other magickal systems, from the chakras to the seven planets, seven metals, and seven days of the week.

CHAKRAS AND THE SUBTLE BODIES

Though the information on energy anatomy presented in Lesson 11 in *The Inner Temple of Witchcraft* was intended to be viewed in light of a human's spiritual bodies, the divine often is personified, and if we truly believe "as above, so below," then the divine hold the same pattern as we do. The Divine Creator's body manifests in seven subtle layers, corresponding to the seven chakras. The chakra lore gives us many correspondences to colors, planets, and gemstones. This concept of the divine body relates quite well to our reality map of the planes of reality.

WITCH'S CIRCLE

When drawn, the witch's circle, and even the altar itself, is a reality map. Called into the circle are all the primal creative forces of the universe. That is why circle magick is so powerful. On the altar are items consecrated to act as conduits for these forces, from the four elements to the Goddess and God and the central flame of the Great Spirit. Various reality-map mandalas can be made, such as one with the elements aligned with the seasons and times of day (*OTOW*, Figure 15) and the elements aligned with the alchemical qualities (*OTOW*, Figure 16).

WHEEL OF THE YEAR

Another powerful reality map is the witch's Wheel of the Year, the eight-spoked wheel, particularly the version in *The Outer Temple of Witchcraft* (Figure 48) with the astrological signs and phases of the Moon also corresponding to the holidays. It shows the cycle of change as we move through various levels of consciousness.

CELTIC CIRCLES OF CREATION

In some versions of Celtic myth and theology, creation is divided into three concentric rings, each with a different character and quality. The concept is much like the shaman's World Tree, but with a horizontal ring structure rather than a vertical axis.

It wasn't until I saw a diagram of this image (figure 77), with the zodiac signs placed within it, that it made sense to me, and I could see it being used as a reality map with both spirit-world and zodiac correspondences. I found this helpful diagram in *The Handbook of Celtic Astrology* by Helena Paterson.

Circle of Abred: Earthly Ring—Mortal Realm and Underworld Annwn

Circle of Gwynvyd: Solar Ring—Realm of Enlightenment or Summerlands

Circle of Ceugant: Galactic Ring—Realm of Pure Divinity, Galactic Core

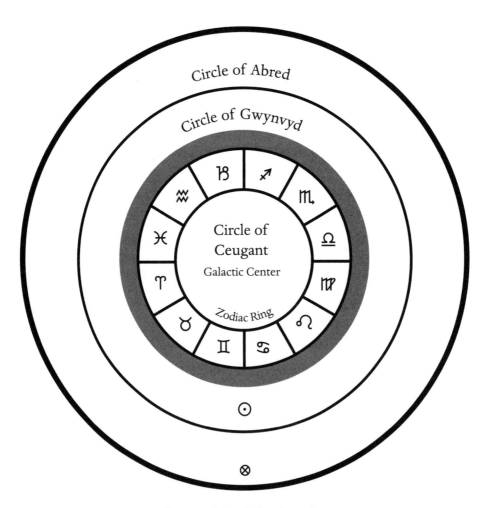

Figure 77: Celtic Circles of Creation

Celtic Tree Ladder

The innovative diagram in figure 78 is based on material from the book *Practical Celtic Magic* by Murry Hope. The image depicts the ladder of the cosmos, and each point upon the ladder is associated with a number, an ogham, a planet, and an archetypal image, fusing traditional Western occultism and astrology with Celtic imagery.

Number	Ogham/Tree	Planet	Function/Archetype
1	Beth/Birch	Sun	Absolute Deity
2	Duir/Oak	Jupiter	Dual King
3	Ruis/Elder	Saturn	Triune Queen
4	Ngetal/Reed	Pluto	Double Sun
5	Tinne/Holly	Mars	Humanity
6	Luis/Rowan	Venus	Sacred Fire
7	Nion/Ash	Neptune	Sea
8	Coll/Hazel	Mercury	Mind
9	Saille/Willow	Moon	Moon
10	Muin/Vine	Earth	Earth
11	Gort/Ivy	Transpluto or Venus	Spirit
12	Fearn/Alder	Mercury	Vulcan or Divine Will
13	Uath/ Hawthorn	Uranus	Chaos

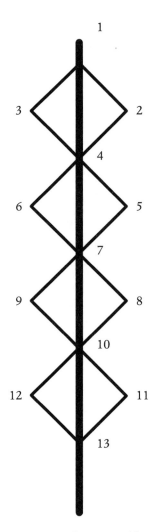

Figure 78: Celtic Tree Ladder

THEOSOPHICAL RAYS

In the traditions of Theosophy, based on the work of H. P. Blavatsky and then the channelings of Alice Bailey (though Bailey broke away from the Theosophical organization), is the concept of "rays" of light, the divine power reflected through a spectrum. These rays are akin to the Qabalist's sephiroth, as each is an emanation of the divine.

The rays emanate to our solar system through our Solar Logos, the divine being of our solar system, and manifest through a trinity of forces, embodied by the image of Father, Son, and Holy Ghost from Christian mythology (figure 79). The rays then first extend from the trinity as the three primary colors of red, blue, and yellow. From the third ray of yellow, the remaining rays emanate—green, orange, indigo, and violet. Each ray has a primary purpose in the development of the universe.

Red: Will, Action, Evolution, Leadership

Blue: Divine Love, Wisdom, Compassion

Yellow: Active Intelligence

Green: Harmony Through Conflict, Art, Nature, Creativity, Faery

Orange: Concrete Science, Technology

Indigo: Devotion, Religion

Violet: Ceremonial Magick

The rays then are directed toward the Planetary Logos, the guiding intelligence of our planet, and divided into a planetary hierarchy of various spiritual beings who direct these energies, including a ruling triad beneath the Logos known as the Manu, Christ, and Mahachohan, and then beneath them, seven *chohans*, or masters, who guide the development of each ray with humanity. These ascended master chohans have other ascended masters working for them in a specific ray "department," and also have incarnated humans who consciously or subconsciously work with them.

The Theosophical rays provide both a diagram of universal powers and a system for understanding how those powers are working in your own consciousness. They are derived primarily from the writings of Alice Bailey, in particular her book *The Rays*

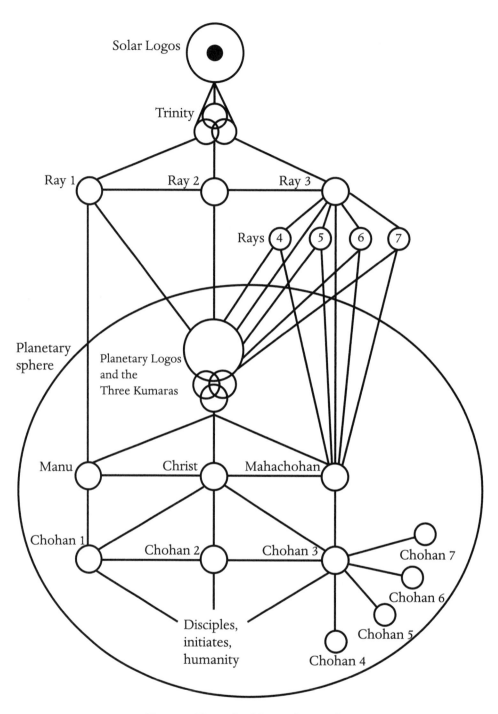

Figure 79: Theosophical Spiritual Hierarchy

and the Initiations. My own book *Ascension Magick* also looks at the rays as a model of reality in modern language for the aspiring witch or magician.

Ladder of Consciousness

The ladder of consciousness is one of the first reality maps I created (figure 80). It is very similar to the World Tree, but instead of using the tree image, it uses the diamond, or two opposing triangles, becoming more and more narrow as the spiritual beings in each stratum become less and less individualized. The strata below, like Underworld beings, are more feminine and intuitive, while the strata above are more logical and masculine. All are surrounded and interpenetrated by the creative spirit. Instead of using worlds, the ladder of consciousness uses rungs on the ladder to describe beings of various states of consciousness. Though it is not a map for magickal correspondences such as herbs or stones, it helped me when I was working mostly through vision and meditation and trying to understand all the beings I was encountering. I made this reality map while researching the material that eventually became my book *Spirit Allies.*

Web Mandala

The web mandala is another reality map I constructed (figure 81). At the time, I was trying to reconcile and integrate many different forms of magick, including my traditional witchcraft, feng shui, astrology, and the runes. I chose the image of a web with the spider in the center, as I often see the Goddess as the Weaver in the center of the cosmos. The web mandala becomes more and more intricate, and in each web "box" I place another corresponding image. By looking at the connections near one another, I would meditate on the links among the elements, the seasons, astrology, and the runes. My original version was done in color, with each box a different shade to denote the color associations I used in magick for each one, but this version has been rendered in black and white for ease of reproduction.

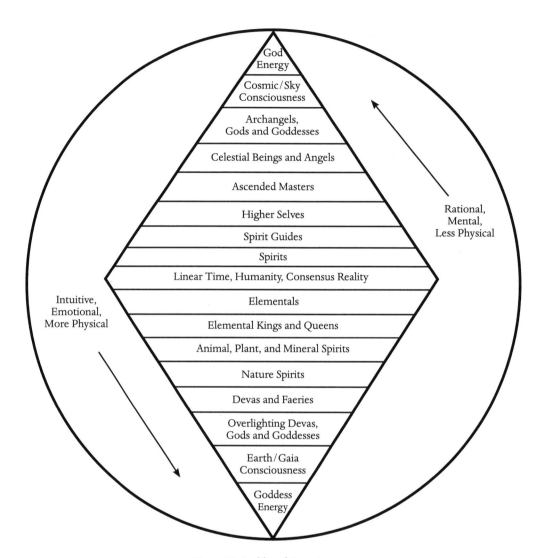

Figure 80: Ladder of Consciousness

Figure 81: Web Mandala

Tree Tattoo

Some students have observed that many of the reality maps are very masculine. The maps often are designed by men, and have a linear, logical feel, compartmentalizing things rather than flowing from a more organic and cohesive process. Not all reality maps are like that. Many are much more creative and organic, but unfortunately, these maps do not reproduce well in books. I've had many students, particularly female students, make maps that were three-dimensional models, dioramas, and sculptures, but they are hard to outline in a book.

One very creative reality map was transformed into a back tattoo design, showing the Goddess of Creation aligned with the student's spine, entwined with the wheel of life / Wheel of the Year and surrounded by the four elements (figure 82). It was designed by my friend and covenmate Ginella Cann. For her, the process of both designing and receiving the tattoo has been a magickal initiation.

Figure 82: Tattoo

Photograph of back tattoo of Ginella Cann by Joyce Cadena Hannon

The Risting: The Grand Circle of Witchcraft

The Risting diagram, credited to S. Rune Emerson, depicts the nine worlds of the Yggdrasil, the World Tree of ancient Germanic myth (figure 83). The six axes in the center represent the six Roads, the means to understanding Nature in all of her seasons:

Wind, the eastern road of Spring: the sweeping of chaos and the preparing of the way

Fire, the southern road of Summer: the quickening time of heat and wildness

Water, the western road of Autumn: the flowing tide of rest, sacrifice, and remembrance

Frost, the northern road of Winter: the time of stillness and solidity, of fortification and necessity

Earth, the lower road of the Wheel: the balance and cycle of all powers, the crossroads and the cauldron

Spirit, the higher road of the Compact: the true dreaming, the realm of desire and initiation

The Seventh World, in the center, represents the melding of powers to create the world of Wyrd, the place of entry, and the land of Dream. It is here that we live, and it is from this place, between the dark and light faces of the Tree, that we witches weave the spells of the Left and Right Hands, the magic of the Craft.

The Moon represents the realm of Sleep, the time of silence and magic. The Sun represents the land of Waking, the time of word and deed. The Runes, the sacred sap that flows through the Tree's roots and branches, are the seeds of the Consort, who is at once the Light and Shadow. The Consort, ever at one with the sleeping Mother, is the life/death force that quickens her womb. The Tree is the egg in the Womb of Nothing, around which can be found the Mother, who is the dark sea of possibility and reality.

Witches of the Risting Tradition use this sigil as the key for all their work, and through study, unlock its many mysteries. For members of the Risting Tradition, this diagram is the great Grimoire, the record of all things and of none.

Figure 83: Risting

Starwell Map

In the Starwell map, Adam Sartwell creates a cosmology combining his favorite elements of the shaman's three worlds with the traditional model of the Tree of Life (figure 84). The upper triangle comprises the Upper World with its transpersonal forces, and its apex is spirit, the source. The lower triangle comprises the Lower World and its own transpersonal forces, with its apex in the void of creation. The center is the hexagram, the intersection of the two worlds, with the four elements arranged as they are in the traditional circle, as well as corresponding to those four points on the Tree of Life (Chesed, Geburah, Netzach, and Hod). The four points also have associations with the realms closest to the land of humanity, such as the ancestors and the fey. The four elemental realms are surrounded by a solar/above world and a lunar/below world, the Middle World's closest links to the Upper and Lower Worlds. The Earth is in the center of this Middle World hexagram. Nine "rungs" are created by the four triangles, corresponding to the seven chakras as well as a higher heart point between the heart and throat and the energy center at the feet. Various "selves" of shamanic cosmology are outlined in several points, with the middle self called the Namer and the highest self called the Watcher.

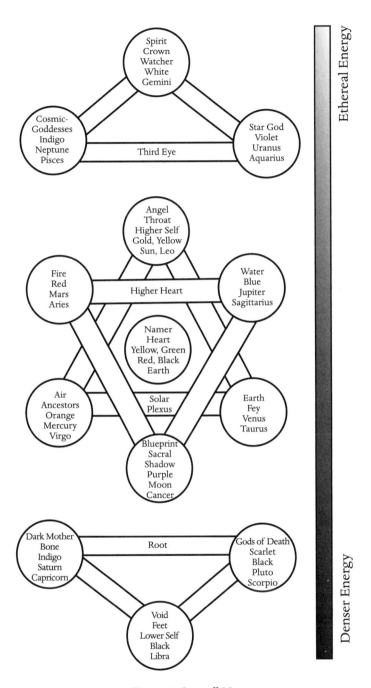

Figure 84: Starwell Map

Magickal House

Jean Pando, a student of mine and a recent graduate of Witchcraft IV, came up with a clever look at reality focused on her house (figure 85). Each section of the house represents a different zone in her reality, but can be applied cosmically. The house is surrounded by the Wheel of the Year, because her home is her focus on the seasonal holidays. She says: "The living space is my Lower World, where my day-to-day activities take place. The resting space and study are my Middle World. The resting space is the place to deal with emotional issues, passions, etc., and the study is where I think, study, communicate, create ritual, etc. The loft and tower are my Upper World. To me they both relate to meditation, sleeping/dreamtime, and altered states. My home is what I love and what makes sense to me."

Tower

Consciousness: Spiritual
Color: White
Deities: Pluto, Hades, Osiris
Animals: Pegasus, Dragon (came to me)
Crystal/Stone: Celestite (connection to the Divine)
Herbs and Incense: Amber (connection to Akasha—pure spirit)
Planet: Pluto (death, resurrection, divine will)
Element: Fire (spark of life)

Loft

Consciousness: Astral
Colors: Purple, Lavender
Deities: Artemis (Moon), Diana (light, Moon, means "brilliant" in Celtic)
Animal: Blue Jay (connection to physical and spiritual)
Crystals/Stones: Amethyst, Moonstone
Herbs and Incense: Sandalwood, Frankincense
Planet: Moon
Element: Water

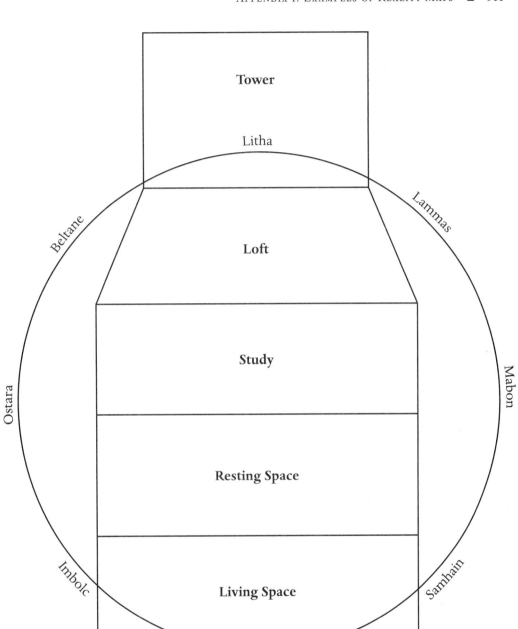

Figure 85: The House

Study

Consciousness: Mental, Mind

Colors: Yellow, Orange

Deities: Hephaestus (smith, creativity), Hermes (messenger, communication), Athena (wisdom)

Animals: Crow, Eagle, Wolf (intelligence)

Crystals/Stones: Bloodstone (enhance creativity), sugilite (wisdom)

Herbs and Incense: Sage (wisdom), Rosemary (mental powers), Rue (mental powers), Benzoin (what came to me)

Planet: Mercury

Element: Air

Resting Space

Consciousness: Emotional, Feeling, Intuition

Color: Light Blue

Deities: Venus (love), Apollo (healing, poetry, song), Aphrodite (love, sex)

Animals: Dolphin, Orca

Crystals/Stones: Rose Quartz, Pink and Green Tourmaline

Herbs and Incense: Rose, Gardenia, Lavender, Myrrh

Planet: Venus

Element: Water

Living Space

Consciousness: Physical

Colors: Green, Brown

Deities: Gaia, Hestia (home), Dionysus (vegetation and fertility), Demeter, Cernunnos

Animals: Dog, Wolf, Squirrel, Turtle

Crystals/Stones: Pyrite, Garnet, Magnetite

Herbs and Incense: Patchouli, Sandalwood, Cinnamon, Salt, Most Culinary Herbs

Planet: Earth

Element: Earth

Appendix II: Variations of the Lesser Banishing Ritual of the Pentagram

Modern magicians have created a variety of pentagram rituals. If you have studied the traditional version of the LBRP (exercise 5), you will notice that it consists of three basic parts: the Qabalistic Cross, the banishing itself, and the angelic invocation. The process is sealed with a repetition of the Qabalistic Cross, making it really a four-part exercise, but based on three different forms.

The purpose of the Qabalistic Cross is to unite the practitioner with the cosmos, yet ground the energy in the material world. Polarities symbolized by the left and right are acknowledged and balanced. The space is then cleared and clearly marked with the use of the four pentagrams and their circle. Unlike a witch's magick circle, the container of sacred space created in the LBRP is not anchored or manifested into a bubble of energy, but rather the boundaries of the cleared space are marked out with a ring of light. A "higher" force, a group of entities associated with those four directions, is called upon, for divine protection, to maintain the space for any further working, or in general to attune the practitioner to these divine forces and make them more readily accessible in daily and magickal life. The entire ritual is referenced, as well as the elusive power of the center as the six-pointed star. The connection between the spiritual and material is then recognized again, and the ritual is complete.

Your own LBRP ritual should contain these basic elements and fulfill the same functions to be truly effective as an LBRP–style ritual.

Temple of Witchcraft LBRP

My own version of the LBRP is the one that many of my students adopt, preferring to use something that has been tested yet not wanting to use the traditional version due to its Hebrew associations. They prefer something more pagan, more witchy.

I meditated on reconstructing the LBRP, and my spirit guides gave me the words and motions. My version is based on Celtic and Greek imagery, as they are two of the most prominent pantheons in my personal practice. Some of the words don't really make sense in a formal language, though to me they sound similar to Latin, but they evoke a power for me, and were divinely given. Sometimes magickal words cannot be translated into a traditional language, but they still are effective.

No blade is necessary for this ritual, as both hands are used for many motions, but if you desire, you can hold your blade in your dominant, projective hand. I prefer to just use my outstretched hands.

In place of the Qabalistic Cross, I use a variation of the Earth and Sky Connection (Exercise 16 in *ITOW*). Instead of doing it in a state of deep meditation, I perform it ceremonially, eyes open and using movement, breath, voice, and visualization.

My version of the banishing is more relaxed when compared to the traditional LBRP, omitting the use of the Sign of the Enterer or the Sign of Silence. Instead of chanting the Hebrew divine names, the vowels associated with the five elements are used. The primary vowels of A-E-I-O-U always have reminded me of the Greek god Aeolus, god of the four winds. Some witchcraft groups use the kings of the four winds as their elemental guardians. I think of Aeolus, and chants based on A-E-I-O-U, as having mastery over the four directions and the subtle fifth element. Whenever I draw banishing or invoking pentagrams (*OTOW*, Chapter 6), I chant the vowel sounds in order of the points I am drawing, starting with the point I am moving toward. In this case, the banishing pentagram of earth moves toward the point of spirit, and then to fire, air, water, and ending on earth, creating a chant of U, I, E, O, and A (figure 86). I also have used variations of sacred syllables for the elements.

Element	Vowel	Modern Syllable	Egyptian Syllable
Spirit	U	Ka	Sa
Fire	I	Ra	Am
Air	E	Leem	As
Water	O	Om	Nu
Earth	A	El	Ta

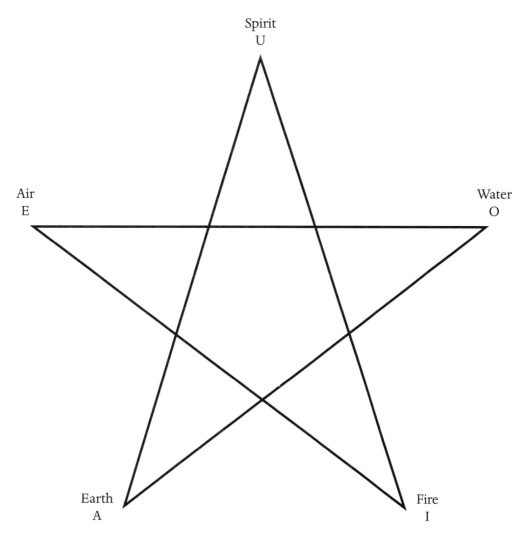

Figure 86: Pentagram with Vowel Sounds

For the calling of the four guardians, I call upon the deities I use in my traditional quarter calls (*OTOW*, Chapter 6) in my personal practice. By calling upon them to be present during my daily LBRP, I build a stronger relationship with them when I call upon them in a more formal magick circle ritual. Some people feel that calling upon deities in this way is disrespectful and trivial. I think that the deities all are capable of being in many places at once, and asking to a build a relationship with them is a sign of great respect. You become attuned to their energy after a time, and there is a part of them always with you. I feel their presence strongly in my life, and if they felt disrespected, I don't think they would come when I ask them to in this ritual.

Earth and Sky Connection

1. Stand straight, facing the north in the center of your circle. Sweep both arms up the sides of your body. Visualize and feel yourself bringing the energy of the Earth beneath your feet up through your body and out your crown and fingertips. Feel the energy reach up and connect to the sky. Look up to the sky and say: **Et Ouranus**.

2. Visualize and feel yourself pull the energy of the sky down through your crown and body as you sweep both arms back down the sides of your body and slightly out to each side, bringing your head down to look at the ground. Say: **Et Gaia**. Feel the energy of the Earth flowing up through you to the sky while the energy of the sky is flowing down through you to the center of the Earth.

3. As you bring your gaze to the east, reach out with your right hand, straight out the right side, and imagine you are holding a ball of golden yellow light connected to a beam of energy from the east. Say: **Et An Ra**.

4. As you bring your gaze to the west, reach out with your left hand, straight out the left side, and imagine you are holding a ball of silvery blue light connected to a beam of energy from the west. Say: **Et An Ma**.

5. Cross your arms over your chest in the God position (the Sign of Osiris Risen, chapter 4), bringing the beams of golden yellow and silvery blue energies across your chest, slightly bowing your head. Say: **Amoura Korey**. Feel a flow of gold energy move through you from east to west while simultane-

ously feeling a flow of silver energy move through you from west to east. Feel the flow of the Earth and sky energies as well, as you are in the center of an energetic cross. Feel your connection to all things.

Banishing

6. While still facing the north, step back with the foot of your dominant side (your right foot, if you are right-handed). Draw a banishing earth pentagram in blue or blue-violet light, and chant **U-I-E-O-A**, with one vowel for each point of the star. Step forward with the foot that stepped back, and plunge your dominant hand into the star, activating it and "pushing" it out to the circumference of your intended circle. In the center of the pentagram, start drawing the circle around you, drawing one-quarter of a circle of light (in white, blue, or violet) until you face the east. Repeat this process in all four directions, completing the circle in the north.

Evocation

7. Standing in the center of the circle and facing the north, with your arms outstretched to either side, evoke the four powers with the following prayer. Imagine each deity standing in the appropriate direction. Feel within your heart chakra the presence of the circle and pentagrams, as well as the hexagram. As you imagine the hexagram, bend your arms at the elbow, bringing your hands in to touch your chest. When you are done, visualize the deities facing out, protecting you from harm.

> **Before me, Cernunnos.**
> **Behind me, Macha.**
> **On my right hand, Lugh.**
> **And on my left hand, Ceridwen.**
> **About me flame the pentagrams.**
> **And within me shines the six-rayed star of perfect love and perfect trust.**

8. Repeat the Earth and Sky Connection.

Modern LBRP

Earth and Sky Connection

1. With your hands raised above your head, say: **Father Sky**. (Picture blue sky energy moving down to your heart chakra.)

2. With your hands directed below, say: **Mother Earth**. (Picture green Earth energy moving up to your heart chakra and mingling with the sky energy. Both energies continue moving through you—sky down to Earth, and Earth up to sky.)

3. With your right arm out, say: **Golden Sun**. (Picture the Sun sending golden energy to your heart chakra. Feel the warmth flow through you.)

4. With your left arm out, say: **Silver Moon**. (Picture the Moon sending you silver energy. The gold and silver energies mingle and then continue on through the opposite sides.)

5. In the center, with your arms in the God position, say: **Blessed be**.

Banishing

6. When you face each direction, draw a banishing earth pentagram. Picture it shining at the boundary of your space. Push your energy and breath into each pentagram. Chant the appropriate words for each point of the star, beginning in the north and tracing one-quarter of a circle in each direction.

North: **To Know.**

East: **To Will.**

South: **To Dare.**

West: **To Be Silent.**

Evocation

7. Say:

> **Before me, Raphael.**
> **Behind me, Gabriel.**

On my right hand, Michael.
And on my left hand, Uriel.
For about me flames the pentagram.
And within me shines the six-rayed star.

8. Repeat the Earth and Sky Connection.

© Alixaendreia. Used with permission.

A Chaos Magick Version of the LBRP

This is a ritual to dispel gloom and seriousness. Use when appropriate, especially on April 15.

Opening

1. Facing east, say: **From the greatest heights.** Reach upward with your right hand, fingers spread in a receiving gesture. Imagine opening a perfect and appropriate channel to the universe.

2. Say: **To the deepest depths.** Sweep your hand vertically from your head toward your feet, feeling the energy enter through your crown chakra and course through your body to your feet.

3. Say: **To the greatest breadths, around and through me. In and of the Universe.** Reach to the right, touch your right shoulder, gesture through your heart chakra, and touch your left shoulder. Feel the support of the universal energy supporting you.

4. Say: **I am centered.** Bring your hands to your heart center. Imagine yourself as balanced, powerful, and centered.

5. Say: **The Universe rolls in ecstasy around me, OM!** Focus on your connection to all.

Banishing

6. Facing east, say: **Bricka Bracka.** Draw a neon-rainbow banishing earth pentagram, then turn clockwise one-quarter of a circle.

7. Facing south, say: **Fire Cracka.** Draw a neon-rainbow banishing earth pentagram, then turn clockwise one-quarter of a circle.

8. Facing west, say: **Cis Boom Bah.** Draw a neon-rainbow banishing earth pentagram, then turn clockwise one-quarter of a circle.

9. Facing north, say. **Bugs Bunny, Bugs Bunny, Rah Rah Rah.** Draw a neon-rainbow banishing earth pentagram, then turn clockwise one-quarter of a circle.

Evocation

10. Facing east again, say:

> **Before me, Buffy Summers.**
> **Behind me, Obi-Wan.**
> **On my right hand, Bugs Bunny.**
> **On my left hand, Jean-Luc Picard.**
> **Before me shines the pentagram.**

Stretch out your arms and legs, and visualize yourself as a banishing pentagram. Say:

> **Within me shines the six-rayed star.**

Visualize a hexagram, a six-pointed star, in the heart chakra. Say:

> **Let Freedom and Joy triumph. Eris be with me for the Greatest Good.**

11. Repeat the opening.

© Penney L. Robinson. Used with permission.

CROSSROADS LBRP

Crossroads Within

1. Point your receptive hand toward the top of your head, visualizing a great ball of light. This ball radiates a pillar down from the heavens and into your body. Say: **I am one with divine will.**

2. Bring your hand down to point at the floor, visualizing the ray of light descending into the Earth below your feet. Say: **In the silence of the kingdom.**

3. Bring your right hand to your heart and extend it to the right horizontally, visualizing a beam of light shooting from your heart to the infinite space to your right. Say: **With power to dare.**

4. Bring your left hand to your heart and extend it to the left horizontally, visualizing a beam of light flowing to the infinite space to your left. Say: **And glory of knowledge.**

5. Return both hands into a gesture of prayer, visualizing a crystalline light from your heart filling your aura. Say: **I weave myself anew. So mote it be!**

Banishing Stars

6. In the east, with your right hand, draw a banishing pentagram, visualizing it in blue flame. When this is done, push the pentagram with your thoughts and gestures until it is at the end of the space that you would like to clear of all unwanted energies. When it is in place, intone the name of the Grigori of the east: **Aldebaran.**

7. Visualize a line of light extending from the horizontal line of the star toward the south as you make a quarter turn. When facing the south, create a pentagram there. Repeat the steps of the eastern pentagram, only intone the name of the Grigori of the south: **Regulus.**

8. Visualize the light circle extending to the next quarter, in the west. Draw the pentagram and intone the name of the Grigori of the west: **Antares**.

9. Visualize the light circle extending to the next quarter, in the north. Draw the pentagram in the air and invoke the Grigori of the north: **Fomalhaut**.

10. Extend the circle of light until it connects with itself as you turn back to the east to begin the invocation of the guardians.

Invoking the Guardians

11. Say:

> **Eko before me, Bran and Branwen.**
> **Eko behind me, Manannan and Cerridwyn.**
> **Eko to my right, Brigit and Lugh.**
> **Eko to my left, Danu and Cernunnos.**
> **Around me and within me burn the flames of the pentagrams.**
> **Above me and now within me burns the six-rayed star.**

12. Repeat the Crossroads Within.

© Adam Sartwell. Used with permission.

OTHER PENTAGRAM RITUALS

Here are a few more pentagram rituals for you to discover and explore.

Star Ruby

The Star Ruby is Aleister Crowley's version of the LBRP, published first in *The Book of Lies* and later, in a slightly different version, in Appendix VI of *Magick in Theory and Practice*, Book 4, Part III. Unfortunately, Crowley didn't leave a lot of information on this ritual, but you can find a commentary, along with instructions, in *The Magick of Thelema* by Lon Milo DuQuette.

Setting of the Wards of Power and Setting of the Wards of Adamant

These pentagram rituals, from the tradition known as Aurum Solis, are similar to the Golden Dawn's style of ritual. Instructions for the rituals can be found in *Mysteria Magica* by Denning and Phillips.

Gnostic Pentagram Ritual

Chaos magician Peter Carroll has his own version of the LBRP, used by many modern magicians. It can be found in his book *Liber Kaos*. One could argue that it was both this ritual and the principles of Chaos magick put forth by Carroll that inspired the next generation of modern magicians to create their own pentagram rituals.

New Hermetics Grounding and Centering

This modern version of the LBRP focuses on the inner experience rather than outer movements, and can be found in *The New Hermetics* by Jason Augustus Newcomb.

Arthurian Ritual of the Pentagram

This Arthurian style of pentagram ritual was written by Gahmuret for the organization known as the Sodalicium Mysteriorum Arthuri, and can be found at http://sodalicium.org/rituals.html.

Appendix III: Variations of the Middle Pillar

Temple of Witchcraft Middle Pillar

I've created a few variations of the Middle Pillar (exercise 9), always trying to find what works best for me. Here are the variations that I have found to be the most successful.

As in my version of the LBRP, I prefer to use simple and primal vowel sounds for the toning, or primal words of power, in my Middle Pillar ritual. By taking the element, and looking at the vowel sound associated with the element, as well as the modern power syllables and those associated with both Hinduism and Egyptian magick, I can arrange the sounds according to the elemental associations of the sephiroth/chakras on the Middle Pillar. This creates a new pattern of tones, different from those used in the pentagrams for banishing and invoking a particular element. In the Middle Pillar, when casting invoking or banishing pentagrams, each vowel is done for one breath and repeated three to four times for each energy center, rather than all five being done in one long breath.

Middle Pillar					
Sephira	**Element**	**Chakra**	**Vowel**	**Modern**	**Egyptian**
Kether	Spirit	Crown	U	Ka	Sa
Da'ath	Air	Throat	E	Leem	As
Tiphereth	Fire	Heart/Solar Plexus	I	Ra	Am
Yesod	Water	Belly	O	Om	Nu
Malkuth	Earth	Feet	A	El	Ta

When performing this modern Middle Pillar ritual, choose one of the sets of sounds listed in the chart above. Perform the Middle Pillar as you would, but use that set of sounds instead of the Hebrew divine names.

If you prefer a Middle Pillar with seven energy centers, you can add the following two vowel sounds to expand the ritual.

Expanded Middle Pillar			
Sephira	**Chakra**	**Vowel**	**Hindu Seed Sylable**
Kether	Crown	U	Aum
Chokmah/Binah	Third Eye	Ah	Ksham
Da'ath	Throat	E	Ham
Chesed/Geburah (Tiphereth)	Heart	Aw	Yam
Tiphereth/Netzach/Hod	Solar Plexus	I	Ram
Yesod	Belly	O	Vam
Malkuth	Root	A	Lam

I've had some students with musical inclinations set the seven-point Middle Pillar to a major scale in Western music, focusing on the light above the head as the upper C and descending in the pattern of B-A-G-F-E-D-C.

Nine Breaths Centering

The Nine Breaths Centering is a modern Celtic practice, from the book *Celtic Sorcery* by Ian Corrigan. It has some similarities to the Middle Pillar ritual, and also some striking differences. Rather than using the five power centers on the Tree of Life, or the traditional seven chakra centers, it focuses on the Celtic imagery of three cauldrons or pools as the power centers—the head, heart, and belly/loins. It also uses two currents, or flows, of power, from the Earth and sky. Here is the practice as written by Corrigan.

- Preparation—Find your comfortable seat for meditation and make your body easy. Take a few deep breaths, perhaps beginning your rhythmic count. When you have taken a few breaths, you begin.

- 1st Breath—Draw the Earth Power up into your body, filling the Cauldron or pool in the loins.

- 2nd Breath—Draw the Earth Power up through the loins to fill the Cauldron in the heart. Feel the cool, nourishing power as it fills you.

- 3rd Breath—Draw the Power through the loins and the heart, to fill the head. See the Earth Power overflowing from the Three Centers through the whole body. For the rest of the work, each breath moves the Power through the Three Cauldrons and the body.

- 4th Breath—Feel the Sky Power shining down through the whole body, and feel the Cauldron in the head kindle with fire of the sky.

- 5th Breath—The Sky Power brightens in the body, and the second Cauldron kindles in its rays.

- 6th Breath—The Power shines brighter, and the Cauldron in the loins kindles. The light fills the water, and the Two Powers flow throughout the body.

- 7th Breath—The combined powers are directed through the body, intensified and concentrated.

- 8th Breath—Turn the palms of the hands upward, and direct the Powers, with the breath, into the palms of the hands. See the Waters overflowing the fingers and the Light or Flame shining up from the hands. (In many cases there may be work to be done with the power at this point. Whenever needed, the Power can now be employed as needed. The Ninth Breath, then, comes when one wishes to end.)

- 9th Breath—Place the palms of the hands together, and allow the powers to recede and re-center, ceasing to flow through the hands.

- Settling—Take a few breaths to relax again, and allow the powers to calm.

Though the Nine Breaths does not use words or sounds to activate the energies, in a later section in *Celtic Sorcery*, Corrigan goes on to describe the use of the "Dord Draoi": "When you wish to intensify the presence of the Two Powers, or to direct with will and vision, you may find it useful to employ the 'Dord Draoi'—the magic chant. The Dord Draoi is an intoning, a buzzing, vibrating call used to move and shape power. Let the breath rise from the belly, making such a tone or drone or buzz as arises by nature. Experiment will find the sound that can be sustained, and which produces the desired feeling of 'vibration' in both the body and in the current of the Two."

EGYPTIAN SUN MEDITATION

A staple in the first-degree training of the Witchcraft as a Science Cabot Tradition is the Egyptian Sun Meditation. It is used to energize the chakras and aura much the same way the traditional Middle Pillar is used. It can be done first thing in the morning, or to recharge yourself after a long day, before you do other spiritual work, or when you simply need more energy. Unlike in the Middle Pillar, there is no outward vocalization necessary.

Get into your meditative state. Cabot witches use a technique known as the Crystal Countdown, which is the basis of my own countdown technique.

Imagine a bright psychic Sun shining directly over your head, about six feet above your crown. Feel the pulsating golden light emanating from it.

Feel the Sun's power, leaping outward, ready to be shared with you and all living things.

Feel a beam of "lasered" solar light descend upon you, enter your head, and go into your pineal gland, the third eye.

Feel a second beam enter your throat chakra.

Feel a third beam of sunlight enter your heart.

Feel a fourth beam of sunlight enter your solar plexus.

Raise your hands, palms upward, as in the Egyptian prayer pose. Each hand should be at shoulder level, fingertips pointed outward to the right and the left. This is similar to the Sign of the Practicus Grade—Air—Hod (traditionally, the Theoricus Grade), but with the arms lower and the fingers pointing outward to the sides.

Feel a fifth beam of sunlight enter the center of your left palm.

Feel a sixth beam enter the center of your right palm.

Feel the golden rays enter your entire body, flowing through your blood, nervous system, and spine, to every organ, muscle, and cell. Continue to let the energy flow through and fill your body until you feel a tingle of warmth or ice in your fingertips or even across the entire body. Touch your feet together and cross your hands over your chest, in the God position or the Sign of Osiris Risen, with your eyes closed. Hold the energy within you, bathing in its warm glow. Repeat the phrase "The Sun gives me physical and psychic energy" over and over again. Sit like this for ten to fifteen minutes, to energize your body, mind, and aura.

Other Inspirations for the Middle Pillar

Sephiroth Variation

The most common modern variation of the Middle Pillar ritual involves the substitution of the divine names associated with each sephira's name. The first name toned is Kether. The second is Da'ath. The third name is Tiphereth, the fourth is Yesod, followed by the fifth, Malkuth. Otherwise, the ritual is executed exactly the same way. Critics would argue that the divine names carry the spiritual vibrations of creation, and the sephiroths' outer names do not, yet I know I've found this variation to be quite effective.

Israel Regardie

Israel Regardie created a simpler version of the Middle Pillar exercise in his book *The Art of True Healing*. It's basically the same as the Golden Dawn version, but replaces the more complex Hebrew words with the following English words, also to be vibrated several times.

>   *Kether:* I am
>
>   *Da'ath:* I see / I speak
>
>   *Tiphereth:* I love
>
>   *Yesod:* I create
>
>   *Malkuth:* I bless

Rousing of the Citadels

This is the Middle Pillar variation of the Aurum Solis tradition. The ritual goes through various stages of development as the student becomes more fully versed in its practice. Instructions for this variation can be found in *Mysteria Magica* by Denning and Phillips.

Appendix IV: Variations of the Four Adorations

Four Adorations of the Temple of Witchcraft

My version of the Four Adorations (exercise 14) is fairly simple. While this is the poetry I first used, and I deliberately kept it simple, I find myself spontaneously talking to each element, direction, and god that I work with when I do the adoration, rather than speaking memorized prose.

Face east when you rise to attune to the element of fire and the rising Sun.

Hold the Goddess position. Say:

> *To the east,*
> *I welcome the rising Sun, guiding my day.*
> *I welcome the god of the Sun as the lord Lugh and the many skills you bless me with.*
> *I welcome you into my soul.*
> *Blessed Be.*

Face south at noon to attune to the element of air and the open sky.

Hold the Goddess position. Say:

> *To the south,*
> *I welcome the sky, watching my path.*
> *I welcome the crow-feathered goddess Macha, the wise crow woman.*
> *I welcome you into my mind and words.*
> *Blessed Be.*

Face west at sunset to attune to the element of water and the setting Sun. Hold the God position. Say:

> *To the west,*
> *I welcome the setting Sun, closing the day.*
> *I welcome the goddess Ceridwen, goddess of the cauldron.*
> *I welcome you into my heart.*
> *Blessed Be.*

Face north at bedtime to attune to the earth element and the darkness. Hold the God position. Say:

> *To the north,*
> *I welcome the Moon and the night.*
> *I welcome the horned god Cernunnos, midnight master of the Underworld.*
> *I welcome you into my home and dreams.*
> *Blessed Be.*

Starwell Adorations

This Celtic variation of the Four Adorations was written by Adam Sartwell. With both Goddess and God in each adoration, this version is a complement to his Crossroads Banishing Ritual (see appendix II).

> *Hail on to thee who art Bran, white raven rising.*
> *Hail on to thee, Branwen, dawn's newborn face.*
> *Follow the trail of the Sun's birth.*
> *Night is ended in the rapture of your splendor.*
> *Hail on to thee from the abodes of night.*

Hail on to thee, Lugh, in the heat of noon.

Hail on to thee, Bridget, inspired spark.

Who art Lugh many skilled.

Who art Bridget poet and smith.

Exultant in the flames of all creation.

Hail on to thee from the abodes of morning.

Hail on to thee, Cerridwyn, cauldron of wisdom's rebirth.

Hail on to thee, Manannan, sailor of the setting Sun.

Who art Cerridwyn of as many shapes as water.

Who art Manannan, ferryman of the isle of apples.

Honored in the fading radiance of the Sun.

Hail on to thee from the abodes of the day.

Hail on to thee, Danu, nourisher of the fertile soil.

Hail on to thee, Cernunnos, shadow of the forest.

Who art Danu, mother to all Fey.

Who art Cernunnos, Lord of the crossroads of life and death.

Dance to the music of the distant stars.

Hail on to thee from the abodes of evening.

Other Versions of the Four Adorations

Kheperu Nu Ra: The Evolutions of Ra

This alternate version of the traditional Four Adorations, created by Chic and Sandra Tabatha Cicero, can be found in their book *Self-Initiation into the Golden Dawn Tradition: A Complete Curriculum of Study for Both the Solitary Magician and the Working Magical Group.*

The Adoration of Belinus

This version of the Four Adorations honors the Celtic god Belinus, and was written by Gahmuret for the practitioners of the Sodalicium Mysteriorum Arthuri. There is a lunar adoration in this tradition as well, known as the Adoration of the Maiden, the Mother, and the Crone. See http://sodalicium.org/belinus.html.

Appendix V: Variations of the Lesser Banishing Ritual of the Hexagram

While the LBRH (exercise 20) represents another foundational stone in ceremonial magick, along with the LBRP, there are fewer variations of it available than there are of the LBRP. I think that pagans often are not as interested in hexagram symbolism as they are in pentagrams, and many do not understand the difference between the two banishing rituals, as oriented to the microcosm and macrocosm, or elemental and planetary formats. Many pagans omit hexagram rituals entirely because they feel the pentagram ritual cleanses and clears as much as is needed. Yet without the hexagram, they are missing the process of alignment to the heavens and planetary powers that will serve them later in their magickal career.

THE TEMPLE OF WITCHCRAFT LBRH

1. Perform the Temple of Witchcraft LBRP (see appendix II).

2. Hold your wand or use your dominant hand in the drawing motions.

3. **Alignment with the Triple Power.** Hold up your arms in the Goddess position and say:

    To the Maiden of the Moon, she who is above us.

4. Lower your arms until they are horizontal to the ground, forming a cross, and say:

   To the Mother of the Earth, she who is with us.

5. Lower your arms further, with palms pointed down to the ground, and say:

   To the Crone of the Underworld, she who is below us.

6. As you recite the words in each of the following three paragraphs, form the three signs of the Alignment with the Triple Power.

   Heaven, Earth, and Underworld,
   May your light guide me in all realms.

   The Morrighan, Hecate, and the Norns:
   Anu, Badb, Macha.
   Artemis, Selene, Persephone.
   Urd, Verdandi, Skuld.

   Sisters, mothers, daughters.
   The three who are one who are three.
   Maiden, Mother, Crone.
   Creator, Sustainer, Destroyer.
   I-A-O.

7. **Formulation of the Banishing Hexagrams.** Face north and draw a banishing hexagram. I usually use the simple all-purpose banishing unicursal hexagram in golden light (figure 87), and do not distinguish the element in the way that it is drawn, though I associate the element of water with the north. You might even perceive the pentagrams behind the golden hexagram. Vibrate: **ARARITA**. Point to the center of the hexagram with your tool, and draw one-quarter of the circle with a line of light, bringing you to the east, just as you did in the LBRP.

8. Face east and draw a banishing unicursal hexagram in golden light, with the element of fire in your consciousness. Vibrate: **ARARITA**. Point to the center of the hexagram with your tool, and draw one-quarter of the circle with a line of light, bringing you to the south.

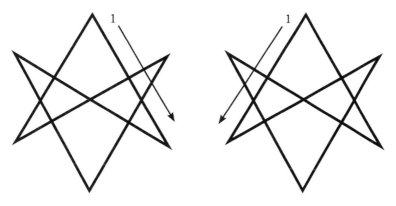

Figure 87: Basic Invoking and Banishing Unicursal Hexagrams

9. Face south and draw a banishing unicursal hexagram in golden light, with the element of earth in your consciousness. Vibrate: **ARARITA**. Point to the center of the hexagram with your tool, and draw one-quarter of the circle with a line of light, bringing you to the west.

10. Face west and draw a banishing unicursal hexagram in golden light, with the element of air in your consciousness. Vibrate: **ARARITA**. Point to the center of the hexagram with your tool, and draw one-quarter of the circle with a line of light, bringing you back to the north, completing the circle.

11. Conclude with a repetition of the Temple of Witchcraft LBRP.

ȘTAR ȘAPPHIRE

A complement to Crowley's Star Ruby, the Star Sapphire ritual is his Thelemic hexagram ritual. It was found originally in Liber XXXVI of *The Book of Lies*, though you also can find a version with excellent commentary and explanation in Lon Milo DuQuette's *The Magick of Aleister Crowley*. Some use the unicursal hexagram figure in the Star Sapphire. Though the unicursal hexagram is associated most traditionally with invoking and banishing the planets, as in the traditional hexagram rituals, some magicians associate the four smaller points with the elements, and draw toward the element, starting at the top or bottom, to invoke with the unicursal hexagram (figure 88). To banish, they start at the element and draw away, toward the top or bottom, reversing the invoking motion. With these hexagrams, you can create banishing or invoking Star Sapphire rituals.

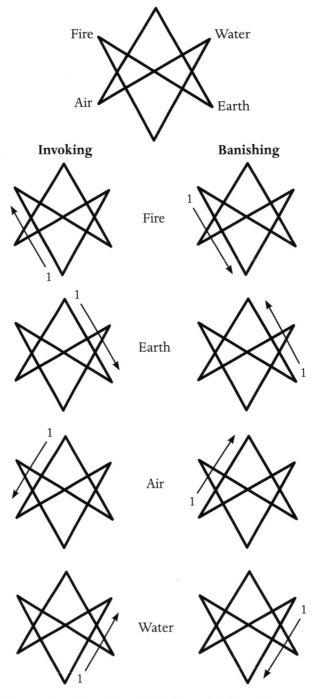

Figure 88: Invoking and Banishing Elemental Unicursal Hexagrams

Appendix VI: Variations of the Greater Ritual of the Hexagram

Temple of Witchcraft GRH

For my Greater Ritual of the Hexagram, I use the basic format of my LRH (appendix V), but substitute the appropriate planetary unicursal hexagram for the basic banishing/invoking unicursal hexagram.

Star Sapphire Ritual: Planetary Form

The Star Sapphire ritual (appendix V) can be adapted to banish or invoke various planetary influences, using the same corresponding associations of the hexagram with the planets, but drawing the unicursal hexagram in one continuous motion (figure 89). The advantage of the unicursal hexagram form is that there is a central point for the Sun, so the entire pattern of all the planets does not have to be performed to invoke or banish the Sun. Otherwise, the form, words, and visualizations are the same.

Some dispense with the use of hexagram symbolism for planetary rituals, preferring to perform septagram rituals, using the seven-pointed star. The star is used by moving clockwise toward the planet you are invoking (figure 90). To banish, start at

Invoking   **Banishing**

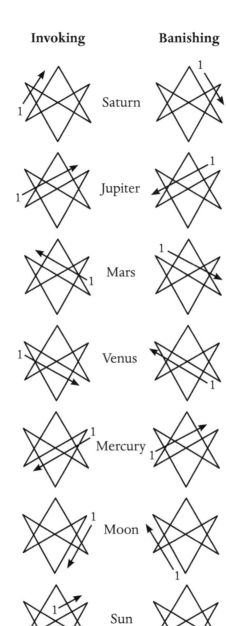

Saturn

Jupiter

Mars

Venus

Mercury

Moon

Sun

Figure 89: Invoking and Banishing Planetary Unicursal Hexagrams

the planetary point and move counterclockwise. You also can draw the planetary glyph in the center of the septagram after completing all seven points. Since this practice is not standardized, like the hexagram correspondences, different magicians and witches place the planets on different points of the septagram, though they usually follow the planetary days of the week, also known as the Chaldean order.

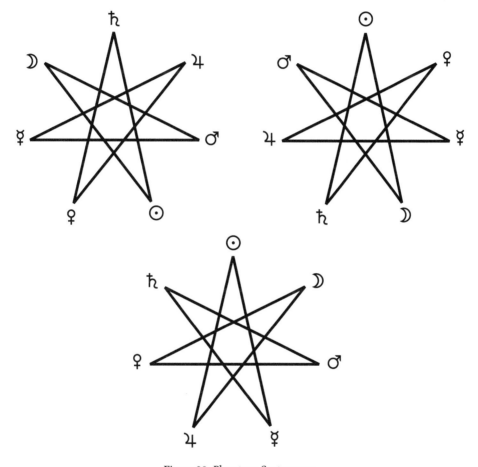

Figure 90: Planetary Septagrams

Appendix VII: Variation of the Bornless Ritual

Rather than focus on the higher-self imagery that is found in ceremonial magick, I prefer to do a version of the Bornless Ritual (exercise 32) that is an alignment of the selves, or souls, and then an invocation to be fully conscious and connected to all three souls. The Bornless Self is identified most with the higher self, but truly it is the self that embodies all selves, beyond division, shape, and form. Ceremonial aspects have an emphasis on the "higher" realms as being the abode of the Bornless One, but through the reworking of Thelemic and Wiccan poetry with the traditional imagery of the Bornless Ritual, I've created something to embody both the Bornless Self and the three selves of shamanic cosmology that I favor.

Temple of Witchcraft Bornless Ritual

1. Create a sacred space through a magick circle ritual, casting a circle and calling the quarters using whatever method is most appropriate for you. You can begin with the LBRP and LBRH.

2. Perform the Great Rite using the blade and chalice.

> *As the sword is to the grail,*
> *The blade is to the chalice.*
> *As the heavens are to the Earth,*
> *Truth is to love.*
> *Let us drink in the power and blessings of the Lady and Lord conjoined,*
> *And let all paradox be resolved.*
> *For there is no part of me that is not of the gods.*
> *So mote it be.*

Drink in the fluid of the chalice, consuming the energies of both Goddess and God, resolving all paradox within you, as you feel the Two Who Move as One in the Love of the Great Spirit move within you.

3. Take a deep breath and hold it for a few moments. Face the heavens and exhale strongly. Feel the life energy of your breath ascend to the heavens and reach your higher self. Feel it descend back again, through your space, aligning your higher, middle, and lower selves, and all of your chakras, making you the perfect conscious vessel for your united souls.

4. **Invocation.** Recite the following:

> *I invoke you, O Bornless One, the Mighty Atman, the Augoedes,*
> *All that was, all that is, and all that ever shall be.*
> *You who have no beginning and no end.*
> *You who create the above and the below.*
> *You who create the heavens and the Earth.*
> *You who create the night and the day.*
> *You who create the darkness and the light.*
> *You are myself made perfect that none has ever seen.*
> *You are matter, destroying to create.*
> *You are spirit, creating to destroy.*
> *You produce by seed and root, by stem and bud, by leaf and flower and fruit.*
> *By Light, Life, Love, and Law, you nourish all that lives.*

And by Liberty, to free all that was bound and open the gates to all wonder.

For you hold the stars of the heavens and the depths of the abyss.

All lie within your being.

For love's sake, you were divided.

And for love's sake, you will be united.

Hear me, for I am yours.

You are myself made perfect.

You are my true self.

I call to the three who are one who are three yet again,

who reside within me, around me, and through me.

I call to the human self, the talker, the namer,

The one who walks on the surface with shining body,

The Uhane, Suld, Thumos, Sa, Ruach, and Emi.

I call to the psychic self, the shaper, the younger,

The one who walks in dreams beneath the world,

The Unihipili, Suns, Epithymia, Ka, Nephesh, and Vivi.

I call to the divine self, the watcher, the deep self,

The winged one who walks with the stars of the heavens,

The Aumakua, Ami, Logos, Ba, Neshamah, and Ori.

I call you forth into alignment, above, below, and center.

For that which is as above, so below, as within, so without.

I am the stars and the dreams and all things in between.

5. Face north, and call to the element you most often associate with the north. Call to the guardians and powers you associate with that element in animal, human, angelic, or deity form. Feel yourself becoming one with the powers of the direction. Feel its powers within you. Feel yourself expand infinitely to the furthest reaches of the outer dark as you recite the sacred words of the Bagahi Rune:

Bagahi laca bachahe — Bah-GAH-hee LAH-ka BAH-khah-hey

Lamac cahi achabahe — Lah-MAHK kah-HEE ah-KHAH-bah-hey

Karrrelyos! — Kah-RREL-yohs!

Lamac lamec bachalyos — La-MAHK lah-MEKH bah-KHAH-lee-ohs
Cabahagi sabalyos — Kah-BAH-hah-gee sah-BAH-lee-ohs
Baryols! — Bah-RREE-oh-lahs!

Lagozatha cabyolas — Lah-goh-zah-THAH kah-BEE-oh-lahs
Samahac et famyolas — Sah-MAH-HAHK EHT fah-MEE-oh-lahs
Harrahya! — Hah-RRAH-hee-yah!

Then say to yourself and the spirits of the north:

O great powers of the universe, hear my words. Make me one with the powers of the north, in harmony and alignment with every spirit, every power, of the north, in the Upper World, Middle World, and Underworld, from here unto the depths of the universe.

Eko, Eko, Aradia! (Or use the name of whatever guardian you associate with the north.)

6. Face east, and call to the element you most often associate with the east. Call to the guardians and powers you associate with that element in animal, human, angelic, or deity form. Feel yourself becoming one with the powers of the direction. Feel its powers within you. Feel yourself expand infinitely to the furthest reaches of the outer dark as you recite the sacred words of the Bagahi Rune (see step 5).

Then say to yourself and the spirits of the east:

O great powers of the universe, hear my words. Make me one with the powers of the east, in harmony and alignment with every spirit, every power, of the east, in the Upper World, Middle World, and Underworld, from here unto the depths of the universe.

Eko, Eko, Azarak! (Or use the name of whatever guardian you associate with the east.)

7. Face south, and call to the element you most often associate with the south. Call to the guardians and powers you associate with that element in animal, human, angelic, or deity form. Feel yourself becoming one with the powers

of the direction. Feel its powers within you. Feel yourself expand infinitely to the furthest reaches of the outer dark as you recite the sacred words of the Bagahi Rune.

Then say to yourself and the spirits of the south:

O great powers of the universe, hear my words. Make me one with the powers of the south, in harmony and alignment with every spirit, every power, of the south, in the Upper World, Middle World, and Underworld, from here unto the depths of the universe.

Eko, Eko Zamilak! (Or use the name of whatever guardian you associate with the south.)

8. Face west, and call to the element you most often associate with the west. Call to the guardians and powers you associate with that element in animal, human, angelic, or deity form. Feel yourself becoming one with the powers of the direction. Feel its powers within you. Feel yourself expand infinitely to the furthest reaches of the outer dark as you recite the sacred words of the Bagahi Rune.

Then say to yourself and the spirits of the west:

O great powers of the universe, hear my words. Make me one with the powers of the west, in harmony and alignment with every spirit, every power, of the west, in the Upper World, Middle World, and Underworld, from here unto the depths of the universe.

Eko, Eko, Cernunnos! (Or use the name of whatever guardian you associate with the west.)

9. Stand back in the center. Feel the power of the center aligned with your three selves, above, below, and center, as well as the four directions. Feel your selves come into alignment. Feel yourself become your divine self, in all worlds. Expand your consciousness in all directions, and recite the Bagahi Rune.

Recite the Eko Eko Evocation in its entirety, using the four traditional names of Azarak, Zamilak, Cernunnos, and Aradia, or, if you have been using other names, substitute those names in the appropriate places in the evocation chant.

Eko, Eko, Azarak!

Eko, Eko, Zamilak!

Eko, Eko, Cernunnos!

Eko, Eko, Aradia!

Eko, Eko, (your magickal name)!

I am the Bornless One.

Being of Holy Formless Fire.

I am matter and spirit.

I am flesh and lightning.

I am the stars and dreams and all things in between.

I am the Light, Life, Love, Law, and Liberty.

I am all that was, all that is, and all that ever shall be.

E-O-A-U-I (vowel formula for invoking active pentagram of spirit)

O-E-I-U-A (vowel formula for invoking passive pentagram of spirit)

I-A-O

10. Feel yourself in complete divine alignment. Do your magickal working or simply commune with your divine self.

11. Thank your divine self, knowing that you are not really releasing it, for it is you. Ground yourself back in the physical world by thanking your divine self and focusing on your grounding root. I also recite the vowel formulas for the banishing pentagrams of spirit:

I-U-A-O-E

A-U-I-E-O

12. Release your sacred space in a manner appropriate for the way you created it, releasing the quarters and the circle.

Bibliography

Anderson, Cora. *Fifty Years in the Feri Tradition.* Self-published. San Leandro, CA, 1994.

Andrews, Ted. *Sacred Sounds.* St. Paul, MN: Llewellyn Publications, 1992.

Ashcroft-Nowicki, Dolores. *The Shining Paths.* Leicestershire, England: Thoth Publications, 1983.

Bailey, Alice. *The Rays and the Initiations.* New York: Lucis Publishing, 1960.

Bardon, Franz. *Initiation into Hermetics.* Salt Lake City, UT: Merkur Publishing, 2001.

———. *The Key to the True Kabbalah.* Salt Lake City, UT: Merkur Publishing, 2002.

———. *The Practice of Magical Evocation.* Salt Lake City, UT: Merkur Publishing, 2001.

Cabot, Laurie, with Tom Cowan. *Power of the Witch: The Earth, the Moon, and the Magical Path to Enlightenment.* New York: Dell Publishing, 1989.

Campbell, Joseph, with Bill Moyers. *The Power of Myth.* New York: Doubleday, 1988.

Carroll, Peter J. *Liber Kaos.* York Beach, ME: Samuel Weiser, 1992.

Cicero, Chic, and Sandra Tabatha Cicero. *The Essential Golden Dawn: An Introduction to High Magic.* St. Paul, MN: Llewellyn Publications, 2003.

———. *Self-Initiation into the Golden Dawn Tradition.* St. Paul, MN: Llewellyn Publications, 1995.

Clark, Rosemary. *The Sacred Magic of Ancient Egypt.* St. Paul, MN: Llewellyn Publications, 2003.

Cochrane, Robert, and Evan John Jones. *The Robert Cochrane Letters: An Insight into Modern Traditional Witchcraft.* Somerset, UK: Capall Bann, 2003.

Conway, D. J. *The Ancient & Shining Ones.* St. Paul, MN: Llewellyn Publications, 1993.

———. *Magick of the Gods & Goddesses.* St. Paul, MN: Llewellyn Publications, 1997.

Corrigan, Ian. *Celtic Sorcery: A Druid's Grimoire.* Starwood Edition, 2005.

Crowley, Aleister. *The Book of Lies.* London: Wieland, 1913.

———. *Magick in Theory and Practice.* New York: Dover Publications, 1976.

———. *777 and Other Qabalistic Writings of Aleister Crowley.* York Beach, ME: Samuel Weiser, 1982.

Cunningham, Scott. *Cunningham's Encyclopedia of Crystal, Gem & Metal Magic.* St. Paul, MN: Llewellyn Publications, 1992.

———. *Cunningham's Encyclopedia of Magical Herbs.* St. Paul, MN: Llewellyn Publications, 1985.

———. *Magical Herbalism.* St. Paul, MN: Llewellyn Publications, 1983.

Dannelley, Richard. *Sedona: Beyond the Vortex.* Sedona, AZ: Vortex Society, 1995.

Davidson, Gustav. *A Dictionary of Angels, Including the Fallen Angels.* New York: Free Press, 1967.

De Grandis, Francesca. *Goddess Initiation.* San Francisco, CA: HarperSanFrancisco, 2001.

Deerman, Dixie (Lady Passion), and Steven Rasmussen (*Diuvei). *The Goodly Spellbook: Olde Spells for Modern Problems.* New York: Sterling Publishing, 2004.

Denning, Melita, and Osborne Phillips. *Mysteria Magica.* St. Paul, MN: Llewellyn Publications, 2004.

DuQuette, Lon Milo. *The Chicken Qabalah of Rabbi Lamed Ben Clifford.* York Beach, ME: Weiser Books, 2001.

———. *The Magick of Aleister Crowley.* Boston, MA: Weiser Books, 2003.

———. *The Magick of Thelema.* York Beach, ME: Samuel Weiser, 1993.

———. *Understanding Aleister Crowley's Thoth Tarot.* Boston, MA: Weiser Books, 2003.

Ea. *Understanding the Bornless Rite.* Class Handout from Pagan Spirit Gathering, Wisteria, OH, 2004.

Falorio, Linda. *The Shadow Tarot.* London: Aeon Books, 2004.

Farrar, Janet, and Gavin Bone. *Progressive Witchcraft.* Franklin Lakes, NJ: New Page Books/Career Press, 2004.

Flowers, Stephen E., Ph.D. *Lords of the Left-Hand Path*. Smithville, TX: Runa-Raven Press, 1997.

Fortune, Dion. *Moon Magic*. Boston, MA: Weiser Books, 2003.

———. *Mystical Qabalah*. York Beach, ME: Samuel Weiser, 2000.

———. *The Sea Priestess*. York Beach, ME: Samuel Weiser, 1972.

Fries, Jan. *Cauldron of the Gods: A Manual of Celtic Magick*. Oxford, UK: Mandrake Press, 2003.

Goddard, David. *The Sacred Magic of the Angels*. York Beach, ME: Samuel Weiser, 1996.

———. *Tree of Sapphires*. Boston, MA: Weiser Books, 2004.

Godwin, David. *Godwin's Cabalistic Encyclopedia*. St. Paul, MN: Llewellyn Publications, 1994.

Greer, John Michael. *Circles of Power*. St. Paul, MN: Llewellyn Publications, 2002.

———. *The New Encyclopedia of the Occult*. St. Paul, MN: Llewellyn Publications, 2003.

Griffin, David. *The Ritual Magic Manual*. Beverly Hills, CA: Golden Dawn Publishing, 1999.

Grimassi, Raven. *The Encyclopedia of Wicca & Witchcraft*. St. Paul, MN: Llewellyn Publications, 2000.

———. *The Witches' Craft*. St. Paul, MN: Llewellyn Publications, 2002.

———. *The Witch's Familiar*. St. Paul, MN: Llewellyn Publications, 2003.

Guiley, Rosemary Ellen. *The Encyclopedia of Witches and Witchcraft*. New York: Checkmark Books, 1999.

———. *Harper's Encyclopedia of Mystical & Paranormal Experience*. San Francisco, CA: HarperSanFrancisco, 1991.

Hall, Manly P. *The Secret Teachings of All Ages*. New York: Jeremy P. Tarcher/Penguin, 2003.

Hine, Phil. *Condensed Chaos*. Tempe, AZ: New Falcon, 1995.

Hope, Murry. *Practical Atlantean Magic*. London: Aquarian Press, 1992.

———. *Practical Celtic Magic*. New York: Aquarian Press, 1987.

Hulse, David Allen. *The Eastern Mysteries*. St. Paul, MN: Llewellyn Publications, 2002.

———. *The Western Mysteries*. St. Paul, MN: Llewellyn Publications, 2002.

Huson, Paul. *Mastering Witchcraft*. New York: Putnam, 1970.

Jones, Evan John, and Doreen Valiente. *Witchcraft: A Tradition Renewed*. Robert Hale Ltd., 1999.

King, Francis. *Modern Ritual Magic: The Rise of Western Occultism*. Dorset, UK: Prism Press, 1989. Originally, *Ritual Magic in England*.

Knight, Gareth. *The Secret Tradition in Arthurian Legend*. York Beach, ME: Samuel Weiser, 1996.

Konstantinos. *Summoning Spirits: The Art of Magical Evocation*. St. Paul, MN: Llewellyn Publications, 1995.

Kraig, Donald Michael. *Modern Magick: Eleven Lessons in the High Magickal Arts*. St. Paul, MN: Llewellyn Publications, 1988.

Leitch, Aaron. *Secrets of the Magickal Grimoires*. Woodbury, MN: Llewellyn Publications, 2005.

Mann, Nicholas R. *Energy Secrets of Glastonbury Tor*. London: Green Magic Publishing, 2004.

———. *The Isle of Avalon*. London: Green Magic Publishing, 2001.

Matthews, John. *Wizards*. Hauppauge, NY: Barron's, 2003.

McLean, Adam. *The Alchemical Mandala*. Grand Rapids, MI: Phanes Press, 2002.

Melchizedek, Drunvalo. *The Ancient Secret of the Flower of Life, Volume 1*. Sedona, AZ: Light Technologies Publications, 1998.

———. *The Ancient Secret of the Flower of Life, Volume 2*. Sedona, AZ: Light Technologies Publications, 2000.

Melville, Francis. *The Secrets of High Magic*. Hauppauge, NY: Barron's Educational Series, 2002.

Miller, Richard Alan, and Iona Miller. *The Magical and Ritual Use of Perfumes*. Rochester, VT: Destiny Books, 1990.

Moore, Alan. *Promethea, Vols. I–V*. La Jolla, CA: America's Best Comics, 2001–2005.

Newcomb, Jason Augustus. *Conjuring the Goetia Spirits: A Simple Advanced Key*. Arlington, MA: Smite! Press, 1999.

———. *The New Hermetics*. Boston, MA: Weiser Books, 2004.

———. *21st Century Mage*. Boston, MA: Weiser Books, 2002.

Orpheus, Rodney. *Abrahadabra*. Boston, MA: Weiser Books, 2005.

Paterson, Helena. *The Handbook of Celtic Astrology*. St. Paul, MN: Llewellyn Publications, 1994.

Rankine, David. *Climbing the Tree of Life*. London: Avalonia, 2005.

Reed, Ellen Cannon. *The Witches Qabala*. York Beach, ME: Samuel Weiser, 1999.

Regardie, Israel. *A Garden of Pomegranates*. St. Paul, MN: Llewellyn Publications, 1951.

———. *The Art of True Healing*. Edited and updated by Marc Allen. Novato, CA: New World Library, 1997.

———. *The Golden Dawn*. St. Paul, MN: Llewellyn Publications, 2002.

———. *The Middle Pillar*. St. Paul, MN: Llewellyn Publications, 2002.

———. *The Tree of Life*. St. Paul, MN: Llewellyn Publications, 2000.

Rheeders, Kate. *Qabalah: A Beginner's Guide*. London: Hodder & Stoughton, 1996.

Runyon, Carroll "Poke." *The Book of Solomon's Magick*. Silverado, CA: Church of Hermetic Sciences, 1996.

Sanders, Alex. *Alex Sanders Lectures*. New York: Magickal Childe, 1989.

Saunders, Kevin. *Advanced Wiccan Spirituality*. Sutton Mallet, England: Green Magic, 2003.

Schneider, Michael S. *A Beginner's Guide to Constructing the Universe*. New York: Harper Perennial, 1995.

Stewart, R. J. *The Miracle Tree*. Franklin Lakes, NJ: New Page Books, 2003.

———. *The Spiritual Dimension of Music*. Rochester, VT: Destiny Books, 1987.

Thorsson, Edred. *The Book of Ogham*. St. Paul, MN: Llewellyn Publications, 1994.

———. *The Nine Doors of Midgard*. St. Paul, MN: Llewellyn Publications, 1994.

Trobe, Kala. *The Magic of Qabalah*. St. Paul, MN: Llewellyn Publications, 2001.

———. *The Witch's Guide to Life*. St. Paul, MN: Llewellyn Publications, 2003.

Valiente, Doreen. *An ABC of Witchcraft Past and Present*. New York: St. Martin's Press, 1973.

———. *Witchcraft for Tomorrow*. Blaine, WA: Phoenix Publishing, 1978.

Watson, Nancy B. *Practical Solitary Magic*. Boston, MA: Samuel Weiser, 1996.

Whitcomb, Bill. *The Magician's Companion*. St. Paul, MN: Llewellyn Publications, 1993.

———. *The Magician's Reflection*. St. Paul, MN: Llewellyn Publications, 1999.

Online Resource

Online Etymology Dictionary, Douglas Harper, http://www.etymonline.com.

Index

CREDITS

Interior Illustrations by the Llewellyn Art Department except the following:

Pages 15 and 21: Magician and High Priestess cards from the *Universal Tarot* by Roberto de Angelis © 2000 by Lo Scarabeo and reprinted with permission from Lo Scarabeo.

Page 55: Permission to reproduce a passage from page 22 of *The Sea Priestess* by Dion Fortune kindly given by Red Wheel/Weiser.

Page 59: Permission to reproduce the Sangreal Prayer by William Gray kindly given by Robert Hale Ltd. First published in Great Britain by Robert Hale Ltd.

Page 70: The Hermetic Universe—Engraving by Matthieu Merian for Johann Daniel Mylius's *Opus Medico-Chymicum*, 1618.

Page 99: Permission to reproduce the passage from *The Chicken Qabalah* by Lon Milo DuQuette kindly given by Red Wheel/Weiser.

Page 169: The Tree of Life with Its Roots in the Heavens—Plate XXI. Arber Sephirotheca, from *Utriusque Cosmi* by Robert Fludd, 1621, Vol. II.

Page 208: Photo of Chic Cicero's personal Earth Pentacle is reproduced by permission.

Page 505: Back tattoo photograph—Model: Ginella Cann. Photograph by Joyce Cadena Hannon. Tattoo art by Jennifer Moore of Sanctuary Tattoo, Portland, ME.

Page 527: Permission to reproduce the Nine Breaths Centering from *Celtic Sorcery* by Ian Corrigan kindly given by Ian Corrigan.